Multicultural China
in the Early Middle Ages

ENCOUNTERS WITH ASIA

Victor H. Mair, Series Editor

Encounters with Asia is an interdisciplinary series dedicated to the exploration of all the major regions and cultures of this vast continent. Its timeframe extends from the prehistoric to the contemporary; its geographic scope ranges from the Urals and the Caucasus to the Pacific. A particular focus of the series is the Silk Road in all of its ramifications: religion, art, music, medicine, science, trade, and so forth. Among the disciplines represented in this series are history, archeology, anthropology, ethnography, and linguistics. The series aims particularly to clarify the complex interrelationships among various peoples within Asia, and also with societies beyond Asia.

A complete list of books in the series
is available from the publisher.

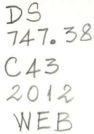

Multicultural China

in the Early Middle Ages

Sanping Chen

PENN

UNIVERSITY OF PENNSYLVANIA PRESS

PHILADELPHIA

Published by
University of Pennsylvania Press
Philadelphia, Pennsylvania 19104-4112
www.upenn.edu/pennpress

Printed in the United States of America on acid-free paper

10 9 8 7 6 5 4 3 2 1

Library of Congress Cataloging-in-Publication Data

Chen, Sanping.
Multicultural China in the early Middle Ages / Sanping Chen. — 1st ed.
p. cm. — (Encounters with Asia)
Includes bibliographical references and index.
ISBN 978-0-8122-4370-3 (hardcover : alk. paper)
1. China—History—221 B.C.–960 A.D. 2. China—Ethnic relations—
History. 3. Ethnicity—China—History. I. Title. II. Series: Encounters
with Asia.
DS747.38.C43 2012
951'.01—dc23

2011035815

To the memory of my mother

Contents

Foreword

Old Wine in New Bottles

Victor H. Mair

After nearly half a century of isolation, China has recently reemerged as an integral member of the global economy and the international political structure. Since its rise has been so explosive, however, knowledge of Chinese culture and society in other countries is still sketchy and often highly distorted. Indeed, so long and so extraordinarily complicated is the Chinese historical record, and so richly complex is Chinese literature, that modern Chinese citizens themselves are often confused about many details of their nation's past.

Virtually everyone has heard of the brave heroine Mulan, who rides off to war (as in the Disney movie), and most of us are familiar with the mythical unicorn that heralds the coming of a sage who will rule justly, yet we see them through a glass darkly. The wonder of this book, *Multicultural China in the Early Middle Ages*, is that it offers a completely new look at many aspects of Chinese history and culture that heretofore may have seemed bewildering or even absurd.

The author of the present volume, Sanping Chen, has the great virtue of being able to examine the past with a fresh eye. He does not take any received text or tradition at face value. Instead, he closely reexamines all the available evidence and subjects secondary interpretations to intense, critical scrutiny. The results of this type of inquiry are frequently surprising and in many cases revelatory. Yet Dr. Chen is not an iconoclast purely for the sake of iconoclasm. Instead, his goal is simply to penetrate the countless layers of obscurity and misrepresentation to get at the truth of what really happened in the past. More than any other Chinese historian that I know of, Sanping Chen is determined to confront historical data directly and without any presuppositions or agenda whatsoever.

From lengthy, ongoing discussions with Dr. Chen over the years, I have come to realize that his unusual approach to Chinese history results from deeply held principles. Among these the most important is that the historian is duty bound to report his findings, regardless of their implications. A corollary of this principle is that the historian may not lie about or color what he discovers concerning the past. For Dr. Chen, this becomes a moral imperative, such that he cannot remain silent when confronted with the facts of history.

Although Dr. Chen not infrequently mentions the prehistoric period (Neolithic, Bronze Age, and early Iron Age), the early period (the classical era or era of antiquity), and the late imperial period, his main focus is on the medieval period (roughly the first millennium AD). Many events that were profoundly formative for the future of East Asian civilization occurred during this period: the advent of Buddhism, the rise of Taoism as a religion, the first stirrings of the written vernacular, the perfection of literary genres, the incorporation into the Chinese body politic of non-Sinitic peoples in all directions, and so forth. Despite the crucial role this period played in the development of East Asian history, it is relatively little studied and, in general, poorly known, whether by specialists or by laypersons. This is particularly so for the first half of the period, and it is precisely that stretch of five or six hundred years upon which Dr. Chen places his greatest emphasis.

What, then, are a few of Dr. Chen's astonishing discoveries that he presents in this book?

1. Mulan was not Chinese.
2. The East Asian "unicorn" was very different, both in appearance and in significance, from the one-horned creature of Western imagination.
3. The royal house of the Tang Dynasty, which constituted the apogee of premodern Chinese civilization, was in large measure "barbaric."
4. Despite general Chinese dislike for dogs, canine imagery and terminology have been positively utilized among certain significant groups in East Asia.
5. Both the Huns and the Bulgars have their congeners in East Asia.
6. Iranian peoples were prominent in trade, religion, and other noteworthy aspects of medieval Chinese society.
7. Naming practices changed dramatically in response to influences from the Steppe.
8. One of China's most revered poets, Bai Juyi, had intimate connections with Central Asia.

Sanping Chen's ability to make, and to firmly document, these remarkable discoveries is due to his open-mindedness and insightfulness, but above all to his persistent inquisitiveness. While not everyone will acquiesce to the entirety of Dr. Chen's findings, no reputable scholar can afford to ignore them with impunity.

Dr. Chen's expositions of his discoveries are captivating in and of themselves. When combined with the solid content that they convey, his chapters make for compelling reading. Above all, these are not mere exercises in the realignment of exotic, alien arcana. Rather, everything that Dr. Chen writes about in this inspiring work has profound implications for our understanding of the present, which is a product of the cumulative past. We are greatly in Sanping Chen's debt for his sustained researches as well as for the creative clarity of his vision.

Introduction

On the afternoon of July 30, 1980, three Chinese historians discovered, on a granite rock face inside a stone cavern in the Xing'an Mountains in northeast China (more exactly at 50°38′N, 123°36′E), an inscription dated September 5, 443, by far the most ancient sample of writing in this part of Asia.[1] This important discovery, or rather confirmation, of the inscription's existence not only helped identify the original homestead of the Tuoba, an ancient nomadic people and the main subject of this book, but also vindicated the accuracy of *Wei shu* (*History of the [Tuoba] Wei Dynasty*), previously considered one of the least reliable Chinese dynastic histories.

However, a seemingly minor discrepancy or rather neglect by the text preserved in *Wei shu* as compared with the actual inscription indicates that, after establishing themselves as the undisputed masters of northern China, the Tuoba monarchs were still known by their nomadic designation *qaghan* instead of the Chinese title *huangdi*, or "son of heaven." This distinction would serve as an important clue to the Tuoba's lasting legacy expounded in this book, as well as a good example of what I would term a Confucianist bias in the written sources on which most of our understanding of the period is based.

The Tuoba first appeared in the history of East Asia as a marginal nomadic group in the second half of the third century. From the beginning, they were regarded as part of the general Xianbei complex or conglomerate, the new dominating yet largely decentralized nomadic power in northern Asia. The Xianbei had displaced the Xiongnu, widely regarded as the forerunners of the Huns who would terrorize Europe several centuries later.

The Tuoba rose to prominence in the late fourth century, especially strong after they destroyed the main forces of the rival Murong power, then the leading Xianbei group in northern China, on December 8, 395, in a superbly executed surprise pursuit under the energetic and daring leadership of the young Tuoba Gui (371–409). Eight months after this decisive military victory, the Tuoba chief formally adopted the Chinese imperial protocol. On this juncture of history, the Yuan dynasty historian Hu Sanxing (1230–1302), in his famous annotated edition of

Sima Guang's immortal Chinese chronology *Zizhi tongjian* (*Comprehensive Mirror for Aid in Government*, abbreviated in this book as *ZZTJ*), made the following incisive comments: "The rise of Tuoba Gui led to the hardening of the North-South partition, which in turn led to the eventual absorption of the South by the North. Alas, from the Sui era onward, sixty to seventy percent of those who were prominent in their times have been descendants of the Tuoba [and other Xianbei and Xiongnu groups led by the Tuoba]!"[2]

In other words, from this point on, the Tuoba and their descendants pretty much set the course of Chinese history, not just politically but also culturally, for nearly a millennium before another nomadic people, the Mongols, swept much of the Asian continent. A reader otherwise well versed in Chinese history may wonder why such an important group was not heard of more frequently in all of the very large volume of history about China. This good question is just one of several issues the current collection tries to address.

Another subject that is often neglected, particularly in comparison with that of the Mongol era, is how these earlier "Barbarian" invasions greatly stimulated the movements of peoples, commodities, and, not least, ideas across the Eurasian continent in the ancient world, especially along but not limited to the Silk Road. In my view, the well-known and much studied cosmopolitanism of the Tang dynasty was the culmination of a chain of events to which the Tuoba had been a major contributor yet for which they have heretofore received little recognition.

The prevailing perceptions of the two most cosmopolitan periods in China's premodern history, namely the Tang and the Yuan, are sharply different. The former is viewed as the accomplishment of an enlightened but largely native Chinese regime, whereas the latter is regarded as the outcome of the conquest of China by a nomadic power. One of the main reasons for this difference is the Sinitic façade the Tang (and its cousin the Sui) royal house had successfully woven for itself, obscuring the family's ethnic and cultural origin and identity. Thus the ethnic identity of the Tang house becomes one of the topics of this collection.

The Tang dynasty, at least during its prime, witnessed unprecedented cultural openness and tolerance, matched only by that of the Mongol Yuan. The best example is the flourishing, albeit not for long, of several foreign religions: Zoroastrianism, Manichaeism, Nestorian Christianity, and finally the establishment of Buddhism in China. There were other important cultural imports and changes. Many are well known and well studied. But some, like the advent and wide adoption of theophoric names, both personal and institutional, have never been noted by historians. No less important, these epochal events can all be traced back to the Tuoba roots of the Sui and Tang houses when one examines numerous earlier cases during the rule of northern China by the Tuoba and its nomadic brethren and/or successors. These cases demonstrate that China's extraordinary cosmopolitanism of that period was in fact driven by factors similar to those evident during the Mongol Yuan.

All in all, these subjects merit a full-fledged treatise. While the pursuit of such a large, complete study remains my desire, in this book I offer only a collection of specific studies of various aspects and hope such a piecemeal product will stimulate further interest and exploration in this fascinating area and epoch.

Chapter 1

The Legacy of the Tuoba
Xianbei: The Tang Dynasty

An Old Open Secret

In late autumn of the thirteenth year of Zhenguan (AD 639), under the reign of the second monarch of the Tang dynasty, Emperor Taizong, a major libel case broke out in the capital: a Taoist priest, Qin Shiying, accused Falin, a leading Buddhist monk in the metropolitan region, of "defaming the royal ancestry" by refuting the official claim that the imperial Li family descended from Laozi, the legendary founder of Taoism.[1] The catalyst of the case was the Tang imperial house's series of actions to promote the "native" Chinese religion allegedly created by their self-claimed sage/sacred forefather at the expense of the "foreign" Buddhism, raising the status of the former above that of the latter and resulting in strong reactions from the Buddhist establishment.

It should be added that the incident occurred in an era during which family origins and clan membership were of critical importance, not just politically, but often more importantly for commanding cultural prestige. A few dozen old Hàn clans with their roots in northern China had for centuries dominated high society and consequently the officialdoms in both northern and southern China. They formed a quasi-aristocracy extremely difficult for outsiders to penetrate, whether ethnic Hàn or "Barbarian." While politically trying to suppress the status of these families, the Tang imperial house was simultaneously compelled to play the same game by claiming its more recent pedigree from the prestigious Li clan of the Longxi region in northern China. Falin's "defamation" of the royal ancestry thus threatened not only the religious halo transmitted from the founder of Taoism but also the self-asserted Sinitic Longxi ancestry. The latter was, naturally, part and parcel of the Tang house's claim to legitimacy for ruling the vast Hàn populace.

Monk Falin was duly arrested and went through several months of court proceedings, defending himself against various incriminating accusations. Finally, on a day in the last month of the Chinese year (January 640 of the Julian calendar), during an inquisition session attended by Emperor Taizong himself, the brave monk plainly declared, "According to my knowledge, the Dashe [clan] of the Tuoba is known in Tang language as the Li. From this descended Your Majesty's family, which did not come from the Longxi (Li) clan going back to Laozi."[2] This blasphemous statement was followed by further scandalous declarations about the self-claimed royal Longxi Li lineage, including the accusation that the clan was the offspring of a slave turned impostor. Quoting Buddhist sutras and metaphors, Falin equated the Tang imperial house's forfeiture of its northern lineage from the "god-king" of the Tuoba of the Yin Mountains in Mongolia, and their adoption of the Taoist pedigree, to "replacing gold with chalcopyrite (copper iron sulfide)," "exchanging fine silk for burlap," and even "abandoning a 'jewel princess' in order to liaise with a female slave."[3]

The emperor was naturally outraged, yet befitting his posthumous fame as one of the most tolerant and just monarchs in Chinese history, with a prankish sense of humor, he granted Falin seven days to practice what the hapless monk had previously preached in a Buddhism treatise, namely that reciting the name of the bodhisattva Avalokiteśvara (Chinese name Guanyin) would produce a religious miracle, saving the pious caller of the sacred name from the executioner's ax. Evidently not quite ready for immediate martyrdom, Falin beat a humiliating retreat, which incidentally made the Buddhist source on which our story is based all the more believable: By claiming, on the day the miracle was due, that he had in the past seven days merely recited the emperor's name instead of that of Avalokiteśvara, Falin secured an imperial pardon, or rather the commuting of the death penalty to exile in remote Sichuan. More intriguingly, faced with the opposition of imperial court judges who wanted to uphold the mandatory capital punishment, Emperor Taizong explained that Falin's defamation of the royal ancestry "was not without foundation."

Emperor Taizong apparently recognized that the imperial clan's genealogical connections to the Tuoba nobles and other "Barbarian" families were open contemporary knowledge. For one thing, his own grandmother née Dugu, his mother née Dou, and his principal consort (and mother of the heir apparent) née Zhangsun were all indisputably of core Tuoba and other Xianbei descent. What monk Falin tried to reveal was that the Li clan's lineage on the paternal side very likely originated from the Tuoba too. The newest proof is the recent archaeological discovery that shows that another prominent Li clan of the period, namely that of Li Xian, a general-in-chief of the Northern Zhou, with the same claim to Longxi ancestry, was in fact of unmistakable Tuoba Xianbei descent.[4]

Nonetheless, Falin's declaration, albeit an open secret to his contemporaries, finally crossed the line the imperial house had drawn in the sand for establishing and defending its legitimacy, that is, being the son of heaven in the Central Kingdom. In this context, Emperor Taizong's handling of the Falin case was a masterstroke, for in sparing Falin's life it showed the imperial benevolence, but in expelling the famous monk with many high-level political connections to a remote place from the metropolis, it sent a clear message about the high price to pay for defaming the royal ancestry. There is little doubt that measures were taken too to eliminate any compromising evidence such as that cited by the brave monk.

The simple fact is that, after Falin's death, or one may say deferred martyrdom, on the twenty-third day of the seventh month in the lunar calendar, or August 15, 740, in Sichuan, barely seven months after his banishment from the Tang capital, the "Barbarian" origin of the Tang imperial house was never openly brought up again until more than five centuries later, in the Southern Song dynasty (1127–1279), albeit at that time few solid records still remained to allow concrete and detailed examination of the real origin and characteristics of the Tang imperial house.

A one-time open secret had become a true enigma.

The Ethnic Identity of the Tang Imperial House

The Tang went on to become one of the most splendid dynasties in Chinese history, as well as one of the most written about. But as foretold by the above story from Buddhist sources, the Tang royal family's own ethnic origin has been a controversy oft debated as a result of conflicting evidence, the well-documented fact that it had intermarried with various Tuoba Xianbei and other non-Hàn families for generations notwithstanding. The best and most important example is perhaps the noted Tang studies authority Chen Yinke (1890–1969), who wrote no fewer than four articles trying to prove the Li clan's native Hàn origin on the paternal side.[5]

It may be observed that Chen's studies were written during a period of Japan's growing military threat to China and encroachment on Chinese territories, which led to increasing sensitivity toward alien rule, ancient as well as modern, in China. Despite his extensive experience in studying abroad, Chen Yinke came from a late Qing aristocratic family with strong nationalistic inclinations. Chen's aged father died in 1937 after refusing food and medicine as a principled protest against the full-fledged Japanese military invasion of China. These events and sentiments certainly colored Chen's studies. Chen's position as a highly respected educator during his lifetime and his near-cult posthumous status as an unsurpassed modern historian certainly impeded any questioning of his results. For example, one of Chen's students, Liu Pansui, hastily concluded a pioneering and stimulating study of the Tang royal family's many "Barbarian" traits by endorsing, without the slightest reservation, his teacher's conclusion of the family's paternal Hàn origin.[6]

Nonetheless, the opposite proposition, namely that the Li descended from the Tuoba Xianbei, had equally solid if not stronger evidence, as acknowledged by, for example, a relatively recent biography by Hu Rulei of Li Shimin, otherwise known as Emperor Taizong, the extremely powerful second emperor of the Tang Dynasty.[7] Moreover, despite Chen Yinke's admittedly politically influenced objective of demonstrating the Li clan's alleged Hàn Chinese origin, the studies by him and others have also shown that the official histories compiled during the Tang had been subjected to much political doctoring in order to conceal the imperial house's "Barbarian" background.

A related and equally portentous issue is the convenient but somewhat arbitrary categorization by which various Chinese dynasties were classified as either a "native" or a "conquest" regime. This dichotomy is largely based on the standard historiography but now appears quite well entrenched. In this scheme the Sui and Tang, though with undoubted strong "Northern influences," were invariably regarded as native regimes. This conclusion is based on the observation that the process of sinicization or sinification, yet another popular but nebulous notion, of the "Barbarian" Xiongnu and Xianbei groups in northern China was considered completed by then.

In his study of "nomadic sinification" in China, David Honey seems to be the only exception, by trying to include the Tang in the "conquest dynasties."[8] Yet in addition to his very curious exclusion of the preceding Sui, he still considers the Tang house "basically sinified." Therefore in his otherwise colorful essay on nomadic sinicization covering the entire Chinese history from the late Shang to the Qing, not a single item or case pertaining to the Tang is included.

From the point of view of sinification, ethnic origin, an issue for which the monk Falin paid a heavy personal price, is not of real significance here. Some persistent or occasional "atavistic" appearances of Northern influences notwithstanding, one could argue that little is found in the standard (i.e., official) histories to suggest that the Li regime was culturally anything but a "native" Chinese dynasty.

To address this issue, one might first ask a different question: Despite the fact that various Xiongnu and Xianbei groups dominated the political arena in northern China for almost three hundred years between the collapse of the Western Jin and the founding of the Sui, and the usually unacknowledged fact that their descendants continued to do so for several hundred more years, as the comments by the Yuan dynasty historian Hu Sanxing quoted in the Introduction clearly stated, why is it that one can learn so little about their cultural heritage in traditional historiography? Even the linguistic affinity of the Tuoba Xianbei remains to this day a matter of controversy, a subject I shall further elaborate in an appendix.

In his narration of the Turco-Persian Ghaznavid sultanate in the eastern Iranian world, David Morgan made this interesting observation: "Although the Ghaznawids were of Turkish origin, there seems to have been little that was identifiably Turkish about the way in which their empire was run, or indeed about the culture they patronized. We should, however, remember that our sources were written by Persian contemporaries, who might have been unlikely to lay much stress on the non-Persian . . . elements that may have been present."[9] Similarly, Herbert Franke, while discussing the legitimation of the most conspicuous "conquest" dynasty in Chinese history, commented, "A Chinese official history like the *Yüan-shi* is not very explicit about the Buddhist and Lamaist elements inherent in Yüan statehood, and one has to turn to the Tibetan and Mongol sources, even though the latter ones are mostly relatively late and sometimes unreliable and fanciful."[10]

As one will see, Morgan's and Franke's observations are also pertinent to the Tang records. However, unlike the case of the Ghaznavids, which was contested by Fuad Köprülü, a modern Turkish historian,[11] there is not a single Xianbei soul left today to question the "all-Chinese" Tang history; and unlike the Yuan world, there were few alternative sources on the Tang, which totally dominated, not only politically, but also culturally, the vast land from Samarkand to the Sea of Japan.

In her study of early modern China, Pamela Crossley contends that the term "sinicization" or "sinification" is an obsolete concept.[12] "Ethnicity," or ethnic study, would appear to be, at least morphologically (and politically), a more correct substitute. However, even she seems to admit that an abstract notion of ethnicity is no more self-evident or more clearly defined than the obsolete concept of sinicization.

The question of appropriate nomenclature notwithstanding, I shall try to demonstrate in the remainder of this chapter the marked contrast between the Tang and other native imperial houses regarding succession and other politico-cultural attributes of a dynasty, as well as the conspicuous cultural gap between the Tang imperial house and the contemporary Confucian gentry class. Finally, I raise serious doubts about the correctness of characterizing the Tang as a "native" or "basically sinified" imperial house. Borrowing the etymology Xianbei < *Särbi first suggested by Edwin Pulleyblank and adopted by Peter Golden, I contend that the first half of the Tang might be more aptly called a Särbo-Chinese (or Xianbeo-Chinese) regime.[13]

The Cultural Gap

The conventional view that the Tang represented a native Chinese dynasty very much depends on the premise that the Lis were either of Hàn origin or had "basically sinified" by the time of the founding of the dynasty. I shall contend that neither was true.

The earlier quotations regarding the Ghaznavids and on the Yuan clearly demonstrate how one-sided sources created biased or even false politico-cultural images of an ethnic regime. Careful examination of the historical sources of the era reveals many cases of the Li clan's non-Hàn cultural traits and identity. What may be more important is the marked distance between the imperial house and the traditional Chinese gentry regarding these issues as well as the contemporary awareness of this difference. Following is a brief summary of some of the most notable examples.

1. Language. In a later chapter I show that the Tuoba Xianbei tongue continued to be used by the Li clan as their first or family language. Moreover, even the term *Guoyu*, "national language," was kept for a while during the Tang. Liu Pansui, Chen Yinke's student, first made this important discovery based on an entry in *Xin Tang shu* (*The New History of the Tang Dynasty*, 44.1160). The contemporary Chinese gentry's attitude toward this was best reflected in a noted passage in *Yanshi jiaxun* (*Family Instructions for the Yan Clan*):

   > There was a court official who once said to me, "I have a
   > son who is seventeen and has quite a good epistolary style.
   > I shall teach him the Xianbei language and to play the *pipa*
   > (a favored foreign instrument), in the hope that he will gain
   > a certain degree of proficiency in these. With such accom-
   > plishments he is sure to gain favour with men in high
   > places. This is a matter of some urgency." At that time I
   > hung my head and made no reply. Strange indeed is the way
   > this fellow teaches his son. Even if, by such means, you
   > could become a minister, I would not wish you to do so.[14]

2. Affinity. The Tang was the last Chinese dynasty before the Manchus to marry off royal princesses to the Steppe khans and chieftains. This practice was clearly documented in the official compilation of Tang officialdom and

institutions (*Tang huiyao* [*Institutional History of the Tang*]). There are also more detailed modern studies.[15] The practice was so prevalent that the word *konchuy,* transcribing the Chinese term *gongzhu,* "princess," was simply regarded by Ziya Gökalp, an early twentieth-century proponent of Pan-Turkism, as an ancient Turkic word for "wife."[16] In the meantime, the leading Chinese gentry families steadfastly refused to establish matrimonial relations with the imperial house. More strikingly, their rejection of the honor of an imperial marriage persisted for more than two centuries, lasting well into the late Tang era, despite the royal family's repeated initiatives (*Xin Tang shu* 119.4306, 172.5205–6; *ZZTJ* 248.8036).[17]

3. Clan relationship. The Tang represented a unique case in Chinese history in which the imperial house bestowed its own clan name, Li, not only on a few Hàn Chinese persons but more frequently on ethnic leaders and chieftains, be they Turk, Tangut, Uighur, Kitan, or Iranian/Persian. In the same study of the marriage practice of Tang royal princesses, Wang Tongling compiled a rather extensive table on this issue.[18] As the Yuan dynasty historian Hu Sanxing particularly noted (*ZZTJ* 172.8879), the Zhuxie Shatuo Turkic tribe founded the Later Tang dynasty based largely on having received this imperial honor. I also add a rather revealing case missing in Wang Tongling's exhaustive table: As late as the Huichang period (841–46), the main business for a Kirghiz embassy, per an imperial edict by Emperor Wuzong (reign 840–46), was to register themselves with the imperial clan office (*Xin Tang shu* 217b.6150), highlighting the alleged common ancestry of the Kirghiz *qaghan* and the Tang house. In his detailed treatise on the collapse of the Uighur Empire, Michael Drompp has documented this interesting relationship.[19] On the other hand, it is well documented and studied that the Tang imperial house made repeated efforts to suppress the leading gentry clans' social prestige and privilege (*ZZTJ* 195.6135–36, 200.6318.). I may even ascribe the emergence of the Chinese civil services examinations under the Sui and Tang to this distrust in old Hàn aristocratic clans.

4. Clothing. It is well known that Tang fashions were under heavy foreign influence. Xiang Da's pioneering study on this subject has been followed up by many other authors.[20] As the famous Tang poet Yuan Zhen's social jeremiad *Faqu* (*Quan Tang shi* [*Complete Anthology of Tang Poetry*] 419.1025) described, the love of exotic style, custom, and makeup became feverish during the reign of Emperor Xuanzong. While most modern authors emphasize the Iranian and Iranic connections and the influence coming from

the Western Regions, I take note of the fact that much of this represented the Steppe heritage, including the nomadic groups' long history of playing the Western Regions card. As a particular example and in sharp contrast to the Tuoba emperor Xiaowen's wholesale sinicization drive, in which the emperor took personal responsibility for abolishing even the leisure dress of the Xianbei women (*Wei shu* 19.469 and 21.536), official records clearly state that most of the so-called regular dresses during the Tang were of the Tuoba military tradition (*Jiu Tang shu* [*The Old History of the Tang Dynasty*] 45.1938, 45.1951; *Xin Tang shu* 24.527–28; and *Tang huiyao* 31.577–78). However, as to how this was viewed by the traditional gentry, I note that the felt hat personally popularized by Zhangsun Wuji, Emperor Taizong's brother-in-law, was later labeled by the Confucian historians as "devilish" (*Xin Tang shu* 34.878). Another telltale case, according to an early Song dynasty source *Tang yulin* (*Anecdotes of the Tang*, 4.101) and corroborated by *Xin Tang shu* (125.4407), was Emperor Xuanzong's feeling of alienation merely because of his chief minister Zhang Yue's "Confucian dress." These incidents again point to a gap between the Tang ruling class and the Confucian gentry in this regard.

5. Social mores. Several notable customs practiced by the Li clansmen, such as breast-sucking and foot-kissing, betrayed the clan's non-Hàn cultural heritage. Again we owe these two important observations to Liu Pansui's already cited pioneering study, albeit Liu's citations are far from complete. The customs' origins are certainly worthy of further exploration, especially a possible relationship between foot-kissing and the well-known ancient Iranian custom of proskynesis documented by Greek authors from Herodotus on down, and particularly with respect to Alexander the Great. But to me the most famous (or notorious) custom was the Li clan's record on levirate and other scandalous matrimonial relations. The practice, as I point out in a later chapter, reflected a key northern legacy in the Tang house, namely the lack of clearly defined and recognized generational boundaries on the Steppe. In addition to the many well-known cases, I note the tomb inscription of the wife of the Türk general Ashina Zhong unearthed in the 1970s, which reveals yet another marriage of Emperor Taizong's with his former in-laws.[21] The case was not reported anywhere in existing records, suggesting even more such incidents that were similarly suppressed in the official histories. As to how this would have been looked upon by the Confucian gentry, suffice it to say that when the Tang house's ethnicity finally became an open issue in the Southern Song,

"violations of the Confucian standard governing a women's proper behaviour" was the first question raised.[22]

6. Another interesting cultural trait was the "Barbarian" childhood names fashionable among the Northern aristocracy, the Sui and Tang houses included. Both Sui emperors Wendi and Yangdi had such names: the father's childhood name was Nanluoyan (*Taisho* No. 2060, 667c) and the son's Ame (*ZZTJ* 179.5577). So did Yang Yong and Li Jiancheng, the two one-time crown princes, under the founding emperors of the Sui and Tang dynasties, respectively. The former's childhood name was Gandifa (*ZZTJ* 179.5575), which can be identified with a similar childhood name, Qizhifa, the "Xianbei-ized" warlord Feng Ba of the Tuoba Wei period (*Wei shu* 97.2126). Li Jiancheng's childhood name was Pishamen (*Xin Tang shu* 79.3540). As shall be discussed later, these two princes shared more than having a "Barbarian" childhood name and being an unsuccessful heir apparent. There is good evidence that many of these names were of Buddhist origin, but the real point is their nonsinicized forms. For example, Sui Wendi's name Naluoyan was also the name of a Central Asian Türk chief (*ZZTJ* 212.6735). An intriguing story is that a passage in *Jiu Tang shu* (64.2415) indicated unmistakably that Emperor Taizong also had such a childhood name. But nowhere could this name be found in any records. One can only conclude that the emperor made sure his "Barbarian" name became an absolute imperial taboo. Another case is the childhood name Zhinu of Li Zhi the future emperor Gaozong (*Jiu Tang shu* 64.2415) His father's use of a proverb "Having borne a wolf . . ." to describe Li Zhi's character (*ZZTJ* 197.6208) leads me to submit that this seemingly Hàn name was but a corrupted or masked proto-Mongolian term for "wolf." This term was well attested as the clan name Chinu, which became Lang, "wolf," in Tuoba emperor Xiaowen's sinicization drive (*Wei shu*, 113.3013). As Peter Boodberg pointed out in "The Language of the T'o-pa Wei," another likely attestation was the popular personal name Chounu.

7. Yet another issue showing the marked contrast between the Tang imperial house and the Confucian gentry was the monarchs' extravagant patronage of the performing arts—music, dance, drama, and other entertainment—much to the horror of the Confucian moralists. Worse still, the Turco-Xianbei emperors often showed little reservation in bestowing on these artists, considered of the same social class as house slaves and prostitutes by the traditional Chinese gentry, prominent and prestigious titles. One such artist was even enfeoffed with a princedom by the Northern Qi (550–57), a precedent the Sui

emperor Yangdi once wanted to follow to benefit his favorite and talented Kuchaean musician Bai Mingda, who would continue to serve the Tang with distinction (*Sui shu* [*The History of the Sui Dynasty*] 15.397). The first two Tang emperors were both criticized by Confucian ministers for giving similar appointments to these artists (*Jiu Tang shu* 62.2375–76, 74.2614–15; *Xin Tang shu* 98.3897, 99.3907–8; and *ZZTJ* 186.5834, 194.6095). The third, Emperor Gaozong, received similar criticism for according the artists undue privileges (*Xin Tang shu* 201.5728.). I further remark that Emperor Xuanzong was the last Tang emperor to show this passion for the performing arts. The emperor's biography by Xu Daoxun and Zhao Keyao, for instance, provides extensive details on this subject.[23] Interestingly and by no means coincidentally, the same royal fervor was not to be observed until the coming of the Shatuo Turkic regimes (*ZZTJ* 272.8904.).

These items illustrate the Li clan's cultural identity in the eyes of the contemporary Chinese gentry class. In addition, I find the views on this subject of two other parties, namely the Türks and the Li clanspeople themselves, suggestive also.

First, the Türks in the Orkhon inscriptions, probably the only independent history source of the era, consistently called the Tang power Tabgach, or Tuoba, fully two centuries after the collapse of the last Tuoba regime.[24] Because of the paucity of data, it is difficult to ascertain the Türks' exact geographic perception of contemporary East Asia. But *Sui shu* (52.1341) clearly showed that the Türks were well aware of the existence of the southern state of Chen. Then, even after several hundred years, al-Kašγari stated unmistakably that Tawγac/Tabgach was only part of Sin or China. Moreover, and against the inevitable analogy of the modern Russian word for China, al-Kašγari also gave an etymology of the name Tawγac: It was "[t]he name of a tribe of the Turks who settled in those regions"![25]

Second, the attitude of the early Tang regime toward the traditional Chinese gentry can be taken as a most useful indicator of its own self-identity. In addition to the regime's persistent efforts to suppress the prestige of the traditional gentry class as mentioned earlier, Li Yuan, the founding emperor, had this explanation for his son Li Shimin's growing political independence and aspiration (*ZZTJ* 190.5959): "This boy has long been commanding troops in the provinces. Taught by educated men, he is no longer my son of the old days." Though the passage has been cited by a great many authors, few have noted the critically important fact that the phrase "educated men" was literally *dushu Hàn*, "educated Hàn," in *Jiu Tang shu* (64.2415–16). Sima Guang, most likely based on a later (Song dynasty) understanding, changed it to the more elegant word *shusheng*, "educated men," editing out the crucial implication. Perhaps wholeheartedly corrupted by the "edu-cated Hàn" as the father had charged, the son, according to a Tang author,[26] would also call the famous courtier Wei Zheng a *tianshe Hàn*, "house-owning Hàn peas-ant," in the privy imperial quarters and in the presence of his consort Empress Zhangsun, who was of Tuoba descent. Again Sima Guang edited it to a mere *tian-she weng*, "old house-owning peasant" (*ZZTJ* 194.6096).

In my view, the two quotations cited earlier are the best reflection of the Li clan's ethnic self-identity, for in the period immediately preceding the Sui and Tang, the term *Hàn* when occurring in such phrases was always a derogatory appellation used by the Xianbei and related Northerners for the Hàn or other-wise sinicized people. In fact, the very etymology of the character *hàn* as a vocative, going back all the way to the era of Tuoba domination, is the reason for the term's persistent derogatory connotation today, more than a millennium after the Tuoba's subjugation of the Hàn people to second-class status. As far as I am aware, the Yuan-Ming scholar Tao Zongyi,[27] apparently prompted by the similarly low status of the Hàn people under the Mongol rule, was the first to observe this connection, followed by many modern authors.[28]

Although the Hàn slur was gradually picked up by other courtiers during Empress Wu Zetian's reign, an episode recorded in a Tang period source, *Chaoye qianzai* (*Popular Records of the Court and Commonalty* 4.89), clearly showed that the traditional meaning and target were not lost on the gentry class. Be-sides, no better classical usage of the term could be found than the father/son's application to "educated men" and "house-owning peasant," typical of a seden-tary, agricultural Central Kingdom but foreign to nomadic tribespeople. These cases are also good examples of how "elegant" editing by historians actually corrupted the original stories.

If one finds the above arguments and evidence fragmentary or argues that the cases represented just the occasional and transient remnants of the imperial house's previous Northern exposure, a far clearer and better focused picture of the imperial clan's ethnic identity can be established by a systematic analysis of the succession struggles in the early Tang, as I show in the following sections.

The Case of Crown Prince Chengqian

First I examine the case of Emperor Taizong's original heir apparent in some detail, because it epitomizes not only some crucial political and cultural issues of the era but also the problems with both standard historiography and modern scholarship in studying these issues. In addition, this episode also sheds light on the so-called process of sinicization.

The case is succinctly described (or one may say glossed over) in *The Cambridge History of China,* which has this to say about Taizóng's first heir apparent: "The prince apparently was intelligent and capable . . . As he grew older, however, the heir apparent began to behave in ways which seemed both abnormal and scandalous to the Chinese courtiers, and he may well be mentally unbalanced. He began to reject his Chinese identity and heritage, used the Turkish language, and dressed himself and his entourage in Turkish costume."[29] This is indeed an accurate narration according to the standard Tang records. But can we take the official lines, especially the alleged "mental problems," at their face value?

Arthur Wright also calls the whole affair a "scandal" caused by Prince Chengqian's "strange neurosis," but he does point out its connections with the Li clan's family history.[30] Edwin Pulleyblank gives what I think is the most relevant observation on this case: he calls Prince Chengqian's "strange neurosis" "atavistic predilections for the Turkish life-style."[31]

I demonstrate here that the whole affair was hardly a "scandal," that Prince Chengqian did not have a "strange neurosis," and that the predilections were not "atavistic." On the contrary, one may find that Prince Chengqian's many acts were not much different from those of other Li boys of the time, just as the young Li Shimin, the future Emperor Taizong, once behaved, and the so-called scandal would seem no more than the norm of the Lis' family life.

Let us look at Li Shimin, the father himself. By many stories, including his own admission, Li Shimin was as "wild" in his youth as Prince Chengqian was reported to have behaved: a passion for archery and horsemanship (which continued throughout his life and were exercised with his largely ethnic, Turkic in particular, imperial guards) but little knowledge of the classics.[32] In fact, Li Shimin continued some of his old habit as an emperor (*ZZTJ* 192.6021–22, 192.6042). Yet the same acts of his son Chengqian were depicted, very likely seasoned with exaggerated or made-up "deviate" details, as scandalous offences.

As for rejecting the "Chinese identity" and taking on "Turkish" things, it can be demonstrated with evidence provided here and in a later chapter that Emperor Taizong himself had a well-established Turkic or tribal identity and was conversant in Turkic. In particular, Li Shimin, while still a prince, became a "sworn brother" of several prominent Türk persons. They include Tuli (Tölis) Qaghan of the Eastern Türk (*ZZTJ* 191.5992); the loyal Türk general Ashina Simo (*Cefu yuangui* [*Prime Tortoise of the Record Bureau*] 980.11516), who was given the imperial clan name Li (*Jiu Tang shu* 194.5156; *Xin Tang shu* 215.6037), and the Western Türk prince, later Duolu Qaghan (*Jiu Tang shu* 194.5183).

If anything, Prince Chengqian could only be accused of being too filial a son of the many aspects of the clan's life his father found best absent from the official history. The suppression of Li Shimin's childhood name in all records is a good example. Chengqian's "scandalous relationship" with an actor-entertainer (*ZZTJ* 196.6191), while hardly exceptional among the long list of imperial homosexual liaisons from the Hàn dynasties on down, also fits the Turco-Xianbei patronage of the performing arts as examined earlier.

This is a typical case of how modern authors tend to go to great lengths to explain things that would have seemed quite natural after the Lis' Turco-Xianbei identity is recognized. Another example is Emperor Taizong's six famous horses whose reliefs were carved at the imperial mausoleum (another Turco-Mongol trait). Edward Schafer in his famous study of the Tang exotica concludes that the six horses "came to T'ai Tsung from the Turks" partly because one of them had the name *Teqin biao*, "prince's roan."[33] This subjective interpretation for the Turkic word *tegin* is hardly necessary after realizing, first, that the term was also a well-recognized Tuoba Xianbei title,[34] and, second, when the horse was being ridden, the future Emperor Taizong was none other than a prince (*Quan Tang wen* [*Complete Anthology of Tang Prose*], 10.124).

Regarding the convenient allegation that Prince Chengqian had "mental problems," it is interesting to notice that the original heir apparent by the Chinese *dizhang* (the eldest son of the principal consort) primogeniture principle of the Qing emperor Shengzu (Kangxi) supposedly had the same disorder.[35] One cannot help thinking of the use or abuse of psychiatry to punish cultural or political dissidents in a more modern context.

Let me further remark that the incoming emperor Gaozong turned out no less "scandalous" than his hapless elder brother Prince Chengqian in "imitating" the Steppe life-style by marrying his father's concubine. Not as well-known but probably more revealing was Gaozong's order that his own sons have Türk companions in their inner palace (*Xin Tang shu* 199.5661; *ZZTJ* 201.6363.). At the very least, we now know that the "mentally unbalanced" Prince Chengqian was certainly not the only Li clan member who liked to speak the Turkic language.

Finally, it is no accident that Prince Chengqian was eventually "rehabilitated" under the reign of Emperor Xuanzong (*Xin Tang shu* 80.3565), the last Turco-Xianbei monarch of the Tang in my view, who, incidentally and despite his ministers' opposition, also liked to have Türk companions during his outings. However, the presence of a Turkic language interpreter in Emperor Xuanzong's entourage

(*Tang huiyao* 27.521) was a sure sign that the Turco-Xianbei period was gradually coming to an end.

To summarize, though his many traits were shared by other "normal" Li boys, Prince Chengqian fell victim to not only the vicious succession struggle but also the joint propaganda efforts by the Confucian historians and the imperial court, prompted by the former's sinocentric views and tendencies and the latter's overt concern, sometimes even obsession, with the historical image and legacy it would leave behind, not to mention the commanding issue of political legitimacy in the Central Kingdom at the time. Moreover, I extract several general observations about the succession struggles and the process of sinicization from this case and many of its precedents, to be elaborated in the following sections.

But before that, let me point to a case bearing a striking resemblance to Prince Chengqian's alleged plots of revolt: the case of the Northern Wei's Crown Prince Tuoba Xun (*Wei shu*, 22.558.). There is, however, a key difference: at that time the Northern Wei was not the only and all-dominating regime in China. It was thus unable to gloss the incident over as perhaps another "family scandal" caused by a "mentally unbalanced" crown prince. In short, it did not enjoy, as its Sui and Tang successors did, a monopoly on historiography: the incident was clearly recorded in *Nan Qi shu* (*The History of the Southern Qi Dynasty* 57.996), the official history of the rival Southern Qi state, as a backlash against the Tuoba emperor Xiaowen's wholesale sinification drive. That effort, according to many people, was motivated by the latter's ambition to end the North-South partition,[36] a deed that was eventually accomplished by the Sui and Tang. In addition to preparing us to address the common threads in these cases, it may also help explain why the two Tuoba political as well as biological heirs were so anxious to claim their alleged Chinese ancestry.

The Succession to the Throne in the Early Tang

The case of Prince Chengqian was hardly an aberration in the imperial family as the official records would have us believe. As I demonstrate, one of many characteristics that set the Tang apart from other native Chinese dynasties was the persistent political struggle concerning the succession of the throne. During a period that covered nearly the first century and a half of the dynasty, not once did the succession follow the time-honored Hàn *dizhang* primogeniture principle. Nor was there a single time that the process ran smoothly, without strife (and indeed bloodshed). Even after that, as observed by Chen Yinke,[37] the position of the official heir apparent (by the *dizhang* rule or not) was anything but firmly established.

It should be pointed out that exactly on this point the supposedly native Tang dynasty was strikingly akin to the Qing regime, a typical conquest dynasty in the conventional categorization. The latter, unburdened by the need to maintain a Hàn Chinese façade, simply (after a period of failed experimentation) abolished the institution of an heir apparent altogether.

This similarity points to the root of the incessant succession struggles of the Tang: the imperial house's Turco-Xianbei Steppe origin and heritage. The magnitude and duration of this entirely unique (among the so-called native dynasties) characteristic are far too great to be ascribed simply to some lingering Northern influences. It is the reflection of the true ethnic/cultural identity of an imperial house that had spared no efforts to present itself as a bona fide Hàn regime in all historical records.

One cannot help noticing the numerous succession struggles in the Western Jin and the Southern dynasties. However, in addition to the Northern influence[38] and often direct involvement, exemplified by the case of Liu Yuan, the founding emperor of the Xiongnu Former Zhao dynasty (*Jin shu* 101.2648 and passim), these incidents all fall into the general feature of every new native dynasty that, largely as the ripple effect of the preceding military campaigns and difficulties in establishing a new imperial order, the first and sometimes the second succession were invariably problematic. In essence, none of the native dynasties mentioned here survived much beyond this bottleneck, whereas the only long-lived native house during the period, namely the Eastern Jin (317–420), was remarkably free of similar trouble. Furthermore, the struggles during the Southern dynasties all had extensive external involvement, while the Tang cases (and many of their precedents in the Northern Turco-Xianbei courts), as observed by Chen Yinke, were all confined to the capital area within the imperial clan.

The disruptive and often bloody succession process of the Turco-Mongol regimes on the Steppe characterized by fratricide and other forms of bloodshed within the ruling house has long been noted. However, the most methodical treatment of the subject appears to be that of the late Joseph Fletcher. He used the term "blood tanistry" for the general principle on the Steppe that the leadership of a tribe or other polity should be passed on to the best qualified member of the chiefly or ruling house.[39] And the eventual choice of a new leader was usually the result of some form of contention. Fletcher discussed in detail how this Turco-Mongol tradition manifested itself in the Ottoman Empire.[40]

Peter Boodberg was among the first to ascribe this characteristic to Turco-Mongol traditions, including the not-unusual father-son enmity in particular, in discussing the Sui imperial succession.[41] In an unpublished presentation on blood tanistry in Ottoman, Indian, and later Chinese (Jin, Yuan, Ming, and Qing dynasties) regimes, Fletcher also mentioned briefly the Sui case and the case of Li Shimin.[42] Nonetheless, as I demonstrate, this tradition was in fact much more than what Fletcher called "traces" in the history of the Tang, which would also reveal some interesting phenomena in what had been traditionally called the process of sinicization.

Let me briefly review the long history of succession struggles in the first two centuries of the Tang.

This uninterrupted stretch started with Li Shimin. The future Emperor Taizong's meticulously planned and impeccably executed maneuver to replace his elder brother Jiancheng as the heir apparent culminated in the famous Xuanwu Gate coup d'état in 626. Later I discuss other aspects reflected in this blatant challenge to the time-honored *dizhang* principle. But not as well known was the observation by the Qing historian Zhao Yi that this murderous fratricide extending to the execution of all male offspring of the two slain brothers almost developed into a case of patricide as well,[43] as is generally believed regarding the Sui emperor Yangdi's accession to the throne.

A very similar drama would be staged under the reign of Taizong by his sons, though with somewhat different endings due to changed circumstances and personalities, whose implications will be discussed later. It is worth noting that in the aftermath of the alleged patricide/fratricide scheme of 643 plotted by Taizong's original heir apparent, Prince Chengqian, the choice of the new crown prince was partially prompted by the need to avoid future fratricide (*ZZTJ* 197.6197, 199.6280–81), which of course did not at all prevent it from happening after the death of Emperor Taizong. Another episode was the promise by one of the players, Li Tai (Prince Wei), to kill off his son if he was appointed heir apparent, so that after his death the throne would go laterally to another son of Taizong (*ZZTJ* 197.6195). This promise did not sound so unnatural to Taizong's ears (and indeed, as we shall see, would be redeemed en masse by a great-grandson of his).

Into the reign of the next emperor, and with the emergence of a strong woman, Wu Zetian, the focus of the succession struggle shifted somewhat from brotherly contest to acute parent-child enmity. Empress Wu showed little hesitation in having two heirs apparent, both her own sons, killed in 675 and 684 respectively (*ZZTJ* 202.6377, 203.6419.). A few modern authors,[44] who contrast her apparent lack of qualms with a mother's natural feelings and argue that one of the princes was perhaps not born of Empress Wu, do not seem to recognize the entrenched tradition of filicide in the Sui and Tang houses and Empress Wu's merciless killing of her own baby daughter and several grandchildren later in her life (*ZZTJ* 199.6286–87, 204.6467, 207.6557).

What is more interesting is that, after having deposed two puppet emperors, both her own sons, and enthroned herself, Empress Wu had put both under house arrest with strict court supervision that effectively cut off all communication with the outside (*ZZTJ* 204.6473, 205.6490). The empress recognized that she would still have to pass on the throne to no one else but her blood offspring in the end (*ZZTJ* 204.6474–75, 206.6526–27). This awkward situation bears a striking resemblance to the Ottoman court's *Kafes* (cage) system.[45] This measure, perhaps in a less draconian form but nonetheless "violating fundamental human relations by incarcerating one's flesh and blood," would be institutionalized by Emperor Xuanzong and enforced at least beyond the year 833 (*ZZTJ* 244.7886).

One may also note that the Ottoman *Kafes* was hardly unique to the Turkic political sphere: the later Ghaznavids in Afghanistan and Northern India also developed a similar policy after incessant succession struggles among the sultan's family members.[46] Corresponding to the birth control measures in the *Kafes*, a remarkable circumstance was the repeated attempts by Emperor Xuanzong (then the crown prince) to abort his consort's pregnancy for fear of further antagonizing Princess Taiping (*Jiu Tang shu* 52.2184). One notes that the incident was recorded due largely to the fact that the pregnancy the future Emperor Xuanzong tried to terminate produced in the end none other than the future Emperor Suzong (reign 756–62).

After the restoration (705) of the Tang dynasty under Empress Wu's son Emperor Zhongzong, we soon see another case of filicide in a succession struggle: the killing of Emperor Zhongzong's heir apparent, Prince Chongjun, after the latter's failed coup attempt against his father (*ZZTJ* 208.6611–12). But not long afterward the emperor in 710 fell victim of viricide/patricide as his empress and his daughter Princess Anle conspired to grab the imperial power for themselves (*ZZTJ* 209.6641–42).

In a typical Turco-Mongol maneuver after the death of the khan, and against the age-old tradition of lineal succession in the Central Kingdom, Princess Taiping, sister of the deceased emperor, and her nephew Prince Longji, the future Emperor Xuanzong (and as some have claimed, the latter's seemingly unambitious father too), together plotted a successful coup to send Longji's father back to the throne. At this time, the principle of blood tanistry, namely letting the ablest heir of all succeed, was so entrenched in the Tang house, prevailing over the *dizhang* principle stipulating instead that the successor be the eldest heir born of the chief consort, that Longji's elder brother Chengqi steadfastly refused to be appointed the heir apparent to avoid an almost certain repetition of the Xuanwu Gate incident (*ZZTJ* 209.6650).

Thus was created a most interesting triangular power structure between the emperor, his full sister Princess Taiping, and the young but capable Crown Prince Longji. The triumvirate showed deep rifts from the very beginning (*ZZTJ* 210.6656–57). Although Prince Longji, later Emperor Xuanzong, apparently made sure that not much was left in the history records that would cast doubt upon his filial relationship with his emperor father, there was ample evidence, for example, the story in *ZZTJ* (210.6673–74), showing that Emperor Ruizong did feel daunted by this intellectually and militarily gifted son, and the menace of patricide, which the Li boys (and girls) often showed little reluctance in plotting and executing, would seem a major factor in Emperor Ruizong's heavy dependence on his sister Princess Taiping against and as a way of balancing his son's power. No sooner had the son forced the aunt to commit suicide by a preemptive military move than the father decided to go into genuine retirement for good.

In many aspects Emperor Xuanzong could be called the last Turco-Mongol or Turco-Xianbei monarch of the Tang ruling house. The military and political expansion continued and reached its zenith during his reign. The emperor also showed remarkable openness and reception to foreign cultures, music and dance in particular, which was eagerly and wholeheartedly imitated by an equally receptive populace, with various Hu (foreign) fashions and styles soon becoming the dominating vogue of the time (*Jiu Tang shu* 45.1957–58). Xuanzong's dependence on and trust in his non-Hàn ethnic generals were also unprecedented (which would eventually cause his fall from grace). It is indeed very tempting to compare the first half of his reign with that of the brilliant Manchu emperor Shengzu (Kangxi), the best emperor the Central Kingdom ever had, according to many. But this would be a little beyond the scope of this chapter.

At issue here is that, just like Emperor Kangxi,[47] Emperor Xuanzong was dogged by the problem of succession and the choice of an heir apparent. What is most remarkable and revealing of his Turco-Xianbei heritage is that, in the spring of 737, the emperor had three of his sons, including his first heir apparent, killed in a single day (*ZZTJ* 214.6829). Such a resolute act of filicide, later indignantly denounced as a "breach of heavenly principles" by the Song dynasty historian Fan Zuyu,[48] would put Xuanzong on an equal footing with, say, the Ottoman sultan Selim I (Selim the Grim), who was believed to have, on November 20, 1514, killed three of his four sons,[49] leaving but one (Süleyman the Magnificent) to succeed him. It can be added that filicide also figured in the succession struggle during the Qing dynasty, in particular that carried out by the eventual successor to Emperor Kangxi, despite some modern authors' effort to whitewash or deny its occurrence.[50]

Emperor Xuanzong's radical measure, plus further act of filicide (*ZZTJ* 216.6916–17), did not relieve him in the end from the by now almost trademark Tang succession trouble. In the wake of the An Lushan Rebellion, another heir apparent son would part ways with Emperor Xuanzong and declare himself the new emperor (Emperor Suzong), handing his father a coup de grace (*ZZTJ* 218.6975–76, 218.6982.). Furthermore, after both had returned to the recovered Tang capital, the now retired Emperor Xuanzong would find himself nearly assassinated in a kidnap plot devised and executed by his son's most trusted courtier (*ZZTJ* 221.7094–95). With all his loyal ministers, attendants, and eunuchs dead or exiled, this retired emperor would eventually die a bitter, lonely, and helpless old man under virtual house arrest.

Such an unceremonious exit of, in my view, the last Turco-Xianbei monarch of the Tang by no means spelled the end of the imperial house's Turco-Mongol-style succession problems. Indeed, even prior to that, Emperor Suzong had to overcome and kill another royal brother, Prince Yong (Li Lin), who, apparently at the encouragement of Emperor Xuanzong (*ZZTJ* 218.6983, 219.7007), began to harbor imperial ambitions too. A side note is that this episode of fratricide had profound effects on the life and career of the two greatest Tang poets, Li Bai (Li Po 701–ca. 762) and Du Fu (712–70): Li Bai signed on with the losing side of this fratricidal struggle for the throne, for which he almost received a death sentence. He was eventually exiled to Yelang, which was by far the most serious crisis in the poet's life (*Xin Tang shu* 202.5763). This in turn led Du Fu to write several immortal poems over his deep concern for his dear friend's fate.

Despite further act of filicide, which saw one of his able sons, Prince Jianning, killed and the eldest, the future emperor Daizong gravely endangered (*ZZTJ* 219.7013.), Emperor Suzong would die, of natural cause or otherwise, amid the chaos of yet another fratricide coup d'état in 762 (*ZZTJ* 222.7123–24).

The Tang's succession troubles and the "unstable institution" of the heir apparent were far from over after this. What is more, there would emerge much more frequent lateral successions than the almost unbroken lineal tradition of the early Tang. However, there were many gradual but important changes in the aspects and circumstances of succession struggles, some of which will be covered in later sections. For my major contention that the early Tang was a Särbo-Chinese regime with strong Turco-Mongol characteristics, the documentation of blood tanistry cases can stop at this point. The following sections will be devoted to various aspects and implications of the Tang succession struggles.

The Oedipus Complex

Arthur Wright first proposed that the Sui emperor Yangdi represented an instance of the Oedipus complex.[51] Victor Xiong later repeated and in fact reinforced the case.[52] In my view, the Oedipus complex depiction here has overstretched the sphere of psychoanalysis. It is obvious from my narration that acute father-son enmity and rivalry were characteristic of the first two centuries of the Tang. In addition to the Sui, one can easily trace the phenomenon back to the Tuoba Wei state and other earlier dynasties established by various tribal groups, as well as in the An Lushan-Shi Siming rebel regime (both leaders were murdered by their respective sons). Boodberg is more to the point: it was a much more general and wider phenomenon on the Steppe.

Wright's Oedipus complex diagnosis would make this father-son adversary a rather personal trait of Emperor Yangdi. Even if the label stuck, it would have to be extended to so many other political figures of Steppe origin or background, both in China and elsewhere, that any utility of the term would appear lost. This father-son enmity was so typical of the Turco-Mongol culture that the vendetta against a dead father or the rush to reverse his policies can be clearly shown in a wide variety of cases, ranging from the Ghaznavid sultan Mas'ud in the Turco-Iranian world,[53] to the late Manchu monarchs such as Emperor Gaozong (Qianlong) of the Qing.[54] But if one invokes the Oedipal drive in the pretext of universal human traits, then in addition to losing the specificity, and hence the very reason for introducing the term, one would face the daunting task of explaining the relative scarcity of similar cases in the two Hàn dynasties as well as in other stable and prolonged native dynasties.

It is my view that the so-called Oedipus complex is in effect a convenient way to bypass the real socioeconomic and politico-cultural issues. I note that even the Shakespearean play *Hamlet*, which has often been cited as a quintessential case of such a complex, may in fact have actual historical succession struggles in the background.[55]

As many modern researchers have concluded, contrary to conventional misconception, pastoral nomadism was a very complex way of life that required sophisticated planning and great effort. In contrast to agriculture, it in fact allowed a much smaller margin of error in decision making and very low tolerance of natural and man-made disasters, as a severe spring storm could easily wipe out one's entire stock in a matter of days. The highly mobile way of life, the relative low economic return on a per-acre basis, and the constant threat of tribal and other warfare meant that tribe and other polity leadership must be very personal and militaristic, without the luxury of a large, permanent, civil bureaucratic establishment. All these factors demanded that the leadership remained with young, industrious, and energetic figures who could respond quickly and forcefully to a change of or emergency in the environment and who would be able to lead the tribes into successful military campaigns.

This leads to the notion that the socio-political life on the Steppe required a faster pace or metabolism in replenishing its leadership than in a sedentary agricultural society, which, with a large civil administration machine feeding on immense and reliable revenues from intensive farming, could afford to have unresponsive and politically uninterested elderly monarchs continue to occupy the throne (incidentally, this was exactly what became of Emperor Xuanzong, the last Turco-Xianbei monarch of the Tang). In my view this was the real root of the semilegendary Steppe tradition of regicide, ritualistic or real, found as far as the Khazar Empire, that a khan had a preordained time limit on his reign, after which he would be murdered.[56]

On this account we see also how Turco-Mongol traditions adapted, or shall we say mellowed, in their transition to the Central Kingdom. Unlike the harsh political realities on the Steppe where a khan normally would have to hang on until his natural or not so infrequently violent death, a sedentary society opened up a less draconian option: the position of a retired emperor, albeit as our examples have shown, life as such would seem not greatly more enviable than the Steppe alternative. Following the Turco-Xianbei traditions of its Northern dynasty predecessors, the Tang, especially in its first century and a half, had numerous such retired emperors, whereas none were found in more than four centuries of the two Hàn dynasties. This is one more reason why the early Tang should be more aptly called a Särbo-Chinese regime.

I further observe that in subsequent major native dynasties, namely the Song and the Ming, only a handful more such cases were found, almost invariably the consequence of catastrophic military invasions from the north.[57] Only in the Qing dynasty did we find another case of a purely domestic nature, which curiously enough was allegedly prompted by the "filial wish" of Emperor Gaozong that his reign not exceed a preset limit, namely the length of the reign of his grandfather Emperor Shengzu.[58]

Having examined the father-son feature, the maternal aspect in the alleged Oedipus complex should also be reviewed to do it full justice. First, once the mother changed herself into a "surrogate father" in the sense that she became a contender for the throne, as in the case of Empress Wu Zetian, the mother-son relation would turn out much less romantic than the complex prescribes, one more indication of the phenomenon's politico-cultural rather than alleged psychosexual root. Also the supposed affection was evidently not always recip-rocal, as political filicide by the mother was noted from the late Tuoba Wei pe-riod onward.

Nevertheless, in comparison with the fate of the fathers, royal matriarchs did seem to fare a lot better, even in extreme cases such as Empress Wu Zetian and the grandmother of Emperor Xiaowen of the Tuoba Wei (*ZZTJ* 134.4187, 137.4302.). However, instead of the either too individual or too universal trait of Oedipal drive, I think a more plausible explanation lies elsewhere. In this regard classical historians would seem more down-to-earth than psychoanalysis-lean-ing modern authors when *Hou Hàn shu* (*The History of the Late Hàn*, 90.2979) provides the following hint in describing the Wuhuan's unmistakable Steppe traits of patricide and fratricide: "[They] kill their father and elder brothers when angry, but would never hurt their mother, for mothers have a clan whereas fathers and elder brothers do not [have someone to take] revenge for them-selves." Here we clearly see remnants of matriarchy at work, which in my view is a more realistic factor on the Steppe than a man's subconscious Oedipal desire for his mother, for this can also explain the Northern women's traditionally strong role, attested by their prominent social status in the Northern dynasties,[59] and culminating in Empress Wu becoming the first and only woman emperor in Chinese history, the latter of which could only happen in a Särbo-Chinese dy-nasty with deeply entrenched Turco-Mongol traditions. A Steppe mother's near-sacred status and complete dominance of her son in my view also provide a most natural explanation for the unprecedented Tuoba Wei custom of killing an heir apparent's birth mother before crowning the prince son. The case of Lady Gouyi of the Former Hàn dynasty (*ZZTJ* 22.744–45), from which the Tuoba custom had allegedly taken its cue, was evidently an exceptional, ad hoc mea-sure. The case of Empress-dowager Hu, the first birth mother of a future Tuoba emperor to escape this fate, demonstrates that the draconian rule was not an unwarranted and overcautious precaution: by her complete domination of her emperor son and her final act of filicide (*ZZTJ* 152.4739), Empress-dowager Hu was blamed for the eventual collapse of the once powerful Tuoba regime in northern China.

Other Aspects of the Tang Blood Tanistry

The established Hàn tradition of having, at least formally, an heir apparent means that the succession struggles in the Central Kingdom usually happened prior to the death of the current ruler and around the institution of heir apparent. This may be the most important departure from the Steppe, where the hell of succession wars normally broke loose with the death of the khan. But as Joseph Fletcher has detailed in his "Turco-Mongol Monarchic Tradition in the Ottoman Empire," such a feature or adaptation to the sedentary society was not unique in China, as it was also attested in other "conquest regimes."

In his pioneering treatise on the political history of the Tang, which provided the first systematic examination of the phenomenon of the unstable Tang institution of heir apparent (to which I owe much of the inspiration for the current chapter), Chen Yinke has analyzed the importance of controlling the Xuanwu Gate in the capital in numerous coups d'état during the early Tang.[60] However, I depart from his theory by considering the discussion of the key factions of people instead of geography in these incidents a more consequential topic. Not only does one see the reason for the notoriety of the Xuanwu Gate in the period, but it also sheds light on the process of how this Särbo-Chinese regime slowly evolved into something more in line with a native dynasty.

For the era under examination, namely the first 150 years of the Tang, one of the key elements in the succession struggle was various imperial guard units. This in my view was the cause for the Xuanwu Gate's prominence in these coups during the period. For blood tanistry struggles in an agrarian society, Fletcher has introduced the term "surrogate nomads" for the equivalent of tribes and tribal military elites who would fight out the succession wars on the Steppe. For the early Tang, the "surrogate" qualifier would seem almost superfluous, because the ranks of imperial guards were filled with people not just of nomadic origin but literally fresh from the Steppe. A good example was the three hundred Türk troops Prince Jiancheng planned to use to attack Li Shimin's residence (*Xin Tang shu* 79.3542).[61] In fact at times these figures were said to be so numerous that they filled half of the positions at court (*ZZTJ* 193.6098), which were apparently mostly military. Many were actually mentioned or even named in succession struggles. Li Duozuo, a prominent imperial guard of Mojie ethnicity (widely regarded as the predecessor of the Manchu), on whom was bestowed the royal family name (*Jiu Tang shu* 109.3296–97), was a typical case. This was hardly the best indication of a "native" dynasty, though the standard records have almost certainly suppressed or played down as much as possible the role of these "Barbarian" figures in setting the course of Chinese history.

Another important dimension of the unmistakable Turco-Mongol trait of the early Tang was its continued military and political expansion in almost all directions. Again a great number of non-Hàn ethnic generals and naturally an even greater number of such troops were used in this endeavor. In fact, the Tang ethnic generals have became a fecund study subject for modern historians.[62] These studies demonstrate that the phenomenon was a rather unusual case in Chinese history. That is, if we exclude the Mongol forces in the Qing's march into Central Asia, an exact repetition of the Tang's advances one millennium earlier. As the imperial guards actively participated in these campaigns, their prestige at the court and their role in the succession struggle continued. The ancient Orkhon inscriptions mentioned explicitly that the Türk troops had fought the wars for the Tabgach/Tuoba emperors.[63] But this complaint masked the other side of the coin: the important role of these Türk generals and soldiers in choosing the very emperors they would serve under as well as the grossly out of proportion positions they filled at the Tang court.

The expansion of the Tang was gradually checked by the advent of two new powers: the Arabs and the Tibetans. A new Uighur power was also emerging on the Steppe. In the meantime, the unstoppable process of sinicization was slowly but steadily taking its toll. One of the signs was the role of personal slaves and eunuchs in the succession struggle. For example, in Emperor Xuanzong's military move to eliminate Princess Taiping's supporters, which culminated in the princess's suicide and Emperor Ruizong's final "retirement," two important players were Wang Maozhong, a family slave of Korean descent, and Gao Lishi, a eunuch (*ZZTJ* 210.6683; *Jiu Tang shu* 106.3252). Emperor Xuanzong, who started as a strong Turco-Xianbei monarch, would gradually turn into an uninterested and disengaged emperor, of the kind of which the later native Ming dynasty would see many. The appearance of the second Eastern Türk Empire was invariably hailed as a conquered people casting off the Tang yoke. Few realize that the development might be more appropriately viewed as the consequence of the growing alienation felt by a (junior) partner in a Särbo-Turco-Chinese joint venture that was tilting more and more toward agrarian traditions. Pulleyblank seems to be the only author to have noted this Turco-Chinese partnership,[64] albeit failing to recognize the crucial Xianbei factor that, like the Manchus, was the key element binding the Steppe and the agrarian communities into a true empire. In my view, the reappearance of an Eastern Türk empire was not unlike the case of Outer Mongolia gaining independence after the end of the Qing, a Manchu-Mongol-Chinese dynasty.

With the onset of the An Lushan Rebellion in 755, the outward expansion of the Tang came to a sudden stop. Yet the stubborn Steppe heritage of succession struggles did not go right out of the political arena with our last Turco-Xianbei monarch, though its fundamental aspects underwent a sea change.

The key transformation was that the court eunuchs replaced the regular imperial guards in deciding the outcome of the succession struggle,[65] a natural development with the end of the glories of the expansion wars. The new power brokers would continue this role until almost the very end of the Tang. Fletcher's term "surrogate nomads" would now do full justice to them. Not by accident, the coming of eunuchal power at the Tang court closely resembled, for example, a similar development in the declining years of the Safavid dynasty of Iran, after the latter's practice of appointing the royal princes to provincial governorship (also an early Tang policy) was replaced by their confinement to the harem (similar measures were adopted by the Tang too, as discussed earlier) in order to avoid succession contentions.[66] With the control of imperial guards gradually falling into the hands of the court eunuchs and the guard ranks filled mostly with rich playboys from the capital (*ZZTJ* 254.8237), the political drama was now played out within the walls of the inner palace. The strategic importance of the Xuanwu Gate, together with the prestige of the many guard units, was soon lost. For example, a late Tang source[67] has an eyewitness report on the deplorable condition during the Yuanhe era (806–20) of an originally prestigious imperial guard office. However, these new changes are mostly beyond the scope of this book.

The Process of Sinicization

The case of Prince Chengqian had many historical precedents and parallels. In addition to Tuoba Xun, the Northern Wei heir apparent, two other prominent cases were that of the Sui heir apparent Yang Yong and Taizong's elder brother Crown Prince Jiancheng, Chengqian's uncle. Careful study of these cases reveals an interesting pattern of succession struggles during the era: the "bandwagon" of sinicization and the patronage of classical Chinese scholarship or other authentic Chinese literature and arts as a most effective tool in such contentions, when the regime was hard-pressed for political legitimacy to rule the entire Central Kingdom.

In the case of Emperor Yangdi of the Sui, we see his marriage at a young age to a daughter of a prominent southern royal family (in fact the daughter of a puppet Later Liang emperor); his patronage of the Southern Buddhist temples; his love of almost everything connected to the south, which before the final unification was seen even by many in the north as the site of the "legitimate" Chinese regime; and, last but not least, his status as an extraordinarily talented man of Chinese literacy[68]—all of this certainly had figured in his successful contention for the throne against his elder brother and the Confucian *dizhang* rule of succession.

Li Shimin's bid for the throne is a very old and thoroughly studied topic. Many factors for his triumph over his elder brother have been proposed: his unmatched military deeds in solidifying the dynasty, his command of a large group of talented followers, his ability to control the crucial Xuanwu Gate, his preemptive strike, and so on.[69] But the issue of sinicization has not attracted enough attention in the context of his eventual command of political legitimacy and its role in the defeat of his brothers. In fact, Li Shimin set up an "academy" in his official residence to patronize classical literature and scholarship as early as 621, while the regime was not yet solidified (*ZZTJ* 189.5931-32). One has to admit that Li Shimin had remarkable political foresight and long-term planning in the struggle for succession.

The situation is perhaps best enlightened by the aforementioned quote of Emperor Gaozu when Li Shimin began to show his independence. It not only indicated the Li clan's ethnic self-identity as discussed earlier but also the notion that Li Shimin's political aspirations were prompted partly by his sinicization— being "taught by educated Hàn."

The case of Prince Chengqian can be studied then in the same context. The hapless Prince was known to have frequently "ignored his learning," whereas his main rival Li Tai was a diligent student and, following in the footsteps of his father, set up a literary "academy" to patronize classical scholarship; his courtyard was then "as crowded as a marketplace." In the spring of 642, he even presented the court with a major work authored under his sponsorship (*ZZTJ* 195.6150, 196.6174). On the other hand, his reported love of hunting and war games aside, there were two interesting episodes indicative of his attitude toward the most important national affair in the Central Kingdom—agriculture. First, he was accused of having "interrupted farming" (*ZZTJ* 196.6168). Second, he was credited with saving the life of an attendant of the imperial manor from Emperor Taizong's order of execution (*Tang huiyao* 4.44). The incident demonstrated Chengqian's quality of decency, something the official history was reluctant to show. The attendant's alleged offense was, interestingly, that he had been ignoring the maintenance of the garden. It should also be noted that, judging by his surname Mu, this hapless attendant was undoubtedly of Xianbei descent.[70]

Proceeding from the cases I have reviewed here, a general rule in the succession struggle can be summarized as follows. The elder sons, Prince Yong, Prince Jiancheng, and Prince Chengqian (and the Tuoba Prince Xun in some sense), tended to be upstaged by their more "cultured" and more "sinicized" younger brothers, Emperor Yangdi, Emperor Taizong, and Prince Tai respectively.

One may find interesting parallels elsewhere. For instance, there were several cases of elder and more militaristic sons being passed over for succession in the Turco-Iranian realm, which has puzzled early Muslim and later authors.[71] Bosworth has suggested they be a reminiscence of the Steppe custom of ultimogeniture. However, as many Mongologists have pointed out, the Mongol practice of *ochigin*, a term with a Turkic origin, regarding the inheritance of property might not necessarily apply to political power (khanship). In the Särbo-Chinese connection, the cultural aspect of these cases would also seem an interesting topic. One notes that, among the Ghaznavids for example, in contrast to the militarist elder brother Mas'ud, the younger brother Muhammad's tastes "were predominately literary and studious."[72]

The paradox back in the Central Kingdom is that what these more sinicized younger sons had to overcome was the very Chinese primogeniture succession principle. Among other things, it created an acute dilemma for Hàn ministers and officials in taking sides. The famous courtier Wei Zheng is a good example. This deep self-conflict could be observed throughout Wei's life, on which most biographies, including Howard Wechsler's fine study, fail to elaborate. Wei Zheng was noted for his loyalty to Emperor Gaozu's original heir apparent, Prince Jiancheng. As shown by an interesting episode in *Jiu Tang shu* (71.2559), he was still quite unwavering on the *dizhang* primogeniture succession rule after many years of service under Emperor Taizong, whose ascension to the throne represented a breach of this very principle.

This politico-cultural aspect of Turco-Mongol conquest regimes, namely enhancing their legitimacy by patronizing the "native" culture and religion at the expense of their own ethnic heritage, was also amply demonstrated by, inter alia, almost all Turkic dominions in the Middle East, at least up to the fourteenth century, as observed by Richard Frye and Aydin Sayili.[73] A similar endeavor would be observed in the Qing's succession struggles, exemplified by the miserable end of both Chen Menglei, the compiler of the voluminous *Gujin tushu jicheng* (*Complete Collection of Literature from Ancient Times to Present Day*), and his immediate royal patron.[74]

However, if the sinicization or patronage of Hàn culture represented the political dimension of the blood tanistry struggle, then the military dimension was equally if not more important. For the support of the imperial guards who would actually carry out the dirty and often bloody job, the military aptitude and valor of the contender were also crucial, as attested by the cases of Emperor Yangdi of the

Sui and the Tang emperors Taizong and Xuanzong. Failure in the military aspect and/or an overkill in sinicization would lead to disastrous results for the contenders, best shown by the case of Prince Tai, whose maneuver led to the downfall of the Crown Prince Chengqian but fell short of Tai's ultimate objective of replacing him. One can note similar effort in patronizing traditional Chinese scholarship by Emperor Gaozong's heir apparent, Li Xian, whose famed annotation of *Hou Hàn shu* (*History of the Later Hàn*) has since become an integral part of that dynastic history. Li Xian's scholarly pursuits, obviously for enhancing his status in the face of his mother Wu Zetian's blatant political challenge to him and the entrenched Hàn patriarchy tradition, proved counterproductive too.

The strong opposition to Prince Li Tai as a replacement for Prince Chengqian also suggests in my view the existence of a political force at the Tang court that was not sympathetic to Tai's overt sinicizing tendency. This, among other things, shows that sinicization was a complex and slow process and was not always one-way. Few authors have noted that the choice of the new crown prince Li Zhi, later Emperor Gaozong, represented a political compromise in this ethnico-cultural context. It can be clearly seen from the fact that Li Zhi was close to Li Yuanchang, a follower of Prince Chengqian in the Li clan, and Zhangsun Wuji was once a friend of Hou Junji, another important member of the Chengqian clique (*ZZTJ* 197.6195 and *Quan Tang wen* 161.1645). Sun Guodong has pointed out that Zhangsun Wuji, Li Zhi's decisive backer, was not a man of letters, while three major supporters of Prince Wei, namely Liu Ji, Cen Wenben, and Cui Renshi, all were, and all had rather miserable ends.[75] Indeed, Zhangsun Wuji carried the Tuoba Xianbei legacy both by descent and in deeds. Instead of being stripped off by the "basically sinified" former tribesmen as David Honey has argued, the "Barbarian" felt hat that Zhangsun Wuji wore soon set the fashion and was later labeled by the Confucian historians as "devilish" as quoted earlier, another indication that Prince Chengqian's alleged neurosis was hardly an anomaly in the ruling aristocracy.

However, the best evidence that this choice was a compromise in the context of sinicization was Prince Li Zhi himself. In addition to ordering Türk companions for his sons as mentioned earlier, he proved himself the ultimate Northern boy by marrying his father's wife as well as allowing her to dominate the court.

The Issue of Legitimacy and the Role of Religion

The issue of sinicization (or patronage of native cultures in the general Turco-Mongol political sphere) as the political arm of the blood tanistry struggle leads to the issue of political legitimacy of the Turco-Xianbei regimes, including the Sui and the (early) Tang, in China.

In his resourceful and often stimulating book on China's frontiers, Thomas Barfield contends that as a universal rule the Steppe nomadic regimes were not interested in settling in and taking over the Chinese heartland.[76] However, this principle would seem at times dependent on disavowing the Steppe identity of the nomads as soon as they crossed to the south of the Great Wall, for they would soon develop a strong interest afterward in doing exactly that. The Tuobas might have originated in the Xing'an Mountains, but the strong Turkic elements, both linguistic (see the Appendix of this book) and political, in them and their successors were hard to ignore. The Turco-Xianbei rulers in northern China certainly did not show great hesitation in aspiring to become true sons of heaven for all those under heaven. As mentioned earlier, the Tuoba Wei's wholesale sinification and transfer of its capital were viewed by many as prompted by such an aim. It is remarkable that the Nüzhen (Jurchen) emperor Wanyan Liang (reign 1149–61) also went through an extensive process of sinicization prior to his disastrous military expedition to unify China.[77]

However, since the collapse of the Western Jin, the political and cultural "legitimacy" had always been regarded, by people in both the south and north, as residing with the Southern dynasties (*Bei Qi shu* [*The History of the Northern Qi Dynasty*] 24.347–48). The Sui/Tang regime spared no effort in overcoming this politico-cultural obstacle. One of the crucial endeavors was to present themselves as having been Hàn Chinese all along. Various post-Islamic-conquest Iranian dynasties of native and Turkic origins did exactly the same to achieve political legitimacy.[78] The appearance of the sinicization bandwagon in the blood tanistry struggles of the Tuoba's Sui and Tang successors is thus a natural extension of this conscious effort.

Few authors have paid attention to the acute ethnic strife, especially in the Northern Zhou domain, just prior to the Sui/Tang unification of the country. An important reason was the cover-up and fence-mending efforts by these two regimes. A good example was the sack by the Northern Zhou forces of the city of Jiangling in 554, the temporary capital of the southern Liang house and an established cultural centre. The brutality, horror, and in particular the large-scale and indiscriminate enslavement of ethnic Southern Hàns, all social strata included, would certainly have paled the atrocities allegedly committed by the Manchus in conquering southern China. But for obvious political reasons, not the least of which was the fact that the fathers and grandfathers of the Sui/Tang ruling clique were active participants in this most savage feat, only sporadic pieces of evidence of the actual atrocity were preserved, while deeds hard to gloss over like the burning of the Liang royal library were conveniently blamed on the victims' own acts (*ZZTJ* 165.5121). Today one can only present very brief discussions of the savageries of the Northern Zhou army based on some sporadic data.[79]

It is simply unbelievable that memories of such atrocities would be forgotten in a matter of a few decades when the Sui, followed by the Tang, came to power. In this context we can understand the obsession these two regimes had with their "politically correct" ethnic images, as well as the utility of the bandwagon of sinicization in succession struggles. For instance, the famed aversion to the character *hu*, "foreign," by the Emperor Yangdi or his father, Emperor Wendi, was therefore in my view not caused by some arrogant sinocentricism as most authors have alleged, but was dictated by the need for political legitimacy as perceived by the Sui rulers and the ethnic skeletons in the Yang family's closet.

It is also interesting to examine the role of religion in this context. Many authors including Arthur Wright have noted that Emperor Yangdi's patronage of the southern Buddhist schools was politically motivated. But few seemed to have recognized the ethnic factor here: the Sui was evidently using Buddhism to help bridge the ethnic divide, a feeling that must have been very strong after the Jiangling atrocity, whose major perpetrators included Emperor Yangdi's very grandfather Yang Zhong. The latter actually bore a "Barbarian" surname, Puliuru, during the Northern Zhou's bloody conquest of the southern state.

The utility of religion became even more evident in the house of Tang. After the short-lived Sui, the early Tang emperors were no great patrons of the "foreign" religion, namely Buddhism, that had failed to prolong their predecessor's mandate of heaven. For the urgent need of political legitimacy, the Tang imperial house found an even better solution than the southern Buddhism schools to mask the clan's non-Hàn origin: to identify themselves as the descendants of Li Er (Laozi), the alleged founder of Taoism.

A striking parallel can be found among the Safavids, the founder of the most splendid post-Turkmen dynasty in Iran that was largely responsible for the now entrenched Shi'a heritage in that country. With a questionable claim of native Iranian (or rather Kurdish) origin,[80] the clan's family language was nevertheless Turkic Azeri.[81] For obvious politico-religious considerations, particularly an authentic Shi'a origin, the family falsified a genealogy from one of the Twelve Imams and "systematically destroyed any evidence" that would imply otherwise.[82] In this regard the Mongols certainly had the fewest worldly obstacles in portraying Genghis Khan as the incarnation of a Buddhist universal emperor to legitimize their rule of a world empire.[83]

This political dimension of religion has important bearings on the issue of blood tanistry struggles, the case between Li Shimin and Crown Prince Jiancheng in particular. Failure to recognize this political and, as we shall see, ethnic aspect led Arthur Wright[84] to question the insightful observation by Tang Yongtong[85] that, in this struggle, the Buddhists were on the side of the elder brother (Wright's erroneous notion has been all but refuted, albeit implicitly, by Stanley Weinstein).[86]

As a "foreign" religion, the Buddhism establishment in China had a vested interest in the imperial house's acknowledgment of its non-Hàn origin and heritage. The church must have actively countered any opposite move. As described before, the famous monk Falin openly slandered the imperial family's ethnic origin claiming its descent from the Tuoba. Proceeding from my examination of the role of sinicization in succession struggles, it was very natural that the Buddhist church was behind the crown prince, as Tang Yongtong has observed. Meanwhile the Taoists rallied to the challenger Li Shimin, as shown by the cases of two Taoist priests (*Jiu Tang shu* 191.5089, 192.5125; *Xin Tang shu* 204.5804–5.). It is telling that when Fang Xuanling and Du Ruhui, the two most trusted followers of Li Shimin, sneaked back to the capital to participate in the Xuanwu Gate coup d'état, they reportedly disguised themselves as Taoists (*ZZTJ* 191.6009). Emperor Taizong's edict of 637 elevating Taoism to a higher status than Buddhism[87] was a most natural reward for this support. Similarly, this could also explain Empress Wu Zetian's patronage of the "foreign" Buddhism in her bid to succeed her husband and become an unprecedented woman emperor against every Hàn Chinese custom and principle.

A Fox Dies with Its Head Pointing to Home Hill

In addition to the incessant succession struggles of the early Tang examined earlier, I add a brief section here on another angle from which to examine the ethnic identity of the Tang royal house.[88]

The Chinese idiom used as the title of this section conveys the general phenomenon that one goes back to one's roots in one's last days. It can also be used to indicate the belief that one's truest feelings are revealed while in death throes. The latter can apply to both people and institutions.

Another heavily studied subject regarding the early Tang emperors hardly touched upon so far in this chapter is the imperial title *tiankehan*, or heavenly Qaghan,[89] first assumed by Emperor Taizong. This imperial title was primarily for symbolizing and embodying a Tang emperor's sovereignty over the tribal groups on the Steppe. It is astonishingly similar to a Qing emperor's epithet of great khan used with the latter's Manchu, Mongol, and other ethnic subjects.

Most historians have represented Emperor Taizong's adoption of the title heavenly Qaghan as a cynical political ploy to neutralize the threat of Türk power in the late 620s. But as Denis Twitchett astutely remarked, it was the emperor's "Turkic identity" that was essential in his accepting this new title. Emperor's Taizong's true feelings in this regard are revealed by what transpired near the end of his life. After his return from the abortive campaign against Koguryo in the autumn of 645, Emperor Taizong was chronically and seriously ill, so much so that when he arrived back in the Tang capital in the third month of 646 he withdrew from his court duties and appointed his heir apparent (future emperor Gaozong) as acting regent for long periods and avoided making decisions himself. Yet he clearly felt that maintaining his standing among the Steppe peoples was of such overriding importance that in the sixth month of 646 he decided to make an exhausting journey to the frontier prefect of Lingzhou for a meeting with the leadership of the Steppe peoples to enable them to reassert their allegiance and proclaim him once more as their heavenly Qaghan, again leaving the heir apparent to act as regent at the capital. The journey took more than two months, and his exertions led to a recurrence and aggravation of his illness, from which he never fully recovered (*ZZTJ* 198–99). This clearly and unequivocally shows the importance he attached to his Turkic connections.

I would add that this "Turkic identity" was further reflected in Emperor Taizong's death. Several authors have observed that certain features of his mausoleum, particularly the large number of stone statues representing real-life personalities, were imitative of the ancient Türk burial custom.[90] I contend that, rather than mere imitation, it in fact reflected the Tang imperial house's Steppe background and identity. For a son of heaven well known for his obsession with posterity and historical legacy in the Sinitic world, Emperor Taizong's mausoleum is a manifestation of his other cultural identity.

The Tang house's respect for non-Hàn burial customs both within and beyond the Chinese heartland was documented. For example, Emperor Taizong once sharply condemned the Eastern Türks' adoption of the (Hàn) tomb burials in violation of their ancestral traditions (*Cefu yuangui* 125.1501),[91] and Emperor Xuanzong issued an edict allowing a surrendered Türk official "to be buried according to the native [Turkic] customs" (*Cefu yuangui* 974.11446).

Nearly three centuries later, when the Tang dynasty was in its death throes, there was another fascinating case of atavistic reflection of its ethnic roots. In the year 904, shortly before his murder by the founding monarch of the succeeding

Liang dynasty (907–23), the Tang emperor Zhaozong (reign 888–904) was forced into a miserable banishment from the Tang capital with a small entourage, a virtual prisoner of the Liang soldiers. In constant fear of regicide and anticipating the final end of the once glorious dynasty, Emperor Zhaozong cited a folk poem lamenting his fate (*ZZTJ* 264.8627), likening himself to a "freezing bird at the peak of Mount Hegan." Interestingly, from hundreds of possible metaphors in volumes of Chinese literature for describing a despondent monarch in his last days, Emperor Zhaozong picked up a folklore icon that originated from the area where Mount Hegan was well known. The final note to this sad episode is that Hegan was an old tribal name found among the Tuoba core followers, and the namesake mountain was actually located in the immediate area of the old Tuoba capital Pingcheng (near present-day Datong in the province of Shanxi), which has had heavy concentrations of ethnic descendants of the Northern nomads ever since the early Tuoba period.[92]

Conclusion

By examining the incessant succession struggles and other characteristics of the period, I demonstrate that the early Tang, far from being a "native" dynasty, was in fact a regime with heavy Turco-Xianbei traits, and hence may be more aptly termed a Särbo-Chinese regime. But for the cause of political legitimacy, the imperial family made enormous efforts to present itself as a bona fide Hàn house and to make sure that no compromising evidence was left in any records.

Two historical factors have contributed to the Tang's near success in maintaining this image throughout history: (a) its status as the all-dominating polity in the vast East-Central Asian continent and the sole custodian of historiography, with hardly any independent cultural entity in existence to provide an alternative view or perspective, and (b) the passing of the time.

Besides being in exclusive control of traditional historiography, the Confucian scholar-officials all but monopolized every genre of writing in classical East Asia.[93] This is reflected in the fact that, in all three major Altaic languages, the early words for "writing" and "books" are generally considered as cognates of the Chinese character *bi*, "pen, writing brush."[94] The long-speculated existence of a Xianbei script[95] must be largely abandoned after the discovery of the Xianbei cavern and other equally rich collections of archaeological findings, especially tomb inscriptions and other artifacts of this period. Without an effective script, let alone a body of existing literature, nomadic oral tradition, albeit rich, was no rival to the tomes of Chinese literature (or "cultural repertoire" in Jack Goody and Ian Watt's words)[96] accumulated since the archaic age.

Conversely, what may have been even more critical were the deliberate efforts by the Northern autocratic families who dominated the political stage in China for centuries. For the specific Sui objective of conquering the south where "legitimate" Chinese dynasties had been maintained, and for the general need for political legitimacy through to the early Tang, a particular task of the Sui/ Tang ruling class was to obscure their non-Sinitic Steppe background and connections. A particular case in point is the contrast between *Zhou shu* (*The History of the Northern Zhou Dynasty*), the official Tang-authorized history of the victorious Zhou regime in the struggle to unify northern China, and that of the loser, *Bei Qi shu*. Because the early Tang ruling clique was dominated by the descendants of the Northern Zhou aristocracy, the chief compiler, Linghu Defen, being the grandson of the Zhou general-in-chief Linghu Zheng (*Zhou shu* 36.643), *Zhou shu* could hardly afford any real impartiality or objectivity. This was noticed and criticized even by the Tang historian Liu Zhiji.[97] Meanwhile, the ruling families of the Qi fared quite miserably after forfeiting their state. Some former royal household members even ended up peddling candles (*ZZTJ* 173.5382), and the Northern Zhou aristocracy's distrust of the people of the former Qi domain persisted well into the Tang times and might even have contributed to the cause of the An Lushan Rebellion.[98] The narration in *Bei Qi shu* was therefore much less inhibited, if not deliberately negative, in describing the Qi regime. As an example of issues pertinent to this study, one can get significantly more information on the Turco-Xianbei cultural and political traits of the Qi ruling clan than of that of the Zhou,[99] whereas in reality the latter was much more "Xianbei-ized" than the former.[100] In view of the "politically correct" ethnic images in *Zhou shu*, one should not be surprised by the even less frequent Northern traits in the Tang records.

On the second factor, of the passing of time, after the death in exile of the Buddhist monk Falin, it was not until the Southern Song that the kind of political atmosphere first emerged in which questions would be raised on this long-established historical image. By that time, few solid records remained to allow concrete and detailed examination of the real origin and characteristics of the Tang imperial house.

This study also tries to show the inherent problem of relying on traditional historiography without critically examining the very source of these records: just like the Arabo-Persian authors who would not write about their ruler's Turkic culture and heritage, even without the attentive interference from a court obsessed with its historical image, Confucian historians would still hardly have found the many Turco-Xianbei aspects of the regime they were serving a worthy topic. Repeated rewriting and editing of the histories for the sake of elegance and concision, if not for some less honest purpose, had made the situation even worse.

By studying several aspects of the Tang blood tanistry struggles, especially its relationship with the so-called sinicization, one can see that, contrary to the conventional view that conquerors would soon melt in the sea of Chinese popu-lace, the sinicization of Steppe people in the Central Kingdom was a long and painful process. The strong reactions to Tuoba emperor Xiaowen's forced wholesale sinicization, culminating in the Six-Garrison Rebellion and the downfall of the Northern Wei, could still see their ripples in early Tang.

Another seemingly entrenched notion challenged in this chapter is the clas-sification of Chinese dynasties into "native" and "conquest" regimes. Even in his otherwise enlightening book on China's "perilous frontier," Thomas Barfield sticks to the conventional view that "the collapse of the [Northern] Wei marked the end of Manchurian rule in China."[101] Yet as I have shown, in many aspects the (early) Tang bore striking similarity to the Qing dynasty. In addition to the succession struggles, the institution of heir apparent, the frontier and ethnic policy, the advance into Central Asia, and even the fate of the "national lan-guage," I may add that the Tang and the Qing were the only two Chinese dynas-ties during which provincial governors held enormous prestige and power. At the very least, these facts suggest that the distinction between a "native" and a "conquest" dynasty is at best a gray area.

Chapter 2

=====

From Mulan to Unicorn

The Ballad of Mulan

Anonymous

Click, click, forever click, click;
Mulan sits at the door and weaves.
Listen, and you will not hear the shuttle's sound,
But only hear a girl's sobs and sighs.
"Oh tell me, lady, are you thinking of your love,
Oh tell me, lady, are you longing for your dear?"
"Oh no, oh no, I am not thinking of my love,
Oh no, oh no, I am not longing for my dear.
But last night I read the battle-roll;
The Qaghan has ordered a great levy of men.
The battle-roll was written in twelve books,
And in each book stood my father's name.
My father's sons are not grown men,
And of all my brothers, none is older than me.
Oh let me to the market to buy saddle and horse,
And ride with the soldiers to take my father's place."
In the eastern market she's bought a gallant horse,
In the western market she's bought saddle and cloth.
In the southern market she's bought snaffle and reins,
In the northern market she's bought a tall whip.
In the morning she stole from her father's and mother's house;
At night she was camping by the Yellow River's side.
She could not hear her father and mother calling to her by her name,
But only the song of the Yellow River as its hurrying waters hissed
and swirled through the night.

At dawn they left the River and went on their way;
At dusk they came to the Black Water's side.
She could not hear her father and mother calling to her by her name,
She could only hear the muffled voices of Scythian horsemen riding
     on the hills of Yan.
A thousand leagues she tramped on the errands of war,
Frontiers and hills she crossed like a bird in flight.
Through the northern air echoed the watchman's tap;
The wintry light gleamed on coats of mail.
The captain had fought a hundred fights, and died;
The warriors in ten years had won their rest.
They went home; they saw the Emperor's face;
The Son of Heaven was seated in the Hall of Light.
To the strong in battle lordships and lands he gave;
And of prize money a hundred thousand strings.
Then spoke the Qaghan and asked her what she would take.
"Oh, Mulan asks not to be made
A Counsellor at the Qaghan's court;
She only begs for a camel that can march
A thousand leagues a day,
To take her back to her home."

When her father and mother heard that she had come,
They went out to the wall and led her back to the house.
When her little sister heard that she had come,
She went to the door and rouged her face afresh.
When her little brother heard that his sister had come,
He sharpened his knife and darted like a flash
Toward the pigs and sheep.

She opened the gate that leads to the eastern tower,
She sat on her bed that stood in the western tower.
She cast aside her heavy soldier's cloak,
And wore again her old-time dress.
She stood at the window and bound her cloudy hair;
She went to the mirror and fastened her yellow combs.
She left the house and met her messmates in the road;
Her messmates were startled out of their wits.

They had marched with her for twelve years of war
And never known that Mulan was a girl!
For the male hare has a lilting, lolloping gait,
And the female hare has a wild and roving eye;
But set them both scampering side by side,
And who so wise could tell you "This is he"?[1]

On January 23, 1999, the Associated Press reported from Istanbul, in an article titled "Turkey Nationalists Protest 'Mulan,'" that a Turkish nationalist party wanted to ban the Disney movie *Mulan* in Turkey, claiming, "This animated film distorts and blackens the history of the Turks by showing the Huns as bad and the Chinese as peace-lovers."

As this chapter demonstrates, it is ironic that the very name of the heroine Mulan, much less the cultural background of the legend on which the Disney film was based, was not even Sinitic or Hàn Chinese to start with, but came from a nomadic and Turco-Mongol milieu. Furthermore, as the title of this chapter suggests, the true meaning of the name Mulan may turn out to be very close to that of another popular figure in animated cartoons. These facts are in addition to another, perhaps bigger, irony—namely that the dominating "Chinese" of the Mulan story were none other than the Tuoba, a Turkic group according to some linguists, ancient as well as modern.

The Name Mulan

The Mulan story comes almost entirely from a folk ballad, "The Ballad of Mulan," of unknown origin and time, but generally believed to be of the Tuoba Wei (the Late or Northern Wei, 386–534) era. Parts of the poem, especially the following six lines, show traces of literati refinement of later periods, hence the speculation that the poem may also be from the time of the Tang dynasty (618–907):

A thousand leagues she tramped on the errands of war,
Frontiers and hills she crossed like a bird in flight.
Through the northern air echoed the watchman's tap;
The wintry light gleamed on coats of mail.
The captain had fought a hundred fights, and died;
The warriors in ten years had won their rest.

But this self-imposed controversy about the exact date of the poem would seem not only a moot issue but also largely a sinocentric idiosyncrasy from a "nomadic perspective," because as examined in the previous chapter, both the Sui and Tang houses were the Tuoba's political and biological heirs and were called Tuoba/Tabγach by contemporary nomadic people. The problem of dating is therefore of little interest to the present discussion.

The background of the poem was clearly the wars between the Tuoba/Tabγach and their former nomadic brethren, most likely the Ruanruan (Juan-juan, Rouran), who remained on the Steppe. As Victor Mair has commented, even the ballad itself may be "first conceived in one of the languages of that land of nomads."[2] The Ruanruan was often identified as the same as, or closely related to, the Avar people in Western sources. This group would later become the oppressors and foes of the early Türks. Therefore, if we take the view that linguistically the Tuoba represented a so-called *l/r* Turkic language (versus the majority of Turkic tongues belonging to the *s/z* group),[3] the Mulan story would become part of the general conflict between the Ruanruan, widely believed to be a proto-Mongol people, on one side, and the "Chinese" and early "Türks" on the other side. This would make the claim that the Mulan story was against the ancient Türks a true irony.

Incidentally, as discussed in the previous chapter, the Mulan story also reflects Steppe women's traditionally strong social role, something not unnoticed in Chinese historiography. It was, furthermore, not at all uncommon for the women of many Steppe groups to go into battle along with their menfolk.

In the poem, a girl named Mulan disguises herself as a man to serve in the military in her father's place when the Qaghan/Son of Heaven mobilizes his army to fight the enemy in the north, because, as the poem says, "My father's sons are not grown men / And of all my brothers, none is older than me." After having served in the north for many years, she is offered a high government post by the Qaghan/Son of Heaven. She turns down the offer in favor of going home and living a peaceful life with her family. After she returns home, she puts back on her lady's clothes and shocks her fellow soldiers, who didn't know that she was a woman during the time on the battlefield.

It is of particular interest to note that in the poem the "Son of Heaven" was referred to repeatedly as *kehan* or Qaghan, but never the authentic Chinese epithet *huangdi*, "emperor." Given that it was originally a folk ballad, the usage demonstrates that at the time even ordinary Chinese-speaking folk in northern China were addressing the emperor as *qaghan*, an interesting custom hardly noticeable from reading the official historiography. But this observation is supported by the rediscovered inscription of 443 at the Tuoba ancestral cavern that used the same royal epithet *qaghan*, not the authentic Chinese title *huangdi*. In addition, it also testifies to the avoidance of the official Chinese term *huangdi* for "emperor" by the Northern rulers of the epoch, which supports my thesis that the Steppe heritage of sacral kingship was not simply a copy of the Chinese counterpart, a topic examined in a later chapter.

The focus of this chapter is the name of the famous heroine, Mulan, as she is called in the poem. This name has presented a perennial controversy regarding what it represented: a family name, a given name, or both? The Disney movie adopted the folk belief that Mulan was a given name, of someone surnamed Hua ("flower," Cantonese pronunciation *fa*, as adopted by the Disney movie). This popular belief has little historical substantiation and comes very likely from the mere fact that *mulan* in standard Chinese stands for some fragrant flower plant. The great ancient poet Qu Yuan (ca. 340 to ca. 278 BC) in his immortal poetic autobiography *Lisao* (*Encountering Sorrow*) first introduced this plant name, which has since figured prominently in numerous literary works. Many people interpret it as representing magnolia, or *magnolia liliiflora*, the term prevailing modern meaning, but the true scientific identity or identities of this ancient plant name have remained a controversy.

This fact, namely that *mulan* in literary Chinese traditionally means a gentle, pure, fragrant, and delicate flowering plant, becomes the starting point of my study. As such, and in addition to the long influence of "The Ballad of Mulan," the notion that Mulan is intrinsically a feminine name is beyond any doubt in China today.

I go further to observe that the character *lan* by itself has traditionally been a popular choice for naming girls in China, when used in its original general meaning of "fragrant plant," covering a wide variety of species ranging from orchid and cymbidium to magnolia.[4] The earliest example was perhaps the name Lanzhi, "sweet grass," in the folk ballad "Southward Flies the Peacock,"[5] presumably based on a true Romeo and Juliet tragedy in the Jian'an era (196–220) of the Later Hàn (25–220; also known as the Eastern Hàn). The popularity of this female name is attested in a Western Jin tomb inscription dated the twenty-fifth day of the fourth month of the first year of Yongkang (May 29, 300), of a concubine, née Zuo, of the first emperor of the dynasty.[6] Similar female -*lan* names were attested in tomb inscription data of the Tuoba Wei era too.

In other words, it can be argued that in a typical Chinese milieu during medieval times, let alone the modern era, a given name like Mulan would be very likely regarded as a feminine name. But this was apparently not the case in the milieu in which the Mulan story first emerged. "The Ballad of Mulan" states unmistakably that, after Mulan has revealed her true gender,

> She left the house and met her messmates in the road;
> Her messmates were startled out of their wits.
> They had marched with her for twelve years of war
> And never known that Mulan was a girl!

This scenario would have been hard to explain if the name Mulan were to be taken in its standard Chinese, hence heavily feminine, context. This is the first indication that the name should not be taken as Hàn Chinese.

Much stronger evidence exists to substantiate the contention that the Mulan of the ode was indeed not a Hàn name, much less a feminine one. In the *Zhou shu (History of the Zhou,* 43.776*)* biography of a noted Northern Zhou general, Hán Xiong, it is stated that "Hán Xiong's 'style' was Mulan. . . . He was very brave while still a youngster and had extraordinary physical strength." Let me first explain that a "style," or *zi*, represents an alternative personal name in premodern China, usually expressing a desirable attribute closely related to the person's formal given name, usually by strengthening or contrasting the latter. As a matter of fact, the name-style relationship is one of the most striking and unusual features of Chinese high culture, observed throughout history from Confucius on down to Chiang Kai-shek and Mao. For example, the late Great Helmsman's style is Runzhi, "to moisten" (in the sense of nurturing plants and crops—an earlier form of this style, somewhat less refined, means "to moisten *zhi* [an auspicious plant]"), which relates to his given name Zedong, meaning, word by word, "marsh/lake east," but more elegantly "to bestow rain and dew upon the east." The name-style relationship can serve as a powerful research tool for studying, among other things, ancient Chinese linguistics. In general, the style was considered a more respectful and polite form than the given name in addressing an individual.

Returning to the above *Zhou shu* passage, we see not only that Mulan was the style of a military man but also that it was coupled with the primary personal name Xiong, meaning primarily "male" but more frequently "grand," "mighty," "powerful," as Hán Xiong's biography elaborates. It is simply impossible that the Chinese word *mulan* in the sense of a noble, fragrant, delicate, and mostly feminine notion was used here to contrast with Xiong's masculinity and prowess. The possibility that Hán Xiong's *zi* was an opprobrious childhood name, a cultural import likely related to Buddhism, for avoiding the gods' jealousy is also out of the question, as *mulan* in Chinese was anything but an unworthy object.

Conversely, two other sources, namely *Bei Qi shu* (*History of the Northern Qi*) and portions of *Bei shi* (*History of the Northern Dynasties*) that were not based on *Zhou shu* and hence not subjected to many political and cultural taboos that affected the latter, give us a clear picture that Mulan was simply the true or "native" name of Hán Xiong, who was born and raised in what later became part of the Northern Qi realm, but who revolted against the state and went to join the rival Northern Zhou regime. These two sources never even bothered with Hán's formal name Xiong, but always called him "Hán Mulan the prefecture resident," or even "Hán Mulan the traitor." Yet according to *Zhou shu*, Mulan was Hán's style, hence always a more respectful form than his formal Sinitic name Xiong.

Let me note a few more points:

1. Hán was one of the "Barbarian" surnames at the time. This was documented in detail in Yao Weiyuan's study of these names.[7] For instance, *Bei Qi shu* (24.294) has included a person named Hán Xiongnu, "Hán the Hun."
2. Even among the "Chinese" Hán clans, the most important home origin was the prefecture of Changli, a frontier area in northeast China, which naturally led to the emergence of many "Barbarianized" Hán clan persons. For example, Hán Feng of the Northern Qi was such a figure from Changli, who loved to call other ethnic Hàn Chinese persons "Hàn dogs" (*Bei shi* 92.3053). The most famous native son of this frontier region during the Tang, by the way, was none other than An Lushan, a "Barbarian of mixed (Turco-Sogdian) origin," who almost toppled the Tang dynasty.[8] Although the celebrated Tang poet, essayist, philosopher, and statesman Hán Yü was from Dezhou in Henan, his ancestors hailed from Changli, and he advertised this fact by choosing Changli as his cognomen.
3. Hán Xiong came from a hereditary military family (*Sui shu* 52.1347), whose even more famous son Hán Qinhu, "Hán the tiger-catcher," later was one of the two generals (the other was Heruo Bi of undisputed Xianbei descent) to conquer the Southern dynasty of Chen in 589, unifying China for the Sui for the first time since the collapse of the Western Jin in 316. Hán Qinhu's achievements were the stuff of legend, as related in Dunhuang manuscript S2144, which was written more than three centuries later.
4. The ultimate proof that Mulan was simply Hán Xiong's original name is nothing other than the remnant of his own tomb inscription dated, in lunar calendar, the eighteenth day of the eleventh month of the third year of Tianhe (December 22, 568), a rubbing of which is preserved in the municipal

library of Beijing.[9] This rubbing states that this general-in-chief of the (Northern) Zhou was simply named Mulan, period, without mentioning at all the Sinitic name Xiong in the officially sanctioned biography. As I noted in Chapter 1, this fits well the pattern that the Northern Zhou was in reality a more "Xianbei-ized" power among the two competing successor states of the Tuoba Wei, yet its official records have been subjected to much heavier sinification doctoring.

5. There was a deep-rooted custom of this epoch among the former "Barbarians" and "Barbarianized" Chinese, including the Sui and Tang royal houses, of keeping one's "Barbarian" name as a "style" or "childhood name," as examined in the previous chapter. A good example of correspondence between a "Barbarian" style and a formal Sinitic name is the case of Hulü Jin. He was an able general of Turkic-Uighur origin of the Northern Qi and has left us with "The Song of Chile (Tölös?),"[10] admired by many today as one of the best poems ever written in Chinese literary history. The late Peter Boodberg was the first to recognize his style Aliudun as the Turco-Mongolian word *altun* for *jin*, "gold."[11]

The evidence cited earlier clearly shows that the name of Hán Xiong, a.k.a. Mulan, was yet another case of a "Sinitic-name with 'Barbarian'-style." Therefore, the name Mulan under the Tuoba regime and its successors was in fact a "Barbarian" name, not a feminine appellation as one would expect based on its standard meaning in Chinese. That was why the name of Mulan, the heroine, which was most likely a surname rather than a given name, a conclusion based on further evidence revealed later, never betrayed her true gender to her comrades in the army. In addition, given the case of Hán Xiong, the Chinese name-style correspondence rule would provide a good clue to what the "Barbarian" name Mulan actually meant, as will be elaborated later.

Variants of the "Barbarian" Name Mulan

Before setting forth to study the true meaning of the name Mulan, first I cite and examine other forms or transcriptions of that name. These forms further strengthen the inference that Mulan was indeed a "Barbarian" appellation. They may also help decode the original meaning of the name.

The most apparent variant is the Tuoba clan name Pulan[12] for the following reasons.

1. It is certainly the rule rather than the exception that a "Barbarian" name had several different transcriptions in Chinese characters. The previously cited superb study of "Barbarian" names by Yao Weiyuan contains numerous examples. In addition to the natural scenario that other versions might have been rendered in different Chinese dialects, or simply with individual taste, it may also reflect the variations among the "Barbarian" tongues.

2. The Middle Chinese pronunciation of Mulan is *muk-lân*, while Pulan was pronounced either *b'uk-lân* or *b'uok-lân*.[13] The closeness of the two names is also vouched for by the fact that in modern southern Fujian dialect, which is also the prevailing local dialect in Taiwan, Mulan is still pronounced something like *b'ok-lān*.[14]

3. Cases of Middle Chinese transcribing a foreign *b-* sound by *m-* are too numerous to list. Two examples are the well-known medieval Chinese transcription *moheduo* for *bayadur*, "hero," and the less known transcription *mole* for *bäliq*, the Turkic word for "fish."[15] Phonetically, it is easy to understand how *b-/m-* interchanges would have occurred, since both are nonplosive labials.

4. The *m-* ~ *b-* equivalence is also attested by the ancient Turkic transcription *ban* and *bou* of the Chinese words *wan* (Middle Chinese *miwan*) and *wu* (*məu*) respectively.[16] This further became the main rule of sound correspondence between different Turkic dialects in al-Kašɣarī's *Divan*, as summarized by Robert Dankoff.[17]

5. The view that the name Mulan in "The Ballad of Mulan" represented a clan name appeared very early and cannot be dismissed as a later fabrication. The long historic era from the two Jin dynasties (265–420) until the end of the Tang was known for its obsession with clan history and genealogical studies. Yet Mulan as a family name hardly ever was mentioned in all these references, much less leaving an attested instance.[18] Meanwhile the surname Pulan (and its sinicized form Pu) has left numerous cases and records.

6. There are several different theories regarding Mulan the heroine's birthplace, with one thing in common: they all point to the region known as Henan ("South of the Yellow River") in contemporary China, which was much greater in size than the modern province of Henan. It is intriguing to note that Henan was also where most Tuoba clans were ordered to settle as their new "native" place after Emperor Xiaowen moved the Tuoba capital from Pingcheng in the north to the ancient Chinese capital of Luoyang in 493–94. Further strengthening my case is the fact that not only Hán Xiong,

a.k.a. Mulan, was from Henan, but so were the Pulan clans since Tuoba times.[19]

7. To the possible argument that Pulan was only a surname, whereas Mulan, at least in the case of Hán Xiong the general, was used as a given name, let me first note that the notion of a surname or clan name was a Chinese one that the Tuoba did not possess even after settling in China. For instance, a Tuoba courtier of Sinitic origin who wanted to dodge his southern compatriots' question regarding his identity made an interesting statement (*Song shu* 59.1600): "I am a [Tuoba] Xianbei, thus do not have a family name." Second, Pulan was in fact also attested as a given name, assumed by none other than a Tuoba nobleman. According to *Song shu* (72.1857 and 74.1924) and *ZZTJ* (126.3979), there was a Tuoba nobleman named Tuoba Pulan. Careful comparison with *Wei shu* (4.104–5, 24.654, and 97.2140) reveals the nobleman's sinified name to be Zhangsun Lan.

All these points combined leave little doubt that Mulan and Pulan were the same item in the contemporary "Barbarian" onomasticon, used as both clan names and given names in northern China during the period.

Another possible transcription of the same root is the popular given name Fulian (*b'iuk-liän*). This name was widely attested, from Tuoba generals to even a *qaghan* of the Tuyuhun,[20] a nomadic people who had migrated from northeast China to the grassland bordering modern Tibet. In transcription data, the character *fu* is frequently interchangeable with *bu* (*b'uo*), *fo* (*b'iuət*, primarily for transcribing "Buddha"), and so on, a subject I visit again. According to Louis Bazin,[21] for transcribing "Barbarian" names the character *lian* (*liän*) represents an original *län*. This is attested by the case of the "Barbarian" name Youlian, which was said to mean "cloud," or Mongol *ä'ülän*.[22]

This probable form provides us with another interesting name-style correspondence. According to *Bei Qi shu* (20.283), an important "Barbarian" figure of the Northern Qi, namely Kudi (or Shedi) Fulian, had a style Zhongshan, "amid the mountains." The relevance of this name will be demonstrated shortly.

Preliminary Notes on the Meaning of Mulan

More than half a century ago, Louis Bazin had already tried to identify the original Altaic word for the name Pulan (*b'uk-lân* or *b'uok-lân*), which as I have shown was just a variant of Mulan. His solutions ranged from *boq*, "excrement," and *buq*, "bad temper," to *boy*, "bag for clothes"—hardly satisfactory, as Bazin himself acknowledged. Even with much expanded historical data at our disposal, such identification remains a difficult task.

One has to first narrow the scope of the search. Given the two name-style correspondences cited earlier, and the strong cultural tradition among the Altaic people, many of whom roamed the Steppes with the herds, or hunted animals in the forests, I submit that the name Mulan/Pulan is most likely to have come from the animal kingdom, in sharp contrast to its meaning in Chinese.

Let us look at the second character *lan*. Bazin took it as representing the Turkic plural suffix *-lar*, which, while phonetically not impossible, was unfortunately not substantiated by any Chinese transcription data regarding the Tuoba. In my opinion, a generic animal suffix *-lān*, to be further examined later, is the most likely interpretation in this case. A less likely possibility is an *-n* suffix in the Tuoba language with unknown grammatical function suggested by several other cases.[23]

This last possibility leads to a root *b'uk-lâ* of the name Mulan/Pulan in Middle Chinese, suggesting an Old Turkic word *buyra*, "camel stallion." But this solution, except for the fact that it meets the "male, mighty" name-style correspondence, has several difficulties, both major and secondary, and is therefore hard to sustain.

First, if we take the name Fulian as another form of the same root, then Kudi Fulian's style Zhongshan, "amid the mountains," is difficult to reconcile with *fulian*, since that is a camel and not a forest animal.

Second, there are both spatial and temporal problems with the "camel" solution. The early camel name attestations in the Altaic milieu, most prominently that of the Karakhanid Bughra Khan,[24] and several persons from the Western Türk Empire,[25] were not only of later periods but also from a region much to the west in Central Asia, where the camel was of great importance, whereas the Tuoba originated in forest regions in northeast China.

However, the principal difficulty with the "camel" solution is cultural. As has been previously stated, after the collapse of the Western Jin, various nomad and former nomad groups dominated the political arena in northern China for many centuries, well into the first half of the Tang. During this long period, the Steppe cultures made enormous inroads into the Central Kingdom. Despite the stubborn sinocentric tradition of Chinese historiography and the heavily biased records, the fact that the descendants of the Tuoba and their northern brethren had dominated the Chinese world until at least the end of the Song, according to the Yuan dynasty historian Hu Sanxing, is bound to betray many of these northern traits, some of which were elaborated in the previous chapter. Chinese onomastics provides another good example, as it contains not only the "Barbarian" elements but also the strong influence of the Iranians and other Western Regions peoples, who had been an almost perpetual ally of the Steppe powers vis-à-vis China, a little studied subject for the Tuoba era. The sudden appearance and popularity of various theophoric personal names as examined in a later chapter is a particular case.

This is where the primordial problem with a "camel" interpretation of Pulan/Mulan lies. Animal origin proper names, a cultural tradition enormously popular with the Altaic people, were widely attested in Chinese nomenclature during that time, reflecting the political dominance of the nomadic groups in northern China. Even animals abhorred or despised in Hàn Chinese culture but respected by the northern people, such as wolf and dog, were attested in the contemporary Chinese onomasticon, not just in surnames, but more importantly among given names (see cases cited in Chapter 3). To this author's knowledge, the camel, with a neutral or even positive cultural image in China and mentioned in "The Ballad of Mulan" ("She only begs for a camel that can march a thousand leagues a day"), was never attested in personal names in northern China during the entire period. The only suspicious case was the old Chinese surname Luo. The character meant a white horse with black mane but later became part of the word *luotuo*, "camel." In *Wei shu* (113.3308) a "Barbarian" clan name Taluoba (*t'â-lâk-b'uât*) was sinified to Luo. In addition to the fact that a single character *luo* was never attested as referring to "camel" during that period, the original name cannot be linked to any Altaic word for "camel" unless one assumes that the middle character (*luo*) was an erroneous insertion and should be dropped. There is no evidence whatsoever for such a contention. The name conversion here follows the standard sound-based pattern of shortening a multicharacter "Barbarian" name to one of its original characters.

As for the "camel" names borne by Turkic personalities of later periods, I am of the opinion that they were the result of Iranic influence. Moreover, I submit that camel personal names originated with the ancient Iranic groups, attested by such early cases as Zarathuštra, the presumed founder of Zoroastrianism. Mary Boyce, among others, interprets the name as "he who can manage camels," based on the Indo-Iranian root *uštra* for "camel."[26]

A Cervid Alternative

A more likely Altaic cognate to Pulan/Mulan, in my opinion, is *bulān* (with phonetic variants like *pulan*, *bolan*, *bülän*, etc.). In various Altaic languages it means "elk," "stag," "moose," "deer," and so forth.[27] The most striking meaning is certainly al-Kašɣarī's definition of "a large wild animal . . . with one horn."[28] The last interpretation is very important, because, as examined by Denis Sinor, it makes *bulān* the only "native" Altaic word for "unicorn."[29] But this word's original meaning, as most scholars seem to agree, has to be "elk," or a large, likely male, member of the Cervidae family.

Semantically, these meanings would fit the name Pulan/Mulan perfectly regarding the two name-style relations revealed earlier, namely "male, mighty" and "amid the mountains." No less important, the "unicorn" or "elk," "deer" interpretation also solves the aforementioned main difficulty with the "camel" solution, namely attestation in the contemporary Tuoba onomasticon.

The "unicorn," or *qilin*, in Chinese (cf. Japanese *kirin*), transcribed into Old Turkic as *kälän*,[30] was a highly respected symbol and semimythic token of auspiciousness since ancient times in China. Confucius was said to have waited for the coming of the unicorn as the sign of the advent of a sage ruler. Other legends associating Confucius with the unicorn developed in later times. Nonetheless, direct use of the full word as a personal name was not attested until the Southern and Northern dynasties. It was certainly more a popular, almost vulgar, name for the common folk rather than a refined and elegant appellation for the educated gentry class,[31] and hence it was rarely observed in standard histories. It is therefore interesting to note that the name Qilin seemed particularly popular among the Tuoba and its ethnic subjects, with at least four direct attestations (*Wei shu* 40.917, 60.1331; *Zhou shu* 19.311, 27.453). Three of them had unmistakable "Barbarian" surnames: Lu (short form of Buliugu, related to the ethnic name Buluoji), Chigan, and Yuwen. The fourth, Hán Qilin, interestingly had the same surname as Hán Mulan and was clearly recorded as hailing from a frontier region with a self-claimed Hàn ancestry, a standard euphemism for an actual "Barbarian" origin. It may not be farfetched to conjecture that Hán Mulan had to be given a different Chinese name, Xiong, because he and Hán Qilin were contemporaries living in the same region.

In addition, a single character *lin* was frequently attested in "Barbarian" names. Without further evidence, it is difficult to ascertain whether the character stood for "unicorn" or merely transcribed some foreign sound. There were, however, near certain examples to show that it was indeed a "unicorn" name. For example, a certain Murong Lin took a reported sighting of a *qilin* as an omen for his imperial ambitions. There was also a Murong Pulin whose name (Middle Chinese pronunciation *p'uo-lien*) came very close to being a variant of *bulān* (*Jin shu* 127.3164; *Wei shu* 15.374).

Table 2.1. Number of Officially Recorded Appearances and
Sightings of *Unicorn*

Eastern Jin (317–420)	*Song* (420–79)	*Southern Qi* (479–502)	*Liang* (502–7)	*Tuoba Wei* (386–534)
1	1	1	0	8

The cultural background here is the previously little noted fact that the Tuoba were particularly obsessed with the unicorn. The following summary, whose statistics cover five dynasties of the period, based on an extensive examination of the respective official histories, namely *Jin shu*, *Song shu*, *Nan Qi shu*, *Liang shu*, and *Wei shu*, clearly demonstrate the point. In Table 2.1, the first four regimes were southern and Sinitic (Hàn), and the Tuoba Wei was the ethnic power in the north. Because all were regional dynasties, sightings outside their respective realm were not counted.

Among other things, this lopsided table reflects the fact that the cervids were, and still are, often considered sacred animals in Altaic cultures.[32] Such beliefs were widespread in ancient Eurasia, extending all the way to northern Europe. The vast range of ancient cervid images and symbols on the Old Continent has led to the notion of a "cosmic deer."[33] One may even further infer that this tradition shared with the Chinese *qilin* ("unicorn") worship a common origin that dates back to before the advent of a deep cultural divide epitomized by the Great Wall, when intensive farming had completely taken over China's economy, a process largely completed during the last five hundred years BC.

In addition to these statistics, there are other examples that demonstrate the "cervid cult" among the ethnic groups in northern China at the time, exemplified by the Tuoba par excellence.

- The Tuoba emperor Taiwu (Tuoba Tao) used the reign title Shenjia (428–31), "sacred/godly (female) deer." This was the only reign title in Chinese history figuring a cervid.
- In addition, there were only three other reign titles in Chinese history that used the character *lin*, "(female) unicorn," as a qualifier. The first two were both Linjia, "auspice of unicorn," first (316–17) used by the self-proclaimed Xiongnu leader Liu Cong of the Former Zhao, and then duplicated (389–95) by the Di/Tibetan leader Lü Guang of the Later Liang. The third was Linde, "virtue of unicorn" (664–65), by

the early Tang emperor Gaozong (Li Zhi). The Tang imperial house was in fact the Tuoba's political and biological heir, as I have shown.

- The Tuoba had an intriguing early legend, recorded prominently twice in *Wei shu* (1.2 and 112b.2927), about their tribes in the process of coming out of the forest region in northeast China, probably during the second or third century AD, being guided by a mysterious sacred animal with "a body like a horse and the voice of a cow" to the rich grassland that had been the "old Xiongnu country." One recalls immediately the celebrated doe that led the Huns across the Cimmerian Bosporus into the Crimea,[34] as well as the famous giant unicorn, "with the body of a deer and the tail of a horse," who stopped Genghis Khan from entering India, directing him to march home instead.[35]

- In sharp contrast to the Chinese tradition of regarding the unicorn as a sign of peace and exhortation against killing, the Tuoba introduced a martial or military dimension of the unicorn symbol by installing forty *qilinguan*, "unicorn officers," to guard the royal palaces (*Wei shu* 113.2974). This, in my opinion, was the likely origin of the Tang's adoption of the unicorn icon, together with the tiger, lion, eagle, and leopard, as the standard insignia for the military uniform (*Jiu Tang shu* 45.1953; see also *Tong dian* 61.1725.). This new "warrior" role of the unicorn, while conflicting with the Sinitic belief, fit perfectly with the ancient deer images on the Steppe and in Siberia.[36]

In the final analysis, behind the façade of the Tuoba's royally decreed sinification were deep-rooted Steppe cultural traditions among the former nomadic people in China, a parallel "Barbarian" nomenclature being one of the traits, exemplified by the "Barbarian" style or "childhood name" born by the Northern aristocracy, including the Sui and Tang imperial houses. Therefore, the Tuoba's unicorn worship and widely attested *qilin* names must have had a "Barbarian" original. Moreover, Denis Sinor's study "Sur les noms altaiques de la licorne" shows that *qilin* as a Chinese loanword did not appear in Altaic languages until after the Uighurs left Mongolia and settled in the Central Asian oases. Let me refer again to his conclusion that *bulān* was the only native Altaic word for "unicorn." Besides, its use as a personal name was attested by that of a Khazar king,[37] much earlier than the case of the Karakhanid Bughra Khan.

I take special note of the Eurasian and Steppe tradition of associating the cervids with maleness. For instance, Enn Ernits's recent study of the Sami reindeer myths in the Kola Peninsula concludes, "In Sami folk religion, the reindeer is associated with *male* lineage."[38] In addition, though Esther Jacobson in her book on deer worship in ancient Siberia tries hard to establish the existence of a deer goddess, she acknowledges that the huge number of so-called deer stones found in many places on the Steppe represent an image that "unquestionably refers to a human *male*," such that "the *male* reference of the stone is beyond doubt." She also cites other scholars' studies from which "the assumption that the antlered deer image referred to the *male progenitor* of the nomadic people and the conclusion that the deer image of the Scytho-Siberians refers to totem, tribal ancestor, *male warrior*, and *maleness* have been derived" (all italics in the quotations here are added by me).[39] Such intrinsic maleness of the deer image on the Steppe resonates naturally with the Mulan-Xiong name-style correspondence cited earlier.

Chinese Transcription Notes

Despite the strong evidence for the existence of a "Barbarian" unicorn name in the Tuoba realm, a phonetic difficulty for linking Pulan/Mulan to this name is the Middle Chinese ending *-k* in the first character. It is therefore legitimate to question whether the Chinese forms could have been a transcription of *bulān* or its variants, which does not seem to show any trace of a velar.

The two Chinese characters of concern, namely *pu* and *mu*, belonged to the old *rusheng*, "entering tone," category, characterized by a final stop (*-t*, *-k*, *-p*), which still exists today in several southern dialects, especially Cantonese. Nearly fifty years ago Edwin Pulleyblank published a study[40] demonstrating the wide use of "entering-tone" characters to represent a single consonant in a foreign consonant cluster or a single final consonant. An additional conclusion of his is that the Chinese name Tujue may have simply represented Türk, not the commonly assumed Mongolic plural form *Türküt ever since the time of Joseph Markwart and Paul Pelliot, prompted by the final *-t* in the Chinese transcription.

This last conclusion faces a technical difficulty that, in all Pulleyblank's well-substantiated examples of foreign consonant clusters, the *rusheng* character always transcribed the first consonant rather than the final as the case of Türk would require. This point notwithstanding, his general contention that such a character so often transcribed a single consonant is certainly valid. What I propose is to advance his observation one step further. If a *rusheng* character could represent only its initial consonant in transcribing a foreign word, it would seem no less natural that it could also represent its initial consonant plus the vowel, that is, the full syllable minus the final stop.

A careful study of the vast Chinese transcription data confirms that such uses of *rusheng* characters, which, by the way, cannot be easily explained by assimilation or other types of absorption into the next syllable, indeed abound. Space considerations prevent me from listing many more than a few illustrative cases most pertinent to my study. Unpronounced final stops are highlighted in boldface. To avoid extensive notes, except as otherwise indicated, the Sanskrit transcription data are based on the several Sino-Sanskrit glossaries in the *Taishō Tripitaka* and P. C. Bagchi's two-volume study of Sanskrit-Chinese transcriptions.

- The ancient Central Asian city transcribed as Mulu (*muk-luk*) (*Hou Han shu* 88.2918 and *Xin Tang shu* 221b.6245) has been identified by almost all scholars (F. Hirth, E. Chavannes, P. Pelliot, etc.) as the modern city of Merv, known as Mûlu in ancient times.[41]
- The Sanskrit name Bhuṭa for Tibet (Bod) was transcribed as Puzha (*b'uk-ta*).[42]
- Here is a sample of cases from *Taishō Tripitaka* (Chinese transcription < Sanskrit word):
  ◊ *boqifu* (*puât-kiət-b'iwak*) < *pakva*, "cooked, ripe."
  ◊ *yutaimo* (*jiu-t'âi-muât*) < *utma*, "high."
  ◊ *shejiedi* (*siät-kiät-tiei*) < *çakti*, "spear."
  ◊ *salishabo* (*sät-lji-ṣat-puâ*) < *sarṣapa*, "mustard."
  ◊ *nalameluo* (*nâp-lât-muâ-lâ*) < *duravala/durbala*, "weak."[43]
  ◊ *naqu* (*nâp-kiwo*) < *dukha*, "pain, hardship."
- Even the famous Buddhist pilgrim-scholar Xuanzang (600–664), well known for having mastered the Sanskrit language and for his rigor in translating Buddhist sutras (as well as for likely being responsible for translating a sutra from Chinese back to Sanskrit)[44] left many such cases. Two examples are *juduo* (*k'iuk-tâ*) for *gupta* in many personal names (the Pali form *gutta* cannot reconcile with the final -*k* of the first character either), and *biboluo* (*piĕt-puât-lâ*) for *pippala*, "pepper."[45]
- The "Nine (Uighur) Tribes" as recorded in the two official Tang histories[46] provide us with a telling pair: Yaoluoge (*iak-lâ-kât*) and Yaowuge (*iak-miuət-kât*). The first was attested in the Saka portion of the famous Staël Holstein scroll as *yah:idakari* and in Uighur Runic inscriptions as *yaɣlaqar*. The second, however, was rendered as *yabūttikari* in the Holstein scroll. W. B. Henning, for one, already wondered how the same Chinese character *yao* (*iak*) could be used in rendering both *yaɣ* and *ya*.[47]

- Pelliot[48] has identified the *Pa-lan-ba Sum-pa* people (*-ba* is a suffix) mentioned in the Tibetan version of the *Inquiry of Vimalaprabha* with the Bailan (*b'ʋk-lân*) tribe in Chinese records.

It should be noted that the first two examples were about the same initial characters as in the name Pulan/Mulan, whereas the last example is a striking parallel to our contention that Chinese *b'uk-lân* ~ Altaic *bulān*.

What may be more revealing is a group of "Barbarian" tribe names with known variants:[49]

1. Chili (*tsiet-lji*) ~ Chilie (*tsiet-liät*).
2. Qifu (*k'iət-b'iu*) ~ Qibu (*k'iət-b'uo*) ~ Qifo (*k'iət-b'iuət*) ~ Qifu (*k'iət-b'iuk*).
3. Pugu (*b'uk-kuo'*) ~ Pugu (*b'uk-kuət*).[50]
4. Dabu (*dât-b'uo*) ~ Dabo (*dât- b'uət*).
5. Hesui (*γâ-zwi*) ~ Heshu (*γâ-dʑ'iuĕt*).
6. Mozhe (*mâk-tśia*) ~ Mozhe (*mâk-tśiät*).[51]

At first glance, the forms with a final *-t* would seem to strengthen the old Markwart-Pelliot theory that the Chinese name Tujue for Türk represented some (proto-)Mongol plural form *Türküt. But after closer examination, in addition to the equivalent forms with an open final syllable, a (proto-)Mongol intermediary cannot be substantiated in most cases, much less accommodate the difficulty with the *-k* endings and the Qiang/Tibetan names (6). On the contrary, these variants lend strong support to the contention that a *rusheng*'s final stop corresponded to an open syllable in many a Chinese rendition of foreign words. The frequent *-t* ending can easily be explained by the simple fact that, among the *rusheng* characters, this type is more numerous, at least in transcriptions. One may note, for instance, that one "Barbarian" clan name was recorded by two different dynastic histories as Fulugu (*b'iuk-luk-ku*) and Buliugu (*b'uo-luk-ku*) respectively,[52] a cognate of Bulgar, the name of the people who founded the medieval Bulgarian kingdom, as we shall see. The avoidance of initial consonant clusters by the Altaic languages makes it clear that the first character in these two Chinese renditions must be transcribing more than just a consonant *b-*. Incidentally, these cases and the Saka form *bākū* for the tribe name (3) Puku (*b'uk-kuət*) strongly support Clauson's seemingly idiosyncratic reading Türkü as the Old Turkic form of the name Türk, a notion heavily criticized by, among others, Pulleyblank.[53]

The clan name transcription Fulugu, by the way, reminds me of the use of the first character *fu* (*b'iuk*) as a frequent alternative, especially in Buddhist theophoric names, to the character *fo* (*b'iuət*), the standard transcription of "Buddha." The final stop -*k* in the former, therefore, had to be silent in such transcriptions.

My thesis that, in transcribing a foreign word, the medieval Chinese "entering-tone" characters often have a silent final stop is in fact not new. After examining similar data, J. Harmatta also reached the conclusion that the Chinese *rusheng* syllables "must have had two phonetic variants" (CVC and CV), so that "[these] two phonetic realizations of the [*rusheng*] syllables permitted their alternative use for representing both foreign syllables with final stop and those without it."[54]

In addition, more than sixty years ago, while studying the Uighur transla-tion of the biography of the Chinese Buddhist monk Xuanzang, Denis Sinor uncovered the same phenomenon from the opposite direction, namely that Chi-nese *rusheng* characters could be transcribed into Old Turkic without the final stop. Interestingly, in three cases documented by Sinor, we have Chinese final -*k* ~ Old Turkic zero.[55]

Between Camel and Unicorn

The above discussions demonstrate the plausibility of a "unicorn" interpretation of the name Pulan/Mulan by the word *bulān*. Yet one has to admit that phoneti-cally the word *buɣra* also sounds like a plausible solution. A comprehensive exposition of the Mulan question, therefore, cannot be closed without reviewing some additional material or old controversies in Altaic linguistics in this regard.

Let us take another look of the word *buɣra*. It is noted that this gender-specific word was not, and still is not, the primary term for "camel" in Altaic languages, as the Turkic word *tevē* and its numerous variations and cognates in other tongues have an undisputed claim in this regard.[56] This leads me to ques-tion the original meaning of *buɣra*.

Even today within the Turkic family, *buɣra* does not universally mean "a camel stallion." In Yakut, the cognate word *būr* stands for "male (deer)." The similar meaning ("male elk") is found in several other Turkic languages.[57] This, plus the Suomi-Finnish word *peura*, "game animal," has led Matti Räsänen to state that "*buɣra* does not mean, originally, male camel, but a male reindeer."[58] In other words, similar to *bulān*, "unicorn," *buɣra* also had a cervid origin. Ger-hard Doerfer appears to accept the possibility of such a "semantic change (*Be-deutungswandlung*)," while disallowing Räsänen's Suomi-Finnish cognates.[59]

Whether Räsänen's conclusion is correct or not, it would seem natural to assume that ancient people might not be overly concerned about the taxonomic accuracy regarding the Cervidae and the Camelidae, or for that matter among many herbivore ruminants. What Räsänen has mentioned is but one example of this disregard of scientific rigor. One can also cite the Yakuts' use of the word *taba*, a cognate of the general Turkic word *tevē*, "camel," for "reindeer."[60] This mix-up of the Cervidae and the Camelidae is also reflected in the Chinese name *tuolu*, "camel-deer," for *Alces alces*, a large cervid. According to an eleventh-century source, this large member of the deer family, and presumably its name too, was from the "Northern Barbarians."[61] I also cite the Chinese character *luo* for *luotuo*, "camel," which originally had nothing to do with Camelidae, but meant a "white horse with black mane," adding an equestrian angle to this linguistic jumble of herbivorous quadrupeds. It may be noted that the meaning of the word *bulān* in Caucasian languages becomes "bison" (e.g., Chechen *bula*, "bison").[62] The original meaning of the English word "deer" may be another example. According to the second edition of the *Oxford English Dictionary*, the word "deer" originally meant "beast: usually a quadruped." The German cognate *Tier*, "animal," certainly attests to this general meaning.

It would not therefore seem farfetched to further Räsänen's theory regarding *buyra* to include also the Tuoba, who originated in a forest region where camels would, to say the least, hardly be a daily concern. Even today we see many seemingly redundant expressions such as *buyra tävä* in Ottoman Turkish, which supports the thesis that the meaning "camel" for *buyra* was not the original. This can also be compared with the Iranian-origin *mäjä*, widely borrowed into Turkic, meaning generally "female animal" and in particular "she-camel."[63]

At this point, a certain parallel if not cognitive relationship can be observed among the Altaic words *buyra*, "camel stallion"; *buyu*, "deer stag"; and *buqa*, "bull," as has previously been both suggested and rebuked by Altaic linguists, and may continue to be debated in the future.[64] A distinct common thread in these words, however, is undeniable, in that all three primarily refer to a male ruminant quadruped.

Finally, let us examine the word *bulān* again. The short vowel length in the first syllable seems to have excluded any possibility of a preexisting velar. Its etymology, befitting a "unicorn," has remained a mystery. After all, according to Chinese tradition, a unicorn is a combination of many animal characteristics, including that of a deer, a horse, a buffalo or bison, and so on. W. Bang, while acknowledging the ambiguous etymology, suggests that the form *bulān* may have been influenced by *qulān*, "wild ass."[65] It is Gerard Clauson who points out that

-*lān* appears to be a generic animal suffix.[66] There are at least seven such names listed by al-Kašɣarī: *pulān*, "elk"; *qulān*, "wild ass"; *arslān*, "lion"; *burslān*, "tiger"; *aplān*, "rat"; *yamlān*, "rat"; and *yilān*, "snake."[67] I can further add *baklān*, "a particular kind of lamb,"[68] and *qaplān*, "tiger."[69] Because these names cut across several animal groups—carnivore, herbivore (both ruminants and rodents), and reptiles—it is very tempting to ascribe the suffix to possible personification or deification of totemic animals. In any case, the real signifying root of *bulān* would have to be *bu-*. As such, its primary meaning of "a large male cervid" would put this word into the same general "stag/bull" category discussed earlier.

Indeed, in his excellent *Etymological Dictionary of the Altaic Languages*, Sergei Starostin proposed an Altaic root **mula*, "a kind of deer," with Tungusic **mul-* and Proto-Mongolian **maral*, "mountain deer," and Proto-Turkic **bulan*, "elk."[70] This root, especially the Proto-Turkic form, would be a near perfect fit for the Tuoba name Mulan.

In conclusion, it is difficult to determine with certainty the original form for any word in the ancient Tuoba language, which has been dead and lost for over a millennium. But it is fairly safe to infer that the name Mulan, transcribing either *bulān* or *buklān*, once belonged to the same "stag/bull" word group in the Altaic family that included, inter alia, the only native Altaic word for "unicorn."

Chapter 3

Brotherly Matters and the Canine Image:
The Invasion of "Barbarian" Tongues

"All within the Four Seas Are One's Brothers"

It is likely that the great sage's leading disciple, Zixia, had in mind Confucius's ideal of a perfect society of "great harmony" and universal human love when he consoled a fellow disciple who complained about "having no brothers (read: none of his brothers behaved in a brotherly way)": "Let the superior man never fail reverentially to order his own conduct, and let him be respectful to others and observant of propriety—then all within the four seas will be his brothers."[1]

This is but one example of the importance of brotherhood, by blood or not, in traditional Sinitic societies. Moreover, with the Confucian emphasis on maintaining the proper societal as well as familial order, a clear distinction between *xiong*, "elder brother," and *di*, "younger brother," was a perennial characteristic of the Chinese language, social mores, and consciousness, in sharp contrast to that of most Indo-European societies. In fact, *xiongdi* or "elder-brother-younger-brother," was one of the five cardinal human relations (*lun*) in Confucianism, the other four being lord-subject, father-son, husband-wife, and friend-friend.

In this historical context, it is rather startling to observe that, while the familial and societal functions of this central kinship notion of "elder brother" have been kept largely intact and even expanded through the ages, the morphologic carrier of this term in China today has been usurped by a different kinship term, *ge* (Wade-Giles *ko*). The latter term permeates all Chinese dialects today and plays a much extended linguistic role beyond a familial vocative. It is indeed amazing to hear this term and its variants in formal speeches, daily conversations, and folk love songs everywhere, from big metropolises like Shanghai to the remotest inland mountain villages. In contrast, the original Sinitic term *xiong* has now been banished to a few archaic and largely literary binomes.

The original Confucian notion of pan-brotherhood is fully embodied in this modern term for elder brother. For instance, a once widespread Qing-dynasty, anti-Manchu secret society was named Gelaohui "Big Brotherhood Society." Any student of contemporary colloquial Chinese would know the popular, largely post–Cultural Revolution vocative *gemen* for "buddy," literally "(elder) brothers," "brethren." In fact, the character *ge* can now serve as a sort of suffix, to be attached with a vocation-specific word to form a general term for (male) workers in that profession. A typical example is *dige*, "(male) taxi driver," formed by adding *ge* to *di*, the short form of the transcription *dishi* (Cantonese pronunciation *tek-si*) for "taxi."

The character *ge* also appears frequently in transcribing and translating the ever-increasing number of foreign-origin words. For instance, cellular phones were once widely known as *dageda*, "big, big brother," a strange term with a dubious origin, now gradually being replaced by the more down-to-earth word *shouji*, "hand machine." The most fanciful use, though, may be the popular transliteration *weige*, literally "awesome brother," for Viagra, the medicine for erectile dysfunction. In fact, a recent collection of essays by a popular Chinese historian is titled *Hello, Weige.*[2]

In this broad social context (despite the sometimes disastrous consequences of the one-child population-control policy in the People's Republic of China, which, if strictly enforced, would have endangered all kinship terms for siblings), and given the number of Chinese-speaking souls worldwide, *ge* must be one of the most frequently used terms on earth, spoken and written billions of times a day. It is therefore surprising that this quintessential Chinese kinship term does not have a Sinitic origin at all! Its invasion into the sea of Sinitic-speaking Chinese populace was the result of the Tuoba and their brethren and progeny, including the imperial Tang clan.

The Proto-Mongolic Origin of Ge and the Case of Agan

Let us look at the Chinese character *ge* again. It was in fact the original form of its homonym signifying "song," "to sing." As the erudite Qing linguist Duan Yucai commented, this character was later borrowed on account of its pronunciation for the meaning of elder brother.[3] Loans similarly motivated by phonetics but serving semantic purposes were of course not infrequent in Sino-Tibetan philology.

As several prominent Qing scholars have observed, the use of *ge* for "elder brother" occurred fairly late: the first recorded such usage did not appear until the middle to late Tang times.[4] *Tang huiyao* (*The Essentials of Tang Institutions,* 5.56) has an anecdotal story, not noted by the cited Qing and modern scholars, about a younger brother of Emperor Taizong, calling the latter *erge*, "the second elder brother." While this is certainly a revealing case of the term's early usage, it should be pointed out that the earliest parts of *Tang huiyao*, completed during the Northern Song dynasty, were compiled no earlier than the reign of Emperor Dezong (780–805),[5] more than 150 years after the conversation allegedly took place.

The origin of *ge* evolving into a kinship term for "elder brother" becomes clear once one appreciates the two basic patterns of kinship terms in colloquial Chinese: those using reduplication, and those with an *a-* prefix. The latter was particularly well represented in ancient times and may well symbolize a common Sino-Tibetan trait. Almost all Chinese characters for kinship relations can in fact be used with an *a-* prefix.[6] Direct attestations are found as early as the late Hàn dynasty period, exemplified by "Beifen shi (Poem of grief and indignation)" composed by Cai Yan,[7] a talented daughter of the Later or Eastern Hàn dynasty's scholar-official Cai Yong (132–92). In that poem, a vocative *amu*, "mommy," was used when the sorrowful poetess described the sad permanent separation from her children, born during her captivity in the Southern Xiongnu territory, after Cao Cao (155–220), the warlord-turned-chancellor of northern China at the time, ransomed her freedom. Not long after, in the folk ballad "Southward Flies the Peacock," which was based on a tragedy in the Jian'an era (196–220), already cited in a previous chapter, we meet at least four *a-* vocatives, namely *amu*, "mommy"; *anü*, "daughter"; *amei*, "younger sister"; and *axiong*, "elder brother." Paul Benedict was certainly misinformed to conclude incorrectly that the usage was a late (ca. 600) development in Chinese language.[8]

Next, one observes that the Middle Chinese pronunciation of *a-ge* as reconstructed by Bernhard Karlgren is *aka*; its close resemblance to the Mongolian kinship term *akha*, which has the same meaning, makes its derivation obvious.

Evidence of the Mongolic kinship term *akha/agha* predates the emergence of Mongolian tribes by many centuries. More specifically, it goes back to the famous story of "The Song of Agan," as narrated in the dynastic history *Jin shu* (*History of the Jin*, 97.2537): During the early years of the Western Jin (265–316), the young and highborn (i.e., of a chief-consort mother) leader Murong Wei of the Murong clan, a group in the general Xianbei conglomerate pasturing in northeastern China, quarreled with his lowborn (i.e., of a concubine mother) elder brother Tuyuhun about the pasture lands for the horse herds of the respective tribes they had inherited. The elder brother finally gave up by swearing to lead his tribes to a place "thousands of miles away" from the lands of his younger brother. This he did, resulting finally in the establishment of the Tuyuhun kingdom in northwestern China that lasted about half a millennium, until the mid-Tang dynasty, before being subjugated and absorbed by the ancient Tibetan kingdom.[9] The younger brother, Murong Wei, was reported to have much regretted such an outcome. Dearly missing his elder brother, he composed the melancholy "Song of Agan." Here *Jin shu* interprets: "*agan* in Xianbei language means elder brother."

The migration of Tuyuhun's tribes was likely a reflection of the Steppe tradition of ultimogeniture, in which the youngest son, the *ochigin*, inherits his parents' homestead. The division of the huge Mongol empire among Genghis Khan's four sons is perhaps the best example of this tradition. The linguistic implication of "Song of Agan" is probably the first appearance of the Mongolic root *akha/agha* for "elder brother" in history.

Paul Pelliot was perhaps the first Western scholar to identify *agan* with this Mongolic root *akha* (*aqa*),[10] to be followed by Peter Boodberg and Louis Bazin,[11] pointing at the Mongolic nature of the Murong's language. A similar observation had in fact been made much earlier by the Qing dynasty Chinese scholar Zhai Hao.[12] The problem here is to explain the terminal -*n*, which is possessed by neither the Middle nor the Modern Mongolian stem for "elder brother." Bazin tried to invoke the plural suffix -*nar* (one could, in fact, do even better by using a postulated Common Mongolian -*n* plural suffix).[13] But this implied solution is contradicted by the historic context in which the word *agan* appeared: all Chinese records indicated that there was no more than a single elder brother in this story. The rendition in *Jin shu* (97.2537) and the word *agan* being used as an official title also preclude the possibility of a genitive or possessive suffix here. More familiar with Chinese records and therefore more circumspect regarding their use for his arguments, Pelliot hinted at the possibility of the common transitory –*n* in Mongolic languages. However, on the key word for elder brother, this seems to be unattested in known historical and modern Mongolian languages. In any case, as remarked elsewhere in this book, the grammatical function of the terminal -*n* attested in many ancient Xianbei words preserved in Chinese literature remains an intriguing puzzle.

One might notice that the word *agan* may also be identified with the Nüzhen (Jurchen)-Manchu term for "elder brother," as the terminal -*n* is well attested in both Middle Nüzhen and Late Manchu languages.[14] Indeed, as noted by Karl Wittfogel and Feng Jiasheng,[15] Edouard Chavannes had called the Tuyuhun "la nation tongouse."[16] But be its origin Mongolian or Tunguz, the crucial point here is that *agan* does not seem to be the word for "elder brother" used by the Tuoba Xianbei. I have two pieces of evidence to support this observation.

First, *Wei shu* (*History of the Wei*, 101.2233), in sharp contrast to *Jin shu*, points out explicitly that *agan* is a Tuhe word, Tuhe being a rather derogatory term used consistently by its author Wei Shou, who served both the Tuoba Wei dynasty and its successor the Northern Qi dynasty, to identify the Murong group. One might remark that Wei Shou was an author quite conscious of the advantage of using deprecating terms for the Tuoba's rivals. Even the authentically Sinitic Hàn powers in southern China were characterized by him (*Wei shu* 97.2129) as being of the *daoyi*, "island barbarians," despite the fact, acknowledged by the Xianbei or Xianbei-ized founder Gao Huan (496–547) of the Northern Qi, that these Southern dynasties were revered by many in the north as the "legitimate" Chinese regime (*Bei Qi shu*, or *History of the Northern Qi*, 24.347).

Second, a cognate of *echi*, the well-known Old Turkic word for both "elder brother" and "father's younger brother," had been used early on by the Tuoba explicitly for the second meaning. This was the Tuoba royal clan name Yizhan, which went back to the very early stage of the rise of the Tuoba, when its chiefs for the first time divided up their growing tribal followings among "seven royal branches" of the Tuoba clan. The name was later sinified to Shusun, "descendants of the paternal uncles" (*Wei Shu* 113.3006). Peter Boodberg in his 1936 study of the Tuoba language seemed to be the first to recognize Yizhan (Middle Chinese pronunciation *iet-tsian*), curiously again with an -*n* suffix, as a cognate of the Old Turkic word *echi*.

There was a deep-rooted ancient Steppe cultural trait reflected in this and similar Turkic kinship terms, namely the lack of clear "horizontal" generation boundaries. As far as I am aware, Kaare Grønbech in a short yet revealing article,[17] was the first scholar to point out this interesting social structure. His finding is that all male members of the ego's extended family whose age was between that of father and ego, that is, father's younger brothers and ego's elder brothers, were given the same kinship appellation regardless of their actual generation. The same went for female kin. This disregard of generational distinction was prominently apparent in the Tuoba regime and its successors, the Tang imperial house in particular, as will be elaborated later. It is thus almost certain that the first meaning of the Old Turkic root *echi*, namely elder brother, was also maintained by the Tuoba.

The Mongolic term *akha/agha* (*aqa/aγa*) was soon to appear. According to Gerard Clauson,[18] it eventually replaced *echi* in almost all Turkic tongues. The same might also have been happening with the Tuoba tribes, as will be argued later. What is more interesting is the close similarity between the Tuoba and the later West Asian Turkic regimes, the Ottoman Empire in particular, where the term became an official title. This historical parallel becomes even more pronounced when one notices that the Tuoba titles survived in Chinese records (*Wei shu* 15.375 and *Xin Tang shu* [*New History of the Tang*] 71.2404) as *nei agan* or *neixing agan*, literally "inside-running *agan*," and the Ottoman title *agha* was assumed by officers of both the "Inner" and "Outer" services of the sultan's household.[19]

Turning to the terminal -*n* shown by several Tuoba terms as compared with their prevailing Altaic original forms, barring grammatical functions yet to be identified as suggested by Victor Mair,[20] it may simply have reflected early nasalized forms in certain dialects, and the Chinese represented them by the final -*n*.

Brother to Brother or Father to Son? Turkic Connections and the Generational Boundaries

Given the close phonetic and semantic similarity, plus the fact that the people who appeared to have left the earliest record of using *ge* for "elder brother" all had some degree of non-Hàn heritage (among them was the great Tang poet Bai Juyi or Po Chü-i), this modern Hàn Chinese kinship term is therefore highly likely a loanword from some ancient Mongolic or other Altaic tongue, just like the same word in most modern Turkic languages mentioned earlier. At the very least one can safely say that the prevalence of this character over the much more classical *xiong* has had a lot to do with influence from the Steppe people and culture.

But that is not my primary focus. The first recorded usage of *ge* as a kinship term in Chinese did not refer to a brother, but was a term for "father." And the users included none other than the Tang imperial family, including Emperor Taizong himself. Among several other examples, one finds in particular the handwritten teachings by this emperor, known for his love of and even obsession with Chinese calligraphy, for the imperial heir apparent Li Zhi, titled *Gege chi*, "edict from *gege*," preserved in the precious calligraphy collection *Chunhuage tie* (*Model Calligraphies Collected in the Pavilion of Chunhua*) compiled in the early years of the Northern Song Dynasty (960–1127). In other words, the emperor used the reduplicative form of the kinship term *ge* to refer to himself in relation to his heir apparent son. Therefore, the recorded use of the Chinese character *ge* as a term for "father" actually preceded that for "elder brother." This strange usage has puzzled many Chinese scholars since the Qing dynasty, with proposed explanations ranging from "special family rule of the Tang time" to a form of teknonymy. None was really convincing, which forced Feng Hanji (Feng Han-Yi), the first modern scholar to perform a scientific study of the Chinese kinship system, to term it a "most perplexing" case.[21]

Many people have correctly attributed the frequent "scandalous" or even "incestuous" marriages involving the Li family to the influence of Steppe mores, particularly the age-old custom of the levirate. But few seem to have reached the heart of the matter: namely, the lack of clear generational boundary in ancient Steppe cultures, as described in the previous section. Yan Zhitui, the Sui dynasty scholar-official, complained about the social impropriety, among the *beiren*, "northerners," of not maintaining the proper generational distinctions: "I have noticed that northerners pay little attention to these matters (generational distinctions). Strangers meeting on a public road immediately call each other 'brother,' guessing ages without considering whether it is a correct form of address or not."[22]

Nevertheless, the Tang imperial family continued to show this disregard for Confucian traditions. In particular, Emperor Xuanzong called a fellow clan member Li Quan (transcribed as Lisün in the Orkhon inscriptions),[23] as *shufu*, "uncle."[24] Quan, however, was clearly documented in both *Jiu Tang shu* (*Old History of the Tang*, 60.2345) and *Xin Tang shu* (70.2016) as being two generations senior in relation to the emperor. And then there was Emperor Dezong, who adopted his grandson Li Yuan as his son (*Xin Tang shu* 82.3624), corrupting one of the five cardinal human relations (*lun*) in Confucianism. As will be examined in Chapter 7, it is also significant that the father of the great poet Bai Juyi, who gave us what appears to be the first authentic record of using *ge* for "elder brother," might have married his own niece.

Incidentally but not accidentally, such disregard of generational boundaries reappeared several centuries later during the Yuan dynasty among the Mongol ruling elite, who would regard younger brothers as sons, aunts as grandmothers, and so on.[25]

However, for the use of *ge* (*ka* in Middle Chinese), meaning "father," which appears to have preceded the now prevailing meaning of "elder brother," there is a much simpler explanation: namely, it was the term for "father" among the Tuoba nobles of the time.

Let us examine the Altaic data. The fact that variants of *akha/agha* could mean "father" in Turkic languages has been recorded by Wilhelm Radloff.[26] This is still reflected in modern Turkish: Sir James Redhouse reported that *agha* may mean "[t]he head of a family."[27] In Yakut, which has long been isolated from other Turkic languages, the term for "father" is none other than the word *agha*.[28] The same holds true for the Dolgans,[29] who, according to Denis Sinor, are probably "Toungouzes turcisés (Tukicized Tunguz)."[30] Further evidence can also be found in Kazakh dialects, which have *ake*, *eke*, "father."[31] There is also a similar term *ake*, "father," in the Kirghiz language.[32] It is interesting to notice that in Khakass *agha* means "paternal grandfather." So does *akka* in Shor. Corresponding to Emperor Taizong's noted "Gege Chi" cited earlier, we have a "characteristic" vocative *kaka*, "dad," in the Turkmen language.

Two superb etymological dictionaries on Altaic and Turkic languages compiled by Russian specialists lend strong support to my proposition. For instance, Sergei Starostin and colleagues reconstruct a proto-Turkic root *(i)āka*, which could mean "uncle, father, grandfather."[33] Ervand Sevortian, in addition, has included several other Turkic tongues in which *ağa* stands for "father."[34]

In sum, there appears to be sufficient ground to make a case that *ge* (*ka*), *gege* (*kaka*), or *a-ge* (*aka*) may have been a Tuoba word for "father." This in turn suggests that the considerable differences found in the meaning of the word *akha/agha* and its variants in contemporary Turkic languages, as remarked by the Russian linguist L. A. Pokrovskaia, may have a very long history. It also strengthens the proposition that the Chinese kinship term *ge* is an Altaic loan. Let me further note the equation uncovered by the Chinese scholar Miao Yue that the Tuoba official title *agan* corresponded to *zhangzhe*, "senior," in Chinese.[35] This is very close to what Pokrovskaia suggested was the primary meaning of the term *akha/agha*.[36]

As for the Turkic term's relationship to, or possible evolution from, the (proto-) Mongolic term *agha/akha* and the sociological implications thereof, I may add a few more examples. First there is a case of the use of the term *xiongxiong* for "father" by members of the imperial family (*Bei Qi shu* 12.160) of the Northern Qi dynasty, a direct successor of the Tuoba. One is tempted to ascribe this isolated incident to a mistranscription of *gege*, assuming *ge*'s meaning for "elder brother," or *xiong* in Chinese, had already been in circulation at the time because of the well-substantiated existence of proto-Mongolic elements in the Tuoba confederation. Second, Gustaf Ramstedt has recorded an interesting case of the status of father being lowered to, and called, "uncle," when the grandfather was still heading the family and given the regular term *etsege*, "father," among the Kalmyks.[37] The same demotion happens with the mother when grandma is still around. Whether the cited *gege/xiongxiong* usage represents a similar sociological phenomenon is an interesting issue too. In this thread I observe my third example: an imperial Northern Qi prince was recorded to have called his mother *zizi* (*Bei Qi shu* 9.125), where *zi* is a Chinese term for "sister."[38]

Related etymological studies can be extended to the prevailing modern Turkic term *ata* via another popular Turkic kinship term, *acha*, both meaning "father."[39] One may also want to look at the Uralic and Finno-Ugric connection and note, in particular, the Samoyed word *aca* and the Lapp term *acci* for "father";

the Lapp term *ække, æge,* "father's brother"; as well as the Samoyed word *agga,* "high," "great."[40] But they are largely beyond the scope of this book.

Though the Tang imperial family had taken pains to eliminate for posterity all traces of evidence that might betray their connections to various non-Hàn groups, it was an entirely different matter to hide this from their contemporaries, as I stressed in Chapter 1. Even the Southern Song dynasty philosopher Zhu Xi (1130–1200), born some five hundred years after such efforts were launched, was still able to observe (*Zhuzi yulei* 136.3245), "The Tang dynasty originated from the Barbarians. It is for this reason that violations of the Confucian standard governing a woman's proper behavior were not regarded as anything unusual."

Thanks to a Tang period contemporary, Lu Yan, we are now able to read in *Taiping guangji* (*Extensive records from the reign of great tranquility,* 184.1379), compiled during the early years of the Northern Song dynasty, the following revealing story:

> Emperor Wenzong (reign 827–840) was choosing a consort for his son the Crown Prince Zhuangke. All the officials at court who had daughters at home found their names listed. This caused anxiety among the officials and the common folks. When the emperor became aware of it, he summoned the courtiers and said, "We wished to arrange a marriage for the Crown Prince, and Our original intention was to ask a daughter from you, the Zhengs and the like, to become the bride. But I have heard that all the ministers here at court are unwilling to become Our in-laws. Why, indeed? We came from a family of hundreds of years of high officials and scholars. [The founding emperor] Shenyao [did something to cast doubts on Our lineage?]. There's nothing We could do about it." The plan was thus shelved.

The vivid description about how the imperial family was viewed by the contemporary traditional Chinese gentry class aside, the last sentence in Emperor Wenzong's quoted speech is difficult to interpret. Chen Yinke quoted an edition in which the puzzling word *luohe* regarding the imperial lineage was given as *heluo,*[41] which indicated that these authors were already having trouble comprehending the emperor's words, and the cited quotation might contain errors.

I have observed repeatedly that the Tang imperial family started as members of the Tuoba nobility. Here the emperor appeared to be challenging his unappreciative courtiers to find a better, meaning higher-born, son-in-law than the imperial prince. He was apparently in an irritated mood and might not have been discreet in choosing his language. Therefore I believe that *heluo,* with its reconstructed Middle Chinese pronunciation *ghala*, might be the correct reading, likely representing the Tuoba word for "son." There is an Old Turkic term, *oghul*, for "son/boy,"[42] as well as a para-Mongolic form **oghala* as conjectured by Sergei Starostin, for the same.[43]

I have further noted that the word *heluo*, otherwise utterly meaningless in Chinese, had earlier appeared in the Former or Western Hàn dynasty (206 BC–AD 25) in the name of a military officer, Ma Heluo, who came from the frontier region. I am tempted to cite Ma's name as perhaps the first attestation of the Altaic root *oghul/*oghala*. It has long been recognized that the Xiongnu term *juci* (**kio-tsiər*)[44] for "princess" preserved in Chinese records was a cognate to the Turkic root *qïz/khïz* for "daughter," "girl."

Intriguingly, Ma Heluo and his brother Ma Tong later played a critical role in suppressing a rare revolt by a Hàn crown prince against his emperor father. According to *Hàn shu* (*History of the Hàn*, 68.2960–61) and *ZZTJ* (22.743–44), during this incident Tong had some intimate contact with the Xiongnu cavalry units serving as palace guards in the Chinese capital Chang'an, strongly suggesting that the Ma brothers were conversant with the Xiongnu language. Even more intriguingly, despite Tong being recorded as Heluo's younger brother, the pair's names make a near-perfect transcription of the Turkic term *tun oghul*, "eldest son."[45]

Returning to the Tang dynasty, the kinship terms are yet another example of the apparent parallelism between the Tang imperial house and the Manchu Qing regime. It is well-known that during the course of the Qing dynasty the ruling Manchu clans lost, gradually but almost completely, their original language. Yet anyone well versed in Chinese literature of the past hundred years knows that even toward the last days of the Qing, Manchu kinship terms such as *ama*, "father"; *gege,* "daughter," "princess"; and *fujin* (corrupted transliteration of Chinese *furen*), "wife," "lady", and so on were still very much in daily use. In fact, these Manchu terms are currently being recycled through the numerous, often vulgar and shoddy Chinese television soap operas based on Qing dynasty figures and events and thus relearned by millions of ordinary Chinese. In other words, the kinship terminology proved to be the most resilient remains of another dying *guoyu*, "national language," of the conquerors in the Central Kingdom.

The Saga of "Slave Talent"

In addition to various Manchu kinship terms, the aforementioned modern soap operas are also refamiliarizing Chinese television viewers with another peculiar

Qing dynasty appellation, *nucai*, a seemingly Chinese term meaning literally "slave talent." During the Qing time and used in front of the Manchu emperor or master, this was the self-appellation meaning "your humble servant/slave," reserved for the "banner people," namely the Manchu regime's original tribal following and their descendants, mostly ethnic Manchu and Mongols and a few Hàn Chinese as well (including the author of the immortal Chinese novel *The Dream of the Red Chamber*). Most Hàn Chinese courtiers called themselves *chen*, "your (humble) subject." This distinction between the Hàn majority population and the "banner people" despite the near-complete cultural and linguistic assimilation of the latter, was but one of several intriguing aspects of the Manchu rule that lasted until the very end.

Notwithstanding the fact that Hàn Chinese courtiers' self-appellation *chen* has the same "slave" etymology that goes back all the way to Shang oracle bones, the term *nucai* used by the Qing "banner people" was in fact a pseudoneologism, whose first appearance in Chinese history went back again to the early medieval period when various nomadic groups, including the Tuoba, dominated northern China. This point has long been raised by several Qing dynasty scholars. But a critical semantic difference between the ancient and near modern usage has hitherto been ignored, namely that when the term *nucai* first appeared in history, it had an utterly different meaning than that of the Qing time and today.

In sharp contrast to the term's near modern connotations describing a person in a state of involuntary or paid servitude, during medieval times *nucai* was used exclusively to refer to an incompetent and therefore contemptible person.

The fact is that when the term was first uttered in early medieval China, interestingly almost always by ethnic figures or their close associates, it was used not as a self-appellation but as a disdainful slur. More intriguingly, the hapless target of the contempt, far from being a bond servant, was always a man of power and importance, including princes and even an emperor, a far cry from the Qing dynasty usage.

For example, the Southern Xiongnu chieftain Liu Yuan (?–310), who later founded the Former Zhao dynasty (304–29), once contemptuously commented as follows on the leadership of Sima Ying (279–306), one of the eight Western Jin imperial princes whose fratricidal intrigues and fighting (the so-called Anarchy of the Eight Princes) not only destroyed the dynasty but also opened the floodgate for northern tribal people to move into and dominate the Chinese heartland in the next several centuries (*Jin shu* 101.2648): "[Sima] Ying did not follow my advice and caused his own miserable rout. He is truly a *nucai*. But I have to rescue him as I once promised."

A reported Di (proto-Tibetan) leader, Li Te (?–303), whose son Li Xiong (274–334) founded the ethnic Cheng-Hàn polity (304–47), reflected upon how the second emperor, Liu Chan (207–71) of the Shu-Hàn dynasty (221–63), surrendered his state to an expeditionary force of the Wei state (220–65), despite the highly favorable geographic positions enjoyed by the defenders: "Liu Chan became a prisoner with such topographical advantages. How could he not be a *nucai*!"[46]

The best example of the fact that those early targeted persons who received the *nucai* label did so not for slave-like attributes is the remark by Wang Meng (325–75), the able advisor to the proto-Tibetan chieftain Fu Jian (338–85), the most successful yet tragic emperor of the Former Qin dynasty (350–94), on the military leadership of Murong Ping, the commander in chief of the troops of the Former Yan (337–70), a polity established by the ethnic Murong Xianbei in northeast China. It is recorded (*ZZTJ* 102.3233) that on the eve of the decisive battle in 370 between a relatively small expeditionary force led by Wang Meng and hundreds of thousands of defending troops under the command of Murong Ping, "Murong Ping was despicably greedy. He even had mountains and springs safeguarded so he could make money by selling firewood and drinking water [to his own soldiers]. He thus accumulated mountain-high piles of money and silk. His soldiers were furious and did not have much will to fight. Wang Meng laughed upon hearing these reports: 'Murong Ping is a true *nucai*. I would not be afraid of him even if he had millions of soldiers.'" Among other things, this talent to accumulate "mountain-high piles of money and silk," such as that shown by the insatiable Murong Xianbei prince, is certainly not that of a slave.

To further make *nucai*, "slave talent," an inappropriate construct as a Chinese slur word, one recalls that since antiquity Chinese slaves were known to have produced talented individuals who rose to become extraordinarily capable chancellors at the royal court. One may cite Yi Yin, the legendary first prime minister of the Shang dynasty, and Baili Xi of the state of the Qin during the Spring-and-Autumn period. Both were said to be former slaves.

Contemporary educated Chinese certainly recognized the awkwardness of this slur word popular among the "Barbarians" and their associates by refusing to ever use it. When some of the cases cited here were retold by Hàn Chinese scholar-authors, the slur *nucai* was either changed to *yongcai*, "mediocre talent" (*ZZTJ* 82.2621), or emended to a more reasonable expression like *nupu xiacai*, "an inferior talent among slaves and servants" (*Jin shu* 107.2796; *ZZTJ* 99.3126). When the Hàn scholar-official Yan Zhitui made a rare exception, using the term to describe the highborn southern Chinese aristocrats who had few useful practical skills, he changed the construct from "slave talent" to a homonymic word meaning literally "inferior horse (nag) talent."[47] These educated edits are an additional indication that the original slur word *nucai* was not a native Chinese term.

A Proto-Mongolic Loanword?

Then where did the word *nucai* come from? It is my opinion that *nucai* is but a cognate of the Mongolian word *noqai/nokhai*, meaning "dog."

There are several angles from which we can demonstrate this etymology. First, one needs to show that long before the meteoric rise of Genghis Khan and the establishment of the vast Mongol Empire, Mongolian-speaking tribes already populated the Chinese frontier, and the Mongolic root for "dog" was already in circulation. This is decisively shown by the Qidan/Kitan group, widely believed to have spoken a Mongolic tongue, who later established the Liao dynasty (916–1126) in northern China, as well as the Karakitan Empire in Central Asia. This important group has not only given us the alternative names Cathay, Kitay, and the Eastern-Slavic (Russian, Ukraine, Bulgarian, etc.) name Kitai and so on for China but also left the term *niehenai*, "dog head," in Liao records. Rolf Stein was the first to recognize *niehe* as a cognate of the Mongol word *noqai* for "dog."[48]

If one argues that the above "dog head" term, related to the Kitan's religious rituals, belonged to a rather late period (tenth to twelfth century), I have a much earlier attestation of the same Mongolic root during the Tuoba Wei period. But I would first have to go back to the Tuoba's sinification drive, launched by the Tuoba emperor Xiaowen (Yuan Hong; reign 471–99) in the last decade of the fifth century.

This famous sinification drive included moving the Tuoba court from Pingcheng in the north to the old Chinese capital Luoyang and formally proscribing the Xianbei language, customs, clothing, and names. This move was apparently driven by the young Tuoba emperor's ambition to put a final end to the north-south division of China. As a result of this drive, almost all "Barbarian" family (i.e., tribe) names, including the very royal clan name Tuoba, were converted to Chinese or Chinese-sounding surnames.

There was, not surprisingly, strong "nationalistic" resistance to this wholesale abandonment of the Tuoba's cultural heritage, forcing Emperor Xiaowen to proceed discreetly and skillfully to alleviate the resentment and opposition of his tribal comrades, as shown by several literal translations of the Altaic names into Chinese. Examples are Chinu to Lang, "wolf," and Youlian to Yun, "cloud."[49] The change of the royal name Tuoba to Yuan presumably also belongs to the same category, though a satisfactory etymology is yet to be identified.

I have uncovered yet another case in this category, namely the change of the clan name Ruogan to Gou, a homonym of *gou*, "dog," but with a "grass" radical replacing the "dog" radical. There is ample evidence that this new Chinese name was a euphemism for *gou*, "dog," as demonstrated below. Therefore the "Barbarian" original Ruogan (Middle Chinese pronunciation *nziak-kan*) must be a cognate of the Mongolic root *noqai*, albeit with, once again, the *–n* suffix.

There were strong cultural reasons for this popular Chinese euphemism for "dog," which were backed by numerous examples. At times the two homonymic characters were in fact interchangeable. The most interesting case was the story narrated by the late Tang dynasty author Feng Yan in his *Fengshi wenjianji* (*Feng's Personal Perceptions and Observations*, 10.133):

> Concurrent (or Honorary) Grand Master of Censors Wei Lun (716–799)[50] was to lead an embassy to Tibet. Censor Gou Zeng (the surname Gou here bears a "grass" radical) was appointed as an administrative assistant in the embassy, and the departure date was set. Someone then warned Lun: "Tibetans regard dog as a (totemic) taboo. Now the entourage of Your Excellence includes a Dog Assistant. How can Your Excellence then seek amity with the Tibetans?" Lun immediately reported the problem to the throne. The emperor instructed Lun to keep the same officer but to change his surname Gou to Xun (by adding one stroke to the Chinese character). After the return of the embassy, Zeng kept the new name Xun and never went back to his old surncame.

According to official records (*Jiu Tang shu* 12.323 and 12.326), Wei Lun led two diplomatic missions to Tibet that departed on September 22, 779, and on June 11, 780, respectively. The "Dog Assistant" story is more likely to have happened in 779 as Wei Lun reportedly succeeded in substantially improving Tang-Tibetan relations during his first mission by bringing back with him some five hundred Tibetan prisoners of war captured by the Tang in previous armed conflicts between the two sides. The repatriation of these prisoners, some held by the Tang for many years, evidently created enough goodwill for a follow-up mission the next summer. At any rate, the described dog taboo was well corroborated by the widely reported dog totem of the Tibetans, a subject I return to later.

The fifth-century Tuoba name-change case thus proved the earliest attestation of the Mongolic root *noqai* in history. It also fit the Steppe custom of canine personal names. For instance, Denis Sinor once commented, "Strange as it may seem to us, 'dog' was one of the Mongols' favourite personal names, attested from a variety of sources, dozens of times."[51] J. Németh further points out that the totem-based canine names were widely used as *noms ethniques* or tribe and clan names.[52] According to the index compiled by Wang Deyi and colleagues, at least twenty-two Yuan dynasty Mongol persons named Noqai can be identified from Chinese records.[53] This is a subject to be discussed later.

The second angle for demonstrating that the medieval Chinese slur word *nucai* came from the Mongolic root *noqai* for "dog" is semantic. As I stated earlier, the key medieval meaning of *nucai* is "an incompetent person," not at all someone in servitude. This happens to be exactly what the dog metaphor frequently referred to in ancient China, whether such usage did justice to the true canine intelligence notwithstanding.

For instance, as recorded in *Hou Hàn shu* (*History of the Later Hàn*, 72.2331), when the warlord-turned-chancellor Dong Zhuo (?–192) was about to be assassinated by one of his trusted officers, he cursed the latter: "How dare you, *yonggou* (incompetent dog)!"

The best example belongs to Cao Cao, the actual founder of the Wei dynasty (220–65), later the dominant state of the Three Kingdoms era. A gifted poet-politician himself, he would redeem the freedom of the poetess Cai Yan from the Southern Xiongnu as mentioned earlier. In the spring of the year 213, when Cao's ambitious efforts to cross the Yangtze to unify China were thwarted by the able military defense of Sun Quan (182–252, style Zhongmou), who later founded the Wu state (222–80), Cao was forced to admire his opponent, the son of a warlord, in contrast to another warlord's feeble son from whom Cao had easily taken over control of the region the latter had inherited from his dead father (*Sanguo zhi* [*History of the Three Kingdoms*] 47.1119): "One should have a son like Sun Zhongmou! Sons like that of Liu Jingsheng are just pigs and dogs."

Another good example of the dog metaphor for incompetence comes from Fu Lang, a distant nephew of the aforementioned proto-Tibetan emperor Fu Jian of the Former Qin dynasty. By all accounts Fu Lang was an utterly sinified, well educated, and extremely talented but haughty person. When the Former Qin was in its death throes after the disastrous Battle of Feishui (383), Fu Lang was forced to surrender to Eastern Jin forces in the year 384 and seek refuge in southern China. Once settled in the Eastern Jin capital and asked by a Buddhist monk whether the newcomer had met with the two brothers from the famous aristocratic Wang clan, Fu Lang answered dismissively (*Jin shu* 114.2936), "Are you referring to the two brothers, one having a man's face and a dog's heart, the other a dog's face and a man's heart?" Fu Lang's reply stemmed from his opinion that one of the Wang brothers was handsome but dumb, the other ugly but smart, and that in ancient China the heart was considered the organ for thinking. One should add that a few years later the Wang brother with "a man's face and a dog's heart" had his revenge by scheming to have Fu Lang executed (*Jin shu* 114.2937). All in all, these and other stories demonstrate that the slur word *nucai* and dog had the same metaphoric interpretation in early medieval China.

The third angle for the *nucai–noqai/nokhai* equivalence is of course phonetic. Ever since the time of the Mongol Empire, the Mongolian word *noqai* has varied little, suggesting that the same pronunciation can be projected back to Genghis Khan's forefathers centuries earlier. According to Bernhard Karlgren, the Middle Chinese pronunciation of *nucai* is *nuo-dz'ai*. Edwin Pulleyblank's reconstructions are not much different: early Middle Chinese *nɔ-dzəj* and late Middle Chinese *nuĕ-tsɦaj*.[54] Hence there is little difficulty in reconciling the initial consonant and the vowel sounds between *nucai* and *noqai*.

The problem is with the second consonant. Karlgren's *dz'* is the voiced form of (Wade-Giles) *ts/ts'*, which is more or less what Pulleyblank proposes for late Middle Chinese (from the Tang dynasty on), and now represented by the *pinyin* letter *c*. However, the *pinyin c* is after all not its medieval Latin counterpart, which represented both velar *k/q* and alveolar affricate *ts/ts'*. But the closeness between Chinese velar and alveolar affricate (dental sibilant) initials is evidenced by their later convergence in numerous characters and many dialects, to what is represented by modern *pinyin* letters *j/q* (Wade-Giles *ch/ch'*).[55] It is true that such convergence is largely restricted to cases with high front vowels or medials (palatalization), not the mid/low front vowels in the second syllable of *nucai*. Yet in one of the most important treatises on Middle Chinese phonology, namely *Jingdian shiwen* (*Interpreting the Text of the Confucian Canon*) authored by the Sui-Tang scholar Lu Deming, the very character *cai* was repeatedly used as the "consonant," in the premodern Chinese spelling system of *fanqie*, for characters with *dz'/ts'* initials that later merged with velar-initial characters.[56]

The problematic equivalence of the second consonant and the close correspondence of the initial and both vowels between *nucai* and *noqai* notwithstanding, it should be stressed that the former was not a direct transliteration of the later: *nucai* after all was presented as a pseudo-Chinese word, thus likely representing some wry form of calque or loanshift.

Incidentally, in medieval European renditions of the Mongolian word for "dog" from Marco Polo on down, the intervocalic -*q*- (-*kh*-) or its voiced equivalent -*γ*- (-*gh*-) was transcribed in a variety of ways, including both -*c*- and -*ch*-.[57]

Cynophobic or Cynophilic? The Images
of the Canine in Ancient Asia

All the facts already discussed regarding the early medieval Chinese slur word *nucai*, namely that it was really a non-word in Chinese, the contemporary circulation of the Mongolic root *noqai*, the phonetic and semantic similarity of the two terms, can only be considered circumstantial evidence for the *nucai* < *noqai* derivation. The strongest evidence for this equivalence comes from a passage in *Jin shu* on the exchanges between a proto-Tibetan Di chieftain and a loyal officer of the Xiongnu Former Zhao regime. Moreover, this passage has important anthropological and cultural implications for the early history of Asia.

In the year 325, in a surprise counterattack, a Di chieftain, Yang Nandi, retook the fort town Chouchi, his old base, from the Xiongnu Former Zhao forces and captured the latter's general-in-chief and regional inspector, Tian Song. *Jin shu* (103.2697; also *ZZTJ* 93.2934) then narrates as follows (italics mine):

> Nandi's guards shouted at Song and ordered him to prostrate himself [before Nandi]. Song yelled back angrily: "*You Di dog*! How can a governor appointed by the Son of Heaven prostrate himself before a bandit?" Nandi said: "Zidai (Song's style), I should work with you to achieve great successes. You are willing to be loyal to the Liu family (the royal Southern Xiongnu clan of the Former Zhao regime). Don't I deserve similar loyalty as well?" Song snarled back furiously: "*You Di nucai bandit*! How dare you seek what you do not deserve! I would rather be a loyal ghost of my nation than submit to you. Why don't you kill me immediately!" He dashed to wrest a sword from a guard and tried to stab Nandi, but missed his target and was killed by Nandi.

This short passage reminds me of "The Ballad of Mulan" discussed in the previous chapter. That folk poem used both "Qaghan" and "Son of Heaven," evidently referring to the same monarch. Similarly, in the current passage, a loyal high official of a Xiongnu regime uttered "Di dog" and "Di *nucai*" to address the same Di chieftain. What further makes the "*nucai* = dog" equation more believable is that the ethnic Di groups, as proto-Tibetan people, also had a dog totem, hence the Xiongnu general-in-chief Tian Song's contemptuous "Di dog" insult.

There are many indications of the Di people's dog totem. For example, a prominent aristocratic Di clan that produced at least two empresses for the Former Qin regime was named Gou (*Jin shu* 113.2884), a homonymic euphemism for "dog." There was also a Di person named Gounu, "slave of dog" (*Wei shu* 101.2232), a perfect theophoric "god's slave" name worshiping the dog ancestor. The most persuasive evidence is the following Chinese record dating from the third century (*Sanguo zhi* 30.858): "The Di people have long had kings. . . . There are various clans and branches, all claiming to be the descendants of Panhu." Here Panhu is the famous "dog ancestor" shared by many people in western and southern China.[58] As a matter of fact, this dog ancestor has either morphed or merged into the creation myths of not only these ethnic groups but also the majority Hàn Chinese today,[59] as this author once learned at grade school. This myth plus the Tibetan dog-taboo mentioned earlier strongly suggests a common canine totem heritage among Sino-Tibetan speakers.

Yet it is also apparent that when the slur word *nucai* first appeared in China, the cultural image of the dog, or of other members of the canine family, was as low as it is today in almost all Sinitic societies. Instead of being a venerated totemic symbol, the dog was used metaphorically, often together with another lowly animal, the pig, to describe incompetent and other contemptible characters by medieval Chinese speakers.

How do we then reconcile these two diametrically opposite historic cultural roles of the canine?

In my view, the evolution of the canine image in China reflected the clash of two opposing cultural traditions in ancient Asia, one of which can be termed *cynophobic* and the other *cynophilic*. These two cultural traditions were also intimately related to or affected by economic development and conditions.

Asian history in the past two millennia, which happened to occupy much of recorded history, has been dominated by a distinct delimitation or "cultural discontinuity" marked by the Great Wall between Inner Asian steppe nomadism and intensive farming in the Chinese heartland. Few people nowadays notice that this basic pattern of Asian conflicts was a relatively late development, more or less solidified during the five centuries before the Common Era. In prehistory and early history, the vast Eurasian continent represented a "cultural continuum" with different patterns of conflicts and exchanges.

The early modern Chinese scholar Fu Sinian (1896–1950), the founding director of the Institute of History and Philology, Academia Sinica, and the former president of National Taiwan University, was the first to observe that, contrary to the last two millennia, the historical conflict pattern in East Asia in the two millennia before the Common Era was east-west.[60] I have no intention of repeating his ingeniously simple yet brilliant observation other than to add my remarks that the cynophobic versus cynophilic cultural clash was part of this general east-west confrontation.

To put it succinctly, most early Sino-Tibetan speakers belonged to a vast "cynophilic complex" in the west. This cynophilic complex extended to Altaic tribes and many Indo-European groups. For the Altaic people, this tradition is amply substantiated by the prevailing and well-known wolf totem among both Turkic and Mongolic groups, as well as the widely popular canine personal, clan, and tribe names found among them, evidenced by, among many other things, the broad distribution of the Mongolic *noqai* as both an ethnonym and personal name.

The Indo-European cynophilic tradition is best exemplified by the pre-Islamic Iranian and Iranic groups, highlighted by, inter alia, the sacred role of dogs in Zoroastrianism. Merely striking a dog would be severely punished, according to *The Avesta*,[61] a tradition corroborated by Herodotus's observation (I.140) that "the Magi not only kill anything, *except dogs and men*, with their own hands, but make a special point of doing so" (italics mine). The Greek "Father of History" also described (Herodotus I.110) how Cyrus the Great, the founder of the ancient Iranian Achaemenid Empire, was an abandoned infant raised by a shepherd and his wife, Spico, the Median name for dog: "The fellow's name was Mitradates, and he lived with another of the king's slaves, a woman whose name in Greek would be Cyno, or bitch." Richard Frye[62] commented that this passage was intended to "let it be known generally that [Cyrus] had been saved by a dog." There are many more examples of the ancient Iranians' love and admiration of dogs. As an example, I quote a recent study: "Dogs have a special place in Zoroastrianism, as they are seen to have a spiritual gaze which frightens and repels the demons. For this reason, they have an important role to play in the *sagdid* ritual which is part of the funeral ceremony. ... The family dog is said to lead the way for the soul and protect it from the attack of demons, in the hereafter. For this reason, in ancient times, Zoroastrian homes would have a dog and this practice holds true to this day for most Zoroastrians."[63]

Given such a sacred role for the dog, we can only imagine how painful it was for the cynophilic Iranians to undergo Islamization after the conquest by the generally cynophobic Arabs. The latter's tradition, however, has also been repaid in modern times.[64]

Interestingly, the pre-Islamic Iranian cynophilic tradition did not seem to be shared by the ancient Indians, whose sacred texts, *The Vedas*, have the following passage on reincarnation according to one's conduct: "Accordingly, those who are of pleasant conduct here—the prospect [in rebirth] is, indeed, that they will enter a pleasant womb, either the womb of a Brahmin, or the womb of a Kshatriya or the womb of a Vaishya. But those who are of stinking conduct here—the prospect is, indeed, that they will enter a stinking womb, either the womb of a *dog* or the womb of a *swine*, or the womb of an outcast (*candāla*)."[65] Such low opinions about dogs and pigs are astonishingly similar to those of medieval Sinitic society and were apparently inherited by Buddhism. I would speculate that the Aryans, after conquering the subcontinent, underwent a cultural conversion similar to that undergone by the early cynophilic Sinitic groups in an environment in which dogs were not of high value, as I describe later. One of the consequences of this cultural resonance between the ancient Hindu and Sinitic worlds was the emergence of opprobrious names in medieval China, a likely byproduct of the introduction of Buddhism, with the dog and pig being the quintessential "unworthy" themes in these names.

On the Iranic side, I cannot help noticing a certain similarity between the pre-Islamic Iranians and early North Asian tribal people regarding the role of the dog in the afterworld. *Hou Hàn shu* (*History of the Later Hàn*, 90.2980) describes the funeral custom of the Wuhuan, an ethnic group generally identified as close brethren of the Xianbei and pastured largely to the northeast of the Chinese heartland, as follows: "Their folk customs value battlefield deaths. Corpses are put into coffins as mourners cry sorrowfully. Yet when it is time for burial, people sing and dance. They raise a fat dog, tie and lead it with color ribbons. They collect the dead person's horse and clothes and burn them all (it was not clear whether the dog was also burned with these items). It is said that they entrust the dog with these items, as well as with the task to protect the dead spirit to return to the Red Mountain."

On the Sino-Tibetan side, proto-Tibetan groups in western China like the Di and the Qiang were generally cynophilic, as can be deduced from the numerous canine clan and personal names recorded by Chinese historians, in addition to the Panhu dog ancestor myth mentioned earlier. Among the Sinitic groups, there are indications that the Zhou tribes who migrated from the west to conquer the Shang, the first veritable Chinese dynasty, originally belonged to the cynophilic complex. For example, the Zhou people had an early tradition of regarding (white) wolves as an auspicious token, and the Zhou king Wu, on the eve of the epochal battle to destroy the Shang polity once and for all, reportedly used a jackal metaphor to depict his troops' valor. As late as the Spring-and-Autumn period (770–476 BC), there still existed canine surnames or clan names such as Lang, "wolf," and Hu, "fox," as well as "dog" personal names among the Sinitic states descended from the Zhou tribes.

Meanwhile, there was a palpable cynophobic tradition among the tribes in eastern China and beyond, extending all the way to the Korean peninsula, that was manifested through the custom of dog eating and professional dog butchers, an occupation found only along the coastal regions in ancient China. This is also the obvious reason that dog was soon lumped together with pig in terms of cultural and metaphoric images. The Shang as a people originating in the east and possessing a bird ancestor myth very similar to that of ancient Koreans, apparently shared this cynophobic heritage, a cultural stance that could only be exacerbated by the existence of many hostile cynophilic tribes to the west, the proto-Tibetan Qiang in particular, as shown by a large number of Shang documents. The oracle bone records on sacrificing dogs in the same manner as sheep and pigs in ancestor-worship rituals[66] further prove the Shang's eastern roots in regarding the dog as a meat source.

It is natural that after their conquest of the Shang and wholesale adoption of much of Shang high culture, particularly the advanced script, Zhou high society must also have inherited some of the Shang court's snobbery toward less civilized fellow "canine tribes" who were left out of the cultural booties of this conquest, a pattern to be repeated by the medieval nomadic invaders, particularly the Tuoba par excellence, who followed the Zhou's footsteps one and half millennia later. For much of the Zhou polity, this smug superior feeling became true abhorrence after one of the Quanrong "Dog Barbarian" groups sacked and burned the Zhou capital in 771 BC, the fact that the plunderers had been invited to attack the Son of Heaven by dissident Zhou nobles notwithstanding. As recorded in the famous *Chunqiu Zuoshi zhuan* (*The Commentary of Mr. Zuo on the Spring and Autumn Annals*, abbreviated in this book as *Zuozhuan*, 4.214), the saying "Barbarians are like insatiable jackals and wolves" soon appeared in the Spring-and-Autumn period, thus starting the equivalence between "Barbarians" and the canine in Chinese politico-cultural language, despite the continued intermarriage and frequent alliance between these "canine Barbarians" and some of the Sinitic states in the west. It is nonetheless interesting to observe that the above famous "jackals and wolves" cynophobic statement was first expressed by the prominent politician Guan Zhong (?–645 BC) of the coastal state of Qi in the east, where one also happens to find the earliest known case of professional dog butchers.

Meanwhile, fundamental economic changes were taking place, with intensive farming gradually entrenching itself in the Sinitic states, accelerating private ownership of arable land and leading to the milestone event of "levying land tax for the first time" in 594 BC in Confucius' home state of Lu (*Zuozhuan* 11.614). In addition to further marginalizing the status of the dog as hunting became economically insignificant, this trend was also the driving mechanism in Owen Lattimore's theory of "progressive differentiation" on the emergence of the nomadism versus agriculture divide in East Asia.[67] As the Sinitic communities brought more and more desirable land under intensive cultivation, their less "civilized" neighbors became progressively barbarized in the following sense: being pushed by the expansion of Chinese agriculture into wastelands, steppes, and deserts to the north, they were forced to rely more and more on animal breeding than on seed cultivation. Eventually this process led to the creation of "pure" pastoral nomadism when the Sinitic groups completely cut the cultural link with their former "canine Barbarian" cousins and in-laws.[68] The eastern cynophobic tradition had vanquished the western cynophilic heritage in the end, and the east-west conflict pattern in prehistoric East Asia was replaced by the confrontations between the agrarian south and the nomadic north now divided by the Great Wall.

When cynophilic nomadic tribes reentered the Chinese heartland during the early medieval era, the dog-abhorring tradition originally prevalent only in eastern regions had already deeply engraved itself on Chinese ideology across the realm. This created an interesting pattern of cultural conflicts. On the one hand, we see a reemergence of canine personal and clan names in China, which was clearly distinct from another emerging fashion, after the introduction of Buddhism, of adopting names of the detested pig and dog, the two animals with "a stinking womb" as depicted in *Chāndogya Upanishad*, as opprobrious personal names used to avoid the gods' jealousy.

On the other hand, and following the example of the victorious cynophilic Zhou tribes who absorbed the cynophobic Shang high culture some fifteen centuries earlier, the medieval sinicizing former nomads from the north and west were quick learners in picking up the Chinese dog slur. Among many other examples, the aforementioned sardonic remark about two brothers having respectively a dog's heart and a dog's face was uttered by none other than a person of Di ethnicity, a proto-Tibetan people with a dog totem. In addition, as cited in Chapter 2, those "Barbarian" or "Barbarianized" figures would call Hàn Chinese *hangou*, "Hàn dogs."

Another revealing yet tragic episode, as recorded in *Luoyang qielan ji* (*The Record of the Monasteries of Luoyang*, 2.76), was that of the Tuoba princess Shouyang. When the Tuoba Wei dynasty was disintegrating, the beautiful princess was accosted by Erzhu Shilong, a tribal warlord of the Jie ethnicity, whom she bravely repudiated: "How dare you *hugou* (foreign dog) degrade a daughter of the heaven king!" The Tuoba princess was strangled afterward for refusing Erzhu Shilong's advances. There are several intriguing issues related to this story, ranging from the Caucasoid physical features of the Jie people to the identification of the Tuoba emperor as the heaven king (*tianwang*), an unmistakable Steppe sacral kingship vestige, as I will elaborate in Chapter 6. The key point here is that a Tuoba princess cursed one of her erstwhile nomadic cousins as a "foreign dog." Such was the politico-cultural environment in which the proto-Mongolic loan *nucai* emerged.

Despite the newly acquired dog slurs, the old cynophilic traits died hard. I have already mentioned that the diminutive name Zhinu of the third emperor of the Tang was very likely a corrupted version of the Mongolic *chinu* for "wolf." In the year 747, during the mid-Tang dynasty, there appeared, I believe, the first-ever documented evidence, albeit in a negative light, of the Korean people's time-honored dog-eating tradition: Gao Xianzhi (?–755), a rising military star in the Tang army, and an ethnic Korean, was cursed (*Jiu Tang shu* 54.3025) by his dog-worshipping proto-Tibetan (ethnic Qiang) superior as a "Korean slave who eats dog intestines and thus dog shit."

Together with the "Di *nucai*/Di dog" name calling, here we hear echoes of the once life-and-death clashes between the cynophobic east and the cynophilic west in East Asia, the long-forgotten ancient battles as old as the Trojan War.

Chapter 4

The Huns and the Bulgars:
The Chinese Chapter

The Zhou shu (History of the [Northern] Zhou)
Biography of the Buluoji: An Annotated Translation

The Jihu are also known as the Buluoji. They represent several separate clans of the Xiongnu and are said to be the offspring of the five branches of [the Southern Xiongnu headed by] Liu Yuan (?–315, the founder of the self-claimed Xiongnu dynasty of the Former Zhao 304–29). Another theory is that they descended from the Mountain Barbarians and the Red Di [of the pre-Qin era]. Spread all the way from the east of Lishi to the west of Anding,[1] in an area of seven to eight hundred *li* [1 *li* » 416 meters] across in each dimension, they live in mountain valleys and have proliferated into numerous tribes and clans. They now have a settled lifestyle[2] and are engaged in some agricultural activities. Their region does not have many mulberry trees and silkworms, but it produces a quantity of hemp fabric. Their men's clothing, as well as their burial customs, is somewhat similar to those of China proper. Their women, on the other hand, wear many shell ornaments such as earrings and necklaces.

Some of their communities intermix with Hàn population. Their chieftains know a fair amount of writing, but their speech is like that of Barbarians. One needs interpreters to communicate with them. Their comportment violates the [Sinitic] norms. They are greedy and cruel. Their mores are lewd and promiscuous, particularly with the unmarried girls, who bid goodbye to their illicit lovers only on the eve of their marriage. The more lovers a girl has, the more prestigious her future husband feels.[3] But once married, the husbands closely watch their wives' conduct. Any extramarital affairs would be punished. Moreover, when a husband dies, his brother always marries the widow.

[The Jihu] are nominally registered households in their respective prefectures and counties. But they are subjected to reduced levels of taxation and corvée labor, and thus are distinct from the regular population. In addition, those who live in remote and deep mountain valleys have not been completely subjugated. Being fierce and protected by a terrain difficult to reach, they rebel frequently.

During the Xiaochang period (525–27) of the [Tuoba] Wei dynasty, there was a [Jihu chief] Liu Lisheng in the Valley of Yunyang,[4] who proclaimed himself the son of heaven, declared a reign title (Shenjia, "sacred auspiciousness"), and appointed court officials. This was during the chaos of the Wei rule, and the government was unable to launch a military campaign [against them]. Consequently, Lisheng divided his troops and dispatched his followers to pillage the sedentary populations. There was scarcely ever a peaceful period in the regions between Fen and Jin.[5]

After the move [of the Tuoba Wei capital from Luoyang] to the city of Ye, [Emperor] Shenwu ("godly martialness") of the [Northern] Qi[6] started plotting secretly against Lisheng. He falsely promised to marry his daughter to the heir-apparent son of Lisheng. Lisheng believed the proposal and dispatched his son to the city of Ye. Shenwu of the Qi bestowed an extravagant amount of dowry (it was in fact a betrothal gift) but delayed the marriage date. Deceived by the promised marriage alliance, Lisheng let down his guard. In the third month of the first year of Datong (535), Shenwu of the Qi launched a surprise attack with a commando force. Lisheng [hastily] led a light cavalry unit to mobilize troops and was killed by his own Prince of the North, who sent Lisheng's head to Shenwu of the Qi. Lisheng's followers enthroned Lisheng's third son, the Prince of the South Sea, and organized military resistance. But Shenwu of the Qi destroyed the regime, captured the bogus monarch, together with his brother, the Prince of the West Sea, his empress and concubines, and more than four hundred persons from princes and dukes on down, and returned to the city of Ye.

Many Jihu who resided to the west of the [Yellow] River,[7] entrenched in their precipitous locations, did not submit [to the Northern Zhou and its predecessor, the rump Western Wei (535–56)]. [The Yuwen regime] was initially battling Shenwu of the Qi for supremacy and could not confront the Jihu. Emperor Taizu [of the Zhou][8] therefore dispatched Gentleman of the Palace Gate Yang Biao to placate the tribes. In the fifth year [of Datong, or 539], the Black-water[9] clans rebelled first, followed in the seventh year (541) by another [Jihu] chief, Liu Pingfu, the regional inspector of the Xiazhou commandery,[10] who took possession of the prefecture of Shangjun.[11] After that, various [Jihu] tribes in the Northern Mountains[12] violently pillaged year after year. Emperor Taizu successively sent off Li Yuan, Yu Jin, Houmochen Chong, and Li Bi (biographies: *Zhou shu* 25.418–22, 15.243–50, 16.268–70, and 15.239–41, respectively) to pacify these rebellions.

At the beginning of the Wucheng period (559–60), the Jihu of the Yanzhou commandery[13] Hao Abao and Hao Langpi ("wolf's skin") led their clans to declare allegiance to the [Northern] Qi. Abao named himself the prime minister, and Langbi appointed himself the Pillar of State. They set up mutual support with another [Buluoji] chief, Liu Sangde. Under the command of the Pillar of State Doulu Ning (biography: *Zhou shu* 19.308–10), the Zhou military units joined the regional inspector of the Yanzhou commandery Gao Lin (biography: *Zhou shu* 29.495–97) to defeat the Buluoji. In the second year (560), Langpi and the remaining collaborators rebelled again. The emperor decreed an expedition led by Grand General Hán Guo (Biography: *Zhou shu* 27.441–42), who captured and killed a large number of rebels.

During the Baoding period (561–65), the Raw Barbarians[14] of Lishi came repeatedly to pillage the northern banks of the Fen river. The regional inspector of the Xunzhou commandery[15] Wei Xiaokuan (biography: *Zhou shu* 31.535–44) built forts in vital locations and stored military provisions in order to block the Jihu's traveling routes. When Yang Zhong[16] joined with the Türks to attack the [Northern] Qi, the Jihu again entertained thoughts of insubordination and refused to supply provisions for the campaign. Zhong then bluffed the Jihu chiefs by threatening to attack them instead, using the Türk troops. The [Jihu] chiefs were intimidated into supplying the provisions. See the [*Zhou shu*] biography of Zhong for details. Afterward, the Jihu clans in the commanderies of Danzhou, Suizhou and Yinzhou, together with another chief, Hao Sanlang of Puchuan,[17] rebelled for years. The emperor successively ordered Daxi Zhen, Xin Wei, and Yu Shi (biographies: *Zhou shu* 19.306–7, 27.447–48, and 15.250–51, respectively) to conduct all-out campaigns against them and to disperse their clans and tribes.

In the second year (567) of the Tianhe period (566–71), the Area Commander-in-chief of the Yanzhou commandery Yuwen Sheng (biography: *Zhou shu* 29.493) led troops to erect a wall around the seat of Yinzhou commandery. Bai Yujiutong, Qiao Shiluo, and other Jihu chiefs plotted to intercept Sheng's troops by surprise. Sheng killed all these leaders and also defeated their other chieftains including Qiao Sanwutong. In the fifth year (570), Commander Liu Xiong (biography: *Zhou shu* 29.503–5) went to examine the rivers and routes in the northern frontier by way of Suizhou.[18] Several Jihu chiefs, including Qiao Bailang and Qiao Suwu, crossed the [Yellow] River to intercept Xiong, but again they were defeated by Xiong.

In the fifth year (576) of the Jiande period (572–77), Emperor Gaozu (Yuwen Yong, 543–78, the fourth son of Yuwen Tai and the third sovereign of the Northern

Zhou), defeated the [Northern] Qi forces at Jinzhou.[19] In hot pursuit of the enemy upon this victory, [the Zhou forces] did not have time to collect the armor and weapons abandoned by the Qi soldiers. The Jihu took advantage of this opportunity and stealthily emerged to steal those pieces of equipment. They set up the grandson, Meduo, of Lisheng as their leader, naming him Emperor Shengwu ("sacred martialness") with the reign title of Shiping ("rock peace").

In the sixth year (577) Emperor Gaozu ("High Ancestor, Progenitor") pacified Eastern China (i.e., destroyed the Northern Qi regime, which had ruled the eastern part of the former Tuoba Wei realm) and wanted to demolish the Jihu regime as well. It was decided that the Zhou forces should pursue them all the way to their deepest hideouts. But [Yuwen] Xian, the Prince of Qi (544–78; the fifth son of Yuwen Tai; biography: *Zhou shu* 12.187–96), observed that there were numerous clans and tribes of the Jihu residing in the mountains and valleys that were difficult to penetrate. It was not possible to annihilate all of them in a royal expedition. One should instead exterminate their leaders and summon the rest to surrender. Emperor Gaozu consented to this suggestion and appointed Prince Xian as the campaign marshal for this expedition, commanding several campaign commanders: [Yuwen] Zhao, the Prince of Zhao; [Yuwen] Jian, the Prince of Qiao; [Yuwen] You, the Prince of Teng;[20] and others to attack [the Jihu]. After stopping at [the Town of] Mayi,[21] Prince Xian divided up the forces to advance simultaneously via different routes. Meduo dispatched his partisan Tianzhu to defend the east bank of the [Yellow] River and his grand general Mu Zhi to guard the west bank of the [Yellow] River, with the intention of defending the crucial locations, and separating and counterattacking Xian's forces. Xian ordered Jian, the Prince of Qiao, to attack Tianzhu, and You, the Prince of Teng, to attack Mu Zhi. Both succeeded in destroying their respective opponents, and beheaded more than ten thousand enemies. Zhao, the Prince of Zhao, captured Meduo, and the rest of the Jihu all surrendered.

In the first year of the Xuanzheng period (578), the Jihu chief Liu Shouluoqian of the Fenzhou commandery rebelled again. Troops under the command of [Yuwen] Sheng, the Prince of Yue[22] (biography: *Zhou shu* 13.204–5), attacked and captured him. Subsequently, the rebellion and pillage have significantly subsided.

The Origin and Ethnic Affiliation

In the early sixth century, when the Tuoba Wei dynasty disintegrated in the wake of the Six-Garrison Revolt, there appeared in northern China a "Barbarian" group with the name Buluoji (Middle Chinese pronunciation *b'uo-lak-kiei*). In Chinese records, this name was often shortened to Jihu, "the Ji-Barbarian." The use of the term *hu*, previously referring specifically to the Xiongnu, but gradually becoming a generic appellation for assorted groups of "Barbarians," is itself an intriguing subject, to be examined later in this chapter. The late Peter Boodberg was the first Western author to study this group.[23] His identification of the ethnonym Buluoji with that of the Volga and Danube Bulgars, though, raises both serious problems and intriguing connections.

A summary account of the Buluoji is found in Chapter 49 of *Zhou shu* (*History of the Zhou*, pp. 897–99), of which I have provided the preceding annotated translation. This most comprehensive description of the Buluoji has been copied or abridged by several classic encyclopedic sources, namely *Tong dian* (*The Comprehensive Statutes*), *Taiping huanyu ji* (*A Description of the World of Great Tranquility*), *Tongzhi* (*General Treatises*), and *Wenxian tongkao* (*Comprehensive Examination of Source Materials*).[24] Brief passages related to the group are scattered in *Bei shi* (*History of the Northern Dynasties*), *Bei Qi shu* (*History of the Northern Qi*), *Zhou shu*, and other minor sources. The near- exhaustive compilation of Xiongnu materials by the Chinese scholar Lin Gan[25] represents perhaps the most complete collection of Buluoji data, while Zhou Yiliang and Tang Changru have each done an extensive study on the Zahu ("mixed or miscellaneous Barbarians"), of which the Buluoji was regarded as a component.[26]

According to the account of the Buluoji in *Zhou shu*,[27] they were "the separate clans of the Xiongnu" and were the descendants of the followers of Liu Yuan, the founder of the Former Zhao Dynasty (304–29). Though Liu Yuan's own ethnicity, especially whether he was a "pureblood" Xiongnu person, is open to debate, the Former Zhao has been generally regarded as a Xiongnu regime.

This earliest account of the origin of the Buluoji appears to be at least partially accurate, namely in that they contained in great part the remnants of the Xiongnu confederation that had not been absorbed by the Xianbei. Besides the *Zhou shu* testimony, additional evidence includes the following:

1. As convincingly demonstrated by Tang Changru (p. 443), the geographic distribution of the Buluoji as reflected in various records matched well that of the Southern Xiongnu during the Western Jin (265–316). In particular, the heavy concentration of the Jihu on the west bank of the Fen River coincided with the region occupied by "the five branches of the Southern Xiongnu" as recorded in *Jin shu*. This strongly supports the

opening statement of the Jihu biography. In addition, the county of Lishi mentioned repeatedly by the Jihu biography happened to be the very first capital of Liu Yuan, the founder of the Xiongnu Former Zhao dynasty.

2. Several Buluoji clan names, particularly those of the leading clan Liu, plus Huyan and Qiao, were well-recognized Xiongnu names.[28]

3. The *Bei Qi shu* (27.378) biography of Poliuhan Chang, whose surname was but a variant of Buluoji, states unambiguously that the clan descended from the Xiongnu.

4. As will be further examined, the Buluoji belonged to a group or groups of "Barbarians" loosely called the Zahu during the Northern dynasties. According to Tang Changru (p. 444), the use of the name Buluoji actually superseded the use of the latter. Tang therefore concludes that the Buluoji represented the final amalgamation of the Zahu. Most Zahu groups can be linked with the Xiongnu in Chinese records. Indeed, this old Xiongnu connection has other implications that will be discussed later.

Conversely, to judge by "the separate clans of the Xiongnu" characterization of *Zhou shu*, it is difficult to argue that the Buluoji represented the original core clans of the Xiongnu or their direct, "pureblood" descendants.[29] On the racial side, there were strong indications that the Buluoji included a conspicuous European or Caucasian admixture:[30]

1. *Taiping huanyu ji* (35.292) quoted a Sui dynasty (581–618) source on a contemporary popular saying that the Buluoji were *Hutou Hànshe* ("Hu-headed but Hàn-tongued"). This shows that, after apparent sinification (Hàn-tongued), the Buluoji still maintained their distinct physical appearance.

2. Several clan names of the Buluoji and Shanhu ("Mountain Barbarians," a contemporary alternative ethnonym for the Buluoji as, will be explained later), such as Bai and Cao, were of typical Central Asian origin. Zhou Yiliang (pp. 151–53) went as far as to conjecture that the Buluoji were originally Central Asians from the Western Regions who migrated to northern China. Tang Changru pointed out that Zhou's claim could not be supported by the Buluoji's geographic distribution and the numerous old Xiongnu clan names. This issue will be further examined.

3. If, as Tang Changru has concluded, the Buluoji were the final amalgamation of various Zahu tribes, then they naturally included the Jie, well known for their Caucasian, "high-nosed and heavy-bearded" physical features (*ZZTJ* 98.3100).[31]

4. Another piece of evidence that the Buluoji's possessed Caucasian traits is the rather sudden change of the primary meaning of the Chinese character *hu* from referring to the Xiongnu to designating the Caucasian Central Asians, which happened to coincide with the appearance of the Zahu.

With regard to their lifestyle, the *Zhou shu* account clearly showed that the Buluoji were mostly settled at the time and partly engaged in agricultural pursuits. However, one may not attribute this entirely to their apparent sinification (adopting Hàn dress and burial customs, etc., and eventually becoming "Hàn-tongued") or to the Central Asian elements among them. Modern archeology has revealed that, contrary to classical records, both the Xiongnu and European Huns had maintained substantial agricultural activities.[32]

Despite the conspicuous Central Asian elements and settled lifestyle, we have solid evidence for the Buluoji's steppe cultural heritage: *Tang huiyao* (*The Essentials of Tang Institutions*), *Jiu Tang shu* (*Old History of the Tang*), and *Xin Tang shu* (*New History of the Tang*) all classified Buluoji music as belonging to the Beidi "Northern Barbarians." Further, it was grouped together with that of the Tuyuhun and the Xianbei. The latter two groups' Altaic affinity is beyond doubt. Last but not least, *Tang huiyao* and *Jiu Tang shu* both noted that the music was of the "cavalry" genre. Given the familiarity and popularity of Central Asian music during the Tang era, exemplified by none other than the famous poet Bai Juyi of Central Asian ancestry, the subject of Chapter 7 of this book,[33] these official records separating Buluoji music from that of the "Western Barbarians" are strong proof of the Buluoji's nomadic past.

The Buluoji's steppe cultural identity is further strengthened by the limited linguistic data. A few surviving and identifiable words of the Buluoji all seemed to be Altaic, Turkic in particular. Peter Boodberg has identified *kuli*, "slave," and *keye*, "fort".[34] I note that the Buluoji word *weiya* (*jwei-nga*), referring to some kind of wetland tree (*Taiping huanyu ji* 35.293) can be identified with middle Turkic *yiγac*, "wood," "tree or shrub."[35] Another toponym, Kutuo, identified by Boodberg with the Mongolian word *kuda*,[36] was also from the area populated by the Buluoji (but note that Edwin Pulleyblank has raised doubts on the claim that the leading elements of the Xiongnu were Altaic. See below.). To this I add yet another piece of data: in describing the music of the "three northern-barbarian states" namely the Xianbei, Tuyuhun, and Buluoji, *Jiu Tang shu* (29.1072) states that their songs sung the name *kehan* or *Qaghan* frequently, and this was particularly the case with a chapter called *Boluohui*, an apparent variant of the root *buluoji*. Thus we learn that the Buluoji called their ruler *Qaghan*, a distinct Altaic trait, though the title itself may not be of Altaic origin.

To summarize, the Buluoji, or the Bulgars of China according to Boodberg, appear to be a group that consisted of the remnants of the Xiongnu confederation that were not absorbed by the succeeding Xianbei conglomerate, with a conspicuous Europoid admixture. Their cultural and linguistic affinity seems at least partially Altaic.

A Mixed Race or "Troublemakers"?

Before we go back to Boodberg's debatable identification of the Buluoji with the Bulgars and the latter ethnonym's equally controversial etymology, there is the intriguing question of whether the Buluoji represented a mixed race.

As presented earlier, the Buluoji not only was one of the many Zahu groups of the era but also signified the final amalgamation of such groups. A general question then is what did Zahu stand for? Here Zahu is the short form of Zazhong Hu, hence often simply rendered Zazhong. The term *zazhong* has had the dual meaning of "miscellaneous races" and "crossbred races." The exact meaning of Zazhonghu thus becomes a perennial controversy between these two interpretations. Such divergence is not unexpected as the Latin root of the English word "miscellaneous" means "mixed."

There is a noteworthy connotative issue that again is not a unique Sinitic phenomenon, namely that *zazhong* has always been a term of insult and spite, in both medieval and modern contexts. For example, in the year 505, Qiu Chi (463–508), an official of the Southern Liang (502–57), wrote a letter to Chen Bozhi, a southern Hàn general who had earlier surrendered to the Tuoba Wei dynasty. This famous letter contained such sinocentric statements as this (*Liang shu* [*History of the Liang*], 20.314–15): "Hence I know that wherever frost and dew are fair and even, the alien races cannot procreate; and the old country of the Ji (the imperial clan of the Zhou dynasty) and the Hàn is never meant to accommodate those crossbreeds (*zazhong*)." Evidently, similar bias against and contempt for "crossbred races" existed in Western culture as well, so much so that, despite Boodberg's learned comment on this issue many decades ago, a noted Sinologist of Western origin, in reviewing an early manuscript of mine on this subject, seriously questioned the possibility that any self-respecting human group would have called itself a "mixed race."

But such Eurocentric and Sinocentric sensitivities may not be appreciated at all by many ancient as well as modern groups who did not find being of a mixed race in any way dishonorable. An example is the medieval tribal group in northern China named Tiefu. *Bei shi* (*History of the Northern Dynasties* 93.3062; see also *Wei shu* 95.2054) records, "In the north, people call by the name Tiefu those whose father is Xiongnu and whose mother is Xianbei. And this has been taken [by themselves] as their clan name." In other words, this is a clear case that a northern group had taken a word meaning "Xiongnu father and Xianbei mother" as their self-identity.

Moreover, a famous chieftain, Helian Bobo (?–425), of this group, who founded the ethnic Xia dynasty (407–31), later thought it necessary to adopt a new royal surname, Helian, meaning "(directly from) heaven." But despite the Sinocentric description of *Bei shi* and *Wei shu* that this was prompted by the "shame" associated with the name Tiefu,[37] Helian Bobo ordered the rest of his fellow clansmen to proudly keep the old "Xiongnu-father-and-Xianbei-mother" clan name, albeit with a more forceful Chinese transcription Tiefa ("Iron-strike"), so that (*Jin shu* 130.3206) "their descendents are as solid and sharp as iron, capable of striking other people."

More than a millennium later and far away from the Old Eurasia, new "mixed races" were created on the New Continent when early European settlers mingled with the aboriginals. And again, words such as Métis and Mestizos, unmistakably meaning "crossbred," have been taken as proud self-identifications of these mixed people in both Americas up to the present day.[38] The conclusion is that, a proud clan name meaning "mixed race" was and is quite normal outside the Sino-European cultural orbit.

Back to the Buluoji and the general Zahu "Barbarians" during the Northern dynasties, there are indeed earlier precedents for *zahu* to mean "miscellaneous barbarians." For example, in *Sanguo zhi* (*History of the Three Kingdoms* 16.512–13), this word was used interchangeably with *zhuhu* ("various Barbarians"). But in the *Hou Hàn shu* (*History of the Later Hàn* 76.2463) passage on *zazhong huji* ("*zazhong* Barbarian cavalry"), a military unit from a group later identified as one of the Zahu groups, indicates that the Zahu of the Northern dynasties was evidently short for *zazhong hu*. As such, the term in all likelihood should be understood in the context of "mixed races." The best example is the case of An Lushan, a self-acknowledged son of a Turk father and an Iranic/Sogdian mother (*Jiu Tang shu* 104.3213, and *ZZTJ* 216.6916). An was thus called a *zazhong hu* (*Jiu Tang shu* 150a.5367), correctly translated by Edwin Pulleyblank as a "*hu* barbarian of mixed race."[39]

In addition, as the translated *Zhou shu* biography states, the Buluoji "represent the separate clans of the Xiongnu, and are the offspring of the five branches of Liu Yuan." It is of particular interest that the other self-identified "mixed race" of the period, namely the Tiefu, later Tiefa, had a nearly identical pedigree, being the descendants of the Xiongnu and coming from the clans of Liu

Yuan (*Jin shu* 130.3201). I would further point out that Liu Yuan's own assertion of noble Xiongnu lineage was rather questionable. Though the claim that Liu's clan was once part of the Southern Xiongnu confederation appears credible, by its very name, Tuge or Xiutuge (also shortened to Xiutu), the group was unlikely to be "pureblood" or unadulterated Xiongnu. It was already called *zazhong* by *Hou Hàn shu* (76.2463) and was later characterized as a Zahu group, which indicated the gradual ethnic blending when the old Xiongnu confederacy began to be supplanted by other nomadic powers, particularly that of the Xianbei, a process leading to the appearance of many "mixed Barbarians." The last piece of the puzzle is the insightful observation by Tang Changru that the Buluoji represented the final amalgamation of such "mixed Barbarians" cited earlier.

To summarize all the evidence, Chinese data including the strong Caucasian elements support the notion that the Buluoji represented a "mixed race." Meanwhile, history records also that the Buluoji and in general the Zahu had been a perpetual "security problem" for the Tuoba Wei dynasty and its successors, namely the Northern Zhou and the Northern Qi, as well as the Sui and the early Tang, to pacify. The histories of these dynasties were filled with incidents of Zahu insurrections and revolts, as well as the government's continued efforts to subdue or mollify them. Indeed, even during the early Tang, the appearance of the name Buluoji was almost always related to such upheavals. The perennial strife between the Zahu/Buluoji on one side, and the Tuoba and its successor states on the other side, appeared to be a carry-over of the old Xiongnu-Xianbei rivalry.[40] In this context, as expressed explicitly by *Zhou shu*, the Buluoji tribes were constant troublemakers in the eyes of the Tuoba rulers of the Northern dynasties and their Sui and Tang successors.

Incidentally, the "Xiongnu-father-and-Xianbei-mother" Tiefu clans mentioned earlier had a similar repute. Not only they were almost always rebelling or fighting against the Tuoba and other Xianbei groups, their leader Helian Bobo gave the name Tiefu a new spin—Tiefa, "iron-strike," a clear warning to his enemies that this "mixed race" was not to be trifled with. One is tempted to ascribe such "troublemaker" character to a mixed group's inherent difficulty in conforming to mainstream populations.

The Xiongnu and the Ethnonym Hu

Whether direct progeny or "separate clans," the Buluoji represented the very last fragment of what was once the mighty Xiongnu conglomerate. As such, they provide some rare input to the perennial question of the Xiongnu's ethnic and linguistic identity. This identity has remained to this day an enigma, despite centuries of extensive interactions with the two Hàn dynasties and their successors, both in violent warfare and through peaceful exchanges. The question is, were the Xiongnu Mongols? Or Turks? Or neither?

Like the linguistic identity of the Tuoba discussed in the appendix of this book, the primary difficulty is that there is precious little linguistic data available, and that mostly in the form of words and names transcribed into (early) Chinese. Ever since Shiratori Kurakichi started the research on this subject early last century, the issue for quite some time was the choice between a Mongolian and a Turkic identity for the Xiongnu. Shiratori seemed to have hesitated between the two characterizations.[41] Then Otto Maechen-Helfen observed that there lived in the Xiongnu Empire the ancestors of the present-day Ket or Yenisei-Ostiaks, and some of the Xiongnu words might have been borrowed from the Proto-Ket.[42] A little later Lajos (Louis) Ligeti made the first attempt to prove the Kettic affiliations of the Xiongnu.[43] Likely enlightened by these attempts, Edwin Pulleyblank in 1963 advanced the theory based on linguistic data that the Xiongnu might not be Altaic at all. He proposed that the Xiongnu language belonged to the Yenissei group, with Kettish as its modern relative.[44] This proposition has kept attracting scholastic attention.[45]

It is of particular interest that the same Yenissei groups have also been linked, with some degree of success, to the Sino-Tibetan linguistic family.[46] The Xiongnu language problem would therefore seem to have come full circle. Indeed, I have observed possible proto-Sinitic linguistic connections of the Xiongnu, including the aforementioned clan name Helian that has survived in China to this day.[47]

Related to this issue is an old yet elusive puzzle in Xeno-Chinese relationships, namely the change of the primary meaning of the character *hu*. From the two Hàn dynasties until well into the Southern-Northern dynasties, Hu as an ethnonym had primarily referred to the Xiongnu (and members of their confederation). For instance, a Jin dynasty source still clearly states *hu* was the general name for the Beidi ("Northern Barbarians").[48] But during the Tang, Hu became largely reserved for Central Asians or "Western Barbarians." This issue has attracted the attention of several prominent scholars.[49] None has provided a satisfactory explanation for this rather sudden change in the meaning of the character *hu*. For example, both Wang Guowei and Cen Zhongmian tried to explain the character *hu*'s double meaning by alleging that the Xiongnu were largely Caucasian or had an Iranic origin, which, while insightful, went beyond what could be supported by historical and archeological data.

Though the Buluoji could not with certainty be traced back to the hardcore Xiongnu, the disintegration and dispersion of the latter under the growing Xianbei pressure and dominance apparently resulted in the appearance of various Hu groups, leading to the summary Zahu designation with the Buluoji as its last representative. This process is relatively well documented in Chinese sources. For example, *Jin shu* (56.1533–34) mentions that the Hu of Bingzhou "had in fact been the Xiongnu." Bingzhou in due course became a major homestead of the Buluoji. The cited studies by Tang Changru and Lin Gan contain other well-documented cases.

While we still cannot answer with certainty the question of ethnic identity, the reconstruction of the process of its breakup inevitably leads to the inference that the original Xiongnu federation had a major Europoid component. For one thing, the largely Indo-Iranic Central Asian oases and city-states had for a long time been under the Xiongnu's direct control, even regarded as its "right arm." Some had demonstrated unwavering loyalty to the Xiongnu under Hàn pressure.[50] Maenchen-Helfen has also demonstrated the increasing Caucasian elements in the Xiongnu during and after the Hàn dynasties.[51] At least we can conclude with much certainty that the end product of the breakup of the Xiongnu Empire included many Altaicized Caucasian groups. The Hephthalites, the War-Huns and/or the White Huns, and so on represented perhaps some of the groups who migrated westward,[52] whereas the Buluoji and other Zahu groups remained behind. It is worth noting that from early on, as claimed by *Sui shu* (84.1862), even the Turks were also known to have descended from the Zahu.[53]

It is my opinion that the Buluoji may serve as the missing link for the change of the primary meaning of the *hu* designation, which happened to coincide with the appearance of the Zahu in the Northern dynasties. A good case is the well-established equation that the Buluoji were widely known as Shanhu ("Mountain barbarians"). The latter name was still popular at least till the early Tang (as shown by *Bei Qi shu*, which was compiled during the Tang and persistently used "Shanhu" to refer to the Buluoji). Along this line I have identified an intriguing datum.

In the year 751, Tang troops led by Korean general Gao Xianzhi suffered a decisive defeat at the hands of the Arabs and local Türk groups on the banks of the Talas River.[54] As a result, many Chinese became prisoners of war and were sent to the heartland of the Abbasid Arab Empire. According to Joseph Needham, this event much accelerated the spread and transmission of Chinese technologies and inventions, papermaking in particular, to the rest of the world.[55] One such prisoner, Du Huan, eventually made it back to China via the ocean trade route and recorded his travels during this extraordinary experience, which included, inter alia, an eyewitness report of Chinese craftsmen working in the Abbasid Arab capital Aqula

(Kufa).[56] Among the few precious remaining pieces of Du Huan's since-lost mem-
oir *Jingxing ji* (*Travel Notes*), which are preserved in *Tong dian*, compiled by Du
Huan's clansman Du You, one finds the following passage (*Tong dian* 193.1041):
"In the countries I traveled through overland [from Central Asia to the Abbasid
capital], there was but one kind of Shanhu ["Mountain Barbarians"], yet several
different religions." Having lived in Central and West Asia for years, Du Huan was
undoubtedly very familiar with the cultures and linguistics of this region. For example, his accurate comments on Iran having been conquered by the Arabs more
than one hundred years earlier were quoted by Du You to correct the out-of-date
Chinese account of the old Sassanid Persia (*Tong dian* 193.1042). In addition, Du
Huan's brief description of the three major religions current in the region appears
rather precise.[57] Du had also accurately recorded the location of the Khazar
"Turks" (*Tong dian* 139.1044). Therefore, his choice of the name Shanhu instead of
the standard Tang period designation *Hu* for Iranic Central Asians is intriguing. In
my view, Du's wording has both racial and linguistic underpinnings and very possibly reflects the flourishing of, if not the Buluoji per se, at least many Turkicized
Iranic groups in the area, which was consistent with the subsequent Turkicization
of much of the region.

To recap, the fact that Buluoji was the last name for the Zahu was not a mere
accident. As examined earlier, the evolution of the Zahu included the increasing
Caucasian elements in the former Xiongnu groups. With the continued intermix-
ing between the Xiongnu remnants and the Indo-Europeans both native in northern China and from Central Asia, coupled with the westward movement of many
such groups, the name Hu acquired in a relatively short time its new primary designation. This may also have been a harbinger of Central Asia's Turkicization.

Parallels between the Buluoji and European Bulgars

Peter Boodberg's suggestion that the name Buluoji is a cognate of Bulgar raises
two intriguing questions. The first is of course the solidity of this cognitive relation, and the second is whether the two ethnic groups were related. On the one
hand, there are scant data to support either claim, especially the second one. On
the other hand, there are two interesting parallels between the Buluoji and the
Bulgars that may be of some value to the study of both groups, and even to disprove a direct link between them.

First a brief digression to the enormously popular identification of the European Huns with the Xiongnu in Chinese records: W. B. Henning's study of the

"Sogdian ancient letters,"[58] particularly about the Sogdian name *xwn*, was once acclaimed as having finally proved such a link.[59] But Otto Maenchen-Helfen soon pointed out the problems in this "final proof."[60] While Iranologists tend to support Henning's conclusion,[61] Altaicists continue to discount this evidence and consider the theory yet unproven.[62]

The foremost parallel between the Buluoji and the Bulgars is in their respective progeny in relation to the Xiongnu and the Huns. As I have presented, the link between the Buluoji and the Xiongnu confederation is well substantiated in that the Buluoji were clearly one of the remnants of the earlier Xiongnu Empire (but unlikely to have descended from whose dominant clans). Conversely, the Bulgars' connection to the European Huns has also been recorded ever since their first appearance in European history. In fact, contemporary European sources kept equating the Bulgars with the Huns,[63] so much so that the modern scholar D. Detschev simply assumed that Bulgar was the name given to the descendents of the Attilanic Huns by the Gepids and Ostrogoths.[64] Modern studies have also identified the name "Irnik" on the Bulgarian Princes' List with the youngest son of Attila, Ernach.[65] Gyula (Julius) Németh interpreted these old records as the intermingling of European Hunnic elements with newly arrived Oğuric Turkic groups.[66] At the very least, the Hun-Bulgar connection is much more tangible than the Hun-Xiongnu identification.

However, this parallel tends to disprove a direct link between the Buluoji and the Bulgars, especially in the case of the yet questionable Hun-Xiongnu equation. This is because the European Huns could only be the descendants of the Northern Xiongnu, whereas the Buluoji were clearly, albeit very likely partially, descended from the Southern Xiongnu. In addition to the original differences that prompted their permanent schism in AD 48, the two branches of the Xiongnu had further undergone centuries of radically different migrations, interminglements, and evolutions[67] in diverse parts of the Eurasian continent before the advent of the Buluoji and the Bulgars.

The second parallel is the meaning or etymology of the two ethnonyms. It is true that Boodberg's suggested cognitive relation between Buluoji and Bulgar lacks solid linguistic proof and may remain forever a conjecture.[68] But an intriguing similarity can be observed between the two names. This is the controversial etymology of the name Bulgar. In the early days of modern scholarship, there was the seemingly unanimous opinion that *bulγa* means "to mix, to become mixed." Related to the first parallel, it is worth noting Maenchen-Helfen's conclusion that the European Huns were already "racially mixed."[69] However, several alternative etymologies have since been proposed.[70] Of particular interest is the etymology "to incite, to rebel," later preferred by Németh who had earlier advocated the "mixed" theory.[71] Having earlier agreed with the old "mixed race" interpretation, Peter Golden too has switched to the new "disturbers" etymology.[72] However, as presented earlier, these two rather different interpretations may not necessarily be mutually exclusive and can in fact coexist in the case of the Buluoji in China: the group represented both a "mixed race" and a persistent "troublemaker." Moreover, about a century earlier, a "Barbarian" chieftain, Helian Bobo, declared that his tribal name, Tiefu, originally interpreted as "Xiongnu father and Xianbei mother," also stood for Tiefa "iron-strike." This is clearly another case of similar double-meaning of a Steppe-origin ethnonym.

These parallels do not substantiate any direct link between the Buluoji and the Bulgar groups. Nonetheless, one cannot help mentioning the latter's following possible contacts with the medieval East Asian world.

First there was the Arab author al-Nadim's statement that the Bulgars had once used the Chinese script as well as the "Manichaean script."[73] This rather extraordinary story can be discounted by al-Nadim's poor repute in reliability. However, the Bulgars' use of the twelve-animal cycle is beyond doubt, as clearly shown by the famous Bulgarian Princes' List.[74] This is not the place to delve into the origin of the animal cycle. But as argued elsewhere in this book, recent archaeological discoveries and the Austroasiatic link uncovered by Jerry Norman[75] make the China-to-Steppe transmission route of the animal cycle indisputable.

Omeljan Pritsak[76] may have gone too far by attempting to identify the most prominent clan, Dulo, on the Bulgarian Princes' List with the (Southern) Xiongnu clan name Tuge (Old Chinese pronunciation *d'o-klak) that happened to be the ancestor of the Buluoji and the name of an important Zahu group to boot.[77] The use of the animal cycle by the Bulgars may also be attributed to their belonging to the Oğuric (l/r- according to Gerard Clauson) Turkic grouping who shared with the present-day majority "Common Turkic" peoples the heritage of an ancient calendar based on the twelve-animal cycle as documented by Louis Bazin.[78] The challenge to such an explanation is the historical fact that all other Inner Asian peoples, namely the Turks, the Tibetans, the Mongols, and various ancient Indo-Iranic groups who used the animal cycle, had been in direct contact with the Chinese cultural world. One perhaps needs more convincing arguments why the Bulgars, of whose calendar the animal cycle was a centerpiece, should be an exception.

The Buluoji in China had an enormous impact on Chinese history, political as well as cultural, which went largely unrecognized in the traditional sinocentric historiography. I have already touched upon the Buluoji's political role. The best example must be the Six-Garrison Revolt, which eventually brought down the Tuoba Wei regime. It was first started and led by a person named Poliuhan Baling (*ZZTJ* 149.4674). This somehow could be viewed as the final revenge exacted by the former Xiongnu groups on the Xianbei, who had earlier replaced the Xiongnu as the dominating power on the Steppe.

What may have been neglected even more were the Buluoji's significant contributions to China's cultural and religious heritage. For example, arguably the most prominent real-life figure in the vast Dunhuang grotto arts was the Buddhist monk Liu Sahe, who was of well-documented Buluoji ethnicity.[79] But perhaps the least noted case was Lu Fayan, author of the single most important historical treatise on Chinese phonology, namely *Qieyun* (*Tonic Rhymes*). The late Chinese scholar Chen Yuan had only pointed out that Lu was a Xianbei person,[80] without recognizing that the original form Buliugu of the sinified clan name Lu was yet another variant of the root Buluoji. Even today, one cannot but marvel at the great accomplishments of such a presumably marginal "mixed Barbarian" group in medieval China.

Chapter 5

The Mystery of the "White-Drake" Oracle: The Iranian Shadows

"Using Aliens to Check Aliens": When the Tables Were Turned

The late John K. Fairbank summarized the rule of the several so-called non-Chinese dynasties of conquest as follows: "Once in power at Peking, though such non-Chinese dynasties made many innovations, on balance they utilized the Chinese tradition in governing China and to a large extent in conducting their foreign relations."[1] Though Fairbank's description of their foreign policies may also be open to serious challenge, this chapter takes issue with his characterization of the domestic policies of the "conquest dynasties." I submit that the ethnic regimes in China deviated substantially from the "Chinese tradition in governing China." Oddly enough, it may be said that many of these "conquest dynasties" turned around the "Chinese tradition in conducting foreign relations (or rather frontier affairs)" and applied it to the dynasties' domestic administration of the Central Kingdom.

For much of the time over two millennia, "Chinese foreign policies" were essentially Sinitic frontier policies, whose traditional guiding principle was *yiyizhiyi* or its several variations, roughly translated as "using Barbarians to check/rule/govern Barbarians." This principle can be summarized as a combination of the doctrines of "divide and conquer" and "my enemy's enemy is my friend." Despite its very long history going back to the Hàn dynasty (206 BC–AD 220), its practice had generated some limited, short-term, and transient effects at best, and not a few calamities at worst. The latter are exemplified by the two diplomatic follies of the Song dynasty (960–1368) that led to or accelerated the establishment of the Jurchen Jin dynasty (1115–1234) and the Mongol Yuan dynasty (1260–1368).

Contrary to what Fairbank has described, many Steppe-origin "conquest powers" in Chinese history can be said to have turned the table in this regard and adopted, in "governing China," a policy of "using the 'civilized' to check the 'civilized.'" Moreover, the former nomads' clever manipulation of Chinese domestic politics led to far-reaching and long-lasting legacies in China, which are still felt by every Chinese today.

The Mongol Yuan polity is perhaps the best-documented case of this smart policy. In dire need of sedentary talents and administrative experience, yet with little trust in the newly conquered natives in China, the Mongol court set up discriminatory laws and rules and effectuated a social class structure that greatly favored the so-called Semu people, mostly of Central and West Asian origins, at the expense of native Sinitic and sinicized groups. The special status and treatments translated into unprecedented opportunities for these foreigners such that the floodgate was opened for them to flock to China. The result was that, in the words of Samuel Adshead, "Probably more non-Chinese came into China under the Yuan dynasty than in any other period of Chinese history till the nineteenth century."[2] The family of Marco Polo was just one example. Faithfully fulfilling their designated role in the Mongol Yuan regime's politico-social scheme of "using the 'civilized' to rule the 'civilized,'" these Semu people were termed by Adshead, quite aptly, as "assistant conquerors."

As it is beyond the scope of this book, the Mongol Yuan case will be examined in detail elsewhere. I mention here only the most important legacy of the Mongol policy: the permanent establishment of the Islamic faith in the Central Kingdom. Despite the Yuan dynasty's very short time span, which lasted not even a full century in orthodox historiography, the influx of the enormous numbers of Central and Western Asian Muslim "assistant conquerors" brought on by the Mongol court's "domestic policy" rapidly grew to a critical mass. This critical mass was sufficient for many Islamic communities, particularly those in western China, to weather and survive the post-Yuan persecutions and "de-Barbarization" efforts. This is not the place to delve into the long, fascinating, and torturous story of how Muslim communities in China endured and in fact grew in the centuries after the Mongol rule. The upshot is that today the Hui, the sinicized Muslims, are recognized as the second largest "nationality" in the People's Republic, with all the domestic and geopolitical influences that implies.

A Lost Chapter of East Asian History: The Duration of the Central Asia Card

The Mongol Yuan's clever game of employing "assistant conquerors" to help rule the conquered is a well-known and extensively studied subject. What I contend in this chapter is that it was in no way the first such scheme in East Asia. Long before Central and Western Asian Muslims filled the Yuan court in Beijing and provincial administrations all over China, other Steppe and Steppe-origin regimes in East Asia had already adopted and even perfected this game of "using the 'civilized' to check the 'civilized.'" In other words, the Central Asia card played by the Steppe and Steppe-origin polities vis-à-vis China or the Chinese heartland was a perennial phenomenon or geopolitical game in East Asia ever since the construction of the first Great Wall.

However, until now, the Mongol Yuan remained the only prominent case of this deliberate strategy, while all its precedents rest in oblivion or the historical dustbin. Put differently, the role and influence of the pre-Islamic Iranians and other Indo-Iranic groups who populated Central Asia at the time is a lost chapter in East Asian History. This fact is an intriguing subject in its own right, worthy of special attention. Here I propose only two primary reasons for this void.

First, as I have already commented on the Sinitic façade of the Tang, the pre-Islamic Iranic influence occurred unfortunately during an era when Chinese Confucian gentry and scholar-officials were the sole custodians of historiography and virtually all forms of writing in classical East Asia. This monopoly was first broken by the Chinese Buddhist literature, which was centered around ancient India and the Indic cultures. The independent medieval sources and cultural entities that greatly helped to propagate the Mongol Yuan case came too late for the pre-Islamic Iranians and Iranic groups.

The second major reason was the suppression and loss of ancient Iranian and Iranic culture records after the Arab conquest of Sassanian Iran and Central Asia. We now possess limited quantities of these precious records, many of them in fragmented form, especially in comparison with the corpus of ancient Sinitic, Indo-Buddhist, Greco-Byzantine, and Arabic records. This sorry situation was aggravated by the westward Turkicization of the vast Iranic-speaking areas in Central Asia and beyond, a process almost parallel to the eastward Islamization of the region. Much of the non-Islamic Turkic literature also suffered similar deliberate suppression or unintentional abandonment.

The oldest case of playing the Central Asia card was by the Xiongnu. In fact, for a long time, the Hàn-Xiongnu conflict centered around control of Central Asia, or the Western Regions as it was known then, and dubbed "the right arm of the Xiongnu." The Xiongnu made full use of the material and human resources of the Western Regions, especially those provided by the sedentary city-states. Nicola Di Cosmo's 1994 study of the Xiongnu Empire's economic basis touched upon the material resources, but the subject of the Xiongnu's human resources from Central Area remains understudied, due largely to the lack of data. Given the historical pattern of the Central Asia card, there is little doubt that the Xiongnu also profited amply from the human resources of the Western Regions, which also provides an important case for strong Caucasian elements among the Xiongnu, in addition to indigenous Indo-European tribes that may have inhabited north and northwest China in prehistoric times.

The pattern of the Central Asia card became clearer in the post-Hàn era. Despite the continuing near-monopoly of historiography in East Asia by the Confucian literati, traces of Central Asians and other Hu immigrants in the various ethnic polities that emerged in northern China became more and more noticeable. While the provenance of a growing number of these alien figures may be tracked all the way to the subcontinent, after the advent of Buddhism in East Asia, the great majority were undoubtedly Iranian or Iranic-speaking.

Of these forerunners of the "assistant conquerors" of the Mongol Yuan time, the Sogdians certainly occupied the center stage. The Sogdians spoke an Eastern Iranic language and were natives of Sogdiana, the large region in Transoxania that covers much of the territory of today's Tajikistan, southern Uzbekistan, and even northern Afghanistan. The Sogdians were best known as successful traders and merchants along the ancient Silk Road, "going wherever profit is to be made" according to the official history of the Tang. Consequently, a "Sogdian trading network" has been universally attributed to the extensive distribution of Sogdian travelers, communities, and colonies from Crimea to Manchuria. The most extensive modern treatise on their history is, unsurprisingly, Etienne de la Vaissière's *Histoire des marchands sogdiens*.[3] But in addition to commerce, the Sogdians "were also interpreters, entertainers, horse breeders, craftsmen, and transmitters of ideas."[4] In the words of Frantz Grenet, "the Sogdian influx [was] a major factor in the cultural history of China,"[5] an observation supported not only by early modern scholarship but also by a growing body of new archaeological findings. Yet so far, few authors have noted the political dimension of the Sogdians and other Iranian-speaking immigrants in medieval China, which is exemplified in the following puzzle regarding a children's rhyme.

The Rooster Puzzle: Vox Populi, Vox Dei

Since the dawn of history, folk songs have played an important role in China. The best example is *Shijing* (*Classics of Odes*, or *Book of Songs*), one of the six (five still extant) books of the Confucian canon. The great majority of the poems preserved therein are folk songs. Not only were kings and government administrations sup-posed to collect and monitor folk songs to gauge public opinion and to ameliorate their rule accordingly, but Confucian historians also looked to these songs to help evaluate the deeds of ancient and contemporary rulers. This reflects the somewhat idealized political theory of the Zhou conquering kings who overthrew the alleg-edly tyrannical Shang dynasty: the king's power comes from a mandate of heaven; heaven sees and listens through the eyes and ears of the people. In other words, this is the ancient Chinese version of "vox populi, vox Dei."

This adage came originally from an alleged proclamation of King Wu of the Zhou, made on the eve of the decisive battle to topple the Shang dynasty.[6] The au-thenticity of this proclamation, likely a piece of the Zhou propaganda after it had overthrown the Shang, or the preserved text version, is naturally in serious doubt. However, Mencius cited this passage in his argument for justifying the overthrow of unworthy monarchs (*Shisanjing zhushu*, p. 2737), proving the saying's antiquity.

Of all folk songs, children's ballads or rhymes occupied a particularly im-portant place: they were often regarded as "vox Dei," or oracles from heaven. One may view this as a logical extension of the previously mentioned post-Zhou conquest political doctrine: heaven speaks through the mouths of uncorrupted and unbiased people, that is, innocent children. Chinese history is thus perme-ated by stories of how these supposedly spontaneous children's songs presaged future events, especially the rise and fall of rulers and regimes.[7] As such, this time-honored tradition soon also became a much-exercised political maneuver: creating and spreading, or collecting, and then interpreting children's rhymes, were often part of a "political campaign" conducted by ambitious or scheming individuals.

For instance, shortly before a meticulously planned coup d'état culminating in the sensational murder of the dictatorial warlord-turned-chancellor Dong Zhuo (?–192) of the Later Hàn dynasty, a children's rhyme circulated in the capital region (*Hou Hàn shu*, or *History of the Later Hàn, zhi* 13.3285): "O so green is the grass of a thousand miles, yet your imminent doom is presaged by a tenth-day divination." Here the "grass of a thousand miles" and "tenth-day divi-nation" were clever decompositions or "anagrams" of the two Chinese charac-ters *dong* and *zhuo*, respectively. Only a naïve observer would fail to see the Machiavellian hand of the coup plotters in this children's rhyme.

In a similar context, *Bei Qi shu* (*History of the Northern Qi*) recorded a per-plexing story with a peculiar explanation of the name Buluoji, which, as I identi-fied in the previous chapter, was the designation of some "Barbarians of mixed origin" in northern China and a likely cognate of the name Bulgar. Gao Zhan

(537–68, formal reign 561–65), the ninth son of the actual founder of the dynasty, Gao Huan (496–547), and the fourth sovereign of the Northern Qi, had the *xiaoming* ("childhood name") Buluoji. Around the year 561, while Gao Zhan precariously held the position of right chancellor under his elder brother Emperor Xiaozhao (Gao Yan; reign 560–61), the following children's ballad reportedly circulated in the Northern Qi (*Bei Qi shu* 14.183.):

> There lives in the Zhongxing Temple an old white *fu* bird
> Whose harmonious singing was earnestly listened to everywhere.
> A monk rings the bell at night after hearing it.

As the spin doctors of the day explained in *Bei Qi shu*, the chancellor's residence was exactly where the Zhongxing Temple used to be, and the *fu* bird, meaning "rooster," referred to Gao Zhan's childhood name, Buluoji. The ballad was therefore an omen of Gao Zhan's ascendance to the throne.

Of particular import in this case is the political connotation of the rooster. Starting in the Northern dynasties (386–589), a golden rooster was a token of the imperial voice, especially in proclaiming a royal amnesty, a standard act celebrating the enthronement of a new emperor. A mid-Tang dynasty source *Fengshi wenjianji* (*Mr. Feng's Personal Perceptions and Observations*) tells us (4.39–40),

> When the state has a general amnesty, an imperial guard officer, under the command of the Royal Armory, is ordered to erect a golden rooster in front of the royal palace. The head of the rooster is made of pure gold. The rooster is erected underneath a tall pavilion and is only removed after the announcement of the imperial edict of amnesty. . . . [This tradition] was not known prior to the Wei and Jin dynasties, and is said to have originated during either the Later Wei (i.e., the Tuoba) dynasty or the Lü Guang regime (the Later Liang, 386–403, a polity in northwest China established by the Lü clan, an offshoot of the proto-Tibetan Former Qin dynasty 350–394). . . . During the Northern Qi dynasty, every time there was an amnesty, the golden rooster was erected in front of the principal gate (Changmen) of the royal palace for three days. Ten thousand people would strive to fetch a small amount of earth around the post on which perched the golden rooster, claiming that carrying this earth would bring good luck. The authorities could not disallow such acts and the place was thus turned into a pit in days.

This custom was corroborated by official records (e.g., *Xin Tang shu*, or *The New History of the Tang*, 48.1269). Apparently the erection of the golden rooster was a festival-like public event widely participated in by the general population. It should also be noted that in an imperial amnesty, almost all criminal offences ranging from rebellion to petty crimes were mitigated or pardoned, thus touching upon the lives of thousands of families whose members had for one reason or another run afoul of the law. In short, in an era with no mass media such as newspapers, radio, or television talk shows, one of the most effective ways to market a person's imperial potential and image to the general public might well be to link the person to the golden rooster. Actually the same Tang source (4.40; see also *Bei Qi shu* 11.146) continues with a story later during Gao Zhan's own reign as the Northern Qi emperor, in which one of Zhan's prince nephews was similarly linked with a rooster in a children's rhyme, presaging the latter's imperial fortune. Not to take any chances, Gao Zhan immediately had the nephew put to death.

Returning to the "White-Drake" oracle, the key "rooster" link in the children's rhyme that allegedly prophesies Gao Zhan's enthronement has two difficulties. First, the character *fu*'s meaning, "duck," or more generally "water bird," is attested to by such early sources as Ode 258 of the *Book of Songs*. It has hardly ever been attested as referring to a rooster—there does not appear any way to explain this peculiar allusion within classical Chinese literature and linguistics. In fact, *Ciyuan* (*Origins of Words*, p. 1917), a leading modern etymological dictionary of Chinese words, can cite only the Gao Zhan story to substantiate this allusion. Second, while Zhan's childhood name, Buluoji, should support this allusion, as *Bei Qi shu* explicitly states, an extensive search of ancient and modern Turco-Mongol sources nevertheless yields no clue to the word implying or pertaining to "rooster."

Despite Peter Boodberg's pioneering exploration of the ethnonym, Buluoji, including an examination of Gao Zhan's childhood name, and his detailed study of the Northern Qi regime, he completely avoids this "rooster story," which had a conspicuous appearance in *Bei Qi shu* regarding Gao Zhan's accession to the throne. I admit also to having been baffled for years for a solution to the aforementioned double puzzle until I realized that the perennial Central Asia card was the key and started looking into this connection.

I submit that an answer to both difficulties of the "White-Drake" oracle is found in the Iranic root *mwry-* (*mwrgh-*) for "bird."[8] In Chapter 2, I elaborated upon the fact that in Old and Middle Chinese, labials *m-* and *b-* were often interchangeable, particularly in transcribing non-Chinese words and names. Examples include *moheduo* < *bayadur* ("hero"),[9] *Pojie* (Middle Chinese pronunciation *b'uo-tsia*) < Matsya (an ancient people in Northern India),[10] and *mole* (*mua-lǝk*) < *balïq*, a Turkic word for "fish."[11] One may also add the reconstructed ancient Iranic original **buxsux* for *muxu*, "alfalfa," proposed by Berthold Laufer.[12] In the other direction, Chinese *wan* (*miwan*), "myriad," became Turkic *ban* and *wu* (*mu*), the fifth symbol of the "ten Heavenly stems" used in the Chinese calendar, became Turkic *bou*.[13] In our particular case, at least four Chinese transcriptions of the root *bulγa* start with *m-*. The *buly- > mwrγ-* equation leads to the identification of *fu*, "water bird," with *buluoji*, partially answering our double puzzle on linking *fu* with Gao Zhan's childhood name.

But *mwrγ-* is a generic Iranic root for "bird." What about the specific "rooster" insinuation that in fact was the gist of the prophecy in the children's rhyme? The answer lies in the twelve-animal cycle, widely used in Inner Asia at the time. Corresponding to the Chinese year of rooster, the Sogdians used none other than the word *mrγyy*.[14] This fact makes the Iranic/Sogdian equation a perfect answer to the original double puzzle. It is both intriguing and revealing that the *fu*'s "rooster" allusion would be derived from a Sogdian word.

As mentioned in the previous chapter, the popularity of the twelve-animal cycle outside the Chinese heartland has led to theories on the cycle's alleged non-Sinitic origin. These theories, or rather speculations, in fact highlighted the Confucianist bias of traditional Chinese written records, which paid scant attention to popular cultures of the uneducated folk, even though the educated gentry class was hardly insulated from these ordinary traditions.[15] Somewhat ironically, it was the invading nomadic groups who helped bring some of these "vulgar" Sinitic traditions, the twelve-animal cycle in particular, to the fore, or rather to the surface of history: the very earliest record of the animal cycle being used as a "horoscope," or *shengxiao* in Chinese, is the extraordinary letter the powerful regent Yuwen Hu of the Northern Zhou dynasty received, in year 564, from his mother née Yan, then a captive or hostage retained by the rival regime Northern Qi.[16] This letter, likely a Chinese translation or dictation of what was originally narrated in the Tuoba Xianbei tongue and containing some rare vernacular or near-vernacular expressions, not only is a touching and vivid description of the human drama and tragedy in those chaotic years after the collapse of the Tuoba Wei dynasty but also for the first time uses the twelve-animal cycle in reference to a person's birth, in expressions almost identical to those used today.[17]

Despite the popularity of the twelve-animal cycle among former nomads in northern China and their erstwhile Steppe brethren within the sphere of Chinese cultural influence and the above Iranic equation, Gao Zhan's childhood name, Buluoji, was not chronographic, as he was recorded to have been born in 538, a "horse" year.[18] In other words, though the contemporary political "campaign managers" resorted to an Iranic/Sogdian word in order to demonstrate the divine political message, Gao Zhan's "Barbarian" name derived from elsewhere, perhaps either in the Gao clan's questionable ethnic background or from the idea that Gao Zhan himself had been a "troublemaker."[19] While this case is an interesting example of the three-way interaction between the Altaic, Iranic, and Chinese cultures, it does not seem to suggest an additional etymology for the ethnonym Bulgar.

It is intriguing that the Iranic "bird" root *mwry* also appears in Indic languages in the form of *mriga*, but with rather different meanings, referring to various game animals, primarily deer.[20] Such divergent semantics have led to the observation that the root *mrga* is a loanword from some Central Asian source. This root has had a prominent role in Buddhism; the garden in which the Buddha gave his first sermon was named after this very word—*mrigadava*, usually translated as "deer park." The story that Buddha "turned the Wheel of Dharma for the first time in the Deer Park" recurs so frequently in Buddhist sutras that one of the most popular themes in Buddhist art and iconology is two deer perched on each side of the chakra (wheel). One can naturally presume the wide knowledge of this Indo-Buddhist interpretation of the same root in contemporary northern China, where Buddhism reached its zenith, especially among the common folk (whereas in southern China the faith was more or less a fad among the educated and the elite). Therefore, the fact that the "White-Drake" oracle went along the Iranic "bird" path is yet another indication of the relative strength of different "foreign" cultures, if not faiths, in the Northern Qi realm at the time.

The really fascinating point is the sociopolitical implication of the "White-Drake" oracle. For this oracle to have had any social impact there must first have existed a large Iranic-Sogdian immigrant community in the Northern Qi realm; and, second, this Iranic-Sogdian community must have been integrated into the political process of the Northern Qi.

Contemporary examples may help illustrate this sociopolitical situation. In Canada's 2004 federal election, Jack Layton, the leader of the country's then third largest national political party, the New Democratic Party, spoke (badly pronounced) Cantonese and Mandarin Chinese in his campaign ads on television. This development reflects the rapidly rising number of Chinese immigrants and their growing political involvement in Canada. Mr. Layton married a Cantonese-speaking ethnic Chinese wife. In places such as Vancouver and Toronto, Chinese has replaced French as the second most spoken language. Likewise, the *New York Times* reported in 2005 that New York City mayor Bloomberg's campaign for reelection produced television ads in which the mayor spoke in Mandarin to attract votes from the large Chinese immigrant community.[21] A parallel example is the increasing prominence of the Spanish language in the United States, not only in commerce but also in politics, a phenomenon brought on by the fast-growing Latino population in that country, so much so that former president George W. Bush's undoubtedly minimal spoken Spanish has been touted as a huge political asset.

Early medieval China was naturally much different than contemporary North America, principally due to the special circumstance that the Steppe-origin "blue-blood Barbarians" held political sway in northern China. "Political campaigns" using oracles via folk rhymes were also markedly different from modern popular democracy and mass media. But the dual facts mentioned earlier, namely a large Iranic immigrant population and the considerable political power it wielded can be substantiated by historical records, however sinocentric these records may be, and a growing body of archaeological evidence. I do not want to delve into details except to cite several passages from Chinese records in support of my argument that the early medieval situation is but a forerunner or antecedent of the Mongol Yuan case of employing "assistant conquerors."

The famous *Luoyang qielan ji* (*The Records of the Monasteries of Luoyang*), a detailed account of Buddhist monasteries and temples in the Tuoba capital Luoyang during its prime, has this description of the Central and Western Asian immigrant population in that city (3.161):

> From the west of Congling (the Pamirs), all the way to the Great Qin (widely recognized as the Chinese epithet for the Roman Empire), hundreds of cities and states happily submit [to the Tuoba Empire]. Hu merchants rush to the [Chinese] border passes everyday. Countless foreigners from all over the world have fallen in love with life in China and settled [in Luoyang], to the extent that there are more than ten thousand households of such naturalized immigrants in the city.[22]

There are more specific records about the Iranian and Iranic immigrants who followed the Zoroastrian faith. In addition to a prominent case, recognized by many as the beginning of Zoroastrianism in China, of an empress dowager of the Tuoba Wei dynasty worshipping the "Hu heaven god," generally identified as the Zoroastrian supreme god Ahura Mazda, *Sui shu* (*History of the Sui Dynasty* 7.149) describes how the two successor Tuoba regimes—the Northern Qi and the Northern Zhou—competed with each other in attracting people from the Western Regions:

> Toward the end of his rule, the last emperor [of the Northern Qi] worshipped the wrong spirits. He even presented himself in dances honouring the Hu heaven god. This led to many profane temples [in the Northern Qi capital], a custom that has lasted to this day. The Later Zhou, in its scheme to appeal to people of the Western Regions, also established worship of the Hu heaven god, in which rite the emperor participated in person. The ceremony completely followed foreign custom, and was too obscene and obscure to describe.

The above quotations clearly indicate that encouraging people from the Western Regions to come to China was the official policy of the Steppe-origin ethnic regimes and that such a policy resulted in large numbers of Iranian and Iranic immigrants. Both circumstances were repeated centuries later during the Mongol rule of China, motivated by the Mongol regime's deliberate scheme of "using the 'civilized' to rule the 'civilized.'"

There are, naturally, other negative, derogatory, and mostly dismissive descriptions of Iranian and Iranic figures and customs in the Sinocentric official histories. Private Chinese authors, conversely, tended to add exotic sensationalism to traditional Confucianist moral smugness in their occasional remarks about these alien newcomers. The result is that studies of Central and Western Asian immigrants in early medieval China have largely remained nonpolitical in focus, typified by such early titles as *The Golden Peaches of Samarkand*. In recent years, these studies have broadened significantly in both scope and material, aided by the latest archaeological findings.[23] Yet in my opinion they still have not sufficiently recognized these Western Asian immigrants as helpers or "assistant conquerors" of the Tuoba and other Steppe-origin rulers of northern China whose distrust of the native Sinitic population, especially its Confucian elite, ran as deeply and as persistently as that of their Mongol successors.[24]

The significance of the "White-Drake" oracle, therefore, is that it helps expose the political role played by the Central and Western Asian immigrants in a northern China ruled by the Tuoba and their ethnic successors, in addition to solving a millennium-old puzzle. This political role is also revealed by another passing mention by a member of the Confucian literati, Yan Zhitui. In his celebrated family teachings (5.301), Yan remarked casually on the abilities of two very successful Hàn officials serving the Northern Qi court. The special skills that made the duo rare Hàn winners in a regime dominated by Tuoba Xianbei personalities included the ability to speak the Tuoba Xianbei language and the knowledge of *hushu* ("foreign script"). The latter is undoubtedly the popular Sogdian script that flourished along the Silk Road for more than a millennium, which is the source of the Mongolian and Manchu scripts still in use today. Yan Zhitui's fleeting remark thus strongly hints at the dependence of the Xianbei rulers on a non-Sinitic yet equally "civilized" minority group, similar to the Mongols' reliance on the Semu people during the Yuan.

From Azerbaijan to Dunhuang:
The Coming of Fire Worship to China

Just as the establishment of the Islamic faith in China was a major consequence of the Mongol rule of the Central Kingdom, the early medieval "Barbarian" rulers of northern China, via their clever policy of "using the 'civilized' to check the 'civilized,'" greatly contributed to the coming of many foreign religions to China. Buddhism was the most important case, a subject too major and complex to be examined in detail here. However, less well-known faiths were also brought in by the early medieval "assistant conquerors" from the Western Regions, whose converts in China failed to reach the critical mass needed for the religions' long-term survival. Zoroastrianism was one of these faiths.

As shown by the earlier quotations regarding the two successor ethnic regimes of the Tuoba Wei dynasty that vied for the loyalty of Iranic immigrants by honoring and worshipping the "Hu heaven god," Zoroastrianism, whether the orthodox Sassanian denomination or the variant forms practiced in Sogdiana and other Central Asian city-states, undoubtedly flourished in northern China during this period. In a pioneering study, the late Chinese scholar Chen Yuan concluded that Zoroastrianism in medieval China was mainly an alien faith practiced by Central Asian immigrants, not unlike Nestorianism in Mongol Yuan China. This long-accepted thesis has lately been challenged by several authors. However, one of Chen Yuan's principal arguments still holds true, namely that no Chinese Zoroastrian scripture has ever been found. This constitutes a sharp contrast to the case of Chinese Manichaeism, for which a substantial body of Chinese scripture has survived. Even early Nestorian Christianity has left scripture in Chinese language too, in addition to the famous Nestorian Monument preserved in Xi'an.

Let us first spend a few moments on the Zoroastrian supreme "heaven god," or Ahura Mazda, which is represented by a single Chinese character *xian*. This name became synonymous in Chinese with the Zoroastrian religion, or *xianjiao* ("the *xian* teachings"). There is a wide divergence of opinion on the etymology of this character, however. Harold Bailey, in *Khotanese Texts IV*, regards this as a corrupted transcription of Iranic *at(h)ar*, "fire [god]," a subject I discuss later.[25] Bailey's suggestion appears consistent with the fact that Zoroastrianism was often referred to as *huoxian*, "fire *xian*," in Chinese records. The worship of fire is certainly the most prominent aspect of Zoroastrianism in almost all ancient records, Sinitic or otherwise. This tradition goes back to the archaic Indo-Iranian and even Indo-European fire cult. Friedrich Heiler for instance has discussed the role of fire in what he has termed *indogermanischen Religion*.[26] On the Indian subcontinent, this heritage is demonstrated by the ancient Vedic ritual of sacrifice involving the cult of fire, a tradition that has survived to this day in the form of the fascinating ceremony of Agnicayana.[27]

However, with the recent progress in Chinese phonology, *xian* may well be a cognate of the character's phonetic *tian*, "heaven," with a proposed archaic pronunciation *hlin*, a subject discussed in Chapter 6.

This particular character, *xian*, has been used by some recent authors to disprove Chen Yuan's thesis that Zoroastrianism was practiced only by Central Asian immigrants in medieval China. Most notable is Lin Meicun's claim that a Tang popular uprising in southeastern China was led by Zoroastrians, a conclusion based entirely on the alleged appearance of this single character in a tomb inscription.[28] Lin's theory is unfortunately an example of the hasty and far-fetched scholarship now often found in Chinese academia. His entire case collapses once it is realized that the key character *xian* here is almost certainly a popular variant of *yao*, "evil cult," used in government documents, among which one finds the Tang criminal codes dealing with the type of popular uprising that Lin discussed.[29] Usually—quite different context notwithstanding—the two characters appear nearly identical. Other attestations of this variant character for "evil cult," which is of course completely unrelated to Zoroastrianism, abound.[30] Besides, we all know that the Zoroastrian belief soon became mixed with Manichaeism in Chinese records.

What may be more intriguing is that the Zoroastrian "heaven god" later was regarded by Chinese prostitutes as a "guardian deity" of their profession.[31] Moreover, another popular deity in Chinese folklore, the Erlangshen, "younger-master god," which likely originated in Chinese drama, has also been identified as a possible variant of the Sogdian-Zoroastrian god Veshparkar.[32] These cases, however, do not provide direct proof that medieval native Chinese folk followed the Zoroastrian religion.

Yet one more case is Document P.2569 of the Pelliot Collection, which was touted by another recent author[33] as a "Zoroastrian spell," in an apparent effort to fill the marked void regarding Chinese Zoroastrian scripture (or simply any Chinese Zoroastrian document), a major argument for Chen Yuan's thesis. Such a misleading characterization contradicts the simple fact that the document was nothing more than an announcement of a *qunuo* carnival, an age-old Chinese folk custom (and for a long time an entry in the repertoire of official rites and ceremonies) aimed at expelling "evil-spirits."[34] All the figures cited therein, whether mortal or immortal, were from pure (i.e., non-Buddhist) Hàn Chinese tradition. They are, in sequence of appearance, the Mountain God of Sanwei, the Seven Sages from Penglai, the Four White-haired Elders at Mount Shang, and the local city god (*chenghuang*), all of native Chinese origin. The only sign of Zoroastrians was the mention of a *huoxian*, "fire *xian*," team from Ancheng (the city of "An") participating in the carnival. This was not unexpected given the heavy Central Asian influence on Tang cultural life, especially in music and the performing arts, as well as in folk festivals.[35] Considering the cosmopolitanism of the Tang, the enormous popularity of various foreign fashions among the populace, and the simple fact that the name Ancheng clearly showed this to be a community of Central Asian immigrants from Bukhara,[36] it would seem farfetched to take the above announcement as proof that the Zoroastrian faith existed among native Chinese. Indeed *Xin Tang shu* (75b.3445–46) recorded a Central Asian immigrant An family serving as Sabao, which, despite its likely Hindu-Sanskrit origin, was nearly always identified as a Zoroastrian title in Chinese records related to this region during the Northern Zhou and Sui dynasties.[37]

Other evidence cited by these recent authors also tends to show that Zoroastrianism was frequently viewed by contemporaries as an exotic foreign faith. In short, despite the recent claims, the available data fail to provide direct evidence to dismiss categorically Chen Yuan's thesis.

Theophoric Names in China

In order to present the first solid evidence that the Zoroastrian faith had spread to Sinitic populations in medieval China, I must make a short digression concerning ancient Xeno-Sinitic exchanges revealed by Chinese onomasticons. In spite of lack of evidence, the belief that "history begins at Sumer," accompanied by speculations about a "foreign source" of (or at least some form of cultural impetus to) Chinese civilization, presumably originating in the Near East, continues to hold sway. For example, the modern authority on ancient Chinese sciences, Joseph Needham, has ascribed the Chinese notion of *qi* ("air, energy of life"), together with *prana* in ancient India, to a common Mesopotamian origin, without any substantiating data.[38]

As will be further elaborated upon in the next chapter, a hitherto unnoticed simple argument against this "Near-Eastern hypothesis" regarding the origin of Chinese civilization is the complete absence of theophoric personal names in the Chinese onomasticon since the time of antiquity, in sharp contrast to Mesopotamian and all other Near Eastern cultures nurtured or influenced by this earliest cradle of civilization, including Sumerian, Egyptian, Semitic (Akkadian, Assyrian, Phoenician, Aramaic, Hebrew, Arabic, etc.), and Indo-European (Hittite, Hellenic, Indo-Iranic, etc.) cultures, all of which had a rich legacy in theophoric personal names. Indeed, many of these ancient "God's gift" names (e.g., John, Joshua, Theodore, etc.) still flourish in Western nomenclature today.[39] This marked difference between China and all other Old World civilizations no doubt is also related to the lack of a strong theistic religious tradition in the Central Kingdom.

Coinciding with the introduction of Buddhism via Central Asia, this arguably Mesopotamian heritage finally reached China during the Middle Ages, as first noted by the Qing dynasty scholar Zhao Yi (see next chapter). For the purposes of this chapter, I briefly list a few points that will be explained in detail in the next chapter.

1. All principal types of theophoric names found in the Near East, namely verbal-sentence, nominal-sentence, one-word, genitive-construct, and even hypocoristica, were attested. But verbal-sentence (god-gives, god-protects, etc.) and genitive-construct (god's gift, god's son, etc.), followed by the one-word type, constitute by far the great majority of Chinese theophoric names.

2. "Slave/servant" names were particularly popular, apparently the direct result of Iranic (Sogdian in particular) influence. Examples include Tiannu, "heaven's slave"; Shennu, "god's slave"; Fonu, "Buddha's slave"; Sengnu, "Sangha's slave"; and even Sannu (here *san*, "three," clearly stands for *sanbao* or Triratna, the "Buddhism trinity").

3. Though explicit "god-given" or "heaven-given" forms corresponding to Pali/Sanskrit *-datta*, Iranian *-data*, and Greek *-doros* were attested, including the case of the great-grandfather of the founding emperor of the Tang, a more popular type took the "son-of-deity" form. Examples are Fo'er, "Buddha's son"; Fonü, "Buddha's daughter"; Fazi, "son of the

Dharma"; Shenzi, "son of god"; and so on. The deity part again is often from the Triratna.

4. Restricted by the short length of Chinese names, with a formal given name usually consisting of at most two characters,[40] a popular form was to take only the deity's name without adding additional characters. This form was in fact what Zhao Yi first noticed. Thus we read given names like Futu, "Buddha", Pusa, "Bodhisattva"; Jin'gang, "Vajra" or rather "Vajra Buddha"; Luohan, "Arhat"; and so on.

A "Fire Cult" Name

Discovered among the Dunhuang manuscripts, there were several name lists for corvée and other government labor administrations, primarily of the Tianbao era (742–55) of the Tang (P.3559, P.2657, P.3018, and P.2803). These were collected and published in 1936 and have been the subject of extensive study by many scholars.[41] A name found on one of the lists was Fan Touzi. The given name, Touzi, represents an interesting construction in traditional Chinese onomasticon.

I observe that, first, the surname Fan, though not very popular, was clearly Hàn Chinese, attested from the Western Hàn dynasty on down.[42] This family name was somewhat common in the Dunhuang area, with at least seven people bearing this surname appearing as benefactors of several Buddhist grottoes.[43] This name had never been linked to the so-called nine Zhaowu clans and other Central Asian–origin clan names.[44] In fact, it was also in Dunhuang that the remnants of a genealogy of the Fan clan were discovered.[45] The extensive family trees and minute details make it unlikely that these were later inventions or forgeries. Second, *touzi* (literally "head" plus "son," a colloquial noun suffix), as a term for "chief" or "head," was of a much later period,[46] not yet attested at the time, and further, the negative and unflattering nature of the word would have made it quite a bad choice for any name, especially an opprobrious one, because a "chief" can hardly be considered an "unworthy" object if avoidance of god's jealousy was desired. Moreover, the name was not an isolated peculiarity: it also appeared in the names of a government officer (*silang*, "deputy minister") and of another person, Zhang Touzi, in documents unearthed from tombs in Turfan of the Kingdom of Gaochang period (460–640).[47]

Therefore I propose that the name Touzi is very probably another example of the newly introduced theophoric names in China, taking the form of "Tou's son." This proposition is supported by another personal name, Tounu, "Tou's slave,"

found in Turfan.[48] The next question is, what deity does "Tou" represent? I submit
that "Tou" is likely a short form of Atouliu, transcribing Iranian *ātar*, "fire," as
well as the Iranian/Zoroastrian fire god.

First, the fact that *tou*, as in the name Touzi, is an abbreviated form of Atouliu is amply demonstrated by the following onomastic data unearthed at Turfan:
Atouliuzi, Zhao Atouliu, Kuang Touliuzi, Yun Touliuzi, Guo Atouliu, Li Touliuzi, Zhang Touliu'er, Cao Touliu, Wang Touliu'er, Wang Touliuzi, Kui (or Wei)
Touliunu, and so forth.[49] These given names can be translated as "the son of (A)
touliu," "the slave of (A)touliu," or simply "Atouliu," and have been dated to the
late sixth to early seventh centuries.

Next, theophoric names pertaining to *ātar*/Ātar were widely attested in the
ancient Iranian world, likely predating the firm establishment of the Zoroastrian
faith and reflecting the archaic Aryan fire cult, as previously mentioned. More
pertinent to our discussion, in the Hindu cultural word the fire cult was reflected in
theophoric names containing the element Agni, the Hindu god of fire.[50] For
example, the Pali forms are attested by names like Aggidatta, "gift of Fire," and
Aggimittā, "friend of Fire."[51] In an early Iranian example, the Greek author Ctesias
recorded that Cyrus the Great, the founder of the Achaemenid Empire, had been
raised as a young boy by a shepherd named Atradates,[52] the Hellenic rendition of
the popular ancient Iranian name Ātaredāta. The shepherd's name means literally
"given or produced by Ātar" and may also be translated as "the son of Ātar."[53]
Another Greek author, Nicolaus Damascenus, called Atradates the father of
Cyrus.

Theophoric names related to Ātar are naturally attested in *The Avesta*, the sacred book or what remains of the sacred scriptures, of Zoroastrianism. Examples
included the already quoted Ātaredāta, "the gift of Ātar," and Ātarepāta, "protected
by Ātar," two of at least eight such names sung in *Frawardin Yasht* (*Hymn to the
Guardian Angels*). Ferdinand Justi was perhaps the first to include several dozen
ancient Iranian theophoric names pertaining to *ātar* in his *Iranische Namenbuch*,
first published in 1895. Of particular interest is Ātūnbandak, "slave/servant of
Ātar," cited by Justi, a typical case of "god's servant" names widely attested in the
ancient Iranian onomasticon. Another intriguing example is the name Ātūrdūχtĕ,
"daughter of Ātar," for the reason that the male form "son of a deity" was rare in
ancient Indo-Iranian onomasticons, a fact I explored in next chapter.

In an excellent compilation of Middle Persian names of the Sassanian period, *Noms propres sassanides en moyen-perse épigraphique*, published nearly
a century after Justi's pioneering compendium, Philippe Gignoux collected
even more such names, especially in compounded forms. The Sassanian data

were concurrent with the onomasticons of early medieval China, the period under study here. In addition to the familiar Ādurdād, "created by Ādur"; Ādurbandag, "servant of Ādur"; Ādurbān, "protected by Ādur"; Ādurduxt, "daughter of Ādur"; and so on, we have Ādurān-Gušnasp, "Ādurān and Gušnasp"; Ādur-Mihr, "Ādur and Mithra"; Ādur-Ohrmazd, "Ādur and Ahura Mazda"; and even Ādur-Bay, "Ādur [and] Baga."[54]

As suggested by the title of a previous section, the most prominent case is perhaps the name Azerbaijan, which is considered a corruption of Atropatene, after Atropates, "protected by Ātar," the Alexandrian satrap who governed the area for a lengthy period of time.[55] This is especially revealing of the depth of the fire-worshipping beliefs engraved in ancient Iranian cultures, in view of the widely accepted report that the voluminous manuscripts of the original Zoroastrian scriptures were destroyed when Alexander the Great conquered the Achaemenid Empire.

Third, the phonetic evidence and correspondence follow. According to Bernhard Karlgren, the Middle Chinese pronunciation of *atouliu* is *â-d'əu-liuk*. Much like the character *luo*, the character *liu* in medieval China was frequently used to transcribe the *l/r* sound in a foreign word. Examples include Aliudun, the "style" of the Uighur Chile (Tölös?) general Hulü Jin, transcribing *altun* ("gold," or *jin* in Chinese)[56] and the clan name Buliuhan, Poliuhan, and so on, which were alternative transcriptions of the Turkic root *bulγa* and are related to the ethnonym Bulgar. If Arthur Wright's equation to the Mongolian word *burqasun*, meaning a kind of willow, or *yang*, is correct,[57] then one may also add the "Barbarian" surname Puliuru once assumed by the Sui imperial house of the Yang's. In fact, this is a special case of a general phenomenon of characters of the "entering tone" in Chinese transcription of foreign names at the time, exposed and analyzed by Edwin Pulleyblank.[58]

On the other key character *tou*, Luo Changpei's study of northwest dialects of the Tang (618–907) and Five Dynasties (907–60) provides the same pronunciation as that of Bernhard Karlgren, namely *d'əu*. Because the concerned period corresponded roughly to the mid to late Sassanian dynasty in Iran, one of the most important Iranian languages to examine is naturally Pahlevi or Middle Persian, in which *ātar* was written as *'twr*.[59] Both Christian Bartholomae and Harold Bailey thus transcribed it as *ātur*,[60] which corresponds well to the vowel value of *tou*. Perhaps even more significantly, by the Sassanian era, the intervocalic voiceless consonants in Middle Persian had in general become voiced.[61] Therefore, as consistently followed by Gignoux's *Noms propres sassanides* quoted earlier, many scholars have chosen *ādur* as a more precise transcription. This form corresponds perfectly with the voiced dental initial of *tou* (*d'əu*). In summary, contemporary Iranian data strongly support phonetically the inference that *atouliu* is a transcription of the Middle Persian form of the word *ātar*.[62]

Finally, the Chinese onomastic data cited earlier clearly demonstrate that Atouliu represents the divinity part of the apparent theophoric "god's servant" and "god's gift/son" names. There is no Hindu/Buddhist deity, saint, sage, or religious figure or notion with a name that is phonetically close to this Chinese form. This leaves the Iranian fire god Ātar the only solution.

In addition to the somewhat earlier attestations at Turfan, the form Atou(liu) was also found in Dunhuang, in the name Zheng Atou in a document dated 747.[63] Here Zheng was again an authentic Chinese family name. The name was later written as Zheng Tou, confirming that *tou* was a short form of *atou(liu)*.

The first victim of my discovery of sinified theophoric names honoring the Iranic fire god in both Turfan and Dunhuang is the recent revisionist theory that the frequently mentioned "heaven god" in traditional records and Turfan documents worshipped in this early medieval Sinitic exclave at Turfan was not Zoroastrian, but might be related to Taoism.[64] This theory is based on the observation that no scriptures or temples or any written records that relate directly or explicitly to Zoroastrianism have been found at Turfan. Such a claim is certainly no longer tenable given the frequent appearance of the Iranic fire god Ātar in the local onomasticon.

It is also of interest to observe that, in Dunhuang documents of later periods, there are many names with the element Aduo (Middle Chinese pronunciation *atuâ* according to Karlgren) and the familiar Sinitic theophoric form Aduozi ("son of Aduo").[65] This is likely another transcription of the Iranic fire god Ātar. It can be compared in particular with the early New Persian form *ādar*. In addition, largely based on local paintings and the related iconology, Frantz Grenet and Zhang Guangda have already concluded that Dunhuang was "the last refuge of the Sogdian religion," where the Sogdian version of Zoroastrianism may have lasted until the ninth and tenth centuries.[66] If no better alternative to my interpretation of the deity Aduo in Dunhuang can be identified, the relevant theophoric names would provide an interesting terminus a quo on the disappearance of the fire-worshipping tradition in Dunhuang, as the latest attestations of this form came from post-Tang periods, with one even dated to the Kaibao period (966–70) of the Song dynasty (Stein Collection S.2894). This observation is certainly consistent with the conclusions of Frantz Grenet and Zhang Guangda.

Judged by the family names, only one bearer of the Chinese theophoric "Ātar" names, namely Cao Touliu, can be considered to be of Iranic origin.[67]

Interestingly, this name appeared with a group of other Central Asian–sounding names, among which a Cao Fuhe was found. The name Fuhe is almost certainly a transcription of the Iranian *baγa* or Sogdian βγ ("god"), the subject of the next chapter. Other bearers of the Chinese theophoric "Ātar" names had family names like Zhang, Zhao, Wang, Li, Fan, Zheng, and so on, all of which were seldom known to have Central Asian connections. This fact plus the enormous popularity of Buddhist theophoric names adopted by people in both the northwest and the rest of China leads to the natural conclusion that, like Buddhism, the Iranian fire cult had its followers among the Sinitic, Chinese-speaking population, a tradition that may have lasted until the early Song dynasty. Besides Frantz Grenet and Zhang Guangda's study cited earlier, Richard Frye also holds that this was around the time that likely marked the disappearance of Zoroastrians in Central Asia.[68] Given the close association of Zoroastrianism with fire worship in Chinese and non-Chinese records alike, the existence of Chinese theophoric names pertaining to *ātar* is the first solid and direct evidence that the Zoroastrian faith had a native following in medieval northwest China.

Chapter 6

Son of Heaven and Son of God

In the preceding chapter, I pointed out the total absence of theophoric personal names in the Chinese onomasticon since antiquity, in sharp contrast to all other Old World cultures and civilizations. This previously unnoticed fact raises many intriguing questions regarding the origin and evolution of Chinese civilization, as well as its relations with other ancient civilizations on the Eurasian continent both near and afar. This seems to be a new research area that calls for more interdisciplinary scholarly attention, especially from specialists of Near Eastern studies.

There is nevertheless a very old Chinese royal title, *tianzi*, "son of heaven," which is unmistakably a theophoric construct. The antiquity of this title in contrast to the absence of any other theophoric names in archaic East Asia constitutes an interesting question: Where did the by-now quintessential Chinese notion of the "son of heaven" originate?

There is no lack of scholarly interest in this ancient royal title. Julia Ching for instance has given a detailed exposition of the "son of heaven" in ancient China.[1] But despite her statement that the study focused on "mainly the Shang (ca. 1766–ca. 1122 BCE) and the Chou (ca. 1122–256 BCE)," a major shortcoming of the article is that it fails to mention, let alone to discuss, a basic fact that the very concept of "heaven," much less the "son of heaven" and the "mandate of heaven," was not quite a "native" Chinese notion.[2] Such a failure, however, is not at all unusual in the literature regarding this ancient royal title.

In a nutshell, *Tian* or "Heaven" started as a "Barbarian" deity, imposed by the victorious Zhou tribes who conquered the Shang, the first veritable Chinese dynasty. As far as I am aware, Herrlee Creel in a 1935 essay written in elegant Chinese was the first to make this important discovery, followed independently by the oracle bone authority Guo Moruo.[3] Later, in *The Origins of Statecraft in China*, Creel gave another extensive exposition of this issue with more data.[4] Other oracle bone specialists, such as Dong Zuobin, Hu Houxuan, and Chen

Mengjia, heartily concur with this conclusion.[5] The finding is that the character *tian* appeared only rarely in oracle bones, and it can always be interpreted as a variant of *da*, "large, great." Only in Western Zhou bronze inscriptions did *tian* emerge as clearly denoting a deity, followed, naturally, by the appearance of *tianming*, "mandate of heaven," and finally *tianzi*, "son of heaven."[6] Creel's and Guo's conclusion is also supported by the discovery of early Zhou oracle bones in recent years.[7]

Incidentally, the Zhou's use of a Shang character, originally meaning "large," to denote their heaven god can be compared with the ancient Greeks' transcribing the Indo-Iranian *baγa*, "god," as *Μαγα* and *Μεγα*, thus confusing it with *μεγα-*, *μεγας*, "large."[8]

Nevertheless, it is often assumed that *Tian*, the Zhou people's "Yahweh," was the equivalent of the Shang high god *Di* or *Shangdi*, "High *Di*." For example, in Julia Ching's study of the "son of heaven," no clear distinction is made between the alleged Shang "Lord-on-high" and the Zhou "heaven god." There are, however, many problems with this presumption, based largely on Zhou and post-Zhou documents and political concepts. The simple fact that the character *di* was used foremost in oracle bones as an honorific for royal fathers and forefathers has forced Guo Moruo to state that *Di* "was both supreme god and ancestor god(s) in one."[9] This interpretation, however awkward, can certainly never be applied to *Tian*. The distinction is also amply demonstrated by the Chinese terms *tianzi*, "son of heaven," and later *huangdi*, "emperor." Simply put, *Di* could, from the very beginning, represent a (deceased) human or demigod. But *Tian*, at least initially, was always a deity. Robert Eno went so far as to question whether there existed a single supreme deity in the Shang pantheon.[10] While this may be a contention impossible to resolve clearly based on available Shang inscription data, Eno's general conclusion that *Di* was employed as a generic or corporate term and was derived from a root meaning "father" is certainly convincing and amply substantiated by the oracle bone inscriptions.

Sifting through the existing historical political documents composed almost entirely after the Zhou conquest of the Shang, one can indeed find internal evidence that the Zhou heaven deity could not, at least initially, be taken as an equivalent of the Shang "Lord-on-high," the latter's questionable existence notwithstanding. One of the fundamental aspects of Zhou religious practice, as shown in a passage that Allen Chun has quoted prominently in his study of kinship and kingship in the Zhou era, is that "the gods do not accept sacrifices from persons who are not of their own race, while men do not worship those who are not of their own lineage."[11] Among other things, this image of the gods jealously looking after the interests of only their "chosen people" is consistent with other ancient religious traditions, the ancient Semitic/Jewish tradition in particular.

Even if we accept the murky existence of a supreme Shang "Lord-on-high," then, as summarized by Chen Mengjia, "there was no blood relationship between the supreme god and [Shang] kings."[12] Despite the broad meaning of Di, which often meant royal patriarchs and forefathers, a Shang king was never called a "son of Di."[13] Only much later did the great poet Qu Yuan (ca. 340–ca. 278 BC) of the southern state of Chu of the Warring States era (475–221 BC), in his poem "Xiang furen" (The Lady of the Xiang [River]) use the term *dizi* to mean "daughter of a sage/god-king," where the sage-king was the legendary Emperor Yao. In contrast, the Zhou not only was the first concrete case of heaven worship, or one might say, "heaven cult," but it also established for the first time in Chinese history the concept that the king was a "son of heaven." Furthermore, this change was implemented through the equally important political notion that a king's right to rule came from a "mandate of heaven." The latter, as many authors have observed, originally was undoubtedly part of Zhou propaganda in legitimizing their conquest of the apparently more advanced Shang civilization.[14] But it represented perhaps also the Zhou's single most important contribution to Chinese political beliefs ever since. Cho-yun Hsu and Kathryn Linduff, in their *Western Chou Civilization*, even hailed it as having "opened the course for the long Chinese tradition of humanism and rationalism."[15] Other than pointing out that the concept of the mandate of heaven further led to notions like "Heaven sees and listens through the eyes and ears of the people," as quoted by Mencius and cited in the previous chapter, the subject is largely beyond the scope of this book.

On the etymology of *tian*, as observed by Creel, the top interpretation given by China's oldest etymological dictionary *Shuowen jiezi* (*The Explanation of Simple and Compound Graphs*) is not consistent with the character's bronze inscription forms, which clearly show *tian* to be a variant of *da*, a pictograph of "a big man." The projection of a human image on a god is nothing unusual, as vouched for by Genesis. What is worth noting is that the Zhou heaven deity is also known as *haotian*. The bronze inscription form of the character *hao*, again a Zhou creation, shows unmistakable resemblance to *tian*, or yet another variant of *da*. Based on recent progress in reconstructing archaic Chinese pronunciations,[16] I have suggested elsewhere that the original Zhou heaven deity had a multisyllabic name, *gh?klien*, which may have been a cognate of what later became the Xiongnu word Qilian/Helian for "heaven."[17]

At issue here is the little noted fact that despite its extraordinarily long reign and its great success in using its utterly one-sided propaganda to depict itself as a legitimate successor to the Shang, the Zhou was clearly the first example of conquest by "Barbarians" of a more advanced civilization in East Asia. Even after three millennia, traces of the Zhou's "Barbarism" still remain. It is well-known that Mencius referred to King Wen of the Zhou as a *xiyi zhiren*, "Western Barbarian." Edwin Pulleyblank also noted the many "Barbarian" tribes with which the Zhou had allied itself.[18] Further evidence of the Zhou's "Barbarian" traits will be presented later. I shall also demonstrate that the Zhou's heaven worship and the related "mandate of heaven" and "son of heaven" notions had striking parallels in ancient Inner Asia. Traditional Sinocentric views in historiography would naturally ascribe this similarity to Chinese cultural influence. However, given the "conquest" nature of the Zhou dynasty and the aforementioned sharp contrast between Shang and Zhou religious beliefs, in my view it is no less plausible that the so-called Chinese influences may well share a common origin with that of the later Steppe civilizations.

An intriguing case of possible non-Chinese elements in the Zhou polity is the recent discovery at an early Zhou site of two Caucasoid figurines, one of which had been marked as *wu*, generally translated as "shaman." Victor Mair has presented some linguistic and paleographical data that suggest not only the existence of early East-West cultural exchanges in this regard but also the possibility that the Chinese character *wu* is a cognate of the Old Persian *maguš*, referring to the Magi. The role of the magicians and shamans in ancient kingship is well known and will not be repeated here.[19]

Before we move on to the spread of the notion of "son of heaven," I will give some additional etymological notes on ancient kingship names in China. I have already quoted Eno's conclusion that *di* was derived from a root meaning of "father." It can be observed that the other two old names for "king," namely *huang* and *wang*, had similar etymologies. Despite the fact that *huang* later became part of the official name *huangdi* for "emperor," the character continued to be used for a very long time (until the end of the Northern Song)[20] as an honorific for any (deceased) father, as a cursory look of any collection of ancient Chinese tomb inscriptions will show. The character *wang*, being both the phonetic and radical of the character *huang*, naturally had similar meanings.[21] Other old names like *jun* for both "king" and "lord" and *gong* for "lord, duke" had the same "father" meaning. This patriarchal origin of kingship in China is certainly not unique, as can be seen in, inter alia, Yahweh's words to Abraham (Gen. 17:4–5).

After centuries of the Zhou's promulgation of its "heaven-given" right to rule, *tian*, "heaven," gradually came to be used as a metaphor for "king." For example, Confucius (or whoever compiled the *Spring and Autumn Annals*) frequently used the appellation *tianwang* ("heaven-king") to denote the Zhou "son of heaven" whose prestige and authority were rapidly diminishing.[22] Even the broad term *jun* for "lord" was explicitly equated in *Chunqiu Zuoshi zhuan* (*The Commentary of Mr. Zuo on the Spring and Autumn Annals,* abbreviated in this volume as *Zuozhuan*; 10.544) to "heaven." Given the "father" etymology of many old king-ship terms, it is only natural that in the post-Zhou era, even the notion *fu* ("father") can be equated to "heaven."[23] This metaphor is, again, nothing unique, as exempli-fied by the Lord's Prayer (Matt. 6:9–13).

The Spread of "Son of Heaven": The Indo-Iranian Cases

The Chinese conception that a sovereign was a "son of heaven" with a god-given mandate to rule, once established and entrenched by the Zhou conquest and long reign, certainly did not manifest itself only within the Central Kingdom. The most interesting case of its spread is the ancient Kushan kingdom in Central Asia, which was established by one of the five *xihou*s of the Great Yuezhi.[24] Among the many titles of the Kushan king we find *devaputra*, the Sanskrit rendition of "son of heaven." Because the Kushan kingdom soon became a bastion of Buddhism, the term also found its way into Buddhist literature. Sylvain Lévi in his article "Deva-putra," which was called "a learned monograph" by Paul Pelliot, gave a detailed exposition of this title, especially in regard to the Buddhist sutra *Suvarnaprabhāsa*, which was composed under Kushan rule. Lévi convincingly demonstrated why the term, otherwise rarely seen in Sanskrit documents, must be a translation of the Chinese "son of heaven."

Lévi's case is strengthened by the widespread legend of the "Four Sons of Heaven" found in Buddhist and Arabic literatures.[25] The oldest version of this legend, likely originating in ancient India, divides the world into four domains, each ruled by a "great king" or "son of heaven." In the east, there is China, known for its large population; in the south sits India, famous for its great elephants; the Scythians occupy the north with their superb horses; and the west is owned by Romans and produces an enormous quantity of precious metals and jewels. When referring to the Chinese emperor, as Pelliot has shown, the Buddhist records al-ways use the term *devaputra*. This point is further confirmed by a Kharosththi inscription in which the great Kushan king Kanishka was hailed as "*Mahārāja, Rājātirāja, Devaputra, Kaïsara*,"[26] where *Mahārāja*, "Great King," was Indian; *Rājātirāja*, "King of Kings," was Iranian; and *Kaïsara* the Roman emperor, mak-ing the Chinese "son of heaven" the only possible interpretation for *Devaputra*.

Let me also refer to B. N. Mukherjee's relatively recent examination of Kushan coins,[27] which in my view has left little doubt that *devaputra* was not merely a complimentary epithet, but also a formal regnal title.

Another rendition that had a much wider circulation than *devaputra* is what Arabic and Persian records have transcribed as *baghbūr, faghbūr, fayfūr, bagapuhr*, and so on. For example, the tenth-century Arab author al-Nadīm stated, "The meaning of *baghbūr* in the language of China is the 'Son of Heaven,' that is, 'descended from heaven.'"[28] Marco Polo transcribed the term as *facfūr*, on which Pelliot gave a tour de force commentary.[29] Unlike the case of *devaputra*, which was also used by the Kushan kings, in Arab and medieval Persian sources *baghbūr* seemed to refer exclusively to Chinese emperors,[30] so much so that Pelliot found it "difficult to decide whether the Iranian title *fayfūr* was or was not ever used in reference to sovereigns other than the Emperors of China."[31]

As Pelliot has pointed out, both Arabic and Persian forms came from the Sogdian word *βaγapūr* (script *βγpwr*).[32] To my knowledge, the earliest attestation of the Sogdian form is the famous "Sogdian Ancient Letters," which used the word *βγpwr* to denote the Chinese emperor.[33] Note that Henning's dating of the letters to a time after the sack of Luoyang in the year 311 by the Xiongnu leader Liu Cong (reign 310–18), once universally accepted, may seem less conclusive after J. Harmatta's two meticulous studies.[34] As Harmatta has argued, the letters were equally, if not more, likely to describe the events of 190–93 when the warlord Dong Zhuo, whose troops consisted partly of "Barbarian" soldiers, looted and burned the Eastern Hàn capital Luoyang. After Dong's murder, his generals further fought and looted in and around Chang'an, the old capital of the Former or Western Hàn (*ZZTJ* 59.1909–60.1939). The best reference to the involvement of the [Southern] Xiongnu in these events is the famous "Beifen shi" (Poem of grief and indignation) written by Cai Yan (*Hou Hàn shu* or *History of the Later Hàn*, 84.2801–2), the daughter of Cai Yong (132–92). In addition to giving one of the oldest attestations of the *a-* prefix in Chinese kinship vocatives as cited in Chapter 3, the poem is the reflection of Yan's many years living among the Southern Xiongnu after being seized by the "Barbarian soldiers" under Dong Zhuo's command. In either case, the Sogdian *βγpwr* certainly predated the Arabic and Persian *baghbūr* by centuries.

Lévi and Pelliot both noted perhaps the strongest argument why *devaputra* and *βaγapūr*, literally "son of god," must be a translation of the Chinese "son of heaven": the terms represented rare or unusual constructs in their respective languages, at least as an appellative of mortals. Pelliot states that "as a title, [*devaputra*] has never been met with in Sanskrit literature, except in a passage of the *Suvarnaprabhāsa*." Its equivalent in Pali, *devaputta*, as Lévi has noted, was always understood literally, as a *deva* or demigod.[35] The case of *βγpwr* is somewhat different due to the evolution of the meaning of *βγ* and will be discussed in detail later. Its use as "son of god," however, is similarly rare, with the only attestation other than to the Chinese emperor being in reference to Jesus. Lévi even tried to ascribe this reference to the influence of the Chinese notion of "son of heaven," which Pelliot (*Notes*, p. 654) found to be "a much more debatable proposition."[36]

I see in the Indo-Iranian forms of "son of heaven" the underlying notion of theophoric appellatives and names, which as I shall argue later uniquely separated the early Chinese civilization from all other Old World civilizations. Yet it is also in this context that the Indic *devaputra/devaputta* and the Iranic *bagapuhr/βγpwr* stood out distinctly, for the simple fact that the Indo-Iranian word *putra/puthra* was invariantly used literally in names and epithets,[37] yet appeared extremely rarely in theophoric constructs.

On the Indic side, I have examined the entire two-volume *Dictionary of Pāli Proper Names* by G. P. Malalasekera and found *putta*, the Pali form of *putra* (and for that matter *pitā*, "father," and *mātā*, "mother") always used literally in personal names, and not a single time used in a theophoric construct. Similarly, I failed to find a single case of *-putra* in theophoric names listed in Jacob van Velze's *Names of Persons in Early Sanscrit Literature*.[38]

The many compendia of ancient Iranian proper names likewise attest to the fact that *puthra/puhr* too was very rarely an element in a theophoric construct.[39] Nonetheless it is interesting to note that *duχt*, "daughter," was, in contrast, frequently used in theophoric names.[40]

In my opinion, it is because of the scarcity of *puthra/puhr* in Indo-Iranian theophoric names that the use of *bagapuhr* as a personal name, mentioned by Henry Yule and agreed upon by Pelliot,[41] remained rare. Even in cases where it was a personal name, its meaning may be more likely to have been akin to that of the popular Iranian name Shahpūr than "(Chinese) emperor," as will be explained later.

The Altaic Attestations

As noted earlier, Pelliot doubted whether the Iranian title *fayfūr/bagapuhr* was ever used in reference to sovereigns other than Chinese emperors. Though Denis Sinor has cautioned recently that "one always hesitates to take issue with any of Pelliot's points,"[42] it is one of several of Pelliot's points that I will contend with in this study.

My contention is that the Iranian/Sogdian title *bagapuhr/βγpwr* was in fact widely used historically in various nomadic regions bordering the Chinese heartland in reference to leaders of tribes and what Joseph Fletcher has termed supratribal polities,[43] whether or not these nomadic chieftains could be called sovereigns within their respective domains notwithstanding. It is not clear when and where this usage was introduced on the Steppe, but the titles were already widely adopted in the early fifth century when they first appeared in Chinese records. Geographically they spread as far as Manchuria and beyond. But the usage gradually waned during the Tang and Song dynasties, such that it had largely fallen into oblivion by the time of the Mongol conquest. The pre-Mongol disappearance of this title may also have been the major reason why it has never previously been recognized.

This title was attested in the Chinese transcription *mohefu* (Middle Chinese pronunciation *mâk-γâ-piuət*)[44] and *mofu* (*mâk-piuət*). As shall be analyzed later, the phonetic correspondence between the Chinese forms and the Sogdian *βγpwr* is amply substantiated by contemporary transcription data and other evidence. Let us first examine several of the many attestations of the Sino-Altaic forms.

To my knowledge, the first dated appearance of this title in an Altaic milieu is in *Wei shu* (*History of the [Tuoba] Wei* 3.401). In the fifth year (officially 402, but the event was recorded to have occurred in the last month of the Chinese year, thus actually happening in the year 403) of Tianxing (meaning "[May] Heaven empower"), a reign title of Emperor Daowu (Tuoba Gui, formal reign as an emperor 386–408), the Mofu of the Yueqin[45] tribe joined the Tuoba federation with more than ten thousand families. Then in the fourth year (431) of Shenjia ("Sacred Doe") under Emperor Taiwu (Tuoba Tao, reign 423–65), the Mofu Heruogan[46] of the Northern Chile, or Tölös(?), also known as Gaoche "High Carts,"[47] presented himself before the Tuoba emperor. There are several other cases of the title Mofu during the Tuoba Wei dynasty, borne by chiefs from Qidan (Kitan; *Wei shu* 100.2223 and *Bei shi*, or *History of the Northern Dynasties*, 94.3132), Ruanruan (Juan-juan; *Wei shu* 103.2294 and *Bei shi* 98.3255), and others.

Sui shu (*History of the Sui dynasty*, 1.21) and *Bei shi* (11.410) record that in the fourth year (584) of the Kaihuang period (581–600) under the founding emperor Wendi (Yang Jian; reign 581–604), the chieftain of the Qidan, by the title (or name) of Mohefu, sent an envoy to "request submission [to the Sui]." Elsewhere in *Sui shu* (84.1881; also *Bei shi* 94.3128), Mohefu of the Qidan was mentioned in plural form.

All records show that the title Mofu/Mohefu represented a hereditary chieftain. This is clearly implied in the following *Wei shu* (100.2224) passage regarding the Wuluohou, an ethnic group living in Manchuria (and occupying, incidentally, a territory that included the Tuoba's ancestor cavern): "[The Wuluohou] do not have kings. The tribal Mofu's are all hereditary."[48] *Jiu Tang shu* (*The Old History of the Tang*, 199b.5356.) states more or less the same about the Shiwei: "That country has no kings, only seventeen great chieftains, all called Mohefu. They are hereditary." This is also often traced back in the family tree of prominent ethnic Chinese persons. For example, *Zhou shu* (*History of the [Northern] Zhou*; 20.335) mentions, in the biography of Helan Xiang, that his family name came from the fact that one of his forefathers was the Mohefu of the Helan tribe.[49]

The form for the Mojie people, the ancestors of both the Nüzhen/Jurchen and the Manchu (and even some Koreans via the Kingdom of Bohai),[50] is Great Mofu Manduo, as widely recorded in Chinese records.[51] J. Marquart, in his "Über das Volkstum der Komanen," observed many years ago (p. 84) that Manduo might be a transcription of *bayatur*, another puzzling title to be discussed later.[52] It is intriguing to note that the name apparently did not survive in the Jin (1115–1234) and later the vast Qing (1644–1911) records, proving the title's non-indigenous origin.

Another interesting case that suggests perhaps the title's long history on the Steppe is its use as a tribe or clan name. This was with the ethnic group Xi, also known as Kumoxi and always recognized as the brethren of the Qidan, among whom the title Mohefu was prominent. Many sources state that one of the Xi tribes or clans was named Mohefu.[53]

Here one may observe the well-known employment of official titles, particularly foreign ones, as clan and personal names in Central Asia and on the Steppe. An early example is the Xiongnu title *juqu*, later taken as the name of the famous Juqu clan in western China who established the state of Northern Liang (397–439; see *Jin shu*, or *History of the Jin*, 129.3189 and *Wei shu* 99.2203.). The Chinese titles *dudu*, "commander in chief," and *cishi*, "regional inspector," also frequently appeared in Central Asian, Old Turkic in particular, onomasticons.[54] Paul Pelliot referred to this tradition in discussing the possible use of *fayfūr* as a personal name in an Arabic source.[55] A case most similar to the Xi clan name Mohefu is the Jurchen clan name Wanyan. The *Jin shi* (*History of the [Jurchen] Jin*) chapter *Guoyu jie* ("Glossary of the [Jurchen] National Language," p. 2896) has equated this name to Wang, indicating strongly that Wanyan may simply have been a corrupt transcription of *wang*, "king," a fitting name for the Jurchen royal clan. One may also note that several old Chinese surnames such as Wangzi, "king's son"; Wangsun, "king's grandson"; Gongsun, "duke's grandson"; and even Wang all had a similar origin.

Finally, *Bei shi* (94.3127) and *ZZTJ* (135.4234) both record that, in the year 479 under the Northern Wei, a Qidan Mohefu named Wugan led his tribe or tribes to submit to the Tuoba. This is worth noting, first because the famous Yuan dynasty historian and annotator of *ZZTJ* Hu Sanxing made the particular interpretation here that the chieftains of the Qidan were called Mohefu, and second because the incident was recalled in *Liao shi* (*History of the Liao Dynasty*, 32.378) with Mohefu changed to Mefuhe.[56]

The *Liao shi* rendition is interesting for two reasons. First, the same form is quoted specifically in its *Guoyu jie* ("Glossary of the [Qidan] National Language," 116.1547) as an alternative form of Mofuhe, "the title of the chief of various tribes." Karl Menges[57] appears to be the only scholar to have noted this title's relation to the earlier forms quoted in this study. Second, to my knowledge this is the last appearance of the title Mohefu recorded in Chinese history. The *Liao shi* rendition may have been a simple scribal error, as Menges seems to suggest, or a true metathesis in the Qidan language. In either case, it shows that by the time of the Liao (916–1125), the original meaning of, or cultural tradition pertaining to, this title was largely lost.

Chinese Transcription Notes

Here I present the phonetic evidence for why *mohefu* (*mâk-γâ-piuət*) and *mofu* (*mâk-piuət*) must be transcriptions of the Iranian/Sogdian title *bagapuhr/βγpwr*. First, it is universally agreed among scholars that the Chinese rendition *mohe* transcribes *baγa*, widely used in titles and names in Central Asia and on the Steppe, especially in the term *baγatur* ("hero"), transcribed as *moheduo* in Chinese.[58] The transcription *mohe* for the Old Turkic title *baγa* has numerous attestations in contemporary Chinese records (*Sui shu* 51.1332, 84.1865, and 84.1880; *Bei shi* 22.819 and 99.3219, etc.), and this is supported by direct archaeological evidence—the trilingual Qarabalghasun inscription left by the Uighurs.[59] The Old Turkic title *baγa* and its Chinese transcription can in fact be traced back to earlier Steppe groups, Ruanruan for instance (*Wei shu* 103.2296), whose appearance preceded that of the ancient Türks, a subject I discuss later.

There is little doubt that the Old Turkic *baγa* comes from Iranian *baγa/baga*, a topic to which I shall return. Here, however, I would like to note a prevailing tendency, attested from ancient Greece and Asia Minor to early Tibet, to transcribe the Iranian word by an *m-* initial.[60] The Chinese transcriptional data, therefore, were hardly an exception in this regard.

As for the character *fu* (*piuət*) transcribing the Sogdian word *pūr*, "son," let me first note the standard usage of a -*t* final to represent a foreign -*r/l* sound in Chinese transcriptions of the same period, attested particularly in Buddhist literature.[61] Second, according to W. South Coblin's reconstruction based on contemporary colloquial texts and Tibetan transcriptional data, in Tang-period Dunhuang dialects the character *fu* was pronounced *fur (Tibetan transcription *phur*).[62] The Dunhuang area was an important frontier region in which many cultural and political contacts with various foreign people were made. Third, the character *fo* (*biuət*), which was used early on exclusively to transcribe the name Buddha and differed from *fu* only by the voiced initial, was rendered into Old Turkic as *bur*, as attested by the now universal Altaic name Burxan for Buddha.[63] This is the strongest reciprocal evidence that *fu* at the same time must be transcribing an Altaic *pur*. I shall later present supporting evidence for *fu* in these titles to mean "son," representing the Sogdian *pwr*.

The phonetic evidence combined with other historical data below leaves little doubt that *mohefu* and *mofu* represented the Altaic title *baɣapur*, which apparently had come from the Sogdian/Iranian title *βɣpwr/bagapuhr*, as shall be demonstrated throughout this chapter.

The Iranic Influence on the Steppe

One can hardly exaggerate the Iranic influence on the ancient Steppe, starting with the Scythians, widely believed to have spoken an Iranic tongue. One may disagree with some or all of Harold Bailey's Iranian etymologies for the Xiongnu words and titles preserved in Chinese records,[64] but the fact that there was a substantive Caucasoid component in the Xiongnu confederation, as discussed in Chapter 4, is hard to dispute. It is also true that the Western Regions card figured prominently throughout centuries of Sino-Xiongnu conflict, on which I elaborated in Chapter 5.

In the millennium following the rise of the Xiongnu Empire, this Iranic card was a perennial theme among various northern nomadic groups vis-à-vis China, typified by the Sogdians among the Türks and the Uighurs, so much so that the first ever document written under, or literally "erected by," the Türks was the Sogdian inscription of Bugut.[65] J. Harmatta, in his "Irano-Turcica," even attributed the Chinese name for Türk to a Sogdian intermediary. The role of the Sogdians among the Uighurs was no less spectacular, as shown by the latter's (at least the dominating upper class's) wholesale conversion to Manichaeism[66] and the trilingual inscription of Qarabalghasun.

The Central Asians' prominent role in nomadic politics and diplomacy naturally led to the presence of a large number of Iranians and Sogdians among the nomadic people as well as in the frontier regions. Edwin Pulleyblank, for example, has made a detailed study of a Sogdian colony in northern China.[67] These immigrants spread so far that the famous Tang history authority Chen Yinke was puzzled by their heavy presence in northeastern China, at a great distance from Central Asia,[68] a fact not unexpected given the long reach of the title *βγpwr*, which, as cited earlier, included Manchuria.

It can be said that the traditional Central Asia card of the nomads in dealing with the Chinese heartland was inherited and continued by the Mongols, albeit at that time Central Asia had been largely Turkicized and Islamized. That subject is, however, beyond the scope of this book.

It is well known that royal and official titles on the Steppe often were not indigenous, being either inherited from an earlier empire or borrowed from a sedentary neighbor. The perhaps most famous Steppe sovereign title, *Qaghan*, does not have a plausible Altaic etymology.[69] Two other important Old Turkic titles, *tarqan* and *tegin*, were known to have non-Turkic plural forms, which turn out, interestingly, to be Sogdian plurals. But the titles do not seem to be Sogdian either.[70]

The long history of Iranic influence on the Steppe is, as Bailey has attempted to show using Xiongnu data, reflected in the strong Iranian or Indo-Iranic elements in the titles and names found among the early Inner Asian nomadic groups. Again the early Türks and other Turkic groups serve as a good example. The popular title *bäg*, later to become *bey*, is generally believed to have derived from the Iranian *baγa/baga*,[71] a subject to be further examined later. The hereditary title *šad* ("prince") also came from Iranian.[72] The title of the *Qaghan*'s wife, *qatun*, very likely had a Sogdian etymology, *χwt'yn*, "lady."[73] Another frequent Old Turkic title or name, *īšvara*, came from the Sanskrit word *īśvara*, "lord." It is intriguing to note that neither of the two founding *qaghan*s of the First Türk empire had a "native" Turkic name, as they appeared in the Orkhon inscriptions.[74] One of them, Bumin Qaghan, was strangely recorded as Tumen Qaghan in Chinese sources, a peculiarity that "remains unexplained" according to Denis Sinor.[75] I have in a linguistic note concluded that Tumen, representing the Altaic word *tümen*, "myriad," "large numbers," was likely the Tuoba Xianbei form of the name Bumin, which I attributed to the Sanskrit *bhuman*, "earth, territory." The notion underlying the name is the concept of the universality of the king (or "the king of kings").[76] I now realize that the name Bumin is more likely to have come from the Old Persian word *būmi*, "land," "empire," which was used as early as Achaemenid times precisely for the concept of the king's universality.[77]

These examples strengthen the inference that the Steppe title transcribed as *mohefu* and *mofu* came from the Iranian/Sogdian *bagapuhr/βγpwr*, originally "son of god," denoting the Chinese "son of heaven."

The Evolution of the Meaning of Bagapuhr

As the Sogdian Ancient Letters and other ancient manuscripts clearly demonstrated, the Iranian/Sogdian *bagapuhr/βγpwr* originally meant "son of god" in both a social and religious sense. Nonetheless, it is rather doubtful that the same title on the Steppe, at least when it was widely adopted and eventually became a clan name during the Tuoba era, still had this original meaning. I shall argue that, like so many other royal titles on the Steppe and elsewhere, the Altaic form of the original Iranian/Sogdian title *bagapuhr/βγpwr* had been subjected to an "inflation process" and lost much of its original value. In the end, it meant no more than "prince," "of noble origin," or simply "chieftain."

That *mohefu* or *mofu* meant primarily "tribal chief" is amply demonstrated by the various Chinese data cited earlier. That it is a far cry from the "king of kings" is indicated particularly by the title's appearance in plural forms (e.g., *Wei shu* 40.902 and 100.2224; *Sui shu* 84.1881). Moreover, it is explicitly recorded (*Sui shu* 84.1883; *Bei shi* 94.3130.) that *mohefu* was a rank lower than *moheduo* or *baγatur*.

It should first be noted that a royal title being gradually devalued in its original meaning and importance is in fact a widespread phenomenon present in almost all ancient cultures. The Chinese title *wang* is a case in point. Back in the early Western Zhou dynasty, *wang* was synonymous with "son of heaven." But this prestigious meaning was soon lost during the Eastern Zhou, when more and more feudal lords, beginning with the king of the initially non-Sinitic state of Chu, usurped this title, forcing Confucius (or whoever compiled the *Spring and Autumn Annals*) to introduce the adjective *tian* to distinguish the *tianwang* ("heaven-king"), meaning the nominal Zhou "son of heaven," from all other undeserving and sometimes upstart rulers who also had styled themselves as a *wang*.[78] The irreversible devaluation of the title *wang* was the major reason behind the creation of the new title *huangdi*, "emperor," by the founding emperor of the Qin dynasty (221–206 BC). The various Indo-European "king of kings" titles, for example, the Achaemenian *χshāyathiya χshāyathiyānām*, the Sanskrit *Mahārāja*, the Greek *βασιλέως βασιλέων*, the Indo-Parthian *rajatiraja*, and the Latin *rex regum*, were evidently also partly a response to this inflating process of royal titles.

On the Steppe, the devaluation was exemplified by the royal Xiongnu title *Chanyu*. As the once unified Xiongnu Empire gradually lost its cohesion and eventually disintegrated, the title *Chanyu* saw itself assumed by more and more frontier chieftains and ethnic leaders in northern China. Not long after the collapse of the Western Jin (265–316), *Chanyu* further declined from representing roughly a prince,[79] already a far cry from the days when the Xiongnu *Chanyu* constituted the equivalent of the Hàn emperor, to simply being juxtaposed with such titles as *dudu*, "commander in chief"; *jiangjun*, "general"; and even *cishi*, "regional inspector."[80] The appearance at about the same time of another steppe regnal title, *qaghan*, representing what *Chanyu* had once stood for is therefore not surprising at all.

It is very tempting to ascribe the devaluation on the Steppe of the title *bagapuhr/βγpwr*, from referring to "Chinese emperor" to simply meaning "tribal chieftain" to the same process that saw the parallel degeneration of the Xiongnu sovereign title *Chanyu*. This certainly fits the historical scenario in which the great Hàn Empire did not long outlive the great Xiongnu Empire. In all likelihood, the prestige of the Chinese emperor, or *bagapuhr* as he was known in Central Asia and presumably on the Steppe too, had followed the same downward spiral as that of the Xiongnu *Chanyu* throughout the last years of the Eastern Hàn Three Kingdoms period (220–65) and the very short Western Jin (265–316), and certainly afterward, as attested by the famous Sogdian Ancient Letters: "Sir, the last Emperor (*βγpwr*)—so they say—fled from Saraγ (Luoyang) because of the famine. And his fortified residence (palace) and fortified town were set on fire. The residence burnt down and the town was [destroyed]. So Saraγ [is] no more, Ngap (the city of Ye) no more!"[81]

The fate of the last two emperors of the Western Jin, namely the emperors Huaidi and Mindi, captured by a "Barbarian" ruler (in 311 and 316, respectively) and forced to perform the duties of house slaves, including serving as lavatory attendants (*ZZTJ* 88.2790 and 90.2851), certainly made a strong impression on both the Hàn Chinese population and the Steppe "Barbarians."

It is worth noting that in the centuries that followed until the Sui unification (589), the only Chinese monarchs who could have made their power strongly felt in Central Asia and on the Steppe were the Tuoba emperors who had called themselves *qaghan*s, as revealed by the rediscovered inscription in the Tuoba ancestor cavern (see the Introduction to this book), as well as "The Ballad of Mulan" (Chapter 2). This tradition is still reflected in the *tiankehan*, "Heavenly Qaghan" (*tängri-qan*?), titles assumed by the early Tang emperors, as examined in Chapter 1. That the Chinese emperors were still known as *qaghan*s on the

Steppe into the eighth century is shown by the Orkhon Turkic inscriptions. There was also an intriguing tendency among the Steppe-origin "sons of heaven" to avoid the Chinese title *huangdi*, as discussed below.

However, an equally if not more plausible interpretation for *bagapuhr/ βγpwr*'s relatively low standing on the Steppe is another devaluation process, namely that of the word *baγa/baga* within the Iranic cultural sphere. At issue here is the divinity of kingship in ancient Iran. According to Richard Frye, the Achaemenian kings were not deified.[82] While it may or may not be due entirely to the influence of Hellenism,[83] the fact appears to be that, soon after Alexander's conquest, the word Θεος, "god," began to appear in the regnal name of various successors of Alexander from Egypt to Bactria,[84] and then in the title of the Parthian kings, who, at least initially, were partially Hellenized.[85] According to *Ammianus Marcellinus*, the founder of the Parthian dynasty, Aršak, was the first to be so deified.[86] It is therefore quite natural to see the corresponding Iranian term *baga-* appear in sovereign titles in the Iranian world. By the time of the founding of the Sassanian dynasty in the early third century, the deification of Iranian kings was well entrenched, as shown by the Inscription of Shapūr I at Naqsh-e Rustam in Fars[87] and *Ammianus Marcellinus* (vol. 2, pp. 332–33, corresponding to XVII 5, 3),[88] which reveals that Shahpūr II called himself "partner with the stars, brother of the Sun and Moon."

Then the same devaluation process as that of royal titles elsewhere was set in motion, which has been succinctly described by W. B. Henning as follows: "The appellative *baga-* 'god' came to be applied to the Great King of Kings of the Persians initially. Later it suffered a social decline, which was most marked in Sogdiane [*sic*]. The local king adopted it, then the kinglet, then the owner of a castle, finally any gentleman laid claim to it."[89] The Turkic title *bäg* or *bek* was likely related to, if not the above final result, something close to the sense of "lord" in this inflation process.[90] The same can also be applied to the Steppe title *bagapuhr/βγpwr* with the interpretation "king's son" or "lord's son." In other words, *bagapuhr* was fairly close in meaning to the popular Iranian name Shahpuhr, the Sanskrit name Rajaputra, and the Khotan Saka title *rris-pūra*, meaning no more than "prince." In fact, Harold Bailey has given *βγpwr* this alternative interpretation of "prince" in addition to "divine son."[91] In the next section I present evidence to show that the same interpretation may also have been true in an Altaic milieu.

A striking parallel as well as supporting evidence is the name *Tängri* for the Xiongnu-Altaic heaven- or sky-god. From the beginning, it appeared as part of the Xiongnu *Chanyu*'s regnal name in the context of "son of Tängri," according to *Hàn shu* (*History of the Hàn,* 94a.3751), an interpretation I shall contest later. The ancient Türks and Uighurs continued this tradition with the word *tängri* always forming a part of the *qaghan*'s formal royal title.[92] Finally, in the Old Turkic text found at Turfan, the Uighur Bügü *Qaghan* was recorded to have simply stated *mn tngri mn* or "*Ich bin Tängri* (I am *Tängri*)," as translated by W. Bang and A. von Gabain in their "Türkische Turfan-Texte."

Then the devaluation process set in. In his noted article "Tängrim > tärim," Paul Pelliot convincingly demonstrates how the honorific *tängrim*, literally "*mon Dieu* (my god)," degenerated from its original use in addressing the *qaghan*'s spouse to eventually meaning "*toute femme d'un certain rang* (all women of a certain rank)." Even *tängrikän* (< *tängri qan*), originally meaning "*göttliche König* (godlike king),"[93] later became "wise, pious man" in al-Kašyarī's *Divan*.[94]

It is worth noting that the Chinese imperial title *huangdi*, unlike its predecessor *wang*, once also assumed by the "son of heaven," has largely preserved its original worth in over two millennia of the title's circulation. A likely explanation for this exception to the seemingly universal rule of the devaluation of almost all royal titles on the Asian continent is the generally uninterrupted centralized power in the Central Kingdom. Few pretenders were allowed to hold onto the ultimate "son of heaven" title for long, usually just during the chaos between two major dynasties. Whereas on the Steppe and in Central Asia, particularly in Sogdiana where the social decline of the appellative *baga-* was "most marked," as Henning has observed, political decentralization was the historical norm.

A Tuyuhun Puzzle

In this section I discuss an old Tuyuhun puzzle that in my view not only provides an interesting semisinicized hybrid construct of *bagapuhr* but also sheds new light on how the term was understood by the contemporary Altaic people. *Song shu* (*History of the Song Dynasty* [420–79], 96.2371) records that, in the fourth century, the Tuyunhun *qaghan* Suixi delegated all his power to his crown prince and son, Shilian. The latter was then called *mohelang. Song shu* explains that *mohe* "means 'father' in the Song language." Similar passages appear in both *Wei shu* (101.2234) and *Bei shi* (96.3179), seemingly to provide multiple sources for the story. But upon further examination, it is very clear that the *Wei shu* passage had been copied almost verbatim from *Bei shi*, as clearly indicated by the Zhonghua shuju edition of the former. The Northern Song (960–1127) scholars, who presumably made up for the lost chapters of *Wei shu* by using material from *Bei shi* and other sources, did not even bother to change the "Chinese language" in the passage to "Wei language," as would have been used had the original *Wei shu* truly contained the passages. *Bei shi*, compiled several centuries after *Song shu* and even further removed from the historical scene depicted, evidently copied the story from *Song shu*. An indication of the copying is that it resulted in an apparently corrupted claim that the whole title *mohelang* stood merely for "father," making it utterly meaningless. The result of the above analysis is that the *Song shu* passage was actually a solitary source for the entire story.

Paul Pelliot took the "father" interpretation at face value. But all he could find was the Mongol term *abaya*, "uncle."[95] Both Pelliot's literal interpretation of the *Song shu* passage and his Mongol word explanation are hardly satisfactory, as examined below. It is rather unfortunate that Pelliot, who later wrote the excellent exposition of *bagapuhr*, "[Chinese] emperor," quoted earlier, missed a title that reads astonishingly similar to that Iranian term.

The key to the Tuyuhun title is the character *lang*, originally meaning a (junior) government official, which Pelliot also seemed to have accepted. But during the period concerned, the character *lang* was more and more being used to refer to "a young lad of prominent descent" or simply "a noble's son," not unlike the Sanskrit word *kumara*.

The etymology for this meaning of *lang*, in my view, came from the Hàn dynasty law of *Renziling* ("the decree for the appointment of sons"), which stipulated that a high-level government official, after at least three years of service at the rank of an annual salary of 2,000 bushels (*shi*) of grain or more, could have one of his sons or nephews appointed as a *lang*.[96] This law was presumably repealed in 7 BC (*Hàn shu* 11.336; *ZZTJ* 33.1060). Yet the practice apparently continued unabated during the Eastern Hàn (25–220), either regularly or on an ad hoc basis, all the way through the Three Kingdoms period (220–65), the Jin dynasties (265–420), and beyond, as widely attested in respective dynastic histories.[97]

This hereditary privilege naturally led to the social phenomenon that youngsters of the upper class were often addressed as *lang* regardless of whether they were actually appointed the *lang* rank. By the time of the Three Kingdoms era, the usage was already widespread; the two perhaps best-known *lang*s were Sun Ce (175–200) a.k.a. Sun Lang (*Sanguo zhi* or *History of the Three Kingdoms*, 46.1101, 1104.), the actual founder of the Wu State (222–80), and Sun's close friend and able military strategist Zhou Yu (175–210) a.k.a. Zhou Lang (*Sanguo zhi* 54.1260). During the Jin dynasty, the usage became even more common, especially by house servants and slaves to address their young masters. Examples abound in *Shishuo xinyu* (*A New Account of Tales of the World*).[98] By the time of the Southern and Northern dynasties, there appeared further the compound *langzi*, "young boy" (*Bei Qi shu* or *History of the Northern Qi,* 41.535, and *Nan shi* or *History of the Southern Dynasties*, 55.1369, 69.1680, etc.), which leaves little doubt about the meaning of the character *lang*.

It should be noted in particular that the above use of the character *lang* was also popular among the "Barbarian" figures in northern China at the time. Examples include the young Tuoba noble Yuan Cha being called Yuan Lang (*Wei shu* 16.406); Dugu Xin being called Dugu Lang "while young";[99] and Zhangsun Sheng, the most brilliant "Türk specialist" of the Sui and the future father-in-law of the best-known Tang emperor-cum-empire-builder Li Shimin (Emperor Taizong), being called Zhangsun Lang at the age of eighteen (by Chinese reckoning; *Sui shu* 51.1329). Conversely, the use of *lang* as an official title in a semi-Sinitic construct is unattested in Chinese records, except the case of *mohelang*.

The above evidence amply demonstrates that the character *lang* in the Tuyuhun title *mohelang* can have only the same "highborn son" interpretation. The remaining obstacle to its being a semi-Sinitic rendition of the Iranic *bagapuhr* is the puzzling *Song shu* claim that *mohe* meant *fu*, "father." As every boy is his father's son, the *Song shu* explanation would make the title *mohelang* nothing more than a *vérité de La Palice* applicable to every lad on earth. Pelliot in his "Neuf notes" seemed to have had second thoughts too when he revisited the Tuyuhun term *mohe*, which he equated with the Old Turkic *baɣa*, the latter naturally having little to do with the Mongol word *abaɣa*, "uncle."

In my view, this puzzle can easily be solved by taking the *Song shu* interpretation *fu* as either an error for *tian*, "heaven," or much more likely a scribe's omission of the first syllable of the word *junfu*. The latter word originally meant "lord and father" but was later almost always used to refer to just the "lord," with its opposite word *chenzi,* literally "subject and son," meaning only "the subject(s)." This was to a large extent due to the general recognition of the emperor as the father of his subjects, as befitting the almost universal patriarchal origin of kingship examined earlier, and explicitly stated as such in *Hou Hàn shu* (58.1872). This was also at times aptly applied to the emperor regarding his relationship with his prince sons (e.g., *Sui shu* 22.627 and 62.1487). With such an emendation, the *Song shu* interpretation becomes a perfect rendition of the Iranian title *bagapuhr* in its somewhat devalued meaning of "lord's son" or "prince."

With the recorded heavy Chinese cultural elements among the Tuyuhun and the aforementioned popularity of the *lang* appellative among the "Barbarian" figures in northern China, there is little doubt that *mohelang* originally was a

Tuyuhun title, an interesting Sino-Iranian compound that arose in the nomadic borderland between the two ancient sedentary cultures.

It is not certain that the Iranian *baga* was always interpreted on the Steppe in its devalued meaning of "lord." This is not the place to delve into the possible link between the Old Turkic *bögü*, "sage," "sorcery," and the Iranian *baga* (also the Russian word *Бог*). But it is notable that the demigod (literally "neither god nor human," as a boy left by or transfigured from a mysterious huge reptile; see *Jin shu* 125.3113) ancestor *qaghan* of the Qifu Xianbei who established the Western Qin state (385–431) in western China was known as Tuoduo Mohe. Peter Boodberg interpreted Tuoduo as the Turkic word *taɣdaqï*, "mountain dweller," and said that Mohe "represents, of course, *baɣa*."[100] This legend, at the very least, reflected the tradition of sacral kingship, or the "godly" or "godlike" khanship on the Steppe. In this context, the two interpretations of *bagapuhr*, namely "son of god" and "king's son," may in fact converge, as I discussed next.

Sacral Kingship and "Son of God-King"

The Iranian title *bagapuhr*, whether interpreted as "son of god" or "king's son," reflects not only the deep-rooted traditions of sacral kingship in Chinese, Altaic, and Indo-Iranian cultures but also the connections between the three cultures in this regard, if not the common origin of all these traditions.

The rendition of the Chinese "son of heaven" by *devaputra* and *bagapuhr* ("son of god") has rather faithfully translated the Chinese concept of sacral kingship that a ruler is someone who has "descended from heaven," as the Arab authors were still able to interpret the title many centuries later. These two renditions are also remarkable in that they were very distinct in their respective languages, deviating from both the usual Indo-European sacral kingship titles and the general theophoric "god-given" names.

I mentioned earlier the paucity of *-putra* and *-puhr* theophoric constructs in Indo-Iranian languages. The same can also be said about the "son of god" regnal titles. It is not surprising that the only other case for *bagapuhr* to be interpreted as "son of god" is the Pahlavi Christian (and Iranian Manichaean) appellative for Jesus, which Sylvain Lévi has also tried to attribute, albeit not very convincingly, to Chinese influence via the Iranians. It is worth noting that the only other "son of god" royal epithet found in contemporary West and Central Asia is the semibarbaric Greek title Θεοπάτορ, literally "god-father," assumed by several Parthian kings.[101] One can compare it with the classic Greek terms υιος Θεου for the Christian "son of god" and Θεοῦ υἱός, the Greek equivalent of *Divi filius*, Augustus's patronym,[102] to see how distinct the Parthian title was.[103] It is further notable that the appearance of this regnal name may simply be due to the fact that a deceased royal father had called himself Θεός.[104] In this sense, Θεοπάτορ would mean not exactly "son of god," but rather something similar to Augustus's patronym *Divi filius* (as the adopted son of Caesar, who had of course already been deified as a *deus*), and the "devalued" title of *bagapuhr* when the Iranian kings started to call themselves *baga*. In other words, it was a form of "son of god-king."

In contrast to the above distinction, however subtle, between the ancient Sinitic and Indo-Iranian civilizations on the manifestation of sacral kingship, there appear to be much stronger parallels between the Sinitic and Altaic civilizations in this regard. The most striking parallel is the Steppe belief in *Tängri*, the universal sky god.[105] From this angle, it is hard to find another religious notion or deity that is as close as *Tängri* to being an equivalent of the Sinitic *Tian*, in both physical and metaphysical senses, among all ancient civilizations. This equivalence is made even more prominent by the opening passage of both the Kul Tegin and Bilga Kaghan inscriptions, in which the blue *Tengri* on high is paired with the brown earth below to give birth to the humans,[106] which parallels the Chinese heaven and earth gods (*Huangtian Houtu*).

This remarkable similarity extends to sacral kingship. The first two aspects of Steppe kingship summarized by Jean-Paul Roux, based on the Orkhun inscriptions, are (a) *Le kagan vient du ciel* (The king comes from heaven), and (b) *Le kagan possède un mandat céleste* (The king has a mandate of heaven).[107] There would seem no better synopsis than these two points in describing the Chinese "Son of Heaven" ever since its inception, interestingly, following the Zhou conquest.

This raises a question of whether this extraordinary similarity was due to Chinese influence on the Steppe. After all, *Hàn shu* (94a.3751) records that the Xiongnu called their ruler *Chengli gutu chanyu*, with the interpretation that *Chengli* meant "heaven" and *gutu* meant "son," seemingly a perfect translation of the Chinese "son of heaven."

But there are two major obstacles to this hypothesis of Chinese influence. The first is that the *Hàn shu* interpretation of the Xiongnu "son of heaven" is a solitary case not repeated by any other sources. The word *gutu*, allegedly meaning "son," has no acceptable Altaic cognate. This in turn forced Edwin Pulleyblank to look at some extinct or near-extinct Yenisei languages, exemplified by the Ket, for a possible solution, which does not sound very convincing either.[108] In fact, a Western

Jin scholar, Huangfu Mi (215–82), consulted his Xiongnu slave on this title, and the slave's answer was simply, "*chengli* means *tianzi*."[109] This is certainly consistent with the previously mentioned direct use of *Tängri* as "*Qaghan*" in Old Turkic.

Further, while the universal sky god Tängri was inherited by all Altaic groups, the questionable Xiongnu, "son of god," construct was conspicuously absent. As a matter of fact, even the same *Hàn shu* chapter a few pages down (94a.3756) revealed that the Xiongnu did not have, or at the very least did not use, the Hàn, "son of heaven," construct. In the year 176 BC, in a letter addressed to the Hàn emperor, the Xiongnu sovereign identified himself as "Heaven-installed Great Chanyu of the Xiongnu (*Tian suoli Xiongnu Da Chanyu*)."[110]

This fact is most evident in the earliest written Altaic literature, namely the various Old Turkic inscriptions and documents. The notion that a *qaghan* comes from heaven is expressed in many forms such as *tängridä bolmïš*, "born from heaven";[111] *Tängri-Qan,* "heavenly king"; *Tängri Ilig*, "godlike king";[112] and simply *Tängri*, "god," but never in a "son of *Tängri*" construct. An interesting case of an Old Turkic rendition of "son of heaven" is *tinsi oylï*, found in the Orkhon inscriptions to refer to Tianshan, "Heavenly Mountain," where *oylï* is the third-person possessive of *oyul*, "son," "boy," and *tinsi* appears to be a direct transcription of *tianzi*, "son of heaven."[113] This mountain was also known as Aq-taγ in Old Turkic and as Baishan in Chinese, both meaning "White Mountain," probably due to its permanent snow cover around the peak.[114] The rather awkward Sino-Turkic compound *tinsi oylï* shows the Türks' recognition of *tian* as an epithet of the Chinese emperor, an understanding certainly in line with both the Xiongnu's and the Türks' use of *Tängri* as the title of their respective supreme ruler. This observation is supported by a *Tang huiyao* (*The Essentials of Tang Institutions*, 73.1309) entry of the year 664 in which a Türk chief told the Tang emperor Gaozong that a *Chanyu* (interpreted as *Qaghan* from the context) was *tianshangzhitian* ("heaven above heaven").

This fact, namely the absence of "son of heaven" constructs in the Old Turkic titulary, is also reflected in the Chinese literature. To my knowledge, the only case in which the title *tianzi* was used directly to refer to a Türk *qaghan* is in *Sui shu* (84.1868; also copied into *Bei shi* 99.3293), which, according to Paul Pelliot ("Neuf notes"), must be a rendition of *tängritäg* ("heaven-like"). In fact, even this *Sui shu* title starts with the phrase *congtiansheng* ("born from heaven"). The most interesting case of translating an Old Turkic "born from heaven" title is an entry in *ZZTJ* (211.6699) in the year 714,[115] in which the Türk *qaghan* Mochuo, in a marriage proposal to Emperor Xuanzong, called himself *tianshang de guobao tiannan*, which Paul Pelliot has translated as "[*le qaghan qui*] *a obtenu au Ciel la récompense, fils du Ciel* (the *qaghan* who has obtained from Heaven the [good] retribution, son of heaven)."[116] This rendition not only demonstrates the influence of Buddhism among the Türks but also helps illuminate the *Jiu Tang shu* (194a.5177) interpretation of the title of Mochuo's grandnephew Dengli, a prevailing Tang transcription of *tängri* as *guobao,* "[good] retribution," which ironically puzzled Pelliot.[117] The rendition *tiannan* (literally "heaven-boy") also reflects the effort by contemporary Chinese translator(s) to preserve the distinctiveness of the Turkic sovereign title in contrast to the Chinese *tianzi,* "son of heaven," an apparent difference also noted by Pelliot, who admitted to being uncertain about the Turkic original. The title of the Uighur *Qaghan tianqin* ("related to heaven"; *Jiu Tangshu* 195.5208; *Xin Tangshu* 217a.6124) is another example. It is also striking to see the title *Tiankehan,* "Heavenly *Qaghan,*" used at least four times in the Chinese portion of the trilingual Qarabalghasun inscription to refer to the Uighur Alp Bilgä *qaghan* (reign 808–21) or his predecessor.[118]

In view of the evidence given above, I contend that the Xiongnu title *chengli gutu* may represent not the uniquely Sinitic genitive form "son of heaven" but the much more common verbal-phrase or other similar theophoric constructs meaning "god-given," "god's gift," and so on, attested in almost all Old World civilizations except early China.[119] This contention is consistent not only with the existing Altaic data and the difficulty in finding a "son" cognate to *gutu* but also with the strong Indo-Iranian elements in the Xiongnu confederation, as remarked in Chapter 4.

The second obstacle to attributing the Steppe sacral kingship to Chinese influence is, in my view, the ample data, even in Chinese sources, showing the Steppe kingship to be a heritage distinct from the Chinese "son of heaven" tradition since the Qin-Hàn era. Nowhere was this separate heritage manifested more strongly than in the proliferation of the title *tianwang,* "heaven-king," among the "Barbarian" regimes in northern China after the collapse of the Western Jin in 316.

This title first appeared in the Xiongnu Former Zhao (304–29) regime, whose rise actually preceded the demise of the Western Jin (*Jin shu* 88.2290, 102.2674). The title was formally adopted by the Later Zhao (319–51; *Jin shu* 105.2746), and it was imitated by many "Barbarian" powers in northern China during all or part of their existence. They included the Former and Later Qin (350–94 and 384–417, respectively; *Jin shu* 112.2869, 2884; *Wei shu* 95.2082), several Yan states,[120] the Xiongnu scion Xia (407–31; *Jin shu* 130.3202), and the Later Liang (386–403; *Jin shu* 122.3060). The short-lived Ran Min regime (350–52) also used it.[121] So did a rebellious Dingling (also known as Chile, i.e., the "High-Carts" Uighurs) chief (*Wei shu* 95.2066). This tradition was carried on almost to the eve of the Sui unification by the Northern Zhou (557–81) and the Northern Qi (550–77) rulers (*Zhou shu* 4.53, 35.616, and *Bei Qi shu* 8.111, respectively).

One may contend that the title *tianwang* was nothing new in China, dating as it did from the Zhou dynasty. But there were clear distinctions regarding its use:

1. Contrary to later claims, *tianwang* was *never* an official or formal title of the Zhou kings. Nor was it that of any other Chinese emperor from the Qin to the Jin, and from the Sui onward, except the "Christian king" Hong Xiuquan (reign 1851–64).

2. An interesting partial exception to the previous sentence, which further strengthens my contention that there was a separate Steppe tradition of sacral kingship, is the early Qidan/Kitan leader Abaoji (reign 907–27), who was called a *tianhuangwang* or *tianhuangdi*, "Heaven Emperor" (*Jiu Wudai shi* 137.1830; *Liao shi* 1.3 and 1.10).

3. As mentioned earlier in this chapter, in literary sources the title was allegedly first used by Confucius, widely admired as the master of using subtle linguistics to make political points, or *weiyandayi* ("sublime words with deep meanings") in Chinese, to distinguish the Zhou king from other pretenders who had styled themselves kings, in the *Spring and Autumn Annals*.

4. The "Barbarian" rulers of northern China not only adopted *tianwang* as their formal regnal title but often also made the deliberate point that it was a different title than *huangdi*, as amply demonstrated by the cases of Shi Le (*Jin shu* 105.2746), Shi Hu (*Jin shu* 106.2762, 2765), and the early Zhou monarchs (*Zhou shu* 4.58, 35.616).

5. The early Northern Zhou monarchs, who were the last "Barbarian" rulers to use *tianwang* as a formal title, not only abolished the Chinese title *huangdi* but also deliberately did away with the Chinese reign-titles, causing a rare break in this uninterrupted Chinese institution since 140 BC.[122] It is notable that a handful of similar exceptions in this regard were none other than the early Mongol khans prior to Khubilai and the first Qidan/Kitan monarch Abaoji.[123]

6. In particular, and amazingly in language identical to what the Uighur Bügü *qaghan* called himself, yet unheard of among "native" Chinese emperors, the Northern Zhou Tianwang Xuandi directly called himself *Tian*, "Heaven," and equated himself with *Shangdi*, "Supreme God" (*Zhou shu* 7.125; also *Bei shi* 10.380)

A detailed study of the "Barbarian" heaven-kings in China is beyond the scope of this chapter. But it is apparent that *tianwang* as a formal title represented a

Xiongnu heritage, first applied to the Xiongnu ruler Liu Yao (reign 318–29). There is also an interesting earlier Xiongnu datum regarding the title, as recorded in *Shiji* (*Records of the Grand Historian*, 110.2905). In 133 BC, a Hàn petty officer captured by the Xiongnu revealed, in the nick of time, a Hàn plot to trap the *Chanyu* in a major ambush, thus saving the Xiongnu from a devastating rout. Thanking heaven for this good luck, the *Chanyu* called the captured Hàn officer *tianwang*.[124]

It should be observed that Shi Le's adoption of *tianwang* as an official regnal title was not only a reflection of his ethnic pride and a deliberate demonstration of his non-Hàn identity but also a natural development in the wake of the miserable end of the last two Chinese emperors of the Western Jin, which must have shattered the prestige of the title *huangdi*, especially in the eyes of the "Barbarians." This was certainly consistent with the Later Zhao's stress on its distinctness from the Hàn Chinese and the need to adopt a different state doctrine or religion, namely Buddhism (*Jin shu* 95.2487–88). As mentioned in Chapter 3, the last northern state to formally adopt the *tianwang* title, namely the Northern Zhou (557–81), initiated many other reactionary measures against the Tuoba Wei's earlier wholesale sinification drive, including restoring the "Barbarian" language, names, and dress in what can only be characterized as a Xianbei revival movement. These facts much strengthen my contention that the *tianwang* title represented a distinct cultural tradition, not merely a Steppe copy of the Chinese "son of heaven."

Given all the evidence, especially the Northern Zhou Tianwang Xuandi's self-designation, a Western Jin Xiongnu slave interpreting *chengli* as *tianzi*, and a Türk chieftain calling *Chanyu/Qaghan*, "heaven above heaven," I submit that *tianwang* was the Chinese translation of none other than the "Barbarian" heaven-god *Tängri/Tengri* throughout the entire period.

Proceeding from the Steppe tradition in sacral kinship, particularly the equivalence of *Tängri* with *Qaghan/Chanyu*, the fact that the title *bagapuhr*, originally translating Chinese "son of heaven," came to mean "prince" on the Steppe becomes a natural inference. In other words, via the vehicle of sacral kingship, the title's meaning evolved from "son of god" to "son of god-king." The honorific *dizi* ("princess," "prince"; literally "child of god-king") mentioned earlier is a striking, albeit poetic, parallel.

The Zhou's "Barbarian" Origin?

Despite an independent tradition of the Steppe sacral kingship, at least by the time of the medieval "Barbarian" invasions, its strong similarities to Chinese "son of heaven" heritage are too evident to ignore. In my view, a common yet remote origin of both traditions is the best interpretation to accommodate this striking parallel. The late Joseph Fletcher was perhaps the most vocal in this regard:

> My working hypothesis is that the idea of a single universal god and a related concept of universal dominion stemmed from the early Aryans and remained in the steppe with those who remained there (Scythians, etc.). Those who entered Iran and India carried it with them, whence it reached the Near East (Jews, Christians, Muslims), Greece (Alexander), and the Romans (one God, one world, one religion, one empire). The "son of Heaven" and "mandate of Heaven" concepts would have reached China either from the steppe nomads or from Iran or India (Asoka).[125]

Fletcher's sweeping conjecture, while ingenious, is nonetheless troubled by anachronism and contradictions. For example, his suggestion that the universal sky god reached China via the court of Asoka would miss the Zhou conquest by centuries. The relatively late appearance of deified Iranian kings also runs against Fletcher's hypothesis, as the early Iranians would have been one of the most natural intermediaries for the Sinitic contact. The highly personal nature of god's favor (*farr*) to Iranian kings[126] is also markedly different than the Chinese notions of the "mandate of heaven" and *zuo*, "imperial fortune," both of which were borne by the entire royal house, not an individual. In short, I only see evidence for a common origin between the Altaic and Sinitic forms of heaven worship and sacral kingship, which might have contained some early Indo-Iranian elements, but is still far from the all-inclusive Indo-European origin of monotheism including Judeo-Christianity Fletcher espoused.

One may not infer too much from the tendency of the medieval northern "Barbarians," in order to justify their many non-Hàn policies and acts, to claim that these traditions came from China's antiquity. For example, *Jin shu* (106.2675) states that Shi Hu's enthronement as a *tianwang* was "in accordance with the Yin and Zhou systems." *Wei shu* (113.2973, as well as *ZZTJ* 113.3575) describes the Tuoba's forgoing the more recent Chinese traditions of officialdom and creating their own titles as "imitating office names from antiquity." This kind of claim included incidentally the Northern Zhou's adoption of the *tianwang* title and many other alleged old (Western) Zhou institutions.[127] This is consistent with the general propaganda by the "Barbarians" intended to identify themselves as the descendents of legendary Chinese sage-kings and/or famous ancient Chinese persons to legitimize their rule of the Central Kingdom. This became almost the standard description of any "Barbarian" leader's ancestry in Chinese records. The opening chapter of *Wei shu* on the Tuoba's family tree is a typical example. Nevertheless, it is also true that the very first "Barbarian" conquest that introduced the sky god, the "son of heaven," and the "mandate of heaven" in China served as a convenient precedent for the medieval "Barbarian" conquerors whose kingship was based on almost identical notions. This can hardly be considered a pure coincidence.

This accordance in my view strengthens the thesis suggested earlier in this chapter that the early Zhou people had a partially "Barbarian" origin and that some of their cultural traditions were shared by many later Steppe groups. This proposition offers a natural explanation for the striking similarity regarding the sky god and sacral kingship between the Sinitic and Altaic civilizations.

In addition to the examples raised earlier in this book, Friedrich Hirth[128] was the first to recognize a cognate to the Xiongnu-Turkic word *kingrak*, "a double-edged knife," among the weapons that King Wu of the Zhou allegedly used to conquer the Shang, albeit that the actual source should be dated to a substantially later period. I point out the Zhou tradition of regarding (white) wolves as an auspicious token,[129] as well as King Wu's *chai*, "jackal," metaphor in depicting his troops' valor.[130] Both were in line with Inner Asian steppe cultures but are hard to reconcile with the Chinese cultural tradition vis-à-vis these two animals.

There is also the little-noted fact that the Zhou people introduced a new kinship term, *kun*, for "elder brother" into Chinese. Unlike its later Altaic successor *akha*, which was the origin of the now prevailing term *ge*, which largely replaced the authentic Chinese term *xiong*, as I discussed in Chapter 3, the Zhou term never caught on, except, as the Qing linguist Duan Yucai observed, in the immediate neighborhood of the Zhou capital, as reflected in the *Wangfeng* (Airs of the king's realm) section of *Shijing* (*Classic of Odes*, or *Book of Poems*).[131] Assuming an old *a-* prefix in Chinese kinship terms, the Zhou term for "elder brother" reckons well with its Altaic equivalents, in particular the Murong Xianbei word *agan* (see Chapter 3) and the Nüzhen-Manchu word *ahun*.

Another interesting piece of evidence is the story of the Zhou king Gugong's elder sons Taibo and Zhongyong, who reportedly migrated to the lower Yangtze basin so their youngest brother could inherit the Zhou throne. This is not only recorded in *Shiji* repeatedly (4.115, 31.1445–47) but also mentioned in the *Taibo* chapter (chapter 8) of *The Analects*. In addition, Gugong was the grandfather of King Wen, hence only three generations removed from the Zhou's final conquest of the Shang. Therefore, the Taibo story cannot be completely a later idealistic invention and must contain a certain element of historical truth. This legend is strikingly reminiscent of the Steppe tradition of ultimogeniture in which the youngest son, the *ochigin*, inherits his parents' homestead. The migration of the Tuyuhun from northeast China to their new home bordering Tibet and the division of the huge Mongol Empire among Genghis Khan's four sons are all examples of this Steppe tradition.

Shiji, in fact, was rather frank about the Zhou people's long "Barbarian" experience, if not origin. Despite their alleged descent from Houji, the legendary sage who discovered agriculture, according to Sima Qian's reckoning the Zhou people lived "among the Rong and Di (Barbarians)" for fourteen generations, during which they often abandoned agriculture. It is only during the leadership of Gugong, King Wen's grandfather, that they started to "shed the Barbarian customs" and to build houses and towns (*Shiji* 4.112–14). Several ancient commentators had long pointed out that the alleged fourteen-generation gap from Houji the agriculture sage to Gugong had to cover more than a thousand years and was thus utterly unbelievable (*Shiji* 4.113, commentaries). In other words, the Zhou's alleged family tree prior to their coming into close contact with the Shang reads amazingly similar to that of all medieval "Barbarian" groups who crossed the Great Wall to settle in the Chinese heartland. Whatever their true ancestry might have been, it is clear that the Zhou people would be no less (and no more) "Barbarian" than the "Barbarians" among whom they had lived for more than a millennium.

A remaining issue is the Zhou's professed heritage, however tangible, in seed cultivation, which was indeed reflected in sources like *Shijing* (*Book of Poems*), and its contrast with the primarily animal-breeding economy of the later "Barbarian" groups. A full exposition of this subject is beyond this chapter. Here let me briefly state that pastoral nomadism as observed in the past two millennia is generally acknowledged as a relatively recent historical development that does not predate the advent of horse riding, much less the Zhou conquest of the Shang. Archeological data clearly show that the vast Eurasian continent represented a cultural continuum in prehistory and early history.[132] During much of the last millennium BC, early "Chinese" and "Barbarians" lived side by side in northern China with heavy political, cultural, and, not least, matrimonial interrelations.[133] This situation lasted almost until the eve of the Qin unification.

The story of Queen-dowager Xuan (?–265 BC) of the Qin, whose son King Zhao (reign 306–251 BC) brought about the series of military victories that eventually led to the unification of the Central Kingdom under his great-grandson, the first emperor of China, in 221 BC, demonstrates how thin the line separating the early "Chinese" and "Barbarians" was. After the death of her husband King Huiwen, the first Qin sovereign to style himself as a king, this Chinese Cleopatra (in a reversed role) cohabited with the *rongwang* ("Barbarian king") of the state of Yiqu and bore him two sons, all for the final objective of subjugating and annexing the "Barbarian" state. This the Queen-dowager ultimately accomplished, apparently with few qualms, at the price not only of her relationship with the "Barbarian king" but also his life.[134] A postscript to this Machiavellian love affair is that Sima Qian, by including this story together with the history of Yiqu in the Xiongnu chapter of *Shiji*, clearly considered that the Yiqu and the Xiongnu belonged to the same "Barbarian complex."

Even after the advent of pastoral nomadism, agriculture was still far from disappearing on the Steppe, as many have mistakenly claimed. For example, Otto Maenchen-Helfen has a full section titled "Hun Agriculture?" in his magnum opus on the Huns, and Di Cosmo has done an extensive study on agricultural production within the Xiongnu Empire.[135] In my view these results lend strong support to Owen Lattimore's ingenious theory of "progressive differentiation," briefly discussed in Chapter 3, which replaces a rather uniform Asian prehistory with the markedly bipolar, nomadism versus intensive-farming division observed throughout much of recorded history.

As a final note on a possible Indo-Iranian role in the Sinitic conception of sacral kingship, let me observe that the Zhou sky god *Tian*, or its more complete form *haotian*, is etymologically built upon the Shang pictograph *da*, "big," "great," "big man." As noted earlier, there is a certain echo of this construct in the ancient Greeks' mixing up the Iranian *baγa* with μεγας.

"Son of Heaven," Theophoric Names, and Iranic Influence

Contrary to Fletcher's sweeping hypothesis about a common Indo-European origin of the sky god and sacral kingship in Eurasia, the Chinese "son of heaven" actually reveals a unique trait of Sinitic civilization, distinct from all other major Old World cultures, Indo-European in particular, namely the absence of theophoric personal names. In sharp contrast, all other major civilizations in the Old World have each had a rich tradition in theophoric names.[136] This marked difference between China and all other Old World civilizations is obviously related to the lack of a strong theistic religious tradition in the Central Kingdom.[137]

The simple fact is that, from the very beginning until the introduction of Buddhism, theophoric personal names had never been attested in China. For a very long time, *tianzi*, "son of heaven," remained the only theophoric appellative in the Central Kingdom.[138] As such it was a rather unique construct as shown by the rarity of the -*puthra* theophoric name in Indo-Iranian cultures, as explained earlier.

Coinciding with the introduction of Buddhism via Central Asia, this arguably Mesopotamian heritage finally reached China during the Middle Ages.[139] The Qing scholar Zhao Yi (1727–1814) in his *Gaiyu congkao* (*Miscellaneous Research after Walking the Steps*, 42.3) was perhaps the first to notice the sudden popularity of naming people after gods and deities during the Southern and Northern dynasties. These names with a Buddhist origin have also received attention from modern scholars.[140] Yet a general treatment of Chinese theophoric names is conspicuously lacking; it will be pursued in a separate study. Here let me recapitulate that all principal types of theophoric names found in the Near East, namely verbal-sentence, nominal-sentence, one-word, genitive-construct, and even hypocoristica,[141] were attested in China. But verbal-sentence (god-give, god-protect, etc.) and genitive-construct (god's gift, god's slave, etc.), followed by the one-word type, constitute by far the great majority of Chinese theophoric names. It should also be noted that, in the case of Buddhist theophoric names, the divinity element often comes from Triratna, the "Buddhism trinity" (Chinese *sanbao*, "three treasures"), namely the Buddha, the Dharma ("Law"), and the Sangha ("Community [of Monks]").[142] In "god-given" or "heaven-given" names corresponding to Pali/Sanskrit -*datta*, Iranian -*dāta*, and Greek -*doros* the Chinese may also take the "son-of-deity" form.[143]

In Table 1 I demonstrate this later style by providing some cursory statistics regarding persons who had a formal entry in the respective dynastic histories with a theophoric name, style, or a diminutive (childhood) name.[144]

The general issue of Chinese theophoric names must be dealt with elsewhere. In relation to *tianzi*, "son of heaven," and *bagapuhr*, "son of god," let me briefly examine the "heaven-given" or "god-given" forms. As far as I am aware, a local lord of the Dunhuang region, Zhang Tianxi, "Zhang the heaven-given," represented the very first such name in China, at least in official records. As a frontier area in the Sino-Iranian exchanges, Dunhuang was certainly not a surprising place to become the beachhead of this Near Eastern tradition. However, because Dunhuang was also a stronghold of traditional Chinese politico-cultural heritage and rituals,[145] Zhang's name was styled in strict but somewhat peculiar Chinese fashion: a rare three-character "style," Gongchungu. This five-character name-style combination, *tianxi gong chungu*, "Heaven bestows big fortune on our Duke," was taken directly from *Shijing* (Ode 300). Similar "god-given" names in the forms of Shenci, "god-given"; Shenzi, "god's son"; Shenguo, "god's fruit"; Tianyang, "raised by heaven"; and so on later abounded in the region and in the

Table 6.1. Number of Persons with Theophoric Names in Several Dynastic Histories

Dynastic History	Number of Persons with a Formal Entry[1]	Persons with a Buddhist Name (%)[2]	Persons with Other Kind of Theophoric Name (%)	Both Kinds Combined (%)
Jin shu	924	5 (0.54)	5 (0.54)	10 (1.08)
Wei shu	1,312	26 (1.98)	34 (2.59)	60 (4.57)
Bei Qi shu	319	6 (1.88)	4 (1.25)	10 (3.13)
Zhou shu	319	10 (3.13)	5 (1.57)	15 (4.70)
Song shu	494	16 (3.24)	9 (1.82)	25 (5.06)
Nan Qi shu	196	10 (5.10)	5 (2.55)	15 (7.65)
Liang shu	317	10 (3.15)	5 (1.58)	15 (4.73)
Chen shu	223	7 (3.14)	1 (0.45)	8 (3.59)
Sui shu	362	7 (1.93)	2 (0.55)	9 (2.49)

[1] As shown by the tables of contents. Buddhist monks and nuns are excluded. So are apparent non-Hàn "Barbarian" names.

[2] Often ambiguity is caused by the characters fa, "law," and dao, "way." The former translates dharma, one of the Triratna, and is frequently used in Buddhist theophoric names. But it can also be used in traditional Chinese names. The latter is the principal concept of Taoism but is widely used in Buddhism, too, sometimes as an alternative translation of dharma. An early name for a Buddhist monk was daoren, "man of the way." I include a name with these characters only when either the name has known Buddhist Sanskrit equivalent, e.g., Fayou corresponds to Dharmamitra (Pali form Dhammamitta), or I have additional evidence, say a sibling's name or a special mention of the family's Buddhist faith, showing the character was indeed used in a Buddhist context.

Chinese establishment further west in Tulufan (Turfan), as revealed by Dunhuang and Turfan documents. It became so popular that the great-grandfather of the Tang founding emperor also bore such a name, Li Tianci, "Li the god-given."[146] Similar "god-protect," "god's power," and "god's slave" names abounded as well.

It is my contention that these "god-given" names, especially the *shen-* ("god-") forms, represented primarily Iranic rather than Indo-Buddhist influence. It is plausible that these Chinese names came from the Sanskrit name Devadatta, transliterated as Tipodaduo or Tiaoda,[147] or even the Greek name Theodore. But the fact that the most famous bearer of this Sanskrit name was none other than a cousin and principal opponent and enemy of the Buddha would seem not very conducive to its popularity among the faithful of the *Triratna*,[148] as clearly demonstrated by the fact that the name does not appear even once in the two-volume *Dictionary of Pāli Proper Names* by G. P. Malalasekera. My proposition that these Chinese "god-given" names came primarily from an Iranian original Bagadāta (which incidentally is also said to be the origin of the name of the Iraqi capital), is further based on the facts that (a) there is no direct Sanskrit equivalent of the Chinese character *shen*, which corresponds perfectly to the Iranian *baga*; (b) a large number of contemporary Chinese *shen-* ("god-") names do not have an apparent Sanskrit equivalent; (c) *shen-* names were borne by numerous people with a Central Asian origin; and (d) *baga* was directly attested in the Chinese onomasticon.[149]

There has been an old controversy regarding the element *baga* in pre-Islamic Iranian names, with a minority opinion claiming that it is not theophoric but merely signifies "lord," "gentleman," that is, the much devalued meaning after *baga* was used to address deified kings.[150] Though Phillipe Gignoux has already convincingly shown the theophoric value in most such Iranian names,[151] the prevalence of *shen-* theophoric personal names in western China under Iranian influence certainly lends much support to Professor Gignoux's thesis.

This rather sudden explosion of theophoric names in medieval China was not limited to personal nomenclature. It is also observed in toponymy, especially in western China. A detailed exposition is again beyond the scope of this chapter, but it may be mentioned that Mogao, the name of the large grotto system at Dunhuang that houses the most famous Buddhist mural arts, also may well be a rendition of the Iranian word *baga*, as suggested by the name of the early Buddhist monastery Xianyansi, "Temple of the Cliff of the Immortals," located at the foot of the Mogao Mountain.[152]

The introduction of theophoric names in China also had a major impact on the uniquely Sinitic institution of reign titles (*nianhao*). It is true that the characters *tian*, "heaven," and *shen*, "god," were earlier used in several reign titles, starting with Hàn Emperor Wudi's Tianhàn (100–97 BC), meaning "Heavenly River (i.e., the Milky Way),"[153] and his grandson Emperor Xuandi's Shenjue (61–58 BC), meaning "sacred bird (i.e., phoenix)," prompted by its alleged sightings. But it is equally true that both characters had always been used as adjectives or qualifiers in these early cases.[154] Their use in a reign title as a subject or object, however, had to wait until after the introduction of theophoric names in China, with the earliest attestations being the Tuoba emperor Daowudi's Tianxing, "Heaven empowers" (398–403) and Tianci, "Heaven bestows" (404–8). The use of the characters *tian* and *shen* in reign titles also became much more frequent. Following is a frequency table of the "heaven-" and "god-" reign titles from 140 BC (the introduction of reign

Table 6.2. *Tian-* and *Shen-* Reign Titles: 140 BC–AD 589

Period	Time Span in Years	Total No. of Reign Titles	Tian-/ Shen- Con- structs	%	No. per 100 Years
140 BC–AD 316	456	135	7	5.2	1.5
317–589: Southern regimes	273	67	6	9.0	2.2
317–589: Northern regimes	273	142	13	9.2	4.8

Note: Including only major dynasties and the "Sixteen States."

titles) to the Sui unification (589), using the demise of the Western Jin (317) as a cut-off point.

The contrast would be even more drastic if we include various minor ethnic regimes in the north.[155] In fact, counting all pretenders, there were only two *Shen-* reign titles, both meaning "phoenix," assumed by two emperors and one popular rebellious leader (for only four month in the year of 303), prior to 316, yet a total of seven from 317 to 589, a much shorter time span, and all proclaimed by ethnic leaders in northern and northwest China. In my view, this is a perfect example of the combined influence of Iranic and Steppe civilizations, especially the former's predominating Baga- ("god-") theophoric names and the latter's sacral "Tängri" kingship tradition.

Nowhere is this influence more evident and longer lasting than on the honorific imperial names, namely the posthumous epithet (*shihao*), temple name (*miaohao*), and, largely since the Tang dynasty, individualized honorific name assumed by a living emperor (*zunhao*).[156] It may sound surprising, but it is a plain fact that the characters *shen*, "god," and *tian*, "heaven," *never* appeared in these personalized honorific names of any "son of heaven" prior to the "Barbarian" invasions in the fourth century.[157]

The first ever appearance of the character *shen*, "god," in these names was the semilegendary Tuoba leader Liwei (*Wei shu* 1.3), who was officially called Emperor Shenyuan, "godly origin." It should be noted first that this chieftain lived more than a century before the Tuoba's rise in the fourth century and the Chinese title was thus a rather late creation. Second, Liwei was said to be born of a goddess or *tiannü* heaven girl,[158] therefore the name Shenyuan, "godly origin," may simply be a translation of his "Barbarian" epithet in this regard. One may notice the striking parallel between Liwei and the Qifu Xianbei's "neither-god-nor-human" ancestor Tuoduo Mohe (*baga*!) cited in an earlier section.

The first genuine Chinese use of the character *shen* in royal titles was the posthumous name Shenwu, "godly martialness," of Gao Huan (496–547), the founder (*gaozu*) of the Northern Qi. Huan himself was never enthroned, as he actually had showed deliberate humility to the puppet emperor under his thumb (*ZZTJ* 160.4958.). The posthumous epithet Shenwu was given in 565 by his grandson Gao Wei (reign 565–76), the fifth emperor of the Northern Qi. This was Huan's second posthumous name and the formal one used in official dynastic history.

The first ever use of the character *tian* in royal epithet is by the Northern Zhou emperor Xuan (Yuwen Yun, 559–78–80) who not only used *tian*, "heaven," as first person, as mentioned earlier, but also proclaimed himself the Tianyuan Huangdi, "heaven-origin emperor." Tianyuan was thus used in all standard sources as his royal epithet.

Once started by these ethnic monarchs of the Northern dynasties, the usage of the characters *shen* and *tian* soon became popular. Of the twenty Tang emperors who were fortunate enough to receive honorific posthumous titles, no fewer than ten had either or both characters appear in one of their individual royal names (either *shihao*, or *miaohao* or *zunhao*).[159] The usage became even more prevalent in later dynasties, with *shen* being used for the first time in a temple name in the Northern Song (960–1127), namely that of Emperor Shenzong, "godly ancestor" (reign 1067–85). During the Ming and Qing, hardly any emperor went without having these two characters appearing in his various honorific names and titles. Yet hardly anyone has so far noted the combined Irano-Altaic origin of this Chinese imperial tradition.

The Case of Bagatur

One of the most widespread names originating in Inner Asia is Bagatur or Bagadur, generally interpreted as "hero," "brave man." It is also one of the oldest. According to some scholars, the Xiongnu Chanyu Maodun represents the earliest attestation of this name.[160] It is certainly found among the Türks and other northern ethnic groups in medieval Chinese frontiers and is usually transcribed as *moheduo*. It has spread not only within the Altaic groups (attested even in the name of Mongolia's current capital) but also to Iran and the Arab world, Russia, East Europe, and the Indian subcontinent.[161]

This name also has a most mysterious etymology with no fewer than eleven theories being proposed for it. As summarized by Gerhard Doerfer, none of them sound really convincing. Among the many theories, one considers the name as come from a hypothesized form *bagaputhra* through dissimilation, making it yet another variant of *bagapuhr*, "son of god." This theory has been heavily criticized by, among others, Paul Pelliot, who argues that "the meanings of *fayfūr* and *bāhādur* are quite different."[162] This is, however, the last of Pelliot's opinions I am taking issue with in this chapter.

Contrary to the above opinion of Pelliot, who unfortunately failed to recognize the widespread Altaic attestations of the title Bagapuhr, several Chinese records show that Bagatur was used in parallel with Bagapuhr, referring to a (hereditary) tribe chief. In particular, the tribe chief of the Northern Shiwei was called *qiyin moheduo*, each assisted by three *mohefu*'s.[163] The hereditary tribe chief of both the Mojie and the Southern Shiwei was called the (Great) Mofu Manduo (*Sui shu* 81.1821, 84.1882; *Xin Tang shu* or *The New History of the Tang*, 219. 6178.). Marquart for one has interpreted Manduo as a variation of *bagatur*.[164] *Tongdian* (*The Comprehensive Statutes*, 196.5367) also recorded that a Wuhuan chieftain had *moheduo* as his title.

As for the divergence of the meaning of the two names claimed by Pelliot, first in being both used as a title of hereditary tribal chieftain, this alleged gap in meaning is certainly small. Second, regarding the "brave man" interpretation of Bagatur, one would expect the same quality to be demanded on a highborn son on the Steppe, where military valor is of the highest social value, and particularly if the highborn son entertains any thoughts of inheriting the power from his father. It is thus not surprising that at least one Chinese source gives the title *bagapuhr* the same *yongjianzhe*, "a brave and strong person," interpretation,[165] as was normally assigned to Bagatur. In fact, as meticulously examined by Fletcher, military prowess or being "brave and strong" was the key qualification of a political contender on the Steppe, another being that he came from "a generally acknowledged khanly lineage."[166] These are exactly the two qualities the *bagapuhr*/Bagatur pair would demarcate.

While the issue of etymology has yet to be tangled with, the data I have presented above strongly suggest that the *baga-* element in the name Bagatur is the same as that of *bagapuhr*, and the two are theophoric constructs related to sacral kingship. In this sense, Bagatur implies the standard marshal qualities of a divine king: god's mighty, heroic, and invincible warrior and conqueror of the enemies, and so on.[167] The same notion is manifested in the first Chinese "godly" imperial honorific Shenwu for the founder of the Northern Qi cited earlier, an epithet recycled repeatedly on many later emperors. They included Emperors Xuanzong (reign 712–56) and Dezong (reign 779–805) of the Tang, Emperor Taizu (reign 907–12) of the Later Liang, and Emperor Mingzong (reign 926–33) of the Later Tang, to name a few. The same word also appeared in the Chinese portion of the trilingual Qarabalghasun inscription honoring the Uighur Alp Bilgä *qaghan*.[168]

The exact semantics notwithstanding, the above points already provide the social or ideological origin of the title Bagatur, namely the legitimization and rationalization of tribal leadership by resorting to the chieftain's godly/khanly origin and qualities. Given this "chiefly" origin, I find another possible early Chinese rendition of the title, namely Buda (Old Chinese pronunciation *b'əg-d'âd*), which was used for addressing a "Barbarian" chieftain during a rather short time span, roughly around the Sixteen-State period (304–439). On the surface, it was a perfect abbreviation of *buluo daren*, "big man of a tribe." But such an interpretation of Buda has the dual difficulty that (a) there would be no reason for its quick disappearance, as *buluo daren* continued to be used for a long time, and (b) *buluo daren* could never be used as a second person in Chinese, whereas Buda was (*Jin shu* 104.2709).

This is not the place to examine the issue of why there remained so few "Barbarian" cultural traits in the Sinocentric Chinese records of an era dominated by non-Hàn ethnic groups. But there is at least one case of a sinified "Barbarian" word from this period: the Chinese slur word *nucai*, literally "slave talent," which I have shown in Chapter 3 to have come from a (proto-) Mongol root meaning "dog" (*noqai* in modern Mongolian). In my view, Buda may also have been a calqued and metathesized form of Bagadur.[169]

It is difficult to conclude this section without venturing yet another plausible etymology for the title Bagatur/Bagadur, namely the possibility of a Greco-Iranian "god-given" compound. Professor Phillipe Gignoux, in a personal communication in May 1998, opposed this suggestion due to its hybrid nature. But I do not see an absolute reason to preclude such a possibility. There are many points, however, to suggest the opposite:

1. Post-Alexander Hellenistic influence on the Steppe was widespread and long lasting.[170]
2. The debasement and "Barbarization" of the Greek language in this long period in Inner Asia were well known.[171] This was even reflected in Chinese artefacts.[172]
3. As far as we know, the name-title Bagatur/Bagadur originated in a "Barbarian" milieu.
4. The Greek -*dore* constructs, especially the name Theodore, had well penetrated Inner Asian onomasticons.[173]

5. Greek colonists in Central Asia were also known to identify local gods with their own.[174]

6. Such semi-Greek hybrid was indeed attested in a largely Hellenistic milieu as shown by the personal name Philammon in Ptolemaic Egypt. Olivier Masson explains: "*il est bien probable qu'on le comprenait 'celui qui aime Ammon'* (it is very likely that one understood [the name] as 'a man who loves Ammon')."[175]

7. It was also under the heavy Hellenic influence that there appeared Milinda's four ministers, whose names, in Caroline Rhys-Davids's word, were "impossible as they are in either Greek, Sanskrit, or Pali."[176] Semi-Greek and semi-Indian titles and names are also attested in numismatic data.[177]

8. In a milieu likely similar to that which saw the appearance of the name Bagatur, there appeared a Sino-Iranian hybrid title *mohelang*, formed by the Iranian root *baga*, "god," "god-king," and a Chinese suffix *–lang*, "lad," "son," as examined earlier.

9. The parallel use of Bagatur and *bagapuhr* on the Steppe strongly suggests that the two have similar theophoric "from god" etymologies.

The Disappearance of Bagapuhr

As mentioned earlier, the use of the title Bagapuhr among the Altaic groups, widespread during the Northern dynasties, waned during the Tang and Song and ceased by the time of the Mongol explosion. The disappearance was so thorough that, except for the brief mention in *Liao shi*, the history of the Qidan who were widely believed to have spoken a proto-Mongol tongue, no trace of the title is found in Nüzhen (Jurchen)-Manchu and Mongol documents and languages, even though the title as an epithet for Chinese emperors continued to be noted by the Arab authors and Marco Polo.

The Steppe title *bagapuhr* in the sense of "son of god-king" reflected a long tradition that royal blood, or "a khanly lineage" in Fletcher's words, was a key qualification for a political career. This tradition can be seen in the Xiongnu's ruling clans being characterized as *guizhong*, "of noble descent" (*Shiji* 110.2890–91; *Hàn shu* 94a.3751), a catchword that continued to appear in Chinese records regarding "Barbarian" leaders (e.g., *Xin Tang shu* 115.4211, 212.5980). Among many other cases, the tradition is also seen in the enormous prestige of the Mongol Genghisid "Golden Lineage," a legacy even Tamerlane found difficult to violate:

Until the last years of Tamerlane's rule, he continued to maintain a puppet khan of the Chaghatay line, and the latter's name was kept on the coins Tamerlane minted until the very end of his rule.[178]

The importance of royal blood is certainly not limited to the Steppe. For instance, Richard Frye has described ("Remarks on kingship" p. 82) that "everywhere in the Iranian cultural area, pride in royal descent was important for rule."[179] In fact, royal descent went much beyond instigating imperial pride, but was a key element of a regime's political legitimacy, as demonstrated by various post–Islamic Conquest Iranian dynasties' claim of a Sassanian ancestry, despite the fact that several were actually of Turkic origin.[180]

Royal descent was of no less import in ancient China. It was first of all a critical prerequisite for occupying the imperial throne, hence often an enormous hurdle for upstart pretenders, as vouched for by the numerous dynastic founders who became resigned to just being a chancellor. Examples include Cao Cao (155–220), Sima Yi (179–251), Gao Huan (496–547), and Yuwen Tai (507–56). Royal descent was also a critical element of the early Zhou sociopolitical structure,[181] long regarded as an ideal model by later political thinkers. Even *junzi*, "gentleman," a core notion in classic Chinese social ideology, came from a term for "son of lord."

It is both natural and intriguing to see the Iranian title *bagapuhr*, originally translating the Chinese "son of god" and later used as "son of god-king" on the Steppe, being replaced by the transliteration of the authentic Chinese title *taizi*, literally "crown prince," yet used on the Steppe in a meaning very similar to that of *bagapuhr*, namely a hereditary noble chief. This title was transcribed back in Chinese as *taiji* during the Ming and Qing, but appeared as early as the Mongol conquest.[182] A more formal title, *huangtaizi*, "imperial crown prince," was also widely attested, from Hentaiji, Huangtaiji, and so on (*Ming shi* [*History of the Ming*] 199.5267, 327.8487, etc.), to the name of the brilliant Later Jin khan cum Qing emperor Huangtaiji (1592–1626–43; temple name Taizong, "Grand forefather"). It should be noted that the Steppe application of the title *taizi*, while deviating from the formal Chinese definition of "crown prince," was nonetheless akin to the title's popular or folkloric use in China, namely a mere "prince" and even just a "highborn son."[183]

The disappearance of the title bagapuhr, conversely, symbolized the gradual but permanent loss of the pre-Islamic Iranian influence on the Steppe and in East Asia after the Arab conquest of the Sassanian Empire. It is true that people from the Western Regions again played very important roles in China under the Mongols. But their influence was felt almost entirely within the sedentary world, with little permanent effect on the Steppe except for the Mongol alphabet

borrowed from the then still largely Buddhist Turkic Uighurs, the former nomads who had settled in Central Asia a few centuries earlier, but not from the
largely Islamized Iranians. In fact, the Uighur alphabet was in turn adapted
from the Sogdian script, thus clearly representing a pre-Islamic heritage.

To a certain extent, the demise of the once prominent and widespread Iranic
influence on the Steppe and in East Asia in general was the direct result of a
rather accidental historical event, namely the famed Battle of Talas in 751 between the Arab and Chinese forces (and their respective local allies). After five
grueling days of fighting on the banks of the Talas River, the battle ended with
the crushing defeat of the Chinese troops when the Karluks soldiers suddenly
reversed their allegiance (*ZZTJ* 216.6907–8). The significance of the Battle of
Talas has long been recognized for having thwarted the Chinese advances into
Central Asia[184] as well as for spreading Chinese technologies, papermaking in
particular, to the West.[185] Yet its effect on the Sassanian Iranians has not been
widely noticed. J. Harmatta seems to be the only author to have expressed the
insightful observation that the battle "rendered possible the liquidation by the
Arabs of the last withstanding centres of the Sāsānian Empire, the independent
petty kingdoms along the Caspian Sea."[186] As hopes of restoring the pre-Islamic
Iranian power evaporated, the perpetual Iranic cultural influence on the Steppe
since prehistory was doomed. The "dog-eating" Korean general Gao Xianzhi,
who commanded the Chinese and allied forces at Talas, might not have realized
its weight, but the far-reaching consequences of his political and military failure
in 751 have in a wry way demonstrated the symbiotic relationship between the
Iranic, Altaic, and Chinese cultures in the ancient world.

Chapter 7

Bai Juyi and Central Asia

On the evening of June 22, 1900, a Taoist monk at Dunhuang in northwest China discovered by accident a small, secret grotto hidden for more than eight centuries. Tens of thousands of handwritten (and occasionally printed) scrolls and booklets in various languages were stored inside. This chance find single-handedly changed the study of medieval China and Inner Asia in a great many critical ways. One of the most important discoveries was of the medieval Chinese literary genre of *bianwen*, "transformation texts." Before that fateful June evening, the very existence of *bianwen* was utterly unknown. It was absent from the tomes and tomes of Chinese documents extant. More amazingly, despite *bianwen*'s heavily Buddhist content, it was also absent from the vast Chinese Buddhist literature dominated early on by what one may term "gentry Buddhism." Nonetheless, following its discovery *bianwen* was shown to be a critically important form of literature for "popular Buddhism," enjoyed by and spread among millions of ordinary medieval Chinese people—yet it has unmistakable Central Asian and Indian origins.[1] Beyond Buddhism, it addressed other themes of Chinese popular culture. The fact that such an important literary genre could be totally forgotten for nearly a millennium demonstrates the depth of the sinocentric as well as the gentry bias of Chinese written records.

The latter kind of bias has also affected records of the twelve-animal cycle, whose Sinitic origin has been proven by recent archaeological finds and other evidence, as mentioned in earlier chapters. But this important element of Chinese popular culture, going back all the way to the pre-Qin unification era, was hardly ever mentioned in written records over the millennia, in spite of the fact that the gentry class who monopolized Chinese writing was in fact not insulated from this "vulgar" tradition.[2]

Partly prompted by such blatant omissions and neglect by Chinese written sources, secular/Confucianist as well as religious/Buddhist, I decided to conduct a critical review of the well-documented Central Asian ancestry of the great Tang poet Bai Juyi (Po Chü-i; 772–846), especially its implications regarding Bai's life and career. To the expected criticism and counterargument that the vast existing written records (including Bai Juyi's own extensive works) hardly ever touched upon the poet's non-Sinitic heritage, the cases of *bianwen* and the twelve-animal cycle provide refreshing precedents for my effort.

No general literary history of China or of East Asia could be written without mentioning Bai Juyi. Nor would his name be absent from any treatise on the politics of the late Tang era. Bai's status in Japan appears to match even that of Confucius and Christ. For example, in Tada Toshio's biographies of six great historical figures in Asia, *Retsuden Ajia no sanga ni* (*Biographies: In the Land of Asia*), Bai Juyi was placed, rightly or wrongly, right after Buddha, Confucius, Christ, and Muhammad. Katayama Tetsu, the founder of Japan's modern Socialist Party and its prime minister after the Second World War, was also a serious Bai Juyi scholar, as attested by his 1961 Bai biography *Taishu shijin Haku Rakuten* (*Popular Poet Bai Letian*). However, for a person exerting such profound influence both within and outside of China, Bai Juyi's well-documented non-Sinitic pedigree, much less its implications for his life and career, has seldom been discussed in any detail in the many volumes of biographies, literary critiques, and political studies of this great Confucian poet-cum-politician. This chapter calls attention to this chronic oversight by presenting an analysis of Bai Juyi's Central Asian connections.[3]

Bai's Ancestry

According to the epitaph in honor of the father of his second cousin, Bai Minzhong, collected in *Bai Juyi ji* (*Collected Works of Bai Juyi* [hereafter *BJ*] 70.1473), Bai Juyi had this to say about their common ancestry: "[Minzhong's father] was named Jikang, with such-and-such a style name. His native place was Taiyuan. He was a descendant of Wu'an Jun [Bai Qi] of [the Kingdom of] Qin [of the Warring States era]. [Specifically] he was a fifth-generation descendant of Bai Jian, the Minister of Five Armed Forces of the Northern Qi." Despite all the evidence against this self-claimed lineage, many modern authors still accept it uncritically. For instance, in his otherwise fine study of the changes of fortune for many prominent clans during the Tang-Song transition, Sun Guodong copied this supposed ancestry verbatim from *Xin Tang shu* (*New History of the Tang*) without raising any questions.[4] Wang Meng'ou, in his article about Bai's ancestry and descendants, also took a rather orthodox or sinocentric view on these standard records in arguing against the well-substantiated theory on Bai's ancestry set forth by Chen Yinke and many other authors.

In an earlier biography of his grandfather (*BJ* 46.981), Bai Juyi traced their illustrious common ancestry further back to an heir apparent of the Kingdom of Chu of the Spring-and-Autumn period, resulting in a glaring anachronism, which was noted by Bai's Southern Song (1127–1279) biographer Chen Zhensun and other early commentators.[5] However, this cousin, Minzhong, "who was to become Po Chü-i's great pride in later life" in the words of Arthur Waley,[6] reportedly later wrote a poem that effectively disavowed what Bai Juyi wrote about their eminent forefathers. According to the study by Chen Yinke, even the information regarding the Northern Qi minister Bai Jian, by far the most credible part of Bai's claimed ancestry, was problematic.[7] As will be further discussed, Bai Juyi's self-claim that his great-grandmother was from the prominent Hán clan of Changli (*BJ* 42.929) does not seem to have figured in, much less helped, his exceptionally cold relations with Hán Yu (768–824), by far the most famous son of the Changli-centered Hán clan during the Tang. The fabricated ancestry of Bai Juyi also reflects on the awkward record of his more recent family history, as will be examined below.

Nevertheless, a modern reader should not be too critical of Bai's blatantly false claim, as it was the vogue at the time for prominent people of non-Sinitic origins to claim descent from famous ancient Chinese figures. Or we can say Bai's claim was no less true than the Tang imperial family's claim of having descended from a noted Longxi clan, as I discussed in Chapter 1, or that the early Tuoba chiefs were the sixty-seventh generation descendants of some offspring of the legendary ruler Huangdi (*Wei shu*, or *History of the Wei*, 1.1). I further advance the general proposition that the custom of claiming preeminent but false ancestry was typical of many nonnative persons, usually of nomadic tribal origins, once they have attained prominence in a sedentary, agricultural society, mainly to achieve political as well as cultural legitimacy in their adopted land. For example, the Turkic ruling house of the Ghaznavid sultanate in the eastern Iranian world fabricated a genealogy from the Iranian Sassanid shahs,[8] with a story line almost identical to similar genealogies claimed by numerous Xiongnu and Xianbei figures in China.

As detailed in his superb study of various Xeno-Sinitic surnames arising during the Northern dynasties, Yao Weiyuan established that the Bai clan originally came from the state of Qiuci (Kucha, around present-day Kuche in Xinjiang) in Central Asia.[9] As mentioned earlier, the most compromising evidence against Bai Juyi's claim came from a poem attributed to his second cousin Minzhong after the latter, relieved of his chief minister's portfolio, was transferred to a provincial position:

Of the Ten Hu clans, I belong to the sixth,
Having once in the golden palace held sway over the realm.[10]

Yao has identified the "Ten Hu clans" with the "Ten Western Türk (Tujue) tribes," with which I can hardly agree. The reason is that Shixing ("Ten-clan") Hu cannot be automatically equated with the Shixing tribes of the Western Türks. Indeed, there was a fine but clear distinction between the names Hu and Tujue at the time, as reflected in the famous exchange between An Lushan, of mixed Sogdian-Türk origin, and Geshu Han, of "pure" Türk background, regarding their respective pedigrees.[11] In addition, the state of Kucha predated the advent and westward migration of the Turks by centuries. The character *hu* at the time was normally reserved for people of Central Asian origins (mostly Indo-Iranic at the time),[12] and Yao's own conclusion that the Bai clan came from Kucha certainly bears this out.[13]

Another contemporary testimony is the grievance of a top Tang politician that all four recent chief minister appointments starting with Bai Minzhong went to persons of foreign origin.[14] They were, beside Bai Juyi's cousin, Bi Xian; Cao Que; and Luo Shao, all of identifiable Central Asian pedigree. The story did not strictly fit the official records of chief minister appointments found in *Xin Tang shu*. But as Yao Weiyuan has stressed, it reflected the preciously preserved views of Bai Juyi's contemporaries on the issue of ethnicity. Here one may also note a most striking feature of the Tang, namely that the regime was never very sensitive about the ethnic origins of its high-level appointees.[15]

Incidentally, Bai Jian (?–576), the most credible ancestor of the Bai clan and an important courtier of the Northern Qi, was in my view a typical product of the Central Asia card played by the Tuoba Wei and its successor regimes in ruling northern China, which I have elaborated upon in previous chapters. In other words, Bai Jian was a predecessor of what later became "assistant conquerors" in the Mongol Yuan dynasty. Despite his very short (two paragraphs) biography in *Bei Qi shu* (*History of the Northern Qi*, 40.532–33), the same official history source accidentally revealed elsewhere (33.447), through a popular saying of the time, that Bai Jian had in fact been one of the two most powerful politicians of the Northern Qi from Taiyuan, the Bai clan's hometown in China. His official biography, meanwhile, portrayed him rather dismissively: "Jian possessed no talents other than being diligent in government affairs."

There have been several recent archaeological finds related to the Bai clan. First, the tomb inscription of Bai Minzhong, first discovered in the early 1960s, was published in 1991.[16] Second, a stone inscription written and erected by Bai Juyi to commemorate the "resettlement" of the "spirit tablet" of one of the alleged Spring-and-Autumn era ancestors of the Bai clan was unearthed near Luoyang in May 2001.[17] Both were consistent with existing descriptions by Bai Juyi about his ancestry quoted earlier. The most interesting discovery, however, was the tomb inscription of the daughter of Bai Minzhong unearthed in October 1997.[18] It was written by the lady's bereaved husband, Huangfu Wei, and dated 859. This inscription mentioned explicitly and proudly that the Tang dynasty general of unmistakable Kuchaean origin, Bai Xiaode (715–80; biography *Jiu Tang shu* 109.3310 and *Xin Tang shu* 136.4593), was a fellow Bai clansman. In other words, Bai Minzhong's son-in-law confirmed beyond doubt that, at the time, the Bai clan still identified with their ancestors' home in Central Asia.

The next natural question is how and to what extent this Kuchaean ancestry affected Bai's family and his own cultural and political life. As far as I am aware, Chen Yinke's study (*Yuan-Bai shi jianzheng gao* [*Draft Commentaries and Researches on the Poetry of Yuan Zhen and Bai Juyi*], hereafter *Jianzheng gao*, pp. 292–302) is the only major work that has seriously addressed the family, whereas the other topics remain virtually untouched.

There is a common notion that, once settled in China, former nomadic tribes-people and other foreign newcomers soon assimilated and in due course became completely "Chinese." It is perhaps for this reason that few researchers are known ever to have looked at the connections between Bai's non-Sinitic ancestry and his works. Even Chen Yinke himself has made his view very clear (*Jianzheng gao*, p. 293) that the non-Sinitic ancestry had no bearing on Bai as a "cultural person."

I beg to differ. A central thesis of this study is the longevity of non-Sinitic ethnicities in premodern China. The survival for centuries of the completely isolated Jewish community in Kaifeng, despite its success in all mainstream "Chinese" pursuits, attests to the resilience of non-Sinitic ethnicity in the Central Kingdom (as well as the high degree of social tolerance in traditional China). That Sino-Semitic community produced numerous successful Confucian scholar-officials who were at the same time active in Jewish communal affairs.[19]

Besides the Sino-Jewish community, another striking case is the recent archaeological discovery, in the county of Yingshan, Hubei province, of several tombs belonging to the Bi clan, whose Central Asian ancestry had been observed by the Tang high official quoted earlier (with regard to Tang chief minister Bi Xian). I am not swayed by the official hubris in China trumpeting the claim that one of the tombs belonged to the Northern Song dynasty commoner named Bi Sheng, who, according to Song dynasty author Shen Gua's (1030–94) *Mengxi bitan* (*Brush Talks from Dream Brook*), had invented movable type for printing,[20] as the possibility of a fortuitous namesake cannot be excluded at this stage. The critical solid finding in my view is the unmistakable indication that the Bi clansmen in Yingshan held Manichaean beliefs, best represented by two important characters, *ri*, "sun," and *yue*, "moon," inscribed prominently onto the tombstone. This was a feature, in the words of a Chinese tomb inscription specialist (italics mine), "*never* seen in other ethnic Hàn Chinese tomb inscriptions from the Hàn (206 BC–220 AD) to the Yuan (1271–1368)."[21] This point, incidentally, also makes the character *sheng* ("rise," especially regarding the sun and the moon), with or without the "sun" radical, a fitting hence popular choice as a personal name for the Bi clan, further increasing the likelihood that the dead person might not be the alleged inventor of the movable type.

As several authors have observed, other features of the tombstones matched those of the Manichaean relics of the Yuan.[22] Most researchers of the Bi tombs have pointed out the link between the Bi clan's Central Asian ancestry and their Manichaean faith. The remarkable fact is that by 1052, the date of the Bi Sheng tomb inscription agreed upon by most scholars, the Bis had lived in China for many centuries. Moreover, the tombstones also betrayed, in a telltale manner, the Bi family's violation of the Sinitic father-name taboo that was deeply entrenched by the Song period if not earlier. This is a subject we shall return to later.

With regard to Bai Juyi's ancestry, I see no solid reason to disallow the scenario that the Bai clan, living in a much more cosmopolitan era than the Northern Song, carried a similar ancestral heritage. Bai Minzhong's poem is not only an unmistakable indication that the Bai clansmen were quite aware of their non-Sinitic heritage but also a clear sign of ethnic pride. It is thus hard to believe that this Central Asian heritage would not have left any mark on the "Confucian" poet-cum-scholar-politician and his work. In addition, this heritage would seem to provide a natural and unifying interpretation for several lingering controversies over Bai's family life, literary work, and political career. They include the marriage of his parents, Bai's own religious belief, his alleged first love affair and general attitude toward women, certain peculiar aspects of his lifestyle, his relationship with other contemporary figures, and so on, some of which are explored in this chapter.

A Confucian Family?

The conventional wisdom in Chinese historiography is that anyone passing the civil examinations and rising in the bureaucracy was ipso facto a "Confucian scholar-official." This would seem to be a typical example of the Confucianist bias mentioned earlier. The Chinese Jewish community in Kaifeng is a case in point. Chen Yinke also discovered another successful Tang "Confucian scholar-official" family that maintained its apparently foreign religious tradition "forbidding ancestor-worship,"[23] which is, of course, a doctrine common in the Judeo-Christian (-Islamic) monotheistic world.[24] In relation to the discovery of the Song dynasty tombs of the Bi family cited earlier, it is of some interest to link Chen Yinke's finding to the same practice of the Song period Chinese Manichaeans as recorded in Lu You (1125–1210), corroborated by another Song author, Zhuang Chuo (fl. 1101–39), and later, seemingly, by Marco Polo as well.[25]

Misled by a line in one of his later poems (*BJ* 11.217), "I was a son from a Confucian family," many people have accepted as given that Bai was foremost a "Confucian."[26] In my analysis, the "Confucian family" characterization would appear to be as reliable or plausible and as necessary as his claim of an eminent ancestry for a former member of "the sixth among the Ten Hu clans" who happened to be in critical need of powerful political patronage and family connections. For instance, despite Bai's well-documented lifelong devotion to Buddhism, Stanley Weinstein has pointed out the length to which our poet would go to denounce Buddhism in order to pass an important civil examination.[27]

I note the following sentence in the celebrated letter (*BJ* 45.962) Bai wrote to his best friend and confidant Yuan Zhen (779–831): "I first learned about the *jinshi* ("Presented Scholar") examination when I was fifteen or sixteen (Chinese reckoning) and started working hard [for it]." As Chen Yinke observed in his study of Tang political history, a *jinshi* degree commanded such eminence and other benefits at the time that failure to secure it topped the idiomatic "Three [life-long] Resentments" for the literati.[28] The degree's prestige spread well beyond the Tang border, so much so that a twelve-year-old Korean student reportedly had set it as his ultimate goal, even before embarking on his journey to study in Tang China.[29] Bai's words therefore reflect, if not an extraordinary profession of innocence, at least the true politico-cultural background of this "Confucian family" in order to account for this much belated aspiration of a son who "started composing poems at the age of five or six and understood the rules of sound and rhymes at nine" (*BJ* 45.962; all ages Chinese reckoning).

Let us take a closer look at the "Confucian family" image. Luo Zhenyu first developed the case that Bai's parents represented an uncle-niece union, which Chen Yinke further elaborated.[30] Cen Zhongmian in his *Sui Tang shi* (*History of the Sui and Tang Dynasties*, pp. 404, 415–16), with some vehemence if not extremism in his indignation, disputed their evidence. This controversy continues to be hotly debated. While many modern authors agree with Luo and Chen,[31] others find such an "incestuous" union difficult to accept, apparently from a modern

sinocentric viewpoint.[32] In the final analysis, Cen's contention requires more assumptions than the opposite notion does. Hiraoka Takeo, relying on a rare Japanese edition of Bai's works, proposes another solution.[33] However, in addition to
the necessity to emend, perforce, all existing editions of Bai's works, Hiraoka's
proposal would still put Juyi's mother one generation younger than his father. In
view of the false or highly suspicious claims regarding both his clan's remote and
more recent (i.e., Northern Qi dynasty and the Changli Hán clan grandmother)
ancestors, Bai's stories about his immediate family certainly should be subject to
such critical scrutiny as Luo and Chen had initiated. The case is clearly supported
by the Bai family tree drawn up by Arthur Waley, apparently independently of
Luo and Chen's work, albeit Waley failed to notice this important point.[34]

I would argue that, taking into account the Bai clan's Central Asian heritage, this marriage would not at all appear *jixing*, "abnormal," as some modern
Chinese researchers rather painfully characterize it. In Chapter 3, I pointed out
the ancient Steppe tradition of not maintaining clear "generational boundaries"
and its relationship with levirate and other "scandalous" marriages that were
frequently visited on the Tang imperial house, which was closely connected to,
if not directly descended from, the Tuoba and other former nomad clans. The
marriage of Bai's parents can then be similarly linked with their Central Asian
origin, particularly in view of the Central Asia card played by the nomadic and
former nomadic groups vis-à-vis the Sinitic world, which led to extensive intermingling of Central Asians with Steppe nomads.

Let me further remark that the uncle-niece union, while not actively promoted
or widely favored, was a well-accepted practice among people in South and West
Asia at the time. In fact, this tradition has remained in India to this day.[35] It was
permitted among the Jews.[36] One may also note the pre-Islamic Arab custom of
bint 'amm marriage of patrilineal parallel cousins.[37] This favorite matrimonial relationship is said to have expanded to non-Arab Muslim societies.[38] As suggested
by the case of Ali ibn Abi Talib, who was the Prophet's both cousin and son-in-law,
such marriages, in addition to being between two individuals bearing the same
surname, could cut cross generational boundaries, thus becoming the equivalent
of uncle-niece union in the eyes of generation-sensitive Sinitic pedants, as Yuan
dynasty Confucians would later accuse. One may note that the practice was still
quite popular among aristocratic families in early modern Europe, attested by
such major monarchs as Philip II and Philip IV, both of Spain, and Leopold I, the
Holy Roman Emperor. All three married a full sister's own daughter.[39]

In pre-Islamic Central Asia, there was furthermore the custom of *xvaetvadatha*, "next-of-kin marriage," practiced by early and medieval Zoroastrians

and widely reported by ancient Greek authors.[40] Thus *Sui shu* (*History of the Sui*, 83.1856, 83.1849) accuses the Sassanian Iranians of "marrying their own sisters," and the city-state of Bukhara, another bastion of Zoroastrianism, of having "mothers and sons behave like beasts to each other [i.e., have sexual relations]." This long-disappeared custom is even said to have contributed to the prevalence of consanguineous marriages in modern Iran.[41] In this connection, I have noted another case supporting the Luo-Chen conclusion: the Sino-Pahlavi bilingual tombstone of the wife née Ma of Su Liang, a Tang general of Central Asian origin, which was discovered at Xi'an in 1955. Corresponding to the Chinese word *qi*, "wife," the Pahlavi text offers a curious word choice: *BRTH*, meaning "daughter." As pointed out by W. Sundermann and W. Thilo, this difference in wording strongly suggests the possibility of a next-of-kin marriage not infrequent among the Central Asians, mostly Iranic, at the time.[42] It also suggests a deliberate effort by the author(s) of the inscriptions to conceal the fact, presumably the same dilemma faced by Bai Juyi.

In addition to the prevalence of uncle-niece marriages in both ancient and modern India, one may observe a Buddhist connection here. The most prominent fact is that, in comparison with traditional Confucianism, incestuous relations were a much less prohibitive taboo in Indian Buddhism than in China. This was a cultural gap that had tormented early Chinese translators of the Tripitaka, as observed by Chen Yinke.[43] Mother-son incest, though condemned, was a recurring theme in Indo-Buddhist literature, likely a reflection of the alleged universal or Indo-Aryan Oedipal complex.[44] Other less severe forms of incestuous relations such as brother-sister marriage were recounted in neutral or even approving tones.[45] A most striking story relevant to the marriage of Bai Juyi's parents is the following elaboration, narrated in a tone of praise, on the origin of the Sakyas, the clan of the Buddha: "Then the princes settled there, and, mindful of the words of their father the king that they seek to *marry within their own clan*, they were not able to find brides. Each accepted a *maternal aunt* and her sisters, and took them as wife, according to the rites of marriage. In the first place they desired to follow the instructions of their father the king, and in the second place *they feared introducing corruption into the lineage of the Śākyas*" (italics mine).[46] This would seem a perfect religious guide for the Buddhist Bai family on how to maintain their own non-Sinitic lineage (see below).

It is also worth noting the supporting evidence used by Chen Yinke that Bai Juyi suffered public accusations (and a "conviction," of sorts) that he violated the Confucian ethics in connection with some family scandal involving his mother (*Jiu Tang shu* 166.4344). One should further note not only that Bai has left us no written record in his own defense against the accusers (except for a rather ambiguous and meek passage in a letter to a relative in *BJ* 44.947–48) but also that the incident served as a crucial divide in Bai's political life and philosophy. Thereafter Bai was never again the same aggressive and assertive official he had been prior to the incident. It would be tempting to ascribe this sea change to the most serious charges one could possibly make regarding his mother and Confucian ethics: it had hit Bai's soft spot, if not his Achilles heel.[47]

Whether uncle-niece or first cousins, it is beyond any doubt that the Bai clan practiced cousin marriages for generations. This was certainly not the practice among the contemporary prominent Hàn Chinese clans who would consider marrying into the imperial house something of a disgrace, as I noted in Chapter 1. I would contend that, contrary to the traditional myth of "sinification," Bai clan's practice might have represented a conscious and serious effort to maintain their ethnic identity through endogamy. Besides the story reflected in the Sino-Pahlavi tombstone, numerous other Tang tomb inscriptions showed descendants of immigrants marrying each other for generations.[48] In addition, we possess more recent data on the Jewish community in Kaifeng confirming the same custom, albeit with questionable success.[49] Such practice within a small group of kindred people would inevitably lead to what may be termed *nepogamy*, or marriage of close kin regardless of the degree of consanguinity. During the Mongol Yuan dynasty, this was one of the harsh criticisms the Hàn Chinese literati leveled at the Huihui (Muslim) communities,[50] whose practice of *nepogamy*, disregarding basic generational boundaries, was confirmed in Fujian by a modern Muslim author who reports that such practice often led to two sisters marrying two men who were uncle and nephew.[51]

All these behaviors ran against Confucianist morals and social mores. In this context, it does not seem coincidental that the tombstones of the Bi clan in Yingshan, cited earlier for the evidence of their Manichaean belief, also revealed that family's violation of the deeply entrenched Sinitic father-name taboo.[52]

Another case that casts doubts on Bai's "Confucian family" image is the erotic verse "Dale fu" (Rhapsody of great pleasure) discovered among the Dunhuang manuscripts (P. 2539) and attributed to Bai Xingjian, Juyi's younger brother. Robert van Gulik saw "no valid reason to doubt [Xingjian's] authorship."[53] Indeed, I shall later propose additional evidence to support this authorship. Prior to the entrenchment of neo-Confucianism, China had been quite liberal in this regard, with many sex manuals appearing in the guise of medical texts and Taoist classics. However, not only would "Rhapsody of Great Pleasure" with its at times highly literate verse seem to introduce a new genre of erotic literature, the Bai brothers also happened to witness a "Confucian revival," generally considered to be the direct or indirect precursor of Song neo-Confucianism.[54] Even measured by the tolerant or exotic social mores of the Tang, it would still appear very hard to reconcile "Rhapsody of Great Pleasure" with a "Confucian family" environment.

The Central Asian Heritage

Let us recall the most crucial role Central Asia has played in China's history. Few would dispute that this was in the realm of religion: from early times until almost the previous century, Central Asia has been the beachhead that enabled various faiths and ideological visions to spread to China:[55] Buddhism, Zoroastrianism, Nestorianism, Judaism, Manichaeism, and Islam. And Central Asians have been rightly associated with these movements, from the early Buddhist missionaries[56] to the Chinese name of Islam.[57]

The surname Bai was closely associated with the state of Kucha,[58] which is the basis of the argument set forth by Yao Weiyuan to reach his own conclusion regarding the Bai clan. Historically a great center of Buddhism, Kucha was noted for its critical contribution to the spread of Buddhism to China.[59] One of its roles involved the large number of Buddhist missionaries. For a long while, monks with the surname Bo (a variant of Bai) were identified as coming from Kucha.[60] As pointed out by Chen Yinke, Bai Juyi revealed a clue regarding this link. In an essay commemorating a Buddhist temple in Mount Wozhou, he mentions two abbots who shared with him the surname Bai and the commission of his essay by one of them, Bai Juyi (*BJ* 68.1440), and goes on to wonder whether "the Bai clan was not destined to be associated with Mount Wozhou generation after generation." Bai Juyi's self-identification was in fact noted as early as *Nanbu xinshu* (*New Book of the South*, 7.64) by the Song dynasty author Qian Yi (fl. 1017).

Both Bai's interest in Buddhism and his devotion to it were well attested.[61] Nevertheless, almost every Bai scholar I have read has stressed that Bai was foremost a Confucian scholar-official. Indeed, in a formal "debate among the Three Teachings" at the Tang court in 827, Bai was the designated spokesman for Confucianism (*BJ* 68.1434–40). Many authors thus tend to regard Bai's active patronage of Buddhism as a development in his later life and his devotion to that faith an "acquired" attribute, particularly after he suffered much political frustration. They then try to search for hints in Bai's works for the time of the onset of his Buddhist inclinations.[62] However, it should be noted that Confucianism was mandatory for any seeker of a political career. Bai Juyi himself said explicitly that his role representing Confucianism at the court debate was by an imperial edict.[63] I would further contend that, befitting his Central Asian/Kuchaean heritage, Buddhism was in fact a traditional creed in his family. Perhaps the clearest indication is that Juyi's youngest brother, who died a minor (at age nine, or eight by Western reckoning), had a *xiaozi*, "childhood name," Jin'gangnu, "slave of Vajra Buddha," a typical Buddhist theophoric name, as examined in Chapters 5 and 6. His two surviving brothers, in an endearing elegy some twenty-two years after his death (*BJ* 40.894 and 42.930–31), still clung to this childhood name rather than his formal Sinitic name, Youmei.[64] Together with Chen Yinke's example of a noted Tang family's failure to practice ancestor worship and the Yingshan Bi clan's failure to observe the father-name taboo on the tombstones, we can see that the non-Sinitic heritage among the immigrants died particularly hard on the very question of death.

There is a fascinating recent archaeological discovery on the site where Bai Juyi's villa once stood in Luoyang: the remnants of a stone pillar or mini stupa were unearthed in 1992, on which were inscribed texts from two dhāraṇī sutras:[65] "Dhāraṇī of the Jubilant Buddha-Corona"[66] and "Dhāraṇī of the Bodhisattva with a Thousand Hands and Eyes Who Regards the World's Sounds with Great Compassion."[67] The inscriptions likely represent the only surviving sample of the great Tang poet's handwriting. It is intriguing to observe that the inscribed texts are nothing more than transcriptions of Sanskrit spells in Chinese characters. Unlike most mantras, dhāraṇīs have verbal meanings. But to an average Chinese believer who did not know Indian languages, the transliterated texts had no literary significance whatsoever. So why did a highly educated man of letters endowed with such a keen aesthetic sense for both literature and music choose to inscribe these passages that were utterly meaningless in Chinese? Adding the *Jiu Tang shu* biography's emphasis (166.4345) that Bai had "mastered in particular the Buddhist canon," it would not seem farfetched to deduce that Bai Juyi was at least partially literate in Sanskrit and that such knowledge was related to his Central Asian heritage.[68]

Another intriguing issue vis-à-vis religion is Bai Juyi's little-noticed connection to Manichaeism. That faith had its birthplace in West Asia but spread to China via Central Asia, particularly through Iranian-speaking converts.[69] The Southern Song author Hong Mai (1123–1202) reported, as cited by the Buddhist historian Zhipan, that the Song Manichaeans in southern China quoted the following poem, allegedly composed by Bai Juyi, enthusiastically lauding Manichaeism, at the beginning of their scripture:

I calmly examine the record of Sulin,
The Doctrine of Mani is amazing,
The Two Principles display their dignified silence,
The five Buddhas accompany the light,
The Sun and Moon render their homage,
Heaven and Earth acknowledge their origin.
In the matter of self-discipline and purification,
[The Manichaeans] do not lag behind [the Buddhists].[70]

Both Hong and Zhipan regarded the poem, absent from existing editions of Bai's works, as a forgery, though Zhipan's argument that this was because Bai was a Buddhist is rather weak if one recalls Bai's not-so-frivolous interest in Taoism. The modern authority on medieval Chinese Manichaeism, Samuel Lieu, while acknowledging this probability, considers the poem plausibly authentic.[71] Either possibility would lend support for Bai's Central Asian heritage. Regarding the first possibility, Lieu's explanation that it was perhaps because Bai "had mentioned Manichaeism in favourable terms in a letter he wrote to the Uighur Khaghan" appears tenuous and superficial. A more plausible interpretation for this attribution in my view was his contemporaries' knowledge of Bai's Central Asian heritage. Even as late as the sixteenth century, Chinese Manichaeans still knew well that their canon had been propagated in Bosi (Persia) and Tokhara before it came to China.[72] Lieu's other hypothesis, namely that Bai Juyi had actually written a preface for one of the Manichaean scriptures, would be an even stronger indication of our poet's special feeling toward Central Asia.

Let me return to Monk Zhipan's point that the alleged Bai poem praising Manichaeism was a forgery because Bai was a Buddhist. Such an argument in fact does not hold water, because medieval Central Asia was known for its syncretism in religious beliefs. For example, *Xin Tang shu* (221b.6244) recorded that the Sogdians worshipped both the Buddha and the Zoroastrian god, an observation shared by Richard Frye.[73] I revealed in Chapter 5 theophoric names pertaining to the Zoroastrian fire god in medieval Chinese communities with simultaneous deep devotion to Buddhism. The aforementioned Song-era Manichaean faith of the Bi clan who descended from Central Asian immigrants is another piece of supporting evidence.

Another important item of Central Asian heritage, perhaps next in prominence only to religion, was music. Kucha, the ancestral land of nearly all Bai clan members in China, was particularly famous for its musical tradition. Indeed, Kuchaean music and musicians had enormous influence on the cultural scene of the Tang,[74] exemplified by, among others, another member of the Bai clan, namely the famed Sui court musician Bai Mingda (*Sui shu* 15.397).

Among contemporary literati, Bai Juyi's musical talent was certainly signal.[75] It does not seem accidental that a large number of Bai's poems were ballads. As one of the first writers of a new genre of song-poems (poetic ballads), he even coined the very term *xinyuefu*, "new folk-song."[76] In the much recited "Pipa xing" (Ballad of the lute), Bai set an unsurpassed example in the masterly use of Chinese poetic language to describe the *pipa*, "Chinese lute," music. It is notable that the instrument was not native to China either, its repertoire being especially rich in Central Asian content, Kuchaean in particular.[77] Bai was also among the very first authors to have experimented with the completely new genre of Chinese poetry, *ci* ("lyric poetry," written to various specific tunes), whose creation had an unmistakable Central Asian influence.[78] It would be difficult to name another Tang literary figure embodying such a wide spectrum of musical talents. One finds it hard not to relate this rather unique case to Bai's Central Asian heritage.

This brings up a problem typical of the failure to recognize the Bai clan's Central Asian background: Chen Yinke once established, with solid evidence, that the popular Tang music piece "The Song of *Nishang yuyi* (Rainbow-skirt and plume-blouse)" was of foreign (in fact partly Kuchaean) origin. Another Chinese scholar, Ren Bantang, contested this well-substantiated conclusion, ironically using the argument that Bai Juyi, a quintessential "native Chinese poet," was, in Ren's opinion, a connoisseur of "The Song of *Nishang yuyi*."[79]

Even acknowledging the possibility that Bai had acquired all these extraordinary musical skills merely as an extremely gifted and diligent scholar, the warm feelings and genuine affection toward musicians and other "entertainers" frequently shown in Bai's poems constitute a marked contrast to the traditional Confucian bias against the same artists or *changyou*, "singers and actresses," whose ranks at the time swarmed with people of Central Asian origin.[80] This sympathetic attitude toward a social class full of the Bai clan's former compatriots from Central Asia, who were regarded by mainstream Confucian literati as equivalent to house slaves and prostitutes, was certainly a familial trait: the heroine in the celebrated love story "Liwa zhuan" (Biography of the beautiful girl Li), authored by Juyi's brother Xingjian and acclaimed as "probably one of the world's finest specimens of early prose fiction,"[81] was a "sing-song girl" who was to become the respected wife of a successful scholar-official and eventually be ennobled as "the Lady of the Dukedom of Qian." At the very least, this ethnic factor helps us to better understand Bai Juyi's deep sympathy toward a former prostitute lute player who once worked in the red-light district of the Tang capital, let alone the identification of her fate with the poet's own, in his immortal poem "Pipa xing" (Ballad of the lute).

Indeed, on this particular issue one sees another parallel between Bai and the ruling autocracy from the Northern dynasties on down to the early Tang. As shown in Chapter 1, the successive imperial houses with their undeniable Steppe origins often showed little reservation in bestowing on those artists prominent and prestigious titles, even though they were considered to be of the same social class as whores and gigolos by the traditional Chinese gentry. One such artist was even enfeoffed with a princedom by a Northern Qi emperor, a precedent the Sui emperor Yangdi intended to follow for the benefit of his favorite, the talented Kuchaean musician Bai Mingda (*Sui shu*, 15.397). The first two Tang emperors were both criticized by Confucian ministers for similar appointments. The same fervor could be observed in the Shatuo Turkic regimes later.

An additional case is Bai's famous nomadic-style tent, about which he wrote many affectionate poems.[82] Recently Wu Yugui conducted an extensive study and identified thirteen such poems plus one letter.[83] Wu observed that Bai had spent, rather extraordinarily from the year 829 until the poet's death in 846, a total of eighteen long winters in his cherished tent. While Wu attributed this matter to the alleged "foreign customs" of the Tang society, he admitted that such intense affection shown in so many poems on the same object, namely Bai's tent, was a "very rare" phenomenon. Worse still, Wu concluded that Bai's attachment to the Steppe lifestyle "went against common sense."

Wu's points in my view reflect the deficiencies of studying Bai Juyi as a typical Tang poet without considering his non-Sinitic family origin. For instance, the "very rare" phenomenon of Bai's love of the Steppe-style tent makes perfect sense once we realize the ancestral culture heritage that was still strong in the Bai family. Most indigenous populations in the Western Region were believed to be Indo-Iranic and sedentary. It is also true that ever since the founding of the great Xiongnu Empire, if not earlier, this vast area had always been at the center of sedentary versus nomadic conflicts, and, when not under Chinese control or influence, it would invariably be under the rule of a Steppe power. It had indeed been for a long time a part of the Western Türk Empire prior to the Tang, hence Yao Weiyuan's aforementioned erroneous identification of *hu* as part of Tujue or Türk. The area's later Turkicization certainly bears out this enormous nomadic influence on Central Asians at the time. There was also the issue of the Central Asia card, a deliberate policy of the nomadic and former nomadic groups that may well have enticed Bai's ancestors to come to China, as I have argued in the previous chapter, and which is strongly suggested by the career of Bai Jian, the Bai clan's prominent forefather of the Northern Qi.

The most important Central Asian and/or Buddhist influence on the great Tang poet, however, was probably Bai's conscious efforts to promote his trademark, epoch-making, plain-and-simple style of writing, which I shall examine in more detail later.

Silk Road—"Umbilical Cord" to the Ancestor Land?

It would not be practical to offer in this short chapter a full discussion of the entire corpus of Bai's works and explore the influence of his Central Asian ancestry on his writings. The pervasive presence of foreign elements in the Tang world dictates that any such discussion be made with a point of reference. It is my contention that the life of Bai Juyi represented not the outcome, as Wu Yugui and other authors have concluded, but rather a source of Tang cosmopolitanism. There could be no better choice of a point of reference than Bai's lifelong friend and fellow scholar-official Yuan Zhen. Both had a very similar social background. Being a tenth-generation descendant of the Tuoba Xianbei chief Shi-yijian (posthumously given the title Emperor Zhaocheng [*Jiu Tang shu* 166.4327]), Yuan Zhen's claim to be a bona fide Chinese was not much more solid than his friend's. But in general, the Yuan family did appear to have a longer history than the Bais of acculturation, if not complete assimilation, into the Central Kingdom. We should also note another famous poet, Liu Yuxi (772–842), who later also became Bai Juyi's close friend. It is not an accident that this friend was a descendant of the Xiongnu or the (Tuoba) Xianbei.[84]

I thus find some of their *xinyuefu* ("new folk-song" or "new ballad") poems illuminating through their contrasting attitudes.[85] In particular, there are several poems, namely "Faqu(ge)" (Song of ceremonial music), "Huxuan nü" (Hu whirling girls), "Libu ji (Dancers from the standing section), "Xiliang ji" (Dancers from West Liang), and a number of new titles that Bai derived from Yuan's originals, in which foreign cultural themes, style, fashion, and so on were mentioned.

All in all, Yuan Zhen was strongly negative and hostile to the Hu and their cultural influence on Tang life, so much so that Liao Meiyun has summarized it as an accusation that the Hu influence might have been responsible for most of the Tang's calamities.[86] Bai, with a much wider range of subjects, seemed far more restrained and objective, if not reluctant, on the Hu question. I may add that one reason for Bai's great popularity was his integrity, in both his political and personal life, at times in sharp contrast to that of his friend Yuan Zhen, who later sacrificed the basic gentry-class principles in order to be nominated chief minister through the backing of powerful palace eunuchs. Chen Yinke (*Jianzheng gao*, pp. 94–96) has exposed Yuan's hypocrisy even in his personal life. After all, the fact that the clan was still identified as Hu notwithstanding, Bai could not have been accused of hypocrisy after having proudly entertained his friends in his nomadic-style tents.[87]

Such a contrast is exemplified by Yuan Zhen's outburst against the alleged Hu cultural fashion prevalent at the time in "Faqu." In the last eight verses, the character *hu* was repeated no fewer than eight times, together with the derogatory expression "Fur and fleece, rank and rancid, have filled the [two Tang capitals]."[88] This repeated pejorative use of the character *hu* was apparently meant to create an impression of aggressiveness and arrogance.[89] Such sensational and simplistic scapegoating for an extremely complex series of historical developments is rightly dismissed by Xu Daoxun and Zhao Keyao as mere juggling with words.[90]

Bai's "Faqu(ge)" is much milder in this respect.[91] And it is significant that Bai has omitted all mention of "Hu fashion." Instead, in a separate poem, "Shishi zhuang" (Fashion of the current world), apparently derived from Yuan's subject, Bai objectively and accurately, albeit implicitly,[92] attributes the vogue to Tibetan influences. Even more strikingly (and linguistically quite correctly), in contrast to Yuan, Bai did so without once using the character *hu* in a total of fourteen verses in that poem. Moreover, in contrast to Yuan Zhen's indiscriminate condemnation of the Hu, Bai appears to have been selective when criticizing the Tibetans.[93] His possible motivation will become clear in my discussion of the poem "Xiliang ji."

By comparison, "Huxuan nü" (Hu whirling girls) is Bai's only poem in the group in which the character *hu* appears frequently. But it does so always as part of the proper name *Huxuan* (Hu whirling dance). This is a poem that also shows some of the most striking contrasts between Yuan and Bai. Following are excerpts from their respective poems bearing the same title:

Excerpts of "The *Hu* whirling girls"
(Yuan Zhen's version)
> With the Tianbao (Heavenly Jewel) era (742–55) drawing to a close,
>   the Hu were ready to rebel.
> [Hence] the Hu presented to the throne the Hu whirling girls.
> The girls whirled and whirled 'til the wise Monarch was infatuated
> And the demon Hu came right to the [inner] Palace of Long Life.[94]

. . . .

Let me tell those whirling with their eyes and their hearts:
You ought to be condemned by all who cherish family and the land.

(Bai Juyi's version)

. . . .

With the Tianbao era drawing to a close, the time was ready to
    change:
Every man and woman at court started whirling.
Lady Taizhen (Emperor Xuanzong's favourite consort) in the
    Palace, and General Lushan of the provinces
Were said to be the best at the Hu Whirling Dance.

. . . .

Oh, Hu whirling girls, do not just dance in vain:
Pray repeat this song of mine to awaken the wise Monarch.[95]

Bai's avoidance of the term "Hu" in any pejorative sense could not be more obvious. What is more, in Yuan's original, the *Huxuan* dance was said to have started as something of a Hu conspiracy in preparation for rebellion, with derogatory accusations like "the demon Hu came right to the Palace of Long Life." Bai was more objective and candid, pointing out the dance's existence long before that time.[96] Whereas Yuan concluded his poem by calling for universal condemnation of the dance, Bai in the end asked instead the *Huxuan* girls to "awaken the wise Monarch." Such a sharp contrast between the two authors in handling the same subject is unmistakable.

However, something even more revelatory of Bai's psyche may be found in the poem "Xiliang ji" (Dancers from West Liang), again a title both Yuan Zhen and Bai used. First I note that, though Bai tried to distance himself from the incessant clique struggles current at the Tang court, his sympathy for the Niu Sengru faction is well substantiated. Despite their often sharp differences on many major issues, two noted authorities on Tang political history, namely Chen Yinke and Cen Zhongmian, both concluded that the Li Deyu and Niu cliques also represented, respectively, the hawks and doves regarding Tang military policy.[97] Bai Juyi's renowned lifelong adherence to pacifism, as reflected in his many poems, court memorials, and essays, would then be further strengthened by his inclination toward the Niu clique. Given this political context, Bai's social jeremiad "Xiliang ji" (Dancers from West Liang) constitutes a rare and extraordinary deviation from his pacifist conviction. For it was an overt critique of, not the Tang's militarism, but the lack of it.[98]

First the title. It implied the "blue-bearded, deep-eyed" Hu dancers from the West whose identity Bai elaborated but Yuan ignored. Here I call attention to the first half of the ballad that depicted two youthful Hu dancers emotionally lamenting the loss of Liangzhou and, more importantly and symbolically as I shall demonstrate, the severance of their homebound path. This is a theme completely absent in Yuan's poem. Its significance seems to have been ignored by most commentators, who always regard it as mere preparation for the second half.[99] Ren Bantang appears to be the only scholar to have expressed wonderment at this sharp contrast between the two close friends' handling of the same subject at about the same time.[100] But his attempt to ascribe it to a time lag, arguing that Yuan was describing a pre–An Lushan Rebellion performance whereas Bai was writing about its contemporary form, sounds singularly farfetched.

In my view, the contrast between Yuan's concision and Bai's elaboration reflects a fundamental difference in attitude toward the dance and its circumstances. First, from *Sui shu* (15.378), the dance had its musical root in Kucha, which also happened to be the ancestral land for the Bai clan. But the truly telling point was conveyed via the impassioned words of the two Hu dancers. The issue that prompted Bai's unusual call for military action—the Anxi Path, the traditional Silk Road—had been made too perilous for Central Asians to make periodic or permanent return trips to their homeland. One may further note that Kucha, the *Urheimat* of most Bai families in China, was the seat of the vital Anxi Protectorate from the year 658 on.[101] This is the crucial issue that set Bai Juyi, the son of Central Asia, apart from Yuan Zhen, the descendant of the Tuoba from the Steppe.

The Tibetans' lethal stranglehold on the traditional Silk Road, which linked the two Tang capitals to the Western Regions, is too major a political and economical development to be discussed in detail here. One of its immediate consequences was that it had cut off many ethnic Hu individuals' return route to their homeland (*ZZTJ* 232.7492–93). However, most such stranded guests seemed to be not very heartbroken over this situation. When given a chance of repatriation via the Uighur territory, the vast majority of them opted to settle in the Chinese heartland for good (*ZZTJ* 232.7493).[102] Indeed, here I note a near contemporary Tang poem "Huteng'er" (Hu hop-dancer) by Li Duan[103] with an almost identical story line: the performance of Hu dancers from Liangzhou moved some officials who were previously stationed in Anxi to tears. But the key difference is this: the poet was bemused in the end by the Hu dancers' apparent indifference to their loss of a functional homebound route.

In this context, such strong feelings and the appeal of the Central Asian homeland expressed through the words of the Hu youths in Bai's poem can hardly be ignored. Poets expressing what they would like to say through the *personae dra-matis* in their works has been a time-honored tradition in China. In fact, both Bai and Yuan implied it in their respective introductions to the new genre of poetry, *xinyuefu*, "new folk-song." One may then conclude that the words of the two young Hu dancers represented also atavistic regression and yearning for one's *Urheimat* in the subconscious of a poet whose clan could still recall vividly that they be-longed to the "Sixth of the Ten Hu clans," and proudly paraded the Hu general Bai Xiaode from Anxi, who had died barely decades ago, as one of their clansmen. The physical severance of the political and cultural bond to the land of his fore-fathers was the last straw that shattered our Buddhist poet's pacifism.

Linguistic Observations

In Chapter 3, I advanced the notion that the modern Chinese kinship term *ge* for "elder brother" was an Altaic loan with Turkic connections. I also pointed out that kinship terms often proved to be the longest-surviving reminder of a given individual's nonnative heritage. I then noted that Bai Juyi left what seemed to be the first authentic record of a writer using it for this purpose, and in a most for-mal genre of classical writing—an elegy for his deceased elder brother—giving one more indication of his non-Sinitic heritage. As it happened, all other early usages were by the Tang imperial clan members, and most other early records of using the term for elder brother were of third-party or anecdotal nature, whereas Bai Juyi had carefully compiled and edited his own collected works during his lifetime, which included the said elegy.

This foreign-origin kinship term, *ge*, in my view, can also lend some tangible support for the alleged authorship of the erotic tale "Dale fu" (Rhapsody of great pleasure) mentioned earlier:[104] the vocative *gege* has a prominent appearance in this otherwise "classic" piece, as noted by one of its first modern annotators, Ye Dehui.[105] It should be noted that other than the Bai brothers and the Tang imperial family members, the vocative *ge* was very rarely used in formal Tang literary writings.

Earlier in this chapter I suggested, based on recent archeological finds, that Bai Juyi was likely literate in Sanskrit, and such knowledge was related to his Central Asian heritage. One notes that Sanskrit learning was once highly devel-oped in Kucha, a bastion of Buddhism in early medieval times. In fact, one of the pioneer translators of Buddhist sutras into Chinese language, Kumarajiva, was of mixed Indian-Kuchaean parentage.

I present two additional linguistic cases to substantiate Bai Juyi's Central Asian link, which may have some intriguing implications on the history of the cultural exchanges between Tang China and the rest of the world. During his tenure as prefect of Suzhou, Bai wrote a poem bidding farewell to several "sing-song girls" (*BJ* 24.551). In the poem he used the word *bahan*, which was rarely if ever employed by other noted Tang poets. Fortunately, the term was found in an old dictionary and interpreted as "a [large] foreign horse."[106] Despite the "horse" radical, the word does not have any plausible Chinese etymology, and I fail to find in numerous Bai anthologies any elaboration of the term beyond the standard *Yupian* (*Jade Chapters*—an old Chinese dictionary) entry.

In light of Bai's non-Sinitic heritage, *bahan* is undoubtedly a foreign, likely Central Asian, word. However, a rather extensive search in various Indo-Iranian and Altaic languages[107] also leads me to conclude that the term does not have a transparent equestrian origin. Rather, its etymology is like that of the English words "Arab" and "Labrador": it refers to the geographic origin of the breed concerned.

In all likelihood, the word *bahan* stands for the Central Asian state Ferghana, generally identified as Dayuan of Hàn times,[108] famed for its "blood-sweating horse."[109] Indeed, even Bai's contemporaries were very well informed about Ferghana's famous export. Zhang Zhuo (ca. 660–ca. 741), in his *Chaoye qianzai* (*Popular Records of the Court and Commonalty*, 5.120), recorded a rather tortuous story about one such "thousand-mile horse" reportedly sent as tribute by the Central Asian state to Sui China.[110] The most direct evidence for this identification of Bai's word is several transcriptions of Ferghana of the Sui-Tang era: Pohan, Bahanna, Peihan, and so on.[111]

Once *bahan* has been identified with Ferghana, this famed breed of horse, by its more sinicized name *Dayuan ma*, "Dayuan horse," was certainly not such a rare and remote subject. Besides the *Chaoye qianzai* story, another famous poet, Gao Shi (ca. 702–65), described the breed's frequent military use on the Tang frontier (*Quan Tangshi* 213.501). Yet in Bai's poetry, which was widely noted for its "easy comprehensibility," a singularly uncommon appellation was employed instead. This, together with the theory that Dayuan was a transcription of *Tokhar(o)*,[112] the famous ancient Indo-European people who were also said to have populated Kucha,[113] would seem rather illuminating on the issue of Bai's ancestral land as well as its lingering spell on our poet.

A more intriguing case is found in Bai's "Yinshan dao" (Mount Yin route), one of his *xinyuefu* or "new folk-song" poems on the Uighurs' "trading" their horses for China silk. It was composed in 809, the year that he also drafted a letter on behalf of Emperor Xianzong (reign 806–20) on this issue.[114] Bai Juyi opened his social jeremiad as follows: "Mount Yin Route, O Mount Yin Route / [Where] *geluo* is thick and luxuriant, and springs plentiful." The word *geluo* is utterly meaningless in Chinese. It is obviously a foreign word.[115] To the best of my knowledge, Chen Yinke seems to have been the only author to make a serious attempt at interpreting the word.[116] He first concluded, quite rightly, that by context and internal analogy the word can only mean "grass." Since the poem was about the Uighurs, Chen apparently deduced that the word must be Turkic. Either misled by this unproven "Turkic" assumption or due to a misreading of Classical Chinese, he then suggested that *geluo* be read *kara* and that the next character *dun*, "deep, thick," should also be Turkic. He thus strained to break up a perfectly good construct, *dunfei*, "thick and luxuriant," and rendered a very poor reading of the verse, something a great poet noted for his rigor and elegance could hardly have countenanced, even if the Turkic equation would hold true. Moreover, Chen's Turkic construction *kara tuna* is neither natural nor attested, the problem with the rest of the verse notwithstanding. All things considered, a "Turkic solution" does seem a formidable task in this case.[117] Given the Bai clan's ancestry, I submit in general that an answer to this puzzle must be found in Central Asia and beyond.

This leads to various ancient Indo-Iranian and Tokharian tongues for a possible origin of the elusive word *geluo*, apparently meaning "pasture or grass grazed by horses." I list several such possibilities below, all of which seem to have some technical difficulties.

1. Pahlavi and Parthian words *car, carag*, "pasture, graze."[118] But the *c-* initial is difficult to reconcile with the Chinese transcription.
2. The root *xwr-*, "to eat," "food," attested in all ancient Iranian idioms.[119] While the root no doubt could mean "animal feed," I have yet to find a single attestation in ancient texts of this root referring to "pasture," or in the context of "water and grass" as in Bai's case.[120]
3. The word *'alaf*, "grass, pasture," widely attested in medieval Iranian literature, especially in the context of "water and grass."[121] Unfortunately, the Iranian word represents a typical post–Arab Conquest loan, thus leading to major chronological difficulties unless used in the context of direct Arab contact.
4. These difficulties compel me to look beyond the Indo-European family, with the following two admittedly rather speculative correspondences from the Semitic languages.

5. The well-attested Arabic word *kala'* or *kalā'*, with plural form *aklā'*, "grass, pasture, or what cattle etc. feed upon."[122] It was used by Tamin ibn Bahr[123] to describe the availability of springs and pasture on the Steppes. It appeared in a report written after Tamin paid a visit to the very Uighur court to which Bai Juyi addressed his official letter of 809 in the name of Emperor Xianzong on the matter about the horse-silk exchanges. Tamin described the silk trade with remarkable accuracy, even giving the figure 500,000 as the number of pieces of silk the Uighurs would receive annually from the Tang court. This was, of course, exactly the number given by Bai Juyi in the official letter on how much the Tang owed the Uighurs for their horses, although Bai added that the Tang court could repay only half of that number due to domestic strife.[124] The principal difficulty with this solution is that the term *kala'*, though found in Farsi as a result of the massive Arabic invasion of that language during Iran's Islamization, was not a native Iranic word. Nor was it Indic. Therefore, this proposed equation does present implications on or problems about the progress of Arab influence in Central Asia and on China's frontiers. For one thing, though Arab military influence had long been felt in the area,[125] at the time much of Central Asia as well as the Uighur domain was not Islamic, at least not yet. There was also a telling incident in 758 that showed the lack of mutual respect, to say the least, between the Abbasid Arabs and the Uighurs.[126] Even in the territories under direct Arab rule, namely Iran and Transoxania, feelings of religious and cultural hostility against the Arab conquerors ran deep.[127]

6. If one allows another channel of the Arab influence, namely that via the Radhanite Jewish merchants, perhaps the forerunners of those who founded the Jewish community in Kaifeng,[128] then the Biblical Hebrew term *kar*, appearing in Psalm 65:13 and Isaiah 30:23, may provide another potential match for *geluo*. This word may not have the same etymological origin as the Arabic word *kala'*,[129] but it means "fat pasture,"[130] exactly what Bai Juyi intended by the word *geluo*. The antiquity of the Hebrew word is attested by its Akkadian and Ugaritic cognates.[131] This solution, however, may further depend on the historical controversy about a suspected Uighur origin of the Khazars.[132] The date of the Khazars' conversion to Judaism is usually given as "in the middle of the eighth century," or more precisely circa 740.[133] The appearance of a Hebrew term in an "Uighur affair" would seem only natural if there were continued interchanges between the Jewish Khazars and their alleged Uighur brethren, as hypothesized by Róna-Tas.[134]

Granted, all above possible foreign origins of the word *geluo* are at present speculations, not proven facts. There are other potential issues that might result from Bai Juyi's use of Central Asian origin words.[135] But one simple fact stands out: the foreign-origin words were found in the works of a poet best known in folklore for his insistence that his poetry be easily understood by the common folk. To the best of my knowledge, the two rare words examined here were not taken up by any of Bai's fellow literati. Given the enormous volume of Tang poetry, it is very hard to attribute Bai's such individuality to pure coincidence, having nothing to do with the clan's non-Sinitic ancestry. It is also worth noting that both words, namely "horse" and "grass," were of the most critical importance on the Steppe, as pointed out by Denis Sinor.[136] Together with the Altaic kinship term *ge*, in Bai Juyi they would seem to fit the pattern that many Central Asians came to China via serving a Steppe or semi-Steppe power, from the Tuoba regime and its heirs, to the Mongol Empire.

Bai's Legacy

Finally, I discuss briefly the profound and widespread popularity Bai's poetry enjoyed among the people of his time (even before his death), both within and outside of the Chinese heartland. Bai's popularity among contemporaries in Korea and Japan has been well known and well studied. But similar phenomena in Central Asia have long been obscured and ignored, probably as a result of the interruption of Chinese political control of the area after the Tang era.[137] Judging from Yuan Zhen's remarkable story about a Korean chancellor purchasing Bai's poems at a high premium (*BJ*, Yuan's foreword.), Bai must have taken pride in the spread of his fame to these "uncivilized" lands, a feeling seemingly also echoed in his admiration of the deeds of his two great poetic predecessors, Li Bai and Du Fu (*BJ* 15.331): "Their poems will be read for thousands of years, / And their fame strike all four uncivilized corners."[138]

A natural question then poses itself: Did Bai Juyi consciously strive for such renown not just within the Central Kingdom but also beyond the confines of the Sinitic heartland? While acknowledging that a definite answer to this question appears elusive given the available data, I contend that the issue may be intimately related to Bai Juyi's celebrated insistence on the use of simple and easily understandable language for his poetry.[139] I feel rather confident in submitting that, at least on this second issue of writing style, Central Asian and/or Buddhist influence cannot be dismissed out of hand.

Victor Mair has convincingly demonstrated that the appearance of written vernacular, in not just China but also other East Asian states, had its roots in Buddhism.[140] In particular, it may have been prompted by the strong missionary zeal of Buddhism and the desire to rapidly spread its doctrine and ideology among the populace. While Mair seems to have stressed only the role of Buddhism, I point out that some of the Chinese Nestorian texts are also composed in a colloquial style,[141] suggesting a somewhat broader picture than Mair has proposed.

In this connection, Bai Juyi's unique, legendary *su*, "vulgar," writing style, commented on by many noted men of letters including Su Shi (1036–1101),[142] would hardly seem a mere coincidence, completely unrelated to his Central Asian heritage or to his Buddhist background.[143] Just like the vernacular Buddhist writings, Bai's poetry in plain style and simple language soon penetrated all social strata, especially the lower classes, and even to the lands beyond the Tang border. It is worth noting that Juyi's younger brother Xingjian happened to be among a few pioneering authors of a new genre of narrative love stories "based on an oral tradition."[144]

One may also wonder what had really contributed to the sharp contrast between Bai and another great man of letters, Hán Yu, and the striking lack of close relation and interaction between the two,[145] despite their being contemporaries and even colleagues at the court, as well as both being leading literary figures of the era.[146] As mentioned earlier, this becomes even more puzzling given Bai's claim that he had a great-grandmother from the same Hán clan as Hán Yu, in an era noted for valuing clan relationships.[147] The prevailing interpretation for this distinction appears to be based on their differences in personality and philosophy.[148] Charles Hartman is among the few who have attempted a political explanation.[149] But his speculation that it might have been caused by enmity involving the Wang Shuwen clique can hardly stand scrutiny in view of Hán's celebrated friendship with Liu Zongyuan, who had never shown remorse for his membership in that clique. Nor could it be explained by Hán's famous antagonism to Buddhism, which Bai patronized, for Hán had quite willingly overlooked his personal feeling to socialize with some monks at Liu Zongyuan's request.

Hán Yu, however, was generally regarded as a banner holder for Confucian orthodoxy, a fierce defender of Chinese tradition against all foreign intrusions. I submit that Hán's strong sinocentric stance was likely the real cause for his lack of enthusiasm toward another great man of letters who was still very much attached to the Hu heritage.

Regarding the possible motivation for Bai's unique writing style, besides reaching out to the "sing-song girls and cowboys" in China, was Bai also anxious that his forefathers' compatriots be able to read and enjoy his works? An answer may well lie in the foreign-origin words found in his works examined earlier and in the following verse in a poetic elegy generally attributed to Emperor Xuānzong (reign 847–60) in honor of the passing of a great poet whose influence transcended political and cultural boundaries (*Quan Tangshi* 5.31): "Even Hu lads ably sing [Bai's] 'Ballad of the Lute.'"

Appendix

Turkic or Proto-Mongolian?
A Note on the Tuoba Language

As discussed in various chapters of this book, the Tuoba, or Tabγach, as they are recorded in the Orkhon inscriptions, played a critical role in the history of China, not only for founding the Northern (or Late) Wei dynasty (386–534), but also and perhaps more importantly for having created two heirs, both political and biological, the Sui (581–618) and the Tang (618–907). The linguistic affinity of this important group, however, has remained to this day an enigma. As Denis Sinor summarizes the situation in his *Introduction à l'étude de l'Eurasie centrale*, most scholars agree that the Tuoba language belonged to the Altaic family.[1] But controversy and contention arise with the simple question: Were the Tuoba Turkic or proto-Mongolian?

There are prominent names among the proponents of either of the two rival claims. For proponents of the Turkic theory, one can cite Paul Pelliot, Peter Boodberg, and Sir Gerard Clauson,[2] among others. Wolfram Eberhard in his *Das Toba-Reich Nordchinas* was also of the opinion that the Tuoba had a Turkic majority among its members.[3] The more recent opinion of Hakan Aydemir that the ruling stratum of the Tuoba spoke "Bulgharic" is essentially the same as that of Clauson.[4] The list of proponents of the opposite, proto-Mongolian theory includes Louis Ligeti ("Le tabgatch, un dialecte de la langue sien-pi") and Karl Menges (*The Turkic Languages and Peoples*, p. 17). Perhaps encouraged by the archaeological discovery in 1980 in the Xing'an Mountains of a cavern once occupied by the Tuoba's ancestors, the Mongolian theory seems lately to have been gaining momentum.[5]

The primary reason for this controversy is the scarcity of relevant linguistic data. The secondary reasons are twofold. First, there is evidence for both Turkic and proto-Mongolian elements in the Tuoba federation, as can be expected of most Steppe empires. The other factor is that the Tuoba is usually regarded as having formed part of the Xianbei complex or conglomerate, which was generally considered, with good evidence, to be largely proto-Mongolian.[6] Ligeti's quoted study, for instance, suffers from a failure to carefully differentiate the Tuoba data from that of the Xianbei in general.[7]

Given time and luck, some future archeological breakthrough, or another chance find like the Dunhuang hoard stumbled upon in the early twentieth century, may finally solve this mystery. But before this takes place, if it ever does, one may still uncover new linguistic evidence pertinent to this issue by adopting a novel and perhaps unconventional perspective from which to examine the known historical data. This study is a tentative step in this direction.

The Tuoba's Sinification Drive

In the last decade of the fifth century, the Tuoba emperor Xiaowen (Yuan Hong; reign 471–99) launched his famous sinification drive, moved his court from Pingcheng in the north to the old Chinese capital of Luoyang, and formally proscribed the Xianbei language, customs, clothing, and names. This move was no doubt driven by the young emperor's ambition to put a final end to the north-south division of China.[8] What this appendix discusses is the conversion of almost all "Barbarian" family (i.e., tribe) names, including the very royal clan name Tuoba, to Chinese or Chinese-sounding surnames.

One should first mention the strong "nationalistic" resistance to this wholesale abandonment of the Tuoba's cultural heritage, something that Emperor Xiaowen was fully aware of and indeed anticipated. As discussed earlier in this book, the opposition proved so strong that even Emperor Xiaowen's eldest son and heir-designate, Yuan Xun, became entangled in the resistance movement that eventually cost the young crown prince his life. It was also amply attested in a "Xianbei revival movement" after the collapse of the Northern Wei, in the wake of the Six-Garrison Rebellion started by frontier garrisons disillusioned with the sinified Tuoba court in Luoyang. All these reactions indicate that Emperor Xiaowen must have proceeded discreetly and skillfully to alleviate the resentment and opposition of his tribal comrades apparently still very much attached to their Steppe heritage. His careful and tactful approach is evidenced by the provisions and exceptions the emperor had granted to the "older folks,"[9] as well as the so-called wild-goose courtiers (*yanchen* in Chinese) who migrated between the Tuoba's new capital and their tribes like wild geese (*Wei shu* [*History of the Wei*] 15.378 and *ZZTJ* 141.4410).

It is therefore natural to deduce that the same discretion and care had been taken in replacing the "Barbarian" tribe names with "Chinese" family names, in order not to exacerbate the hostility felt by the name bearers. In fact, a royal commission was formed by an imperial edict in 495 to deliberate this matter (*Wei shu* 113.3014–15) before the announcement of the name-change decree in the spring of 496 (*ZZTJ* 140.4393). All four named members of the royal commission were Tuoba Xianbei nobles. In other words, the name change must have accorded adequate respect to fellow tribespeople's ethnic pride and culture, as shown by some literal translations of the Altaic names into Chinese (see below).

Let us make a short digression to the history of the Tuoba's tribal followings. *Wei shu* (1.1) narrated that, dating back to a semilegendary *qaghan* Mao, fortuitously a namesake of the twentieth-century Great Helmsman, the Tuoba started with thirty-six "states" containing ninety-nine "big tribes" (*daxing* in Chinese) that apparently formed the core of the Tuoba polity. By the time Wei Shou (506–72) compiled *Wei shu*, he could no longer provide a full account of all these clans. Nonetheless he listed all those he could still identify who had followed another partly legendary Tuoba *qaghan* named Liwei, allegedly born to a goddess, and "migrated inward" (*neiru*, read southwestward) in the third century to the southern part of the Mongolian Plateau and rose as a major military and political power soon afterward. In Chapter 113 of *Wei shu*, these and the Tuoba royal clans were clearly differentiated from the so-called four-corner (*sifang* in Chinese) tribes conquered or otherwise subjugated by the Tuoba, which resulted in two distinct groups of clan names.[10] The clear division of Tuoba subjects into "inner" and "outer" tribes is so typical of nomadic rule that Wolfram Eberhard has termed it the "Turkish type of organization."[11] This division will serve as a key to this study.

Change of Tribe and Clan Names

As listed in Chapter 113 of *Wei shu*, with the exception of those names that remained unchanged and a handful of unclear cases, there are three main patterns or categories in replacing a "Barbarian" clan name with a Chinese one.

1. Literary translation of an Altaic word into Chinese. Examples are Chinu to Lang "wolf", Youlian to Yun "cloud",[12] and Ruogan to Gou, a euphemistic homonym of *gou* "dog" as examined in Chapter 3. The change of the royal name Tuoba to Yuan presumably also belongs to the same category, though a satisfactory etymology has yet to be identified.

2. Linking of a steppe clan name to a common Chinese surname based on some politico-cultural traditions that may no longer seem clear today.[13]
3. A great majority, or 93 out of the 121 names listed, represents a shortening of an original two- or three-character "Barbarian" name to a single character that is either one of the original characters or its phonetic variant or derivative.

The third category is what I will examine for the remainder of this discussion. This category clearly represents a multisyllabic clan name being shortened to a single character representing or deriving from one of the original sound elements. This original sound element in most cases should represent a full syllable. The reasons for the last claim are (1) due respect for the original name as previously argued, (2) the single character likely representing what the name changers believed should be articulated, (3) the well-known aversion to consonant clusters of the Altaic family,[14] and (4) only a small minority, or seventeen, of the new names being of the "entering tone (*rusheng*)," which according to Edwin Pulleyblank may be more likely than other characters to represent just a foreign consonant in a Chinese transliteration.[15]

Another issue is whether the original two- and three-character names may already represent an "abridged" form. The large corpus of Old Turkic (including Uighur), Sogdian, Tibetan, and other non-Chinese records attest to the popularity of two-syllable, followed by single- and three-syllable, proper names, which together represented the absolute majority of tribal and clan designations on the Steppe. There are also many names in Chinese transcription, including the first category above, that have been successfully identified with their foreign originals. These facts plus the dominance and ethnic pride of the Xianbei in the upper echelons of the Tuoba hierarchy prior to the sinification reform lead me to submit that a great majority of the Tuoba names recorded in chapter 113 of *Wei shu* (with the extensive editorial corrections by later scholars based on other sources) represent a largely faithful and full transcription of the original form.

I have long noted that among the core Tuoba clans, there appears a strong preference for category 3 name changes to derive the single-character Chinese name from the final character of the original name, whereas, among the "four-corner" tribes, it seems to be the exact opposite, namely a propensity to use the first character or its phonetic variant as the Chinese name. Prompted by some readings regarding accentuation in Altaic linguistics, I decided to examine this interesting contrast in detail. Table A.1 summarizes the ninety-three category 3 names in this regard.

In order to combine the evidence from two- and three-character names without resorting to complex probabilistic modeling, and also because the medial character

Table A.1. Single-Character Constructs of New Clan Names
(*Wei shu*, chapter 113)

Original Character Position		*First*	*Medial*	*Final*
Core clans	2-character names	17	—	28
	3-character names	5	7	8
"Four-corner"	2-character names	12	—	4
	3-character names	4	2	5

Table A.2. Single-Character Constructs of New Clan
Names: First-Character Derivation versus
Final-Character Derivation

Original Character Position	*First*	*Final*	*Subtotal*
Core clans	22	36	58
	(37.9%)	(62.1%)	(100%)
"Four-corner"	16	9	25
	(64.0%)	(36.0%)	(100%)

is of no interest to this discussion, I further restrict the analysis to a subset of cases for which the name transformation is based on either the first or final character,[16] and thus obtain our second table.

The striking difference between the core Tuoba clans and the "four-corner" tribes now becomes apparent, as the relative percentages of using the first and the final character are almost in a perfect opposing pattern between the two groups.

However, one may also argue that all these numbers could be attributed to coincidence, and the name transformation might well have been conducted in an arbitrary and haphazard fashion. If we indeed go to this rather extreme end and assume that our data had occurred simply by chance, and all data were in fact largely random to start with, we can formulate three hypotheses in accordance with classical hypothesis-testing theory in statistics:

Hypothesis A: There was no actual difference between the core clans
and "four-corner" tribes in the likelihood of using either the first or
the final character for the new Chinese name.

Hypothesis B: Among the core clans, the likelihood of deriving the new
name from the first or the final character was the same.

Hypothesis C: Among the "four-corner" tribes, the likelihood of deriving the new name from the first or the final character was the same.

We can then apply standard statistical methods and calculate the so-called
observed significance level, also known as p-value, under each hypothesis,
which is in essence the probability of the actual data happening purely by
chance under the respective hypothesis. They turn out to be the following:[17]

1. For Hypothesis A, $p = 0.034$ based on Fisher's Exact Test, and $p = 0.029$
   based on the Chi-square test.
2. For Hypothesis B, $p = 0.044$ based on exact binomial distribution.
3. For Hypothesis C, $p = 0.115$ based on exact binomial distribution.

Therefore, at the conventional critical significance level (α-value) of 0.05, both
Hypotheses A and B are rejected for being too unlikely to be true. The p-value
for Hypothesis C is not as small, even though the first-versus-last-character "im-
balance" is more severe than that for the core clans. This is largely due to the
insufficient number of cases, but the p-value is nonetheless "marginally significant" as well.

Naturally, this kind of probabilistic analysis requires a few mathematical
assumptions that may or may not hold rigorously true in reality. There may also
be other factors at work in the name-change process. Nevertheless, the above
statistical analysis does provide a quantitative assessment of the strength of the
collective evidence reflected in Tuoba name-change data. It also demonstrates
that the likelihood the observed patterns could have happened purely as random
phenomena is very small.

I may also mention that the use of statistical analysis in historical linguistics is
nothing new. As Denis Sinor cited in his *Introduction à l'étude de l'Eurasie centrale*, more than half a century ago, Björn Collinder already used probability calculation to demonstrate that concordances between the Altaic and Uralic languages
cannot be attributed to chance.[18] There have been many other probabilistic and
statistical models employed for the purpose of linguistic analysis, most much more
complex than mine, and there is even a full text devoted to this subject.[19]

All in all, albeit perhaps still far from being beyond any doubt, given the earlier observation that the character chosen for deriving the Chinese surname very
likely represents a syllable in the original name, the evidence uncovered by my
analysis does suggest the following: the core Tuoba clans were more likely to ar-
ticulate the final syllable of their name than the first, whereas the "four-corner"

tribes within the Tuoba federation tended to stress the first syllable of their name rather than the last. One may naturally infer that this pattern of articulation or stress can be extended to other words in their respective languages.

Accentuation in Altaic Languages

It has been theorized that, due to its agglutinative nature and sound harmony, the proto-Altaic language, if there ever existed such an entity, had prima accentuation, in that the root syllable always retained the stress.[20] The same is also claimed of the proto-Uralic and proto-Finno-Ugric languages, as is still maintained by major members of the Uralic family: Finnic, Hungarian, Yenisei, and so on.[21]

According to Karl Menges, Mongolian languages to this day have retained prima accentuation. This is supported by Gombojab Hangin, a native speaker who claims that "[the stress in Mongolian] automatically falls on the first syllable."[22] James Bosson also states, "Stress in Mongolian is expiratory and falls on the first syllable, whether its vowel is short or long."[23] Nonetheless, other experts mention a tendency in Modern Mongolian to shift the stress to noninitial long vowels and diphthongs.[24] However, regular long vowels and diphthongs in Mongolian languages developed from earlier multisyllabic constructs and only appeared in Modern Mongolian, which began in the sixteenth century.[25] Our period of concern belongs to what Nicholas Poppe has termed Ancient Mongolian, which ended around the twelfth century and "was almost identical with Common Mongolian."[26] Therefore, for that period it is safe to concur, at the very least, with Isaac Schmidt who conducted what has been called "the beginning of linguistic work on Mongolian on a high level."[27] In a grammar published some 180 years ago on Written Mongolian, which, in the words of Nicholas Poppe, "reflects the Ancient Mongolian well from the point of view of its phonetic and morphologic development," Isaac Jacob Schmidt stated unmistakably, "Bei weitem die meisten zwei- und dreisylbigen Mongolischen Wörter haben den Accent auf der *ersten* Sylbe (By far most two- and three-syllable Mongolian words have the accent on the *first* syllable) (italics in original)."[28]

Turkic languages, conversely, are a different matter. In fact, the Turkic group has supposedly undergone the historical process of developing an originally secondary accent on the last syllable, such that it today has an ultima accentuation "slightly reminiscent of French," with a few exceptions easily explained by their nonsuffixal, enclitic nature.[29] The question is when this process was completed.

The presence of alliteration in some Turkic folk poetry has led to the speculation that prima accentuation might have survived down to historical times.[30] But no hard evidence exists. On the contrary, there are solid data indicating the opposite:

1. The phonetic data of the Orkhon inscriptions, the earliest existent Turkic texts, has led Telat Tekin to infer that in Orkhon Turkic in general the accent fell upon the last syllable.[31]

2. Several Uralic languages' accentuation of the final syllable has been attributed to the influence of neighboring Turkic idioms, attesting to the long history of the ultima accentuation of Turkic.[32]

3. As Otto Böhtlingk stated in his famous 1851 grammar, Yakut, a Turkic tongue that has been separated from all other Turkic languages for many centuries,[33] and has been under strong influence from the prima-accentual Mongolian,[34] has nevertheless had the stress on the final syllable.[35]

4. Chuvash, the only surviving member of the so-called *l/r*-Turkic, also has ultima accentuation.[36] Many scholars contend that Chuvash should be separated from Turkic, with a "Pre-Turkic" or proto-Turco-Chuvash as their common ancestor.[37] At the very least, the presumed Chuvash-Turkic unity ended long before the Tuoba era.[38] Incidentally, Gerard Clauson, a major proponent for the Turkic affinity of the Tuoba, classifies the Tuoba idiom as an *l/r* language,[39] belonging to the Chuvash subfamily.

To summarize, in addition to the celebrated temporal and spatial stability of Turkic in recorded history, it seems safe and justified to contend that for the historical era under study, namely the Tuoba Wei period, Turkic languages were already largely ultima-accentual, in sharp contrast to the contemporary proto-Mongolian.

Conclusion

The conclusion follows naturally from the combination of the Tuoba name-change data and the opposite accentuation rules of the Turkic and (proto-) Mongolian languages. However, before drawing the conclusion, we also have to face the fact that no nomadic or nomadic-origin power was ever ethically or linguistically homogeneous. Even the ruling core of a steppe polity may not always be "pure-blood." For example, the "imperial maternal uncles," namely the Xiao clan of the proto-Mongolian Qidan/Kitan regime, were believed by many to have been Turkic.[40] Nevertheless, given the new evidence uncovered from the Tuoba's onomastic data, and the diametrically opposite accentuation rules in Turkic and Mongolian languages, the core Tuoba clans now would seem more likely to have spoken a Turkic (or an ultima-accentual) language or to have contained stronger Turkic elements than the "four-corner" tribes. The latter represented more or less other Xianbei groups within the Tuoba federation and may have included more proto-Mongolian constituents than Turkic ones. This conclusion is not entirely new, if we believe, inter alia, the eleventh-century claim by al-Kāšγarī that the name Tawγāč came from a group of Turks who had settled in China.[41]

Naturally, one may choose not to accept my interpretation of the Tuoba name-change data. The question then is to find an alternative and more probable explanation for the striking contrast between the core Tuoba and the "four-cor-ner" clans vis-à-vis the name-change patterns, a daunting task in my view. Quoting almost verbatim from David Keightley, "I make no apologies for the 'probable'; we are dealing with the probabilities that sound historiographical practice requires us to assess."[42]

Notes

Introduction

1. The discovery was originally reported in *Wenwu* in 1981 by Mi Wenping, one of the three discoverers. Later Mr. Mi also published recollections of his persistent efforts to find the cave and his eventual success. See Mi, "Xianbei shishi de faxian" (The discovery of the Xianbei rock chamber), and "Qiangu zhi mi Da Xianbei shan" (The Great Xianbei Mountain: A millennium-old enigma).

2. *ZZTJ* 108.3429. Translation of this passage is by Dr. Chung-mo Kwok, via personal communication.

Chapter 1

This chapter is an expanded version of the author's 1996 essay on the ethnic identity of the Tang imperial house, published in the *Journal of the Royal Asiatic Society,* ser. 3, 6: 379–405.

1. The story is largely based on a detailed biography of Falin written by the Tang dynasty Buddhist monk Yanzong, The Taishō Tripitaka (*Taishō shinshū daizōkyō*; abbreviated throughout this book as *Taishō*), no. 2051, 198b–213b.

2. No definite date was given by Falin's biography except that it was between January 13 and 18, 640.

3. Literally *baonü*, translating Sanskrit *Kanyā-ratna*, "precious maiden(s)," one of the seven treasures of the *Cakravertin*. See Soothill and Hodous, *Dictionary of Chinese Buddhist Terms*, p. 477.

4. Ningxia Zizhiqu Bowuguan , "Ningxia Guyuan Bei-Zhou Li Xian fufu mu fajue jianbao" (A brief report on the excavation of the Northern Zhou tombs of Li Xian and his wife at Gu yuan in Ningxia). This implication of Li Xian's recently unearthed tomb inscription on the ethnic origin of the Tang imperial family was pointed out to me by Dr. Chungmo Kwok via private communication.

5. They are "Li-Tang shizu zhi tuice," "Li-Tang shizu zhi tuice houji," "San lun Li-Tang shizu wenti," and "Li-Tang Wu-Zhou xianshi shiji zakao." All can be found in his collected works *Chen Yinke xiansheng lunwenji.*

6. Liu P., "Li-Tang wei fanxing kao" (Evidence that the imperial Li house of the Tang was of foreign origin).

7. Hu R., *Li Shimin zhuan* (*A Biography of Li Shimin*).

8. Honey, "Stripping off felt and fur: An essay on nomadic signification."

9. Morgan, *Medieval Persia, 1040–1797*, p. 22.

10. Franke, *From Tribal Chieftain to Universal Emperor and God: The Legitimation of the Yüan Dynasty*, p. 60.

11. Bosworth, *Ghaznavids*, p. 3.

12. Crossley, "Thinking about ethnicity in early modern China."

13. Pulleyblank, "Chinese and their neighbors in prehistoric and early historic times"; and Golden, *Introduction to the History of the Turkic Peoples,* p. 69.

14. The Beijing 1993 edition, 1.50–51. The translation here is adapted from that by Wright, *Sui Dynasty*, p. 36.

15. Wang T., "Yang-Sui Li-Tang xianshi xitong kao" (Examining the ancestry lines of the Sui and Tang imperial houses), was the first modern author to compile an extensive list on this subject.

16. Gökalp, *Principles of Turkism,* p. 110. This goes back to the famous eleventh-century dictionary of Turkic languages by Mahmud al-Kašyari, which interprets the term as "princess, noblewoman." See the translation by Dankoff and Kelly, *Compendium of the Turkic Dialects (Türk Siveleri Lügati)*, vol. 3, pp. 147 and 262. See also Clauson, *Etymological Dictionary of Pre-thirteenth-century Turkish*, p. 635.

17. For a modern analysis, see Chen Yinke, *Tangdai zhengzhishi shulun gao* (*A Draft Treatise on the Political History of the Tang Era*), pp. 57–59.

18. Wang T., "Yang-Sui Li-Tang xianshi xitong kao," pp. 20–23.

19. Drompp, *Tang China and the Collapse of the Uighur Empire: A Documentary History*, ch. 5, especially p. 126.

20. Xiang, *Tangdai Chang'an yu Xiyu wenming* (The Tang Chang'an and the civilizations of the western regions).

21. "Tang Ashina Zhong mu fajue jianbao," originally reported in *Kaogu* (1977.2), and reprinted in Lin G., ed., *Tujue yu Huihe lishi lunwen xuanji* (*Selected Papers on the History of Turks and Uighurs*), vol. 2, pp. 408–19.

22. *Zhuzi yulei* (*Teachings of Master Zhu Xi Categorized*) 136.3245. The passage will be quoted in Chapter 3.

23. Xu and Zhao, *Tang Xuanzong zhuan*, pp. 409 and passim.

24. See, for instance, Tekin, *Grammar of Orkhon Turkic*, pp. 373–74.

25. Al-Kašyari, *Compendium of the Turkic Dialects*, vol. 1, p. 341.

26. Liu S., *Sui Tang jiahua* 1.7; Liu S., *Da Tang xinyu* (*New Talks of the Great Tang*) 1.13.

27. Tao, *Nancun chuogenglu* 8.104.

28. See, e.g., Chen Yuan, *Tongjian Huzhu biaowei* (*Uncovering the Subtleties in Hu Sanxing's Commentaries on Comprehensive Mirror for Aid in Government*), pp. 323–24.

29. Twitchett, *Cambridge History of China*, vol. 3, p. 236.

30. Wright, "T'ang T'ai-tsung and Buddhism," p. 253.

31. Pulleyblank, "An Lu-shan Rebellion and the origins of chronic militarism in Late T'ang China," p. 37.

32. See, e.g., *ZZTJ* 192.6034; *Quan Tang wen* 9.106; Wang P., *Tang huiyao* 26.506; and Lie, P., *Da Tang xinyu* 9.133, etc.

33. Schafer, *Golden Peaches of Samarkand: A Study of T'ang Exotics*, p. 65.

34. Boodberg, "Language of the T'o-pa Wei." See also Luo Xin's new study "Bei Wei zhiqin kao" (A study of *zhiqin* [*tekin*] of the Northern Wei).

35. Wu, *Passage to Power: K'ang-hsi and His Heir Apparent, 1661–1722*, pp. 133–36.

36. See, e.g., Chen Q., *Li Daoyuan yu Shuijing zhu* (*Li Daoyuan and the Commentary on the Water Classic*), pp. 31, 34–35.

37. Chen Yinke, *Tangdai zhengzhishi*, pp. 52–53.

38. Chen Yuan, *Tongjian Huzhu biaowei*, p. 252.

39. Fletcher, "Mongols: Ecological and social perspectives."

40. Fletcher, "Turco-Mongolian monarchic tradition in the Ottoman Empire."

41. Boodberg, "Marginalia to the histories of the Northern dynasties," p. 266.

42. Fletcher, "Blood tanistry: Authority and succession in the Ottoman, Indian Muslim, and Later Chinese Empires."

43. Zhao Y., *Nian'ershi zhaji* (*Notes on the Twenty-two Histories*) 19.410.

44. For example, see Hu J., *Wu Zetian benzhuan* (*A Proper Biography of Wu Zetian*), pp. 60–61.

45. Alderson, *Structure of the Ottoman Dynasty*, pp. 32–36; Goody, *Succession to High Office,* pp. 20-21. For a detailed description of this part of the Ottoman palace, see Penzer, *Harem,* pp. 197–201.

46. Bosworth, *Later Ghaznavids: Splendour and Decay*, p. 38.

47. Wu, *Passage to Power*.

48. Fan Z., *Tang jian* (*Reflections on the Tang*) 9.78.

49. See Alderson, *Structure of the Ottoman Dynasty,* p. 30.

50. Meng S., "Haining Chenjia," pp. 324–26. The recent efforts by Yang Zhen (*Qingchao huangwei jicheng zhidu*, ch. 5) to argue that the prince son died of natural causes impress one as being singularly anemic.

51. Wright, "Sui Yang-ti: Personality and stereotype."

52. Xiong, "Sui Yangdi and the building of Sui-Tang Luoyang."

53. Bosworth, *Ghaznavids*, pp. 230-34.

54. Feng E., *Yongzheng zhuan* (*A Biography of Emperor Yongzheng*), pp. 555–59.

55. Winstanley, *Hamlet and the Scottish Succession*, and lately, Kurland, "Hamlet and the Scottish succession?"

56. There is an amazing convergence of early Chinese and non-Chinese sources on this subject. For Chinese sources, read Linghu, *Zhou shu* 50.909; Li Y., *Bei shi* (*The History of the Northern Dynasties*) 99.3287; and Du Y., *Tong dian* (*The Comprehensive Statutes*) 197.1068. For non-Chinese sources, see Frazer, "Killing of the Khazar kings"; and Dunlop, *History of the Jewish Khazars*, p. 97. An extensive exposition of ritual regicide can be found in Frazer, *Golden Bough*, vol. 4, pp. 9–119.

57. A comprehensive summary of most such retired emperors can be found in Zhao Y., *Nian'ershi zhaji* 13.281–86.

58. See, for instance, Hummel, *Eminent Chinese of the Ch'ing Period (1644–1912)*, p. 372.

59. Wang L., *Yanshi jiaxun jijie* (*An Annotated Edition of Yan's Family Instructions*) 1.48. Wright, *Sui Dynasty*, p. 35, has also noted Yan's observation.

60. Chen Yinke, *Tangdai zhengzhishi*, pp. 41–44.

61. Wechsler in *Mirror to the Son of Heaven: Wei Cheng at the Court of T'ang T'ai-tsung*, p. 71, noted this particular incident.

62. Two rather influential ones are Chen Yinke, "Lun Tangdai zhi Fanjiang yu fubing" (On the Foreign Generals and Militia of the Tang Era); and Zhang Q., *Tangdai Fanjiang yanjiu* and its sequel.

63. Tekin, *Grammar of Orkhon Turkic*, p. 264.

64. Pulleyblank, "An Lu-shan Rebellion," p. 40.

65. Chen Yinke, *Tangdai zhengzhishi*, pp. 50–51.

66. Jackson and Lockhart, *Cambridge History of Iran*, vol. 4, p. 366; Lockhart, *Fall of the Safavi Dynasty and the Afghan Occupation of Persia*, pp. 17, 29–32. The appointment of princes of the ruling house/clan to provincial governorships under the tutelage of an older, "surrogate" father was practiced in a number of Turkic societies, including the Seljuk and the early Ottomans, whence the term *atabeg* ("father-commander").

67. Zhao Lin, *Yinhua lu* (Old Talk Recorded) 5.35.

68. Read, e.g., Wright, "Sui Yang-ti," pp. 161–62.

69. See, e.g., Hu Rulei's biography of Emperor Taizong, pp. 78-89.

70. Yao W., *Beichao huxing kao*, pp. 25–28.

71. Bosworth, *Ghaznavids*, pp. 45 and 228.

72. Bosworth, *Later Ghaznavids*, p. 18.

73. Frye and Sayili, "Turks in the Middle East before the Saljuqs."

74. Hummel, *Eminent Chinese of the Ch'ing Period*, p. 94

75. Sun Guodong, "Tang Zhenguan Yonghui jian dangzheng shishi."

76. Barfield, *Perilous Frontier*, p. 197.

77. Tao, J.-S., *Jurchen in Twelfth-century China*, pp. 42–47.

78. Meskoob, *Iranian Nationality and the Persian Language*, pp. 36-37.

79. Wang Zhongluo, *Wei-Jin nanbeichao shi* (vol. 2, p. 983), has a very short discussion on this subject. Still, the intense savageries of the Northern Zhou forces speak for themselves.

80. Togan, "Sur l'origine des Safavides"; Mazzaoui, *Origins of the Safawids: Šiʻism, Sufism, and the Gulat,* pp. 47–48.

81. Braun, "Iran under the Safavids and in the 18th century," p. 188.

82. Holt et al., *Cambridge History of Islam*, vol. 1, p. 394; Mazzaoui, *Origins of the Safawids,* pp. 46–52.

83. Bawden, *Mongol Chronicle Altan tobci*, pp. 128–29; Franke, *From Tribal Chieftain to Universal Emperor and God,* pp. 64–69.

84. Wright, "T'ang T'ai-tsung and Buddhism."

85. Tang Y., *Wangri zagao* (*Miscellaneous Manuscripts of Yore*), p. 10; *Sui-Tang Fojiao shigao* (*Draft History of Buddhism of the Sui-Tang Era*), p. 14.

86. Weinstein, *Buddhism under the T'ang*, pp. 11-12 and 155n2.

87. Song, *Tang da zhaoling ji* 113.586.

88. This addition was largely inspired by a personal communication from the late Professor Denis Twitchett in March 1997, after the publication of my essay in the *Journal of the Royal Asiatic Society*, on which the current chapter is based. I express my deep gratitude to Denis Twitchett for his kind encouragement and his suggestion of this new and stimulating point from which to examine the Tang house's identity. Many passages of this section come straight from his communication.

89. The most detailed exposition of this fascinating topic is Yihong, *Son of Heaven and Heavenly Qaghan*.

90. For examples, Cen, *Sui Tang shi*, pp. 140 and 142, has claimed that this feature of Emperor Taizong's mausoleum was imitative of the Turkic burial custom, a notion followed by Howard Wechsler, *Offerings of Jade and Silk*, p. 81.

91. See also Ecsedy, "Ancient Turk [T'u-chüeh] burial customs," pp. 276–77.

92. Yao W., *Beichao Huxing kao*, pp. 132–33.

93. See Pulleyblank, "Chinese and their neighbours in prehistoric and early historic times," pp. 414–15.

94. Middle Chinese pronunciation *bit*. For a dissenting view, see Sinor, "Altaica and Uralica."

95. See, e.g., Mair, "Buddhism and the rise of the written vernacular in East Asia: The making of national languages."

96. Goody and Watt, "Consequence of literacy."

97. Zhao Lüfu, *Shitong xin jiaozhu,* pp. 457, 960.

98. Pulleyblank, *Background of the Rebellion of An Lu-shan*, pp. 75–81.

99. For examples, see Dien, "Yen Chih-T'ui (531–91+): His life and thought," p. 12; and Holmgren, "Politics of the inner court under the Hou-chu (Last Lord) of the Northern Ch'i (ca. 565–73)," pp. 269–330. Both have used the standard "exemplary history" arguments to explain this contrast.

100. Eberhard, *History of China*, p. 152; Wright, *Sui Dynasty,* p. 36.

101. Barfield, *Perilous Frontier*, 126.

Chapter 2

This chapter is an expanded version of the author's 2005 essay of the same title, published in the *Journal of Asian History*.

1. Adapted from Arthur Waley's translation, in Mair, *Columbia Anthology of Traditional Chinese Literature*, pp. 474–76. For a different translation, see Frankel, *Flowering Plum and the Palace Lady: Interpretations of Chinese Poetry*.

2. Mair, *Columbia Anthology of Traditional Chinese Literature*, p. 474.

3. Clauson, *Etymological Dictionary of Pre-thirteenth-century Turkish,* Intro.

4. Whereas when used in (Hàn Chinese) masculine names, it usually only has the derived meaning of "fine offspring."

5. For an English translation (by Anne Birrell), see Mair, *Columbia Anthology of Traditional Chinese Literature*, pp. 462–72.

6. Zhao C., *Han-WeiNanbeichao muzhi huibian*, p. 10.

7. Yao W., *Beichao huxing kao*, pp. 126–28.

8. See, e.g., Pulleyblank, *Background of the Rebellion of An Lu-shan*.

9. Zhao C., *Han-Wei Nanbeichao muzhi huibian*.

10. For a translation of this remarkable poem, see Mair, *Columbia Anthology of Traditional Chinese Literature*, p. 476.

11. Boodberg, *Hu Tien Han Yüeh Fang Chu,* no. 5.

12. *Wei shu* 113.3307 has the name without the "grass" radical, but almost all other sources have it. See Yao W., *Beichao huxing kao*, p. 57.

13. Unless otherwise indicated, all ancient Chinese pronunciations cited in this book are based on Karlgren, *Grammata Serica Recensa*.

14. I am much obliged to Mr. Cheong Song Hing, of Singapore, who kindly supplied this telltale piece of linguistic data. See Xiamen University, *Putonghua Minnan fangyan cidian*, p. 549.

15. Boodberg, "Early Mongolian toponym."

16. Gabain, *Alttürkische Grammatik*, pp. 107, 326.

17. R. Dankoff's translation, vol. 3, p. 276.

18. Except for a very short quotation in passing in *Yuanhe xingcuan* (*The Yuanhe Compendium of Surnames*) 10.1481, citing another now-lost book titled *Xingyuan* (*Garden of Surnames*) compiled by He Chengtian of the Liu Song dynasty (420–79) that stated that such a surname existed in Rencheng (in the modern province of Shandong), without citing a single person bearing the name. It is worth noting that the county of Rencheng during much of the period belonged to the Tuoba-controlled north.

19. See, e.g., Yao W., *Beichao huxing kao*, p. 57.

20. Here are several cases: Shen, *Song shu* 50.1449; *Wei shu* 2.39, 31.743, 111.2239; and Wei Z., *Sui shu* 39.1159.

21. Bazin, "Recherches sur les parlers T'o-pa," p. 289.

22. First recognized by Boodberg, *Hu Tien Han Yüeh Fang Chu*, no. 1, p. 75.

23. As will be cited in more detail in Chapter 3, these are, briefly, (1) the clan name Yizhan (*iet-tśiän*), meaning "uncle's descendants," a cognate of the ancient Turkic term *echi*, "elder brother or father's younger brother"; (2) a clan name Ruogan (*ńźiak-kân*), later changed to Gou, a euphemism for *gou*, "dog," which can be identified with the Mongol term *noqai*, "dog"; and (3) the official Tuoba title Agan (*a-kân*), translated as *zhang*, "senior, elder," which can be identified with the Mongol word *aqa*, "elder brother." One may also note that the ancient Turkic word for "wolf" was transcribed in Chinese as both *fuli* and *fulin*.

24. Roux, "Le chameau en Asie centrale," pp. 60–61.

25. Transcribed in Chinese as Puluo (*b'uk-lâ*). See Liu X. et al., *Jiu Tang shu* 97.3046; Ouyang Xiu et al., *Xin Tang shu* 122.4364, 221b.6245, 221b.6252.

26. Boyce, *Zoroastrianism*, vol. 1, pp. 182–83.

27. Sinor, "Sur les noms altaiques de la licorne," p. 175; Clauson, *Etymological Dictionary of Pre-thirteenth-century Turkish*, p. 343; Räsänen, *Versuch eines etymologischen Wörterbuchs der Türksprachen*, pp. 87–88; Doerfer, *Türkische und mongolische Elemente im Neupersischen*, Band 2, pp. 356–58 (no. 810).

28. This is quoted in almost all references given here. One can also read R. Dankoff's translation of the *Divan*.

29. Sinor, "Sur les noms altaiques de la licorne," p. 176.

30. Ibid., p. 168.

31. It was not uncommon for a member of the latter to be named with a single character, either *qi* or *lin*, but not both. The oft-quoted gender distinction of the two characters was likely a late invention and rarely observed in practice. Indeed, *qilin* was undoubtedly originally a pure bisyllabic word of which neither syllable had independent morphemic or semantic signification. Precisely the same process of gender distinction was also later applied to the bisyllabic name of another well-known mythical creature, the *fenghuang,* "phoenix."

32. For example, Szyszman "Le roi Bulan et le problème de la conversion des Khazars," p. 71; and Jacobson, *Deer Goddess of Ancient Siberia*.

33. Huntington, "Range of the 'cosmic' deer."

34. See, for instance, Maenchen-Helfen, *World of the Huns: Studies in Their History and Culture*, p. 444.

35. *Yuan shi* 146.3456. See also Tao Z., *Nancun chuogeng lu* 5.55.

36. Jacobson, *Deer Goddess of Ancient Siberia*, pp. 32 and 228.

37. Szyszman, "Le roi Bulan et le problème de la conversion des Khazars"; Peter Golden, *Khazar Studies*, vol. 1, pp. 169–71.

38. Ernits, "Folktales of Meanash, the mythic Sami reindeer," part 1.

39. Jacobson, *Deer Goddess of Ancient Siberia*, pp. 32 and 235.

40. "The Chinese name for the Turks." For more recent discussions, see Beckwith, "On the Chinese names for Tibet, Tabghatch, and the Turks," and "Frankish name of the king of the Turks."

41. Chavannes "Les pays d'Occident d'après le *Heou Han chou*," p. 177n5; Pelliot, *Notes on Marco Polo,* vol. 1, p. 494; Hulsewé, *China in Central Asia, the Early Stage: 125 B.C.–A.D. 23*, pp. 115–16.

42. In addition to the Buddhism sources, see Bailey, *Culture of the Sakas*, p. 82.

43. For *n- ~ d-*, see P. Bagchi, *Deux lexiques sanskrit-chinois*, tome 2, p. 441.

44. Nattier, "Heart sutra: A Chinese apocryphal text?"

45. See Ji, *Da Tang xiyuji xiaozhu* (*An Emended and Annotated Edition of Records of the Western World of the Great Tang*) 4.385, 8.670, 9.722, and 9.747.

46. Liu X. et al., *Jiu Tang shu* 195.5198; Ouyang et al., *Xin Tang shu* 217a.6114.

47. Henning, "Argi and the 'Tokharians,'" pp. 555 and 557.

48. Pelliot, *Notes on Marco Polo,* vol. 2, p. 691.

49. The best reference on these names is Yao W., *Beichao huxing kao*. To avoid extensive footnoting, I do not list individual page numbers, as Yao's work has an excellent index, a rarity in modern Chinese scholarly books.

50. This was a well-known "High-Cart" Uighur tribe, attested in the Saka portion of the famous Staël Holstein scroll as *bākū*, reconstructed by Henning as **boqu* or *buqu*. "Argi and the 'Tokharians,'" p. 555. This name is strikingly close to a name also given to a former Zhao emperor, Liu Yao: Pugu (*b'uk-kuk*) King. Here Pugu was described as Liu's *huwei*, translated by Pulleyblank ("Consonantal system of Old Chinese: Part II," p. 264) as "Liu Yao's barbarian rank," which does not make sense for a person who had been recognized as an emperor for more than ten years. In my view, here *wei* either was an error for *ming*, "name," or stood for Liu's (heavenly or horoscope) sign. Unfortunately, neither Liu's year of birth nor his age at death (329) was preserved, which deprives us of a possible datum regarding the language of Liu's group, generally accepted as the Xiongnu or its progeny.

51. This was an old Qiang/Tibetan tribe always in close contact with Hàn Chinese. Therefore a "Proto-Mongol intermediary" was out of the question.

52. Yao W., *Beichao huxing kao*, pp. 28–29.

53. Pulleyblank, "Chinese name for the Turks," p. 124.

54. Harmatta, "Irano-Turcica," p. 269.

55. Sinor, "À propos de la biographie ouigoure de Hiuan-tsang," pp. 578–79 (nos. 52, 54, and 87).

56. See, e.g., Menges, "Die Wörter für 'Kamel' und einige seiner Kreuzungsformen im Türkischen"; and Roux, "Le chameau en Asie centrale." It is interesting to compare forms like *dävä* (and *tüö* in Kazakh) with the Chinese character *tuo* (*d'â*), "camel," which appeared fairly late (during the Hàn dynasty).

57. Doerfer, *Türkische und mongolische Elemente im Neupersischen*, Band 2, pp. 295–96 (no. 747); Räsänen, *Versuch eines etymologischen Wörterbuchs der Türksprachen*, p. 86.

58. Räsänen, "Uralaltaische Forschungen," p. 25.

59. Doerfer, *Türkische und mongolische Elemente im Neupersischen*, Band 2, p. 297.

60. Menges, *Turkic Languages and Peoples*, p. 53; Roux, "Le chameau en Asie centrale," p. 39.

61. *Ciyuan* (*Origins of Words*), p. 1879, quoting *Piya*.

62. Doerfer, *Türkische und mongolische Elemente im Neupersischen*, Band 2, p. 356 (no. 810).

63. Menges, "Die Wörter für 'Kamel,'" p. 519.

64. Joki, "Die lehnwörter des Sajansamojedischen," p. 105; Doerfer, *Türkische und mongolische Elemente im Neupersischen*, Band 2, p. 300.

65. Bang, "Über die türkischen Namen einiger Großkatzen." Bang assumes *bülän* to be the original form.

66. Clauson, *Etymological Dictionary of Pre-thirteenth-century Turkish*, p. 314.

67. R. Dankoff's translation, vol. 3, p. 250.

68. Clauson, *Etymological Dictionary of Pre-thirteenth-century Turkish*, p. 314.

69. Doerfer, *Türkische und mongolische Elemente im Neupersischen*, Band 4, p. 295 (no. 2073).

70. Starostin, Dybo, and Mudrak, *Etymological Dictionary of the Altaic Languages*, vol. 2, pp. 951–52.

Chapter 3

This chapter is adapted, in places with considerable additional material, from the English article "A-gan revisited: The Tuoba's cultural and political heritage," and the Chinese article "*Nucai* as a proto-Mongolic word: An etymological study," coauthored with Dr. Chung-mo Kwok.

1. Legge's translation of *The Four Books.*

2. Yi, *Nihao, Weige* (*Hello, Viagra*).

3. Duan, *Shuowen jiezi zhu* (*An Annotated Edition of the Explanation of Simple and Compound Graphs*) 5.204.

4. For examples, Qian, *Hen yan lu* (*Notes on Perpetual Words*) 3.73, and Liang, *Chengwei lu* (*Records of Names and Appellations*) 4.145. Han-Yi Feng's classical study *The Chinese Kinship System* is a good source in English.

5. See, e.g., Twitchett, *Writing of Official History under the T'ang*, pp. 109–10.

6. Two early Western articles on this issue are Maspero, "Sur quelques texts anciens du chinois parlé," and Laufer, "The prefix *a-* in the Indo-Chinese languages."

7. See, e.g., Lu Q., comp., *Xian-Qin Han Wei Jin Nanbeihao shi*, 7.199–201.

8. Benedict, *Sino-Tibetan: A Conspectus*, p. 156.

9. For a source in English, see Carroll, *Account of the T'u-yü-hun in the History of the Chin Dynasty.*

10. Pelliot, "Notes sur les T'ou-yu-houen et les Sou-p'i," p. 329.

11. Boodberg, "Language of the T'o-pa Wei," p. 171; and Bazin, "Recherches sur les parlers T'o-pa," p. 311.

12. Zhai, *Tongsu bian* (*Collection of Common Sayings*) 17.197.

13. See Sinor, "On some Ural-Altaic plural suffixes," pp. 208–9; and Poppe, *Introduction to Mongolian Comparative Studies*, p. 183.

14. For references in Western languages, see Kane, *Sino-Jurchen Vocabulary of the Bureau of Interpreters*, for Middle Jurchen; and Norman, *Concise Manchu-English Lexicon*, for Manchu.

15. Wittfogel and Feng, *History of Chinese Society: Liao*, p. 105.

16. Chavannes, *Documents sur les Tou-Kieu (Turcs) occidentaux*, p. 280.

17. Grønbech, "Turkish system of kinship."

18. Clausen, *Etymological Dictionary of Pre-thirteenth-century Turkish*, p. 20.

19. Gibb et al., *Encyclopaedia of Islam*, vol. 1, p. 246.

20. Personal communication.

21. Feng, H.-Y., *Chinese Kinship System*, p. 75.

22. Translation taken from Wright, *Sui Dynasty*, p. 35.

23. See, e.g., Tekin, *Grammar of Orkhon Turkic*, p. 246.

24. Radloff, *Die Alttürkischen Inschriften der Mongolei*, Zweite Lieferung, Plate II, column 17.

25. See Wang Shumin, *Nian'ershi zhaji jiangzheng* 30.708.

26. Radloff, *Versuch eines Worterbuches der Türk-Dialecte*, vol. 1, p. 676.

27. Redhouse, *Turkish and English Lexicon*, p. 146.

28. Krueger, *Yakut Manual,* p. 232.

29. Popov, "Semeinaia zhizn' u dolgan," p. 73.

30. Sinor, *Introduction à l'étude de l'Eurasie centrale*, p. 85. Menges, *Turkic Languages and Peoples*, pp. 16 and 52, further suggests that they were Samoyeds who had been Tungusized prior to the "Jakutization."

31. Krader, *Social Organization of the Mongol-Turkic Pastoral Nomads,* p. 390.

32. For this and the next several cited Turkic kinship terms, see Pokrovskaia, "Terminy rodstva v tiurkskikh iazykakh," pp. 26 and 35.

33. Starostin, Dybo, and Mudrak, *Etymological Dictionary of the Altaic Languages*, vol. 1, p. 281.

34. Sevortian, *Etimologicheskii slovar tiurkskikh iazykov*, vol. 1, pp. 70–71.

35. Miao, *Dushi cungao (Saved Reflections on Reading History)*, p. 69.

36. Pokrovskaia, "Terminy rodstva v tiurkskikh iazykakh," p. 36.

37. Ramstedt, *Kalmückisches Wörterbuch*, p. 38.

38. It should also be pointed out that the claim by the Qing author Liang Zhangju in his *Chengwei lu* (3.113) that a Northern Qi emperor called his uncle *axiong*, seemingly a perfect correspondence to the Turkic term *echi*, is in fact incorrect. See Li B., *Bei Qi shu* 11.149.

39. See Krueger, *Tuvan Manual*, p. 210.

40. For the Samoyed words, see Katzschmann and Pusztay, *Jenissej-Samojedisches Wörterverzeichnis*, p. 21 (*aca*) and p. 23 (*agga*). For the Lapp terms, see Collinder, *Fenno-Ugric Vocabulary: An Etymological Dictionary of the Uralic Languages*, p. 24 (*acca*), p. 26 (*ække, æge*). One may also observe the etymology of *agh*, "aufsteigen," of uncertain origin proposed for Turkic terms *aghary*, "empor" and *agharu*, "hoch, oben," by Räsänen, *Versuch eines etymologischen Wörterbuchs der Türksprachen*, p. 7.

41. Chen Yinke, *Tangdai zhengzhishi shulun gao*, p. 57.

42. See, e.g., Malov, *Pamiatniki drevnetiurkskoi pis'mennosti*, p. 403; and Gabain, *Alttürkische Grammatik*, p. 349.

43. Starostin, Dybo, and Mudrak, *Etymological Dictionary of the Altaic Languages*, vol. 1, p. 612. Modern Uighur forms *oghal* and *ughal* might be later variations, though. See Jarring, *Eastern Turki-English Dialect Dictionary*, p. 212.

44. Ban Gu et al., *Hàn shu (History of the [Former] Hàn Dynasty)* 94b.3807–8; Karlgren, *Grammata Serica Recensa*, pp. 34 and 148.

45. Despite this blemish during the Former Hàn dynasty, Ma's family would keep its prominence in the Later Hàn dynasty by producing a famous general Ma Yuan (14 BC–AD 49; biography: *Hou Hàn shu*, 24.827–52), as well as the general's more influential empress-daughter (*ZZTJ* 44.1437). Therefore, the family was naturally described as descended from a famous Sinitic general of the Warring States era. Nonetheless, the underplaying of the

"Barbarian" elements and connections is a long tradition in Chinese historiography. For example, I have yet to see any study on the "Barbarian" (Xiongnu) ancestry on the maternal side of the famous Later Hàn dynasty Ban family of historians and generals, whose legacy included the very first dynastic history of China, *Hàn shu.*

46. Li Daoyuan (?–527), *Shuijing zhu* 20.395.

47. Wang L., *Yanshi jiaxun* 3.148.

48. *Liao shi* (*History of the Liao Dynasty*) 116.1542, and Rolf Stein, "Liao-Tche," p. 23. I thank Professor Denis Sinor for pointing out this important early attestation, in a personal communication.

49. Boodberg, "Language of the T'o-pa Wei," was the first to make these two identifications, which Bazin, "Recherches sur les parlers T'o-pa," followed.

50. Biography: *Jiu Tang shu* 138.3780–82; *Xin Tang shu* 143.4687–88.

51. Sinor, "Mongol and Turkic words in the Latin versions of John of Plano Carpini's journey to the Mongols (1245–1247)," p. 546.

52. Németh, "Noms ethniques turcs d'origine totémistique."

53. Wang Deyi, Li, and Pan, *Yuanren zhuanji ziliao suoyin*, pp. 2502–4.

54. Pulleyblank, *Lexicon of Reconstructed Pronunciation in Early Middle Chinese, Late Middle Chinese, and Early Mandarin*, pp. 44 and 227.

55. See, e.g., Baxter, *Handbook of Old Chinese Phonology*, p. 51. Examples abound in Pulleyblank, *Lexicon of Reconstructed Pronunciation*, pp. 137–69 and 244–63.

56. Lu D., *Jingdian shiwen* 8.111, 8.112, 8.123, 9.129, 9.138, 10.145, 10.155, etc. Meanwhile, in "spelling" characters with *dz'/ts'* initials followed by mid/low vowels, including a near-homonym of character *cai* (with a voiceless initial), consonant characters that later merged with velar-initial characters were frequently used (3.37, 5.60, 5.67, 6.71, 6.84, 7.98, 24.345, etc.).

57. Pelliot, *Notes on Marco Polo*, p. 121; Skelton, Marston, and Painter, *Vinland Map and the Tartar Relation*, p. 71.

58. Mair, "Canine conundrums: Eurasian dog ancestor myths in historical and ethnic perspective," has a very detailed discussion of this myth in ancient China.

59. Again see ibid., especially pp. 14–16.

60. Fu, "Yi-Xia dongxi shuo" (The East-West conflicts between the Yi and the Xia: A theory).

61. See, e.g., Nigosian, *Zoroastrian Faith: Tradition and Modern Research*, pp. 55 and 56.

62. Frye, *History of Ancient Iran,* p. 82.

63. Kotwal and Mistree, "Court of the lord of rituals," p. 383n3.

64. It was widely reported that the U.S. military in Iraq made use of the traditional Arab abhorrence of dogs during the interrogations and abuse of Iraqi prisoners. See, e.g., Frank Rich, "It's all *Newsweek*'s fault," *New York Times*, May 22, 2005; and Josh White, "Abu Ghraib dog tactics came from Guantanamo," *Washington Post*, July 27, 2005.

65. *Chāndogya Upanishad* 5.10.7, taken from Hume, *Thirteen Principal Upanishads*, p. 233. I have italicized the words "dog" and "swine" in the passage.

66. For instance, see the oracle bone text of "offering, in the tenth month, one hundred sheep/goats, one hundred dogs and one hundred pigs" to an ancestor, in Guo Moruo et al., *Jiaguwen heji* (*Complete Collection of Oracle Bone Texts*) no. 15521.

67. Lattimore, *Inner Asian Frontiers of China*, pp. 54–61.

68. See also Peter Boodberg's fine elaboration of Lattimore's insightful theory in a 1942 University of California, Berkeley, lecture, "Turk, Aryan and Chinese in ancient Asia," in particular p. 7.

Chapter 4

1. Both Lishi and Anding are names of *jun*, usually translated as commandery, an administrative unit above *zhou* ("prefecture"). The seat of the prefect of Lishi is the modern county of Lishi, Shanxi Province. The seat of the prefect of Anding is located on the north bank of the Northern Jing River in the modern county of Jingchuan, Gansu Province. The principle references for the geographic identifications are Tan et al., *Zhongguo lishi dituji* (*The Historical Atlas of China*), and Wei Songshan et al., *Zhongguo lishi diming da cidian* (*The Grand Dictionary of Chinese Historical Toponyms*).

2. The particular word *tuzhu* used here usually referred to former nomadic people settling in a place and no longer migrating. See Xu F. et al., *Gu Hanyu dacidian* (*A Grand Dictionary of Old Chinese*), p. 598.

3. There may be more than traditional Sinitic moral snobbery in this story. Several centuries later, a Southern Song emissary Hong Hao (1088–1155) who spent many years as a prisoner in the Jurchen domain in the north had a similar description about the marriage customs of the Turkic Uighur tribes that still lived in northern China (*Songmo jiwen* [*Recollections about the Pine Deserts*], 1.15): "Parents would brag to a visiting matchmaker: 'Our daughter has had intimate relations with such and such men.' The more lovers the daughter had, the better. This is their universal custom."

4. The Valley of Yunyang is located in the modern county of Zuoyun, Shanxi Province.

5. Both Fen and Jin are names of rivers, as well as of corresponding commanderies. The river Jin is a branch of the Fen, which in turn is the second longest branch of the Yellow River. It is somewhat confusing that the Tuoba Wei dynasty commandery of Fen (Fenzhou) was not the commandery of the same name set up by the rump Western Wei dynasty under the thumb of the Yuwen clan, who later took over the throne and changed the dynasty name to Northern Zhou. The seat of the former became the modern county of Fenyang (meaning "the northern bank of the Fen River"), Shanxi Province. The seat of the latter commandery is in the modern county of Yichuan, Shaanxi Province. Given that the narrative of *Zhou shu* is always centered in the Western Wei and the Northern Zhou, the name Fen here, if referring to a commandery, should normally follow the Northern Zhou definition. The complication is that this *Zhou shu* chapter later also mentions the commandery of Danzhou, which was the new name of the Western Wei commandery of Fen since the year 554. We have a similar confusing situation regarding the commandery of Jin, as both the Northern Qi and the

Northern Zhou maintained their respective but distinct commanderies named after the Jin River. The seat of the Northern Qi commandery of Jin becomes the modern city of Linfen, Shanxi Province. The seat of the Northern Zhou namesake is in the modern county of Jiang-xian, Shanxi Province.

6. This was only a posthumous imperial title of Gao Huan (496–547), because a pup-pet Tuoba emperor was maintained on the throne throughout Gao Huan's lifetime, until Huan's second son Gao Yang declared the new dynasty of [Northern] Qi in 550. For Gao Huan's biography, see Li, *Bei Qi shu* 1.1–29.

7. During much of the period, the Yellow River formed the boundary between the two successor and rival dynasties, namely the Northern Qi and the Northern Zhou, of the Tuoba Wei.

8. Just like the title Emperor Shenwu of the Northern Qi, this was a posthumous impe-rial title of Yuwan Tai (507–56), who never was enthroned himself. For biography, see Linghu, *Zhou shu* 1.1–44.

9. Places bearing the name Heishui or Black Water were too numerous to be identified with certainty. The most likely candidate, however, is the modern river of Madong or Yu-nyan, to the east of the county of Ganquan, Shaanxi Province.

10. The seat of the commandery of Xiazhou was formally the Tuoba garrison fort of Tongwan ("command myriads," or rather the Chinese transcription of the Altaic word *tümen*, "ten thousand"), which in turn had been the capital city of the Xia dynasty (407–31), founded by the Xiongnu scion Helian Bobo. It has been identified as the ruin at Baichengzi in the northeast part of the modern county of Jingbian, Shaanxi Province.

11. At the time, the Hàn dynasty prefect of Shangjun ("Upper Prefecture"), with its seat located southeast of the modern city of Yulin, Shaanxi Province, was part of the prefecture of Guizhen. Given the date of *Zhou shu*, it could also refer to the Sui dynasty prefecture of Shangjun, with its seat located in the modern county of Fuxian, Shaanxi Province.

12. "Northern Mountains (Beishan)" was a semigeneric toponym. It often referred to the mountains on the north side of the Gansu-Qinghai Corridor. Whether it was used in this sense here is not entirely clear.

13. The seat of the commandery of Yanzhou is near the modern city of Yan'an, Shaanxi Province.

14. The adjective "raw" here is understood in the sense of "untamed," "unsubju-gated," or "unsettled," usually meaning that the "Barbarians" were relative newcomers who had not familiarized themselves with the standard rules of the Chinese "frontier game."

15. The seat of the commandery of Xunzhou is located in the southwest part of the modern county of Jishan, Shanxi Province.

16. Yang Zhong (biography *Zhou shu* 19.314–19) was the father of the founding em-peror, Yang Jian, of the Sui dynasty.

17. Danzhou was a commandery with its seat in the modern county of Yichuan, Shaanxi Province; Suizhou was a commandery with its seat in the modern county of Suide, Shaanxi Province; Yinzhou was a northern Zhou dynasty commandery with its seat

located in the modern county of Hengshan, Shaanxi Province. Puchuan was a place in the vicinity of the modern county of Puxian, Shanxi Province.

18. Here the punctuation of the Zhonghua shuju edition is incorrect. The original text should read that Liu Xiong went to study the rivers (or plains) and routes in the northern frontier, clearly as military preparations (in regard to transport), hence the Jihu hostilities.

19. As mentioned in a previous note, there were two concurrent commanderies named Jinzhou. Given that the war of 576 was a major invasion by the Northern Zhou into the Northern Qi realm, the Jinzhou here should refer to the commandery inside the latter's territory, namely the one whose seat is now the modern city of Linfen, Shanxi Province.

20. All three princes were younger sons of Yuwen Tai. Their biographies are found in *Zhou shu* 13.203–4 and 13.206. All were executed in 580 by Yang Jian, the founding emperor of the Sui dynasty, during the latter's machinations to usurp the throne.

21. The town of Mayi became today's city of Shuozhou, Shanxi Province.

22. Sheng (biography: *Zhou shu* 29.493) was the son of Yuwen Tai, the actual founder of the Northern Zhou. Hence he was a different person than his namesake mentioned earlier (the area commander in chief of the Yanzhou commandery who fought the Jihu in the year 567).

23. Boodberg, "Two notes on the history of the Chinese frontier. II. The Bulgars of Mongolia."

24. Du Y., *Tong dian*, 197.1067; Yue, *Taiping huanyu ji*, 294.646–47; Zheng, *Tongzhi*, 200.3208–9; Ma D., *Wenxian tongkao*, 342.2686.

25. Lin G., *Xiongnu shiliao huibian* (*Compilation of Historical Sources on the Xiongnu*). Lin Gan's inclusion of the Buluoji data in this compilation should be understood in the context of materials related to the Xiongnu Empire or confederacy, not as a presumption of ethnic or linguistic equivalence between the two.

26. Zhou Y., "Beichao de minzu wenti yu minzu zhengce," and Tang C., "Wei-Jin zahu kao" (A Study of the Zahu of the Wei-Jin Era).

27. *Zhou shu*'s other theory, namely that the Buluoji descended from the Rong and Di of the Spring-and-Autumn period, can be disregarded. See Zhou Yiliang, "Beichao de minzu wenti yu minzu zhengce," p. 151. It was popular among the Chinese historians of the time to trace the Northern nomads back to ancient "Barbarians" in early Chinese records. As Pulleyblank has stated in "The Chinese and their neighbours in prehistoric and early historic times," such claims usually had little substantiation. See also Prušek, *Chinese Statelets and the Northern Barbarians in the Period 1400–300 B.C.*, pp. 222–23.

28. Yao W., *Beichao huxing kao*, pp. 277 and 288.

29. However, *Jiu Tang shu* (29.1072) did call the Tuyuhun, a group that started as a genuine branch of the Murong in northeast China, "the separate clans of the Murong." This may be explained by the fact that during the several centuries after they settled in northwest China, the Tuyuhun extensively mingled with various Tibetan and proto-Tibetan tribes and lost some of their Xianbei traits.

30. There were, of course, European or Caucasian components among even the later Xiongnu, as has been shown by see Maenchen-Helfen, *World of the Huns*, pp. 369–74.

31. The Jie people were said to be "high-nosed and heavy-bearded" (*ZZTJ* 98.3100). For an exposition of the Jie's Central Asian traits, see Tan, "Jie kao" (On the Jie People).

32. On the Xiongnu, see Di Cosmo, "Ancient Inner Asian nomads: Their economic basis and its significance in Chinese history." About Hun agriculture, see Maenchen-Helfen, *World of the Huns*, pp. 174–78.

33. Xiang, *Tangdai Chang'an yu Xiyu wenming*.

34. Boodberg, "Bulgars of Mongolia," p. 297.

35. Al-Kašγarī, *Compendium of the Turkic Dialects (Türk Siveleri Lügati)*, vol. 3, p. 225.

36. Boodberg, "Early Mongolian toponym."

37. As I have argued in my essay "Sino-Tokharico-Altaica," Helian Bobo's new "from heaven" imperial name, together with the name Tongwan ("to command myriads," but actually a transliteration of the Altaic numeral *tümän*, "ten thousand, myriad") of his capital, represented a Steppe tradition of sacral universal kingship.

38. Read, for instance, Krauze, "Pride in Memin Pinguin," p. A21.

39. Pulleyblank, *Background of the Rebellion of An Lu-shan*, p. 104n1. However, Paul Pelliot in his "Note sur les T'ou-yu-houen et les Sou-p'i," translated *zhuzazhong* ("various miscellaneous races") in *Song shu* (96.2370) to "les tribus mélangées."

40. Fang et al., *Jin shu* (63.1707), e.g., has a telling incident showing the traditional enmity between the Tuge and the Xianbei.

41. See Shiratori, "Sur l'origine de Hiong-nu." Constantin's work *Were the Hiung-nu's Turks or Mongols: Regarding Some Etymologies Proposed by Shiratori*, is inaccessible to this author.

42. Maenchen-Helfen, "Huns and Hsiung-nu," p. 224.

43. Ligeti, "Mots de civilization de Haute Asie en transcription chinoise."

44. Pulleyblank, "Consonantal system of Old Chinese: Part II."

45. Vovin, "Did the Xiongnu speak a Yeniseian language?"

46. See two works by Starostin: "Praeniseiskaia rekonstruktsiia i vneshnie sviazi eniseiskikh iazykov" and "Gipoteza o geneticheskikh sviaziakh sinotibetskikh iazykov s eniseiskimii severnokavkazkimi iazykami."

47. Chen Sanping, "Sino-Tokarico-Altaica."

48. *Jin zhongxing shu*, as quoted in Lin G., *Xiongnu shiliao huibian*, vol. 2, p. 1046.

49. Wang G., "Xihu kao" and "Xihu xukao." For the essays by Cen Zhongmian and Lü Simian, see Lin G., *Xiongnu shi lunwen xuanji* (*Selected Papers on the History of the Xiongnu, 1919–1979*).

50. See Sinor, *Cambridge History of Early Inner Asia*, p. 128. Also of interest is the "blue-eye" Xiongnu portrait. See Lin G., *Xiongnu shi lunwen xuanji*, p. 81. A potentially fruitful direction for addressing the Xiongnu ethnicity problem is to follow up on Owen Lattimore's ingenious proposition of "progressive barbarization" cited elsewhere in this book. Following Lattimore's theory, it would seem natural to find among the Xiongnu, not only proto-Altaic and paleo-Asiatic components, but also (native) Indo-European and proto-Sinitic elements that had been "progressively barbarized" and forced off their earlier territory by the ever-growing intensive farming in the Chinese heartland.

51. Maenchen-Helfen, *World of the Huns*, pp. 369–74.

52. For a recent survey of some of these groups, see Golden, *Introduction to the History of the Turkic Peoples*, pp. 79–83.

53. This Zahu origin of the Turks was maintained or copied by Li Y., *Bei shi* (57.3286) and Du Y., *Tong dian* (197.1067).

54. For a most extensive examination of this battle and its consequences, see Bai S., "Cong Daluosi zhanyi shuodao Yisilan zhi zuizao de Huawen jilu" (The battle of Talas and the earliest Chinese records on Islam).

55. Needham, *Science and Civilization in China*, vol. 1, pp. 236–37.

56. Pelliot, "Des artisans chinois à la capitale abbasside en 751–762."

57. Two of the religions, namely Daqin and Dashi, can be easily identified as (Nestorian) Christianity and Islam, respectively. The third, Xunxun (Middle Chinese pronunciation *ziəm-ziəm*), requires some explanation. The 1989 edition of *Cihai* (*Sea of Words*) (p. 2788) suggests that it likely referred to Zoroastrianism, claiming, without providing its sources, that the Arabs had called Zoroastrians "Zemzem." I have indeed found that the famous early Arab author Abu-l Hassan al-Mas'udi had reported that a vulgar name, not for Zoroastrians but rather for their sacred book the *Avesta* (*Bestah*), was *zemzemeh*. See *Muru-j al-Dhahab wa Ma'adin al-Jawhar* (*The Meadows of Gold*), vol. 2, p. 123. In view of this evidence, Du's accusation of the Xunxun being the worst offenders of sexual morality leaves little doubt that he was indeed talking about Zoroastrianism, which was famed for practicing *xvaetvadatha*, "next-of-kin marriage." See, e.g., Boyce, *History of Zoroastrianism*, vol. 2, p. 75. In fact, the pre-Islamic Iranian tradition of consanguineous marriages had been observed from Herodotus (3.31) on down, including Chinese historians. *Zhou shu* (50.920) has a similar passage on Persians having "the most immoral" marriage customs among the "Barbarians," whereas *Sui shu* (83.1856) states specifically that Persians "marry their own sisters."

58. Henning, "Date of the Sogdian ancient letters." Henning's dating of the letters to after the sack of Luoyang by the Xiongnu Liu Cong (311), once universally accepted, has been challenged by J. Harmatta's two studies, "The archaeological evidence for the date of the Sogdian letters" and "Sogdian sources for the history of pre-Islamic Central Asia." Harmatta argues that the letters could also be describing the events of 193 when the generals of the murdered warlord Dong Zhuo called in the (Southern) Xiongnu troops for the fighting in and around Chang'an.

59. Read, e.g., Prušek, *Chinese Statelets*, p. 16.

60. Maenchen-Helfen, "Pseudo-Huns." However, Maenchen's use of the Tuyuhun as yet another "Hun" group in his arguments after taking his cue from the Tang-period shortened appellation for the group is misplaced. Chinese records have shown unequivocally that, unlike the Zahu, the Tuyuhun had an unmistakable Xianbei origin. At any rate, the Tang period pronunciation of the character *hun* is certainly quite different from that of *xiong*.

61. For a recent example, see Vaissière, "Huns et Xiongnu."

62. Sinor, *Cambridge History of Early Inner Asia*, p. 179.

63. See, e.g., Maenchen-Helfen, *World of the Huns*, pp. 164, 199, 381, and 431–32.

64. Detschev, "Der germanische Ursprung des bulgarischen Volksnamens."

65. Runciman, *History of the First Bulgarian Empire,* pp. 279–81.

66. Németh, Gyula (Julius), *A honfoglaló magyarság kialakulása* (*The Shaping of the Hungarians of the Conquest Era*), pp. 38, 95–98.

67. One may read Qi Sihe's highly speculative reconstruction of the Northern Xiongnu's migration route from Asia to Europe.

68. Menges, "Altaic elements in the proto-Bulgarian inscriptions," p. 87n3, points out that the Chinese character *ji* showed a terminal *-r* in the last syllable, in support of Boodberg's equation.

69. Maenchen-Helfen, *World of the Huns*, p. 364.

70. See, e.g., Pelliot, *Notes sur l'histoire de la horde d'or*, pp. 224–30; Maechen-Helfen, *World of the Huns*, p. 384; Rudnickij, *Etymological Dictionary of the Ukrainian Language*, vol. 1, pp. 164–65; and Németh, "The meaning of the ethnonym Bulgar."

71. It is somewhat puzzling that as late as 1964, presumably with his consent, the Canadian journal *Onomastica* republished Németh's 1928 article "La provenance du nom Bulgar," repeating the old "mélange, produit d'un mélange" etymology.

72. Golden, *Introduction to the History of the Turkic Peoples*, p. 104.

73. Dodge, *Fihrist of al-Nadim: A Tenth-century Survey of Muslim Culture*, vol. 1, p. 37.

74. See Pritsak's famous study *Die Bulgarische Fürstenliste und die Sprache der Protobulgaren.*

75. Norman, "Note on the origin of the Chinese duodenary cycle."

76. Pritsak, *Die Bulgarische Fürstenliste*, p. 64. This suggestion may require some qualification: Chinese data suggest an original name Xiutuge (**cio(g)-d'o-klak*) for the name Tuge. But Xiutuge may itself be a shortened form of the full name Xiuzhu Tuge. Then Tuge may have been a general clan name with several subclans. See Fan Y., *Hou Han shu* 90.2983 and 90.2990.

77. Yao W., "Dugu ji Tuge kao" (On the Equivalence of the Clan Names Dugu and Tuge).

78. Bazin, "Man and the concept of history in Turkish Central Asia," and more recently his *Les systèmes chronologiques dans le monde turc ancien.*

79. Read, e.g., Vetch, "Lieou Sa-ho et les grottes de Mo-kao." Vetch unfortunately was otherwise uninformed about the Jihu, as shown by her speculation that *ji* in Jihu referred to Kashmir (p. 147n34). Liu Sahe's reported pilgrimage to India and/or the Western Regions may provide further evidence for the Buluoji's links with Central Asia.

80. Chen Yuan, "Ch'ieh-yün and its Hsien-pi authorship."

Chapter 5

This chapter is adapted, with considerable additions, from the author's articles "Some remarks on the Chinese 'Bulgar'" and "From Azerbaijan to Dunhuang: A Zoroastrianism note."

1. Fairbank, "Preliminary framework," pp. 3–4.

2. Adshead, *China in World History*, p. 145.

3. Now in second edition and with an English translation: *Sogdian Traders: A History*.

4. Asia Society, "Monks and merchants: Silk Road treasures from northwest China, Gansu and Ningxia, 4th–7th century."

5. Grenet, "Pre-Islamic civilization of the Sogdians (seventh century BCE to eighth century CE): A bibliographic essay."

6. See, for instance, Ruan, *Shisanjing zhushu*, p. 181.

7. For a premodern collection of ancient Chinese folk ballads, especially those regarded as political prophesies, see Du W., *Gu Yaoyan* (*Ancient Ballads and Sayings*). For a modern annotated collection of ancient children's songs, see Gao D., *Zhongguo lidai tongyao jizhu* (*An Annotated Compilation of Chinese Children Ballads through the Ages*).

8. For ancient attestations of this Iranic root, see Bailey, *Dictionary of Khotan Saka*, p. 336; and Gershevitch, *Grammar of Manichean Sogdian*, p. 8.

9. This well-recognized transcription will be examined in detail in the next chapter.

10. Feng C., *Xiyu diming* (*Toponyms of the Western Regions*), p. 64.

11. Boodberg, "Early Mongolian toponym."

12. Laufer, *Sino-Iranica*, ch. 1.

13. Gabain, *Alttürkische Grammatik*, pp. 107 and 326. See also Chapter 2 for more references on the *m- ~ b-* equivalence.

14. Bailey, "Hvatanica."

15. See the author's essay, "Yuan Hong: A case of premature death by historians?"

16. The full letter is recorded in Linghu, *Zhou shu* 11.169–71. Excerpts are included in *ZZTJ* 169.5243.

17. It is very rare to read in official dynastic histories such an unadorned yet moving document that reveals perhaps the truest human feelings and pain. Zhao Yi, in *Gaiyu congkao* (*Miscellaneous Research after Walking the Steps*) 7.20, commented that after more than a millennium these letters would still read like live events.

18. As Boodberg discussed the case of Gao Yang in his "Marginalia to the histories of the Northern dynasties," errors in these dates were common.

19. The Gao clan claimed a Hàn ancestry. But the family was repeatedly identified by contemporaries as Xianbei. See Yao W., *Beichao huxing kao*, pp. 135–37. Tan Qixiang has suggested the possibility that the Gao was of Korean descent. See Miao, *Dushi cungao*, pp. 93–94.

20. For example, see Lubotsky, "Early contacts between Uralic and Indo-European: Linguistic and archaeological considerations," p. 307.

21. Patrick D. Healy, "Recent experience aside, in politics wealth isn't all," *New York Times*, November 13, 2005.

22. See also *Taisho* 51 (no. 2092, p. 1012b).

23. The collection *Les Sogdiens en Chine* edited by Étienne de la Vaissière and Eric Trombert is a good representative in Western languages.

24. Michael Drompp, "Turks, Sogdians, and the founding of the T'ang Dynasty," is an interesting exception. But he discusses the political role of the Sogdians only as the "collaborators" of the Türks.

25. Bailey, *Khotanese Texts IV*, p. 11.

26. Heiler, *Erscheinungsformen und Wesen der Religion*, pp. 43–50.

27. For possible pre-Aryan elements in this rite, see Converse, "Agnicayana rite: Indigenous origin?"

28. Lin M. "Cong Chen Shuozhen qiyi kan Huoxian jiao dui Tangdai minjian de yingxiang" (The Zoroastrian influence in the Tang population based on the Chen Shuozhen uprising)."

29. Zhangsun, *Tanglü shuyi* (*Tang Legal Code Interpreted*), 18.345.

30. A few examples: *Jin shu* (*History of the Jin*) 106.2773; *Liang shu* (*History of the Liang*) 11.207; *Chen shu* (*History of the Chen*) 4.70, etc.

31. Ma S., *Huaxia zhushen* (*The Chinese Pantheon of Gods*), p. 405. It would be interesting to learn whether this was prompted by the Chinese authors' repeated accusation that the Zoroastrians had the worst sexual morality, based apparently on their (mis)understanding of the latter's custom of *xvaetvadatha*, "next-of-kin marriage."

32. Li Guotao, "Erlangshen zhi Xianjiao laiyuan" (The Zoroastrian origin of the god Erlang).

33. Lin, "Tangren feng Huoxian jiao bian" (Arguments for the Zoroastrian faith among the Tang population), pp. 106–7.

34. On this ancient exorcistic tradition, read, e.g., Gao G., *Dunhuang minsu xue* (*Studies of Folk Customs in Dunhuang*), pp. 483–505, and Li Z., "Dunhuang nuo sanlun" (Free discussions of Nuo in Dunhuang).

35. Again see Xiang Da's pioneering study on this subject.

36. Ouyang et al., *Xin Tang shu*, 221b.6244. See also Pulleyblank, "Sogdian colony in Inner Mongolia," p. 320.

37. The title "Sabao" has attracted a huge amount of interest among sinologists. A few references on this subject are Pelliot, "Le Sa-pao"; Bailey, "Irano-Indica II"; and more recently, two articles by Forte: "Sabao question" and "Iranians in China: Buddhism, Zoroastrianism, and Bureaus of Commerce."

38. *Science and Civilisation in China*, vol. 3, pp. 469 and 637.

39. There is a rich literature on the Near Eastern and Indo-European onomasticon, particularly by early German authors. Here I list only a few major titles. On Sumerian names, see Limet, *L'Anthroponymie sumerienne*. On ancient Egypt, see Ranke, *Die ägyptischen Personennamen*, vols. 1–3. On Hittite names, see Laroche, *Recueil d'onomastique Hittite*. On ancient Indian/Sanskrit names, see van Velze, *Names of Persons in Early Sanscrit Literature*. On various Semitic languages, including Assyrian and pre-Islamic Arabic, see Tallqvist, *Assyrian Personal Names*; Benz, *Personal Names in the Phoenician and Punic Inscriptions*, and many other titles. On Hellenic names, see Fraser and Matthews's extensive two-volume concordance *Lexicon of Greek Personal Names*. On ancient Iranian names, see Justi's classic 1895 *Namenbuch* and E. Benveniste's modern study *Titres et noms propres en iranien ancien*.

40. In fact, starting about the Common Era, single-character given names dominated the Chinese onomasticon for a long time. See, e.g., Bauer, *Der chinesische Personenname*, pp.

66–77. Only extremely rarely were there cases of "three-character" styles, but never formal names, except, of course, with the "Barbarian" figures of the Northern dynasties. Both three-character styles and ("Barbarian") names were subject to ridicule, incidentally.

41. Tao X., "Tang huji bu congji." Wang Yongxing, in his 1957 essay "Dunhuang Tangdai chakebu kaoshi," mistook the surname as Jia, an error he later corrected in "Tang Tianbao Dunhuang chakebu yanjiu" in 1982. The reign title Tianbao itself can also be regarded as a theophoric name, a phenomenon that started in the Southern and Northern dynasties, coinciding again with the flourishing of Buddhism. See the next chapter.

42. Fan Shengzhi, an official at the court of Emperor Chengdi (32–37 BC), was one of the earliest Chinese agriculture scientists. For his works, see Shanghai Library, *Zhongguo congshu zonglu*, vol. 2, p. 777. *The Columbia Anthology of Traditional Chinese Literature*, edited by Victor Mair, contains (pp. 626–28) the translation of the first chapter of Fan's most important work. For other Fan names from the Eastern Hàn to the Jin dynasty, see, e.g., *Er-shiwushi renming suoyin* (*Index of Personal Names in the Twenty-four Histories*), p. 242.

43. Dunhuang Institute, *Dunhuang Mogaoku gongyangren tiji* (*Inscriptions by Benefactors of Mogao Caverns at Dunhuang*), name index, p. 239. All are normal Hàn Chinese names.

44. On the "nine Zhaowu clans," see, for instance, Pulleyblank, "Sogdian colony in Inner Mongolia," p. 320n1. On the general subject of "foreign-originated surnames," see Yao Weiyuan's superb study *Beichao huxing kao*.

45. Stein Collection S.1889. See, e.g., Tang Geng'ou and Lu Hongji, *Dunhuang shehui jingji wenxian zhenji shilu*, pp. 104–8.

46. Guo Zhufeng, *Hanyu da cidian* (*A Great Dictionary of Han Chinese*), vol. 7, pp. 297–98.

47. *Tulufan chutu wenshu*, vol. 3, pp. 46 and150.

48. Ibid., vol. 7, p. 327.

49. Ibid., vol. 2, pp. 318, 333, 334, and 339; vol. 3, pp. 26, 31, 48, 107, 119, and 158; vol. 4, pp. 132, 159, and 188.

50. See, for instance, van Velze, *Names of Persons in Early Sanscrit Literature*, p. 37.

51. Malalasekera, *Dictionary of Pāli Proper Name*, pp. 13–14.

52. Jacoby, *Die Fragmente der griechischen Historiker*, Zweiter Teil A, pp. 361–62.

53. For translating the Iranian *-data* as "son," see Gershevitch, "Island-Bay and lion," p. 89.

54. In a personal communication, Professor Philippe Gignoux has put forward an interesting suggestion that the popular pan-Altaic personal name Baγadur might have come from an Iranian origin baγa- ādur, "god of fire," or a case of the widely attested dual-divinity construct.

55. Frye, *History of Ancient Iran*, pp. 143 and 163. For the element *-pata, -pates* in the pre-Islamic Iranian onomasticon meaning "protected" ("beschützt," "protégé"), see, e.g., Justi, *Iranische Namenbuch*, p. 505; and Benveniste, *Titres et noms propres en iranien ancient,* p. 90. In fact, Christian Bartholomae in his 1904 *Altiranisches Wörterbuch*, p. 318, interprets the name Atarepata as "der vom Feuer geschützte (whom Fire protects)."

56. Boodberg, *Hu Tien Han Yüeh Fang Chu,* No. 5, p. 108.

57. Wright, *Sui Dynasty*, p. 54.

58. Pulleyblank, "Chinese Name for the Turks."

59. Gignoux, "Les noms propres en moyen-perse épigraphique: Étude typologique," and *Noms propres sassanides en moyen-perse épigraphique*. In personal names it was often written as *'twl*.

60. Bartholomae, *Altiranisches Wörterbuch*, p. 316; Bailey, *Khotanese Texts IV*, p. 11n2.

61. I am greatly indebted to Professor Philippe Gignoux for enlightening me on this development in Iranian philology, in a personal communication. Professor Gignoux has further kindly directed me to W. Henning and D. N. MacKenzie regarding this particular transcription *ādur*. See, for example, MacKenzie, *A Concise Pahlavi Dictionary*, p. 5, and Mary Boyce, *A Word-List of Manichaean Middle Persian and Parthian*, p. 8.

62. There are also Chinese transcription data suggesting the less likely possibility that Atouliu might have come from the form *ātar*. In the fourth century Chinese translation of *Lalitavistara* (Chinese *Foshuo puyao jing*), the Sanskrit/Pali name Asita was transcribed as Ayitou. See de Jong, "L'Épisode d'Asita dans le Lalitavistara." There were even contemporary Buddhist scripture data from exactly the same region in which the character *tou* was used to transcribe the Pali *ta/da* sound. Examples include *motouluo* for *mutali*, *titoulaizha* for *dhatarattha*, and *yutoulan* for *uddaka ramaputta*. Coblin, "Remarks on some early Buddhist transcriptional data from northwest China."

63. Pelliot Collection P.2592. See, e.g., Tang and Lu, *Dunhuang shehui jingji wenxian zhenji shilu,* p. 163.

64. Two prominent Chinese scholars advocating this new theory are Lin Wushu and Chen Guoshan. See Rong Xinjiang's review essay "Research on Zoroastrianism in China (1923–2000)."

65. Pelliot Collection P.412, P.3391, P.3707, P.3978, P.4063, and Stein Collection S.1845 and S.6309, etc.

66. Grenet and Zhang, "The last refuge of the Sogdian religion: Dunhuang in the ninth and tenth centuries."

67. Yao W., *Beichao huxing kao*, p. 392.

68. Frye, "Fate of Zoroastrians in eastern Iran."

Chapter 6

This chapter is adapted from the author's article "Son of heaven and son of god: Interactions among ancient Asiatic cultures regarding sacral kingship and theophoric names," *Journal of the Royal Asiatic Society*, ser. 3, 12: 289–325.

1. Ching, "Son of heaven: Sacral kingship in ancient China."

2. Ibid., p. 4.

3. Gu, "Shi *Tian*" (Interpreting Tian); and Guo M., *Xian-Qin tiandaoguan zhi jinzhan* (*Progression of the Concept of Heaven Divine Orders in Pre-Qin Times*). Guo's book was

published under the pen name Guo Dingtang because at the time Guo was a political exile living in Japan. From the date (December 1935) of his supplementary notes, it can be assumed that Guo made the discovery no later than Creel.

4. Creel, *Origins of Statecraft in China*, vol. 1, pp. 493–506.

5. Hu H., *Jiaguxue Shangshi luncong chuji*, p. 328; and Chen M., *Yinxu buci zongshu* (*Summation of Divinatory Inscriptions from the Ruins of Yin*), p. 531. For Dong's opinion, see Creel, *Origins of Statecraft in China*, p. 496.

6. See, for instance, Chen M., *Yinxu buci zongshu*, p. 531, for the specific bronze inscriptions.

7. Wang Yuxin, *Xizhou jiagu tanlun* (*Exploratory Studies of Western Zhou Oracle Bones*), pp. 102, 311.

8. See, for instance, Justi, *Iranisches Namenbuch*, p. 56.

9. Guo M., *Xian-Qin tiandaoguan zhi jinzhan*, p. 17.

10. Eno, "Was there a high god *Ti* in Shang religion?" It is rather unfortunate that Julia Ching's 1997 article does not seem to have consulted Eno's enlightening study of her presumed Shang "Lord-on-high."

11. Chun, "Conceptions of kinship and kingship in classical Chou China." My translation is adapted from that of Sybille van der Sprenkel, *Legal Institutions in Manchu China*, p. 152, translated from a Song dynasty source, which Chun quoted without recognizing the much older origin of this principle. The sentence not merely, as van der Sprenkel claims, "echoes a passage in," but is literally lifted from, an entry in the pre-Qin chronology *Zuozhuan* (5.276), Year 10 of Xigong (650 BC).

12. Chen M., *Yinxu buci zongshu*, p. 580.

13. The construct *dizi* did exist in Oracle bones though, likely referring to royal sons born of the principal consort. As such, the character *di* was merely a loan for a homonym meaning the child born of the principal wife. See, for instance, Qiu, "Guanyu Shangdai de zongzu zuzhi," p. 4.

14. Read, e.g., Creel, *Origins of Statecraft in China*, p. 44.

15. Hsu and Linduff, *Western Chou Civilization*, p. 111.

16. Baxter, *Handbook of Old Chinese Phonology*, p. 792, has reconstructed the archaic pronunciation of the character *tian* as **hlin*.

17. Chen Sanping, "Sino-Tokharico-Altaica: Two linguistic notes."

18. Pulleyblank, "Chinese and their neighbors in prehistoric and early historic times," especially pp. 421–22.

19. Mair, "Old Sinitic **M^{γ}ag*, Old Persian *Maguš*, and English 'magician.'" Julia Ching, for example, has discussed the role of the magicians and shamans in detail regarding kingship in ancient China, though she missed Mair's interesting study on the relationship between China's *wu* and ancient Iranian Magi.

20. For the disappearance of the usage, see Qian, *Shijiazhai yangxin lu* 16.397.

21. See also Vandermeersch, *Wangdao ou la Voie Royale: Recherches sur l'esprit des institutions de la Chine archaïque*, tome 2, pp. 13–18.

22. *Chunqiu Zuoshi zhuan* (*The Commentary of Mr. Zuo on the Spring and Autumn Annals*) 1.3, 1.40, 2.80, 2.116, 5.265, 8.461, etc. (abbreviated hereafter as *Zuozhuan*).

23. From the famous Hàn-dynasty commentaries on *Shijing* (*Classic of Odes*, or *Book of Poems*) by Mao Heng. See for instance *Cihai* (*Sea of Words*), p. 369.

24. The best description of this episode is found in Fan Y., *Hou Hàn shu* 88.2921.

25. Pelliot's unsurpassed "La théorie des quartre Fils du Ciel" remains the best study of this tradition. See also Ferrand, "Les grands rois du monde."

26. Sten Konow, *Kharoshthi Inscriptions with the Exception of Those of Aśoka*, pp. 163 and 165.

27. Mukherjee, "Title Devaputra on Kushana coins."

28. Dodge, *Fihrist of al-Nadim*, vol. 2, p. 839. See also Ferrand, *Relations de voyages et textes géographiques arabes, persans et turks relatifs à L'Extrême Orient du VIIIe au XVIIIe siecles*, p. 131.

29. Pelliot, *Notes on Marco Polo*, vol. 2, pp. 652–61.

30. A particular case is the Pahlevi text of the Tang dynasty bilingual tomb inscription dated 874. According to some readings, it contained the word *bgpwhl* = *bagpuhr*, which referred to the Tang emperor. See, e.g., Humbach, "Die Pahlavi-Chinesische bilingue von Xi'an."

31. Pelliot, *Notes on Marco Polo*, vol. 2, p. 655.

32. Ibid., p. 652. Henning, "Sogdian loan-words in New Persian," certainly agrees with this, as far as the Persian form is concerned (p. 94).

33. See, e.g., Henning, "Date of the Sogdian ancient letters," pp. 601–15.

34. Harmatta, "Archaeological evidence for the date of the Sogdian letters," and "Sogdian sources for the history of pre-Islamic Central Asia."

35. Lévi, "Devaputra," pp. 12–13.

36. Pelliot, *Notes on Marco Polo*, vol. 2, p. 654.

37. Even outside the Indian subcontinent, such usage is still widespread in, say, Southeast Asia, which was once under the strong influence of Hindu culture. One particular example is the name of the Indonesian political leader Megawati Sukarnoputri, the daughter of Sukarno, Indonesia's founding president.

38. Maneka Gandhi in *The Penguin Book of Hindu Names*, p. 100, lists the name Devakumāra, "son of a deva," which appears to be a modern construct, as no ancient source is given for this name. The same can be said about names like Brahmaputra and Brahmaputrā in her book.

39. Ferdinand Justi's classic *Iranisches Namenbuch* and the multivolume *Iranisches Personennamenbuch*, edited by Manfred Mayrhofer. I failed to find a single case of *puthra/puhr* in a theophoric construct. Yet I cannot claim the same thoroughness in examining the ancient Iranian names as I did the ancient Indic names.

40. See for instance Justi, *Iranisches Namenbuch*, pp. 492–93.

41. Yule, *Book of Ser Marco Polo*, vol. 2, p. 148; Pelliot, *Notes on Marco Polo*, vol. 2, p. 656.

42. Sinor, "Western information on the Kitans and some related questions."

43. Fletcher, "Mongols."

44. Middle and Old Chinese pronunciations quoted in this study are from Karlgren, *Grammata Serica Recensa*, unless specified otherwise.

45. It is also recorded in Li Y., *Bei shi* 1.22, with the tribe name mistaken as Yuele, a not uncommon script error. For example, the Chinese transcription *teqin* of the Altaic word *tegin*, "prince," has been written as *tele* in current editions of almost all dynastic histories.

46. Wei Shou, *Wei shu* 4.79 gives the name as Heruoyu, where *yu* is a very common mistake for *gan*. The correct name is given in *Wei shu* 24.635, and Li Y., *Bei shi* 21.798.

47. On the 'High Carts," see Maenchen-Helfen, "Ting-ling"; and Edwin Pulleyblank "The 'High Carts': A Turkish-speaking people before the Turks."

48. The passage also appears in Li Y., *Bei shi* 94.3132 and Du Y., *Tongdian* 200.5489.

49. Two other such ancestral cases are Heba Sheng (*Zhou shu* 14.215) and Husi Chun (*Bei shi* 49.1785).

50. See, e.g., Fang et al., *Jin shi* 1.1–2 on the Nüzhen's ancestry. Pelliot, "À propos des Comans," also agrees that both historically and geographically the Mojie were the ancestors of the Nüzhen.

51. Wei Z., *Sui shu* 81.1821; Li Y., *Bei shi* 94.3124; and Ouyang et al., *Xin Tang shu* 219.6178. *Bei shi* 94.3130 also states the same for the Shiwei. Yet the *Jiu Tang shu* statement quoted earlier and another passage in *Bei shi* (34.3130) indicate the Shiwei's chieftains were known as Mohefu, which suggests Manduo as a subtitle.

52. Marquart, "Über das Volkstum der Komanen," p. 84.

53. Linghu, *Zhou shu* 49.899; Wei Z., *Sui shu* 84.1881; Li Y., *Bei shi* 94.3127; and Du Y., *Tongdian* 200.5481.

54. See, e.g., Clauson, *Etymological Dictionary of Pre-thirteenth-century Turkish*, pp. 417 and 453.

55. Pelliot, *Notes on Marco Polo*, vol. 2, p. 656.

56. The name was also mistaken as Wuyu, a common scribe error as mentioned before.

57. Menges, "Titles and organizational terms of the Qytan (Liao) and Qara-Qytaj (Śi-Liao)," p. 73.

58. Here is a very limited list: Marquart, "Über das Volkstum der Komanen" p. 84; Pelliot, "Neuf notes sur des questions d'Asie centrale"; Boodberg, *Hu T'ien Han Yüeh Fang Chu*, no. 9; Menges, "Altaic elements in the proto-Bulgarian inscriptions," p. 94, and "Titles and organizational terms" p. 73; Molè, *The T'u-yü-hun from the Northern Wei to the Time of the Five Dynasties*, p. 78; Doerfer, *Türkische und Mongolische Elemente im Neupersischen*, Band 2, p. 369.

59. Radloff, *Die Alttürkischen Inschriften der Mongolei*, vol. 1, plate III.

60. Justi, *Iranisches Namenbuch*, pp. 184 and 202; Benveniste, *Titres et noms propres en iranien ancien*, p. 79; Schmitt, *Iranisches Namen in den Indogermanischen Sprachen Kleinasiens*, p. 23; and Thomas, "Tibetan documents concerning Chinese Turkestan."

61. As noted by Pulleyblank, "Chinese name for the Turks."

62. Coblin, "Comparative studies on some Tang-time dialects of Shazhou," p. 314.

63. Clauson, *Etymological Dictionary of Pre-thirteenth-century Turkish*, pp. 360–61.

64. Bailey, *Khotanese Texts VII*, p. 26.

65. See, e.g., Klyashtorny and Livshitz, "Sogdian inscription of Bugut revised."

66. See Mackerras, *Uighur Empire according to the T'ang Dynastic Histories*; and Lieu, *Manichaeism in the Later Roman Empire and Medieval China*.

67. Pulleyblank, "Sogdian colony in Inner Mongolia."

68. Chen Yinke, *Tangdai zhengzhishi shulun gao*, pp. 33–34.

69. See, e.g., Golden, *Introduction to the History of the Turkic Peoples*, p. 71.

70. Clauson, "Foreign elements in early Turkish."

71. Read, e.g., Menges, "Titles and organizational terms"; Bazin, "Pre-Islamic Turkic borrowings in Upper Asia: Some crucial semantic fields"; and Doerfer, *Türkische und Mongolische Elemente*, Band 2, pp. 402–4.

72. Clauson, "Foreign elements in early Turkish"; and Bazin, "Pre-Islamic Turkic borrowings in Upper Asia."

73. Doerfer, *Türkische und Mongolische Elemente*, Band 2, p. 138; Menges, "Titles and organizational terms."

74. Sinor, "Establishment and dissolution of the Türk Empire."

75. Ibid., p. 290.

76. Chen Sanping, "Sino-Tokharico-Altaica."

77. Frye, "Remarks on kingship in ancient Iran."

78. It is well known that Confucius, who was particularly sensitive to the issue of political order and etiquette, first introduced the construct *tianwang* for the marginalized Zhou figurehead "son of heaven" in the chronicle *Chunqiu* (*Spring and Autumn Annals*).

79. Sometimes held by a crown prince (*Jin shu* 106.2769), and sometimes even a great *Chanyu* clearly was lower in rank than the crown prince (*Jin shu* 105.2476).

80. Fang et al., *Jin shu* 109.2816; Wei Shou, *Wei shu* 95.2050, 95.2064; and Li Y., *Bei shi* 98.3270, etc.

81. W. B. Henning's translation in "Date of the Sogdian ancient letters," p. 605.

82. Frye, *History of Ancient Iran*, p. 106n68.

83. Yet see, for instance, Balsdon, "'Divinity' of Alexander."

84. And in the case of Cleopatra, the feminine form Θεα. See, e.g., Wroth, *Catalogue of the Greek Coins of Galatia, Cappadocia and Syria*, pp. 158, 306; Gardner, *Coins of the Greek and Scythic Kings of Bactria and India in the British Museum*, p. xxviii, and several other catalogs of ancient Greek coins.

85. In addition to the Greek language and icons, albeit gradually debased, the word "philhellene" was a near-permanent feature of the Parthian coins, as can be easily verified with any catalog of ancient Greek coins quoted above.

86. Marcellinus, *Ammianus Marcellinus*, vol. 2, pp. 350–51, corresponding to XXIII, 6, 4–5.

87. Frye, *History of Ancient Iran*, p. 371 (app. 4).

88. Marcellinus, *Ammianus Marcellinus*, vol. 2, pp. 332–33, corresponding to XVII 5, 3.

89. Henning, "Sogdian god," p. 249.

90. See, for instance, Doerfer, *Türkische und Mongolische Elemente*, Band 2, pp. 389–410.

91. Bailey, *Culture of the Sakas*, p. 50, and *Dictionary of Khotan Saka*, p. 390.

92. See Wei Z., *Sui shu* 84.1868; Liu X. et al., *Jiu Tang shu* 13.370, 17a.515; Ouyang et al., *Xin Tang shu* 215b.6069, etc.

93. Bang and von Gabain "Türkische Turfan-Texte," p. 412.

94. *Compendium of the Turkic Dialects,* tr. Dankoff and Kelly, vol. 3, p. 185.

95. Pelliot, "Notes sur les T'ou-yu-houen et les Sou-p'i," pp. 323–31.

96. Ban et al., *Hàn shu* 11.337, Ying Shao's commentary.

97. The cases are too numerous to list. Here are some examples: Fan Y., *Hou Hàn shu* 5.232, 9.367, 37.1258, 44.1520, 56.1832, 65.2140, 71.2307; Chen Shou, *Sanguo zhi* 2.59, 45.1075, 56.1308; Fang et al., *Jin shu* 3.72.

98. See for examples Xu Z., *Shishuo xinyu xiaojian*, pp. 329, 352, 377, etc. The example on p. 352 is a clear case for the meaning "son."

99. Linghu, *Zhou shu* 16.263. Dugu Xin was the father-in-law of both the Zhou "heaven king" Yuwen Yu (temple name Shizong; posthumous title Ming) and Yang Jian, the founding emperor of the Sui, as well as the maternal grandfather of Li Yuan, the founding emperor of the Tang.

100. Boodberg, *Hu T'ien Han Yüeh Fang Chu*, no. 5, p. 103.

101. Wroth, *Catalogue of the Greek Coins in the British Museum*, vol. 23, *Catalogue of the Coins of Parthia*, pp. 5, 16, 18, 38, 41, etc. It is interesting to see (p. 61) Mithradates III (reign 57–53 BC) call himself Θεουευπάτορ "[of] god-good-father."

102. Liddell, Scott, and Jones, *Greek-English Lexicon*, p. 1847.

103. According to ibid., p. 790, Θεοπάτορ is only attested as Parthian royal titles.

104. Tarn, *Greeks in Bactria and India*, p. 92.

105. The most extensive study of the subject is perhaps Roux's four-part article "Tängri: Essai sur le ciel-dieu des peuples altaïcs." See also Pallisen, "Die alte Religion der Mongolen und der Kultus Tschingis-Chans," though the latter was based on materials much later than the epoch of our interest.

106. See, e.g., Tekin, *Grammar of Orkhon Turkic*, p. 232.

107. Roux, "L'origine céleste de la souveraineté dans les inscriptions paléo-turques de Mongolie et de Sibérie," pp. 235–36.

108. Pulleyblank, "Consonantal system of Old Chinese: Part II." In fact, Pulleyblank could not find anything acceptable in the still-living Yenisei languages, which generally have a *fyp* root for "son." In the end, he was forced to identify the word *bĭkjàl*, "son," in the extinct Arin language as the cognate to *gutu*, whose Hàn-time pronunciation was reconstructed by him as **kwah-ðah*. He alleged that "*bĭ* appears to be a prefix added to nouns of relationship." In my opinion, a much better correspondence in this direction can be found in the Sanskrit term *kudaka*, "child"; New Persian *kūdak*, "child"; Tamil *kura*, "young"; and Santali *kora*, "boy" with the reconstructed ancient Iranian form **kudak* or **kuðag*. For these Indo-Iranian words, see H.-P. Schmidt, "Indo-Iranian etymological kaleidoscope."

109. Ouyang et al., *Yiwen leiju* (*A Categorized Compilation of Literary Writings*), 80.1371.

110. This passage is actually taken from the earlier *Shiji* chapter on the Xiongnu (110.2896), which further (110.2899) records that, at the instigation of a Hàn eunuch, the Xiongnu monarch later aggrandized his imperial title to "Heaven-and-earth-born, sun-and-moon-installed Great Chanyu of the Xiongnu." There was again no "son of heaven" construct.

111. See, for instance, Tekin, *Grammar of Orkhon Turkic*, p. 231.

112. Bang and von Gabain, "Türkische Turfan-Texte," p. 414, lines 27 and 29.

113. Tekin, *Grammar of Orkhon Turkic*, p. 252.

114. Ouyang et al., *Xin Tang shu* 221a.6230 calls it Ajietian Mountain, apparently transcribing the Old Turkic name.

115. *Cefu yuangui*, ch. 979, is the likely original source.

116. Pelliot, "L'édition collective des œuvres de Wang Kouo-wei."

117. Pelliot, "Neuf notes sur des questions d'Asie centrale," note 29.

118. Radloff, *Alttürkischen Inschriften*, vol. 1, plate III, cols. 12 and 16–18.

119. Or as F. W. K. Müller has suggested, *gutu* may stand for the Turkic word *kut* or *qut*, "Heaven's favor," "good fortune," "majesty," "majestic," as quoted in Pulleyblank, "Consonantal system of Old Chinese," p. 244.

120. Fang et al., *Jin shu* 121.3111 note 8, 125.3128; Wei Shou, *Wei shu* 3.50, *ZZTJ* 111.3506, 112.3527.

121. Fang et al., *Jin shu* 8.196. Ran was supposed to have a Hàn origin but grew up as the adopted grandson of the "Barbarian" heaven-king Shi Hu.

122. This break actually covered the last two puppet emperors of the Western Wei.

123. It is also no accident that the same Qidan monarch called himself "Heaven Emperor."

124. See also Ban et al., *Hàn shu* 94a.3765; and *ZZTJ* 18.582–83. I consider this awkward case likely a mistranslation of Tängri as god, or *tianshen* in Chinese.

125. Fletcher, "Mongols," p. 31n13.

126. Frye, "Remarks on kingship," p. 80.

127. Linghu, *Zhou shu* 2.36, 24.404, 38.685; Wei Z., *Sui shu* 66.1549. Wang Zhongluo's *Beizhou liudian* is the best compilation and study of the Northern Zhou officialdom.

128. Hirth, *Ancient History of China, to the End of the Chou Dynasty*, p. 67. Hirth calls it "the oldest Turkish word on record." This claim is consistent with archeological findings that show striking similarity in bronze daggers found in China and west Siberia. See Okladnikov, "Inner Asia at the dawn of history," p. 86.

129. Sima Q., *Shiji* 4.136 and 110.2881. See also Fang et al., *Jin shu* 87.2264; Shen, *Song shu* 27.764 and 27.809 for interpretations.

130. Sima Q., *Shiji* 4.122. It is interesting to see this changed to "bear" in the *Mushi* chapter of *Shangshu* (*Book of Documents*), making the "bear" appear twice in that short passage. Apparently later literati who edited these ancient classics felt that the original metaphor was repugnant.

131. Duan, *Shuowen jiezi shu*, p. 236.

132. For a somewhat more detailed discussion, see my "Sino-Tokharo-Altaica." For in-depth studies of specific examples, see Goodrich, "Riding astride and the saddle in ancient China"; and Shaughnessy, "Historical perspectives on the introduction of chariots into China."

133. Examples abound in *Zuozhuan* and other early sources. Prušek, *Chinese Statelets and the Northern Barbarians in the Period 1400–300 B.C.,* is a good modern reference.

134. Sima Q., *Shiji* 110.2885, corroborated by *Shiji* 79.2406 and *Zhanguo ce* (*Intrigues of the Warring States*) 5.184.

135. Maenchen-Helfen, *World of the Huns*, pp. 174–78; Di Cosmo, "Ancient Inner Asian nomads."

136. There is a rich literature on Near Eastern and Indo-European onomasticon. Please see note 38 of Chapter 5 for a short list of major references.

137. For the relationship between theophoric names, the so-called personal god, and the Near Eastern religious tradition, see Jacobsen, *Treasures of Darkness: A History of Mesopotamian Religion*; and two excellent focus studies by German authors Vorländer, *Mein Gott: Die Vorstellungen vom persönlische Gott im Alten Orient und im Alten Testament;* and Albertz, *Persönliche Frömmigkeit und offizielle Religion: Religionsinterner Pluralismus in Israel und Babylon.*

138. Another possible early theophoric construct is *shenbao*, "god-protect" (Sima Q., *Shijing*, Ode 219), also written as *lingbao*, "spirit-protect," in *Chuci* (*Elegies of Chu*—a collection of early southern verse). It was traditionally interpreted as an honorific noun meaning the (ancestor) idol (*shi*). Zhu Xi (*Zhuzi yulei* 81.2125) was perhaps the first to interpret it as meaning a sorcerer. But Wang Guowei, *Guantang jilin* (*Collected Works from the Hall of Observations*), vol. 2, 2.81, utilizing bronze inscription data, showed it to be yet another honorific title for deceased ancestors. At any rate, this was not a proper name.

139. One notes the almost simultaneous appearance of opprobrious names, which may also be attributed to similar foreign, particularly ancient Indian, influence. On the latter, see van Velze, *Names of Persons in Early Sanscrit Literature*, p. 26; and Gonda, *Notes on Names and the Name of God in Ancient India*, pp. 9–10.

140. In particular, the Japanese author Miyakawa Hisayuki's far-from-complete collection "Rikucho jinmei ni arawaretaru Bukkyogo," noted by Wright, *Studies in Chinese Buddhism.*

141. The best example of theophoric hypocoristica is the name Suo Shenshen, found in, not surprisingly, the Dunhuang region. See Tang and Lu, *Dunhuang shehui jingji wenxian zhenji shilu*, p. 270, a document dated 847–59.

142. For a discussion of the Buddhism trinity, read, e.g., Oldenberg's classic treatise *Buddha: Sein Leben, Seine Lehre, Seine Gemeinde*, pp. 387–88.

143. An alternative Hellenic form is *-dotos*. See Masson, "Remarques sur quelques anthroponymes myceniens," p. 283. One thus observes that the name Herodotus of the "father of history" means "Hera's gift."

144. It should be noted that a childhood name does not always appear in the person's biography. Due to the sheer size of the dynastic histories (I used the Zhonghua shuju

edition of the nine dynastic histories, which have a total of more than 14,600 printed pages), omissions may occur in this regard despite my best efforts.

145. This is one of several critical conclusions Chen Yinke has drawn in his important work on the origin and sources of the political ideology, cultural heritage, and government system of the Sui-Tang era, *Sui-Tang zhidu yuanyuan lüelun gao* (*A Draft Exploration of the Origins of the Sui-Tang Institutions*), pp. 12–29.

146. Wang P., *Tang huiyao* 1.1; Ouyang et al., *Xin Tang shu* 1.1; Liu X. et al., *Jiu Tang shu* 1.1 gave a slightly different name, Tianxi, of the same meaning.

147. Interpreted as *tianshou* or *tianyu*, both meaning "god-given." See *Eanyi mingyi ji* (*Taishō Tripitaka*, No. 2131, pp. 1062–63).

148. Whereas *deva* could be used as a Chinese theophoric name, as attested by the Northern Qi courtier Mu Tipo.

149. See the name Zang Mohai of a prominent general of the ethnic Juqu regime in northwestern China (*Jin shu* 129.3192ff.). Sogdian *βaγa*- in personal names were rendered as Mojia, Mohe, and so on, with Bohebiduo being the best example, apparently transcribing Bagapāta, "god-protect." The Chinese forms here are quoted from Xiang Da, *Tangdai Chang'an yu Xiyu wenming*, pp. 14, 24, and 90.

150. Gignoux, *Noms propres sassanides en moyen-perse épigraphique*, Introduction.

151. In particular, Phillipe Gignoux's two articles, "Le dieu Baga en Iran" and "Les noms propres en moyen-perse épigraphique: Étude typologiqueé."

152. *Mogaoku ji*, Dunhuang manuscript P.3720, dated 865.

153. Yet Hàn here is also the name of a river, whence the name of the region the founding emperor of the Hàn was first enfeoffed with, hence the dynasty name. The pun was likely intended by this reign title.

154. In addition to the quoted cases, this is also clearly indicated in all such earlier reign titles prior to the Eastern Jin. See Chen Shou, *Sanguo zhi* 47.1142, 1148, 47.1171; and Shen, *Song shu* 31.898.

155. For examples, Mozhe Niansheng's reign title Tianjian (524–27), Jihu Liu Lisheng's Shenjia (525–25), and Moqi Chounu's Shenshou (528–30).

156. Prior to the Tang, *zunhao* stood generically for *huangdi*, "emperor"; *huanghou*, "empress"; *huangtaihou,* "empress-dowager"; etc. It also included *tianwang*, "heaven-king," naturally.

157. Neither was the character *qian*, *tian*'s synonym.

158. Emperor Liwei was famed among the Tuoba ancestors for not having a maternal clan (*Wei shu* 1.2). For the significance of maternal clans on the Steppe, see Chapter 1.

159. Including, not surprisingly, a *tianhuang,* "heaven emperor," title for Emperor Gaozong, which reflected the heavy Steppe heritage in the early Tang, as argued in Chapter 1.

160. For instance, Edward Parker so assumed throughout his *A Thousand Years of the Tartars*.

161. Doerfer, *Türkische und Mongolische Elemente,* Band 2, pp. 371–74; Pelliot, *Notes on Marco Polo*, p. 657.

162. Pelliot, *Notes on Marco Polo*, p. 657.

163. See Wei Z., *Sui shu* 84.1883; Li Y., *Bei shi* 94.3130; and Du Y., *Tongdian* 200.5487.

164. Marquart, "Über das Volkstum der Komanen," p. 84n1.

165. Du Y., *Tongdian* 197.5402 (cf. p. 5421n40).

166. Fletcher, "Turco-Mongolian Monarchic Tradition in the Ottoman Empire" and "Mongols."

167. These are well summarized in Engnell, *Studies in Divine Kingship in the Ancient Near East,* Excursus, particularly pp. 178–89.

168. Radloff, *Die Alttürkischen Inschriften*, vol.1, Plate III, column 1.

169. It is also a possible rendition of the pure Iranian form *bagadāta*, which is not attested in a "Barbarian" milieu.

170. See, among many other titles, Tarn, *Greeks in Bactria and India*; and. Holt, *Alexander the Great and Bactria: The Formation of a Greek Frontier in Central Asia.*

171. This is clearly shown in Greek coins from many places in Asia. See also references cited in Maenchen-Helfen's article in the next note.

172. Maenchen-Helfen, "Parthian coin-legend on a Chinese bronze."

173. Konow, *Kharoshthi Inscriptions*, pp. 2, 66, and 98.

174. Frye, *History of Ancient Iran*, p. 174.

175. Olivier Masson, "Une inscription ephebique de Plotemaïs (cyrenaïque)," p. 254.

176. Davids, *Milinda-Questions*, p. 26.

177. Konow, *Kharoshthi Inscriptions*, pp. xxxiii and xliv (Introduction).

178. Hookham, *Tamburlaine the Conqueror*, pp. 71–72; and Manz, *Rise and Rule of Tamerlane*, p. 57.

179. Frye, "Remarks on kingship," p. 82.

180. Meskoob, *Iranian Nationality and the Persian Language*, pp. 36-37.

181. See, e.g., Chun, "Conceptions of kinship and kingship."

182. Recorded by Rashid al-Din as *taiši*, which may also be transcribing Chinese *taishi*, "grand preceptor." The latter was known as *tayisi* later. See Serruys, "Office of Tayisi in Mongolia in the fifteenth century." But as Paul Pelliot has noted, it was evidently used sometimes as *taizi*, which was directly attested in *The Secret History*. See Pelliot, "Notes sur le 'Turkestan' de M. W. Barthold."

183. For example, in modern Chinese folk arts even the son of Mu Guiying, the legendary female general allegedly of the Northern Song, was referred to as a *taizi*. See He, "Nuo and the fertility cult."

184. Barthold, *Turkestan Down to the Mongol Invasion*, p. 196.

185. Needham, *Science and Civilization in China*, vol. 1, pp. 236–37.

186. Harmatta, "Sino-Iranica," p. 143.

Chapter 7

1. See Victor Mair's two extensive treatises: *Tun-huang Popular Narratives* and *T'ang Transformation Texts.*

2. See my essay "Yuan Hong."

3. There are similar links concerning another great Tang poet, Li Bai (Li Po), which have attracted substantial scholarly coverage. One could read, e.g., Elling Eide's interesting but often speculative paper "On Li Po." In the final analysis, even the assertion that Li was born in Central Asia could not be considered proven beyond any reasonable doubt.

4. Sun Guodong, "Tang Song zhiji shehui mendi zhi xiaorong" (The disappearance of prestigious pedigrees during the Tang-Song transition), p. 289.

5. See, e.g., Zhu, *Bai Juyi ji jianjiao* (hereafter *Jianjiao*), pp. 2833–34 notes.

6. Waley, *Life and Times of Po Chü-i*, p. 26.

7. Chen Yinke, *Yuan-Bai shi jianzheng gao* (hereafter *Jianzheng gao*), p. 294.

8. Frye, *Cambridge History of Iran*, vol. 4, p. 165.

9. Yao W., *Beichao huxing kao*, pp. 374–76.

10. See Wang Dingbao (ca. 870–955), *Tang zhiyan* (*Collected Words on the Tang*) 13.145; and Li F., (925–96), *Taiping guangji* 251.1950–51.

11. Liu X. et al., *Jiu Tang shu* (*Old History of the Tang*) 104.3213; *ZZTJ* 216.6916.

12. See, for instance, Pulleyblank, *Background of the Rebellion of An Lu-shan*, p. 16.

13. One could read Chen Yinke's short but insightful article on the origin of the Chinese term for *bromhifrosis*, "Huchou yu huchou" (Fox-smell and bromhidrosis).

14. Sun Guangxian (?–968), *Beimeng suoyan* (*Trifling Bits of Northern Reverie* 5.32, quoting a Tang dynasty source.

15. In this context, Eide's speculation ("On Li Po," p. 396) about "China's ethnocentrism" being a source of Li Bai's "discontent" would seem farfetched.

16. In Wu G., *Sui-Tang Wudai muzhi huibian Shaanxi juan*. See Meng F., "Taiyuan Bai Juyi kao" (A study of Bai Juyi of Taiyuan).

17. Zhang N., "Ji Luoyang chutu de liangjian Tangdai shike" (Notes on two Tang-era stone inscriptions unearthed in Luoyang).

18. Qian Boquan, "Han-Tang Qiuci ren de neiqian jiqi luosan" (The immigration and dispersion of the Qiuci people during the Han and Tang).

19. Read, e.g., Pollak, *Mandarins, Jews, and Missionaries*, pp. 325–30.

20. For Shen Gua's original passage, see Hu D., *Mengxi bitan jiaozheng* (*An Emended and Annotated Edition of Brush Talks from Dream Brook*) 18.597–98. This possible identification has led to a multitude of articles and at least one conference on this discovery in China. Here I list only a few that are pertinent to this chapter: Wu X., "Bi Sheng mudi faxian ji xiangguan wenti chubu tantao" (The discovery of Bi Sheng's tomb and the preliminary exploration of related issues); Wu X. et al., "Yingshan xian faxian Bi Sheng jiqi houyi muzang kaozeng"; Ren F., "Zaitan Bi Sheng bei de zongjiao secai"; and Lin M., "Yingshan Bi Sheng bei yu Huainan Moni jiao" (The tomb inscription of Bi Sheng at Yingshan and Manichaeism in Huainan).

21. Ren F., "Zaitan Bi Sheng bei de zongjiao secai," p. 38. Lin M., "Yingshan Bi Sheng bei yu Huainan Moni jiao," p. 394, states that the same sun-moon feature was found on the tombstones of Bi's descendants, a claim I have yet to verify with firsthand field reports.

22. In particular, one can compare the picture of Bi Sheng's tombstone (see, e.g., Lin M., "Yingshan Bi Sheng bei yu Huainan Moni jiao," p. 395) to, say, the tombstone shown in Figure 110 in Wu W., *Quanzhou zongjiao shike* (*Religious Inscriptions at Quanzhou*), to see the striking similarities.

23. *Chen Yinke xiansheng lunwenji* (*Collected Papers of Master Chen Yinke*), vol. 1, pp. 505–24.

24. Ancestor worship, or the ancestor cult (but euphemistically labeled "ancestor rites" by the Jesuits and their latter-day apologists), was one of the thorniest problems faced by the Jesuits in converting the Chinese in the late Ming. It was an issue that tried Matteo Ricci's wits to a great extent (Mungello, *Curious Land: Jesuit Accommodation and the Origins of Sinology*, pp. 64-65) and would, together with the so-called Confucian rites, develop into a major and lasting controversy within the Catholic orthodoxy after the rival Franciscans condemned the Jesuits' practices regarding these "rites." See, e.g., Etiemble, *Les Jésuites en Chine: La querelle des rites (1551–1773)*, pp. 90ff.

25. Lu Y., *Weinan wenji* (*Collected Works of Weinan*) 5.64; Zhuang, *Jile bian* (*Notes of Marginal Values*) 1.11. Marco Polo's observations appeared only in the so-called Z manuscript in Latin discovered at Toledo. See *Description of the World*, vol. 2, pp. liii–liv. Lu's note was cited by Cen Zhongmian in his *Sui Tang shi*, p. 312. Oddly enough, although Samuel Lieu ("Polemics against Manichaeism as a subversive cult in Sung China" and *Manichaeism in the Later Roman Empire and Medieval China*, p. 249) has cited Lu You's observations for the resemblance between the spread of Manichaeism to medieval China and the Jesuits' short-lived missionary achievement in the late Ming and the early Qing eras, he failed to discuss at all the part regarding the prohibition of ancestor worship, which not only reflected the extent of the Judeo-Christian elements in Manichaeism but also represented a sharp contrast between the uncompromising Chinese Manichaean church and the accommodating Jesuits of the Ming-Qing period regarding the Judeo-Christian doctrine on idolatry.

26. For example, Feifel, *Po Chü-i as a Censor*, p. 24.

27. Weinstein, *Buddhism under the T'ang*, p. 192n19.

28. Liu S. (fl. 742–55), *Sui-Tang jiahua* 2.28; Wang Dang (fl. 1101–10), *Tang yulin* (*Collected Anecdotes of the Tang*) 4.112. See Chen Yinke, *Tangdai zhengzhishi shulun gao,* pp. 61–63.

29. Choi (fl. 880), *Gewon bilkyung rok* (*Records of Ploughing with Pens in the Cinnamon Garden*), prologue. It should be pointed out, however, that the *jinshi* degree Choi eventually obtained was of the *bin'gong* ("guest contributors") category, set aside by the Tang government specifically to accommodate nonnative contenders. See, e.g., Xie, *Tangdai liu-Hua waiguoren shenghuo kaoshu* (*Examination of the Life of Aliens Who Stayed in China during the Tang*), pp. 124–25.

30. Luo, *Hou dingwu gao*, p. 11. Chen Yinke, *Yuan-Bai shi jianzheng gao*, pp. 292–302.

31. For example, see Yang Zongying, *Bai Juyi yanjiu*, p. 6; and Tanaka, *Haku Rakuten*, p. 10. Zhou Yiliang, in his *Wei-Jin Nanbeichao shi zaji* (*Miscellanious Notes on the History of the Wei-Jin and Southern and Northern Dynasties Era*), pp. 172–76, backed up

Chen's case by pointing out many other marriages, all involving imperial families, in the preceding Southern and Northern dynasties that showed a disregard of "generational correspondence." Deng and Huang in their "Bai Juyi shengping kaobian santi" (Three questions regarding the life of Bai Juyi), found, interestingly, that the daughter of Bai's close friend Yuan Zhen married her remote uncle. Still it should be noted that none of these cases were as "scandalous" as that of Bai's parents, namely an uncle marrying his sister's own daughter.

32. The essay "Bai Juyi fumu jixing hunpei shuo zhiyi" by Yu Liang is a typical example of this sinocentric bias.

33. See Wang Meng'ou, "Bai Letian xianzu," pp. 148–52.

34. Waley, *Life and Times of Po Chü-I*, p. 238.

35. See, for instance, Bittles et al., "Consanguineous marriage and postnatal mortality in Karnataka, South India."

36. Smith, *Kinship and Marriage in Early Arabia*, p. 197.

37. See, e.g., Barakat, *Arab World: Society, Culture, and State*, p. 109.

38. Korotayev, "Parallel-cousin (FBD) marriage, Islamization, and Arabization."

39. These uncle-niece unions, though not a favorite subject in standard history references even if explicitly mentioned as such at all, can easily be deduced from standard royal family trees. For example, see the family trees of the Spanish and Austrian branches of the Habsburgs in Dickens, *Courts of Europe: Politics, Patronage and Royalty, 1400–1800*, pp. 123 and 177.

40. Quotations are too numerous to cite individually. The earliest appears to be from Xanthus Lydus (sixth–fifth centuries BC), who said that "the Magi cohabit with their mothers and their daughters, and according to law have intercourse with sisters." See Müller, *Fragmenta historicorum Graecorum*, vol. 1, pp. 36–44; vol. 4, pp. 628–29. The disputed authenticity of the Xanthus fragment notwithstanding, the observation was certainly vouched for by many other Greek authors. See J. Slotkin's detailed list of early records on this tradition "in old Iran" in "On a possible lack of incest regulations in old Iran."

41. Givens and Hirschman, "Modernization and consanguineous marriage in Iran."

42. Sundermann and Thilo, "Zur mittelpersischen Grabinschrift aus Xi'an" (Volksrepublik China).

43. Chen Yinke, "Lianhuaseni chujia yinyuan ba" (Afterword on Lianhuaseni becoming a Buddhist nun), first published in 1932 and included in *Lunwenji*, vol. 2, pp.719–24.

44. An extensive study of this subject is Jonathan Silk's manuscript "Riven by Lust: Incest and Schism in Indian Buddhist Legend and Historiography." I am much obliged to him for a copy of this remarkable manuscript.

45. See Jonathan Silk's book for detailed examples and discussions. It is particularly intriguing to observe that a story (pp. 138–41) of marriages between full brothers and sisters in the Pali canon came to be about marriages between half-brothers and sisters in the Chinese version.

46. *Abhiniskramana-sutra*, *Taisho* 190, vol. 5, 675, translation by Silk in "Riven by Lust," p. 143.

47. It is also worth pointing out that Bai's aforementioned admission of his ignorance of the most coveted *jinshi* degree of the day until he was fifteen or sixteen was made after the event.

48. For example, see the cases quoted in Xie, *Shenghuo kaoshu*, pp. 86, 88, 92, 276, 278, 280, and 281. Recently Liu Huiqin and Chen Haitao conducted an extensive survey of the marriage patterns of the Sogdians in Tang China based on tomb inscription data in their "Cong tonghun de bianhua kan Tangdai ru-Hua Sute ren de Hanhua" (The sinification of Sogdians who came to China during the Tang era based on the changes of intermarriages). It was evident that, for a long time, the Sogdians in China married primarily within their own and other non-Sinitic clans.

49. Leslie, *Survival and the Chinese Jews*, pp. 49, 63–65, and 105–6; also Siney Shapiro, *Jews in Old China: Studies by Chinese Scholars*, p. 174.

50. Tao Z., *Nancun chuogeng lu* 28.348.

51. Huang, "Qiantan Quanzhou Huizu fengsu" (Preliminary discussions of Muslim special customs in Quanzhou).

52. This was used by Ren Fang in her cited study as an argument for dating the tombstone to post-Song times, possibly the Yuan, against the strong evidence that the partly obliterated reign title on the tombstone started with a character inconsistent with any late date. I regard the Bi clan's non-Sinitic heritage as a much better explanation. Sun Qikang in his "Bi Sheng mubei zhi niandai duanding yu bihui wenti" gives a largely incorrect defense of this violation. The very few so-called other similar cases of the Song dynasty cited by Mr. Sun all involve the common radical of Chinese characters with completely different pronunciations and are thus invalid counterexamples to the long-established sound-based, father-name taboo custom.

53. Gulik, *Sexual Life in Ancient China*, p. 203. The full title of the verse is "Rhapsody of Great Pleasure for Coitus between Heaven and Earth, and between *yin* and *yang*."

54. J.-s. Chen, *Liu Tsung-yüan and Intellectual Change in T'ang China, 773–819*, pp. 1–5.

55. The southeast sea route was much less consequential until, of course, the Opium Wars.

56. One can read, inter alia, Xu Z., *Shishuo xinyu* (*A New Account of Tales of the World*); *Gaoseng zhuan* (*Biographies of Eminent Monks*, Taisho No. 2059); and, on a lesser scale, *Xu gaoseng zhuan* (*Biographies of Eminent Monks, the Sequel*, Taisho No. 2060).

57. In the numerous studies of Li Bai's alleged Central Asian connections and heritage, including the work of Elling Eide cited above, the absence of such a religious link for our sinocentric Taoist poet would appear to be the weakest point.

58. Ouyang et al., *Xin Tang shu* 221a.6230; Yao W., *Beichao huxing kao*, p. 373n1; and Schafer, *Golden Peaches of Samarkand*, p. 293n136, etc.

59. Wright, *Studies in Chinese Buddhism*, pp. 43-44.

60. Zürcher, *Buddhist Conquest of China*, vol. 1, p. 281. It may not be altogether irrelevant to note that Bai was also one of the seventy (or seventeen?) Jewish clans named

by the famous 1489 Kaifeng inscription. See White, *Chinese Jews*, part II, p. 37; and Donald Leslie, *Survival and the Chinese Jews*, pp. 22 and 27.

61. Chen Yinke, *Yuan-Bai Jianzheng gao*, pp. 306–15, was perhaps the first to describe Bai Juyi as primarily a Taoist instead of a Buddhist. His contention was adopted and expanded by other scholars (see, e.g., J.-s. Chen, *Liu Tsung-yüan*, pp. 171 and 186n83). I have major reservations on such efforts to quantify (at the very least to "sort out") Bai's various religious "attributes." For one thing, they could never be conclusively established beyond controversy. For example, both Wang Shiyi, in *Bai Juyi zhuan*, p. 8, and Zhu Jincheng, in *Bai Juyi yanjiu*, p. 251, probably the two most prominent modern Bai Juyi specialists in China, disagree with Chen's opinion that Bai's Taoist leaning was greater than his commitment to Buddhism.

62. See, e.g., Wang Shiyi, *Bai Juyi zhuan*, pp. 5-6.

63. See also Rhee, "Jewish assimilation: The case of the Chinese Jews"; and Weinstein, *Buddhism under the T'ang*, p. 192n19.

64. It is yet another case in which the way family members address each other could be the most lasting indication of non-Sinitic heritage. Another brother of Juyi, Bai Xingjian, had a *xiaozi* Alian, which might also be of Buddhist origin. Read Wang Liqi's comment on the *xiaozi* Alian of Emperor Wu (464–549; reign 502–49) of the Liang dynasty in his *Yanshi jiaxun jijie*, p. 66.

65. Initial report appeared in *Kaogu* (1994.8); for a more detailed study, see Wen, "Bai Juyi guju chutu de jingchuang" (Sutra stele unearthed at the former residence of Bai Juyi).

66. Translated by Buddhapāli and found in *Taishō shinshū daizōkyō*, no. 967, vol. 19, 349–53.

67. Wen Yucheng concludes that the texts are very close to the version translated by Bhagavaddharma and found in *Taishō* no. 1060.

68. The new find on Bai's old home site also strongly suggests our poet's devotion to Esoteric Buddhism, closely related to Tantric Hinduism, with possible sexual implications. For one thing, despite his fascination with proper ways to maintain health and prolong life, Bai was never known to have refrained from enjoying sexual pleasures even late in his life. This would be consistent with his brother's authorship of the erotic verse, "Rhapsody of Great Pleasure," mentioned earlier.

69. Lieu, *Manichaeism*, p. 203.

70. *Taishō* no. 2035, vol. 49. The translation is from Lieu, *Manichaeism*, p. 249.

71. Lieu, *Manichaeism*, pp. 249–50.

72. Ibid., p. 218.

73. Frye, *History of Ancient Iran*, pp. 351–52.

74. Xiang, *Tangdai Chang'an yu Xiyu wenming*, p. 62; Schafer, *Golden Peaches of Samarkand*, p. 52.

75. A rather extensive discussion of Bai's musical education can be found in Yang Zongying, *Bai Juyi yanjiu*, pp. 180-215. Bai himself claimed to have mastered *shengyun* ("sound and rhymes") or *shenglü*, "sound rules," by the tender age of nine. While this may not be directly linked to music education, the unusual "non-Chinese" factor in the

development of Chinese phonology is noteworthy. It is generally agreed that the advent of the *fanqie*, "reverse-cutting," spelling method was closely related to the influence of Buddhism and Sanskrit. In fact, the Song dynasty author Shen Gua in his acclaimed *Mengxi bitan* stated unmistakably that "the theory of 'cutting rhyme' originated in the Western Regions" (Hu D., *Mengxi bitan Jiaozheng* 15.505). For a modern source, read Wei C., *Zhongguo fojiao wenhua lun'gao*, p. 64. Even the discovery of tonality, a fundamental element of the Sinitic (and many other Asian) languages, has been attributed to this foreign influence by Chen Yinke ("Sisheng sanwen" [Three questions on the four tones]). Both the author and the first annotator of the epochal phonology treatise *Qie yun* (*Tonic Rhymes*) were of Xianbei descent. See Chen Yuan, "*Ch'ieh Yun* and its Hsien-pi authorship."

76. You et al., *Zhongguo wenxue shi* (*A History of Chinese Literature*), vol. 2, p. 115. Hans H. Frankel's assertion ("Yüeh-fu poetry," p. 70), based on the standard classification that the poems were not set to music, was a bit too sweeping. In his own preamble, Bai Juyi stated clearly that the poems were so written that they may be "set to musical scores." In addition, Chen Yinke has studied *xinyuefu*'s relationship with popular music, based on the 3-3-7 verse structure common in *xinyuefu*, "new folk-song," and *bianwen*, "transformation texts," song-poems discovered at Dunhuang.

77. Xiang, *Tangdai Chang'an*, pp. 252–74.

78. See, e.g., Mair, *Columbia Anthology of Traditional Chinese Literature*, pp. 300–301, remarks by Mair; and You et al., *Zhongguo wenxue shi*, vol. 2, pp. 219–20.

79. Ren B., *Jiaofang ji jianding* (*An Emended Edition of the Records of the Palace Music School*), pp. 7–8.

80. See, e.g., Xiang, *Tangdai Chang'an;* and Chen Yinke, "Huchou yu huchou."

81. Wu-chi Liu, *Introduction to Chinese Literature*, p. 149.

82. *BJ* 21.474 and 31.703, etc. Schafer (*Golden Peaches of Samarkand*, p. 29) quotes only the second poem. I do not quite agree with Ishida Mikinosuke and Liu Mau-tsai that the tents were necessarily Turkish, a notion adopted by Schafer. For one thing, the Turks did not invent them, nor were they the sole users at the time.

83. Wu Y., "Bai Juyi zhanzhang shi yu Tangchao shehui de hufeng" (Bai Juyi's tent poems and the foreign customs in Tang society).

84. See, e.g., Yao W., *Beichao Huxing kao*, pp. 48–49.

85. Indeed Bai's *xinyuefu* was a response to Yuan's poems, with many titles matching those of Yuan's. Yuan was in turn "matching" Li Shen (?–846), who was acknowledged as the creator of this new genre. Unfortunately, Li's poems did not survive.

86. Liao, *Yuan-Bai xinyuefu yanjiu* (*Studies of the New Folk-Songs by Yuan Zhen and Bai Juyi*), p. 105; Liao could not say the same about Bai's poems.

87. Schafer, *Golden Peaches of Samarkand*, p. 29.

88. Schafer's translation, ibid., p. 28.

89. Liao, *Yuan-Bai xinyuefu*, pp. 203-4.

90. Xu and Zhao, *Tang Xuanzong zhuan*, p. 411.

91. Chen Yinke, *Jianzheng gao*, p. 135, claims that Bai's original title should also be *Faqu.*

92. Ibid., p. 247.

93. Incidentally, Waley, *Life and Times of Po Chü-I*, p. 43, translated the Tibetan war prisoners in Bai's poem "Furongren" (Barbarians in bind) as "Tartars," which might be stretching artistic latitude to the limit. But Edward Schafer's strict interpretation of the term as Turks (*Golden Peaches of Samarkand*, p. 43) went beyond any such limit and was indicative of a serious misreading of Tang history.

94. According to the early Song dynasty source *Nanbu xinshu* (3.27), "the demon Hu" here should refer particularly to An Lushan, the Turco-Sogdian rebel leader who was widely rumored to have had an affair with Lady Taizhen, the favorite consort of Emperor Xuanzong, right inside the Tang royal palace.

95. For Yuan's poem, see, e.g., *Quan Tangshi* (*Complete Collection of Tang Poems*), 419.1025. Bai's poem is found in *BJ* 3.60–61. English translation by Victor Mair of these two poems in full, somewhat different from mine, can be found in *Columbia Anthology of Traditional Chinese Literature*, pp. 485–88.

96. In his most fascinating reconstruction of Tang court music, *Music from the Tang Court*, Lawrence Picken erred (vol. 2, p. 10) in saying that Bai Juyi too implied *Huxuan* "was not introduced to the court until towards the end of the Tianbao period." Bai's contention that the dance existed at the court prior to that is substantiated by Liu X. et al., *Jiu Tang shu* (183.4733).

97. The Chen-Cen dispute was noted by Denis Twitchett ("Composition of the T'ang ruling class," p. 84). For Chen's analysis of the hawks and doves, see his *Tangdai zhengzhishi shulun gao*, p. 72. Cen's opinion was most forcefully expressed in his article "Lun Li Deyu wudang . . . " (On that Li Deyu did not form a clique . . .), though his apparently idiosyncratic theory that Li Deyu did not form a clique has been generally disregarded. Angela Palandri in *Yüan Chen* (pp. 16–17) gives a very concise description of the two factions and their respective political and military policies.

98. Bai's own annotation in the poem, which was copied into *Nanbu xinshu* (6.61), on the Tang government's marking of the distance from the Tang capital to West Liang as 9,999 instead of the dreadful 10,000 *li*, might represent the world's first recorded use of the psychological principle behind what is known as "odd pricing," now widely used in retailing business everywhere.

99. See, e.g., Liao M., *Xinyuefu*, p. 157; and Wang Shiyi, *Bai Juyi zhuan*, p. 276. Waley, *Life and Times of Po Chü-I*, p. 53, ignores this part completely.

100. Ren B., *Tang xi nong (Tang Plays and Music)*, pp. 448–49; also quoted in Zhu, *Jianjiao*, p. 212.

101. This was the third year of the Xianqing era (656–60). See Wang P., *Tang huiyao* 70.1323 and *ZZTJ* 200.6309. The year 649 given by *The Cambridge History of China*, vol. 3, part 1, p. 228, as well as the map on p. 227, is an apparent error.

102. Mackerras, *Uighur Empire according to the T'ang Dynastic Histories*, p. 48, noted this interesting story.

103. *Quan Tangshi*, 284.721. Xiang, *Tangdai Chang'an*, pp. 64-65, quotes the poem from another source.

104. Bai Xingjian's authorship of this piece has been disputed ever since its discovery. Gulik, *Sexual Life in Ancient China*, p. 207, has tried to dismiss these doubts by the somewhat tenuous argument that Xingjian was not a particularly famous name.

105. See Ye's epilogue to his *Shuangmei jing'an congshu* edition of "Dale fu," which was noted by Robert van Gulik.

106. See, e.g., Zhu, *Jianjiao*, pp. 1688–89, Zhu's notes.

107. A good starting point for such a search is a multilingual list of the twelve-animal cycle, as the one given in Bailey, "Hvatanica."

108. For a modern authority, read, e.g., Sinor, ed., *Cambridge History of Early Inner Asia*, pp. 131 and 156–57. Also note that the name *pushao* given in *Shiji* (*Records of the Grand Historian*) for the "heavenly horse" does not seem to correspond to the word *bahan*. Another plausible origin of the term is what has become the modern name of Afghan, particularly if the hypothetical etymology *asvaka*, "horse people," has some basis. See Codrington, "Geographic introduction to the history of Central Asia," p. 39. The Tang Buddhist pilgrim Xuanzang (ca. 596–664) had already mentioned the state Abojian, reconstructed by Samuel Bael as Avakan (*Life of Hiuen-Tsiang*, p. 193). In the same region, Xuanzang had noticed large herds of horses.

109. For a scientific interpretation of this legendary name, see Dubs, *History of the Former Han Dynasty*, vol. 2, pp. 134–35.

110. Earlier *Wei shu* 102.2270 reported specifically that in the third year of Taihe ("Grand Harmoniousness," 479) a Ferghana embassy presented the "blood-sweating horse" to the Tuoba court. Read also the story in *Song shu* 95.2357–58.

111. Wei Z., *Sui shu* 83.1853; Ouyang et al., *Xin Tang shu* 221b.6250; and Feng C., *Xiyu diming*, p. 27.

112. Pulleyblank, "Chinese and Indo-Europeans," in particular p. 22.

113. Read, e.g., Okladnikov, *Cambridge History of Early Inner Asia*, pp. 151–52.

114. *BJ* 57.1224-5; Waley, *Life and Times of Po Chü-I*, pp. 55-56.

115. According to Bernhard Karlgren's reconstruction, the Middle Chinese pronunciation of *geluo* would be *ghuet-la*. But by his proposed equation, Chen Yinke, who was also noted for his work in Chinese phonology, apparently had reconstructed it as *kha(t)-la*. I note that the character *ge/he* is a polyphone. During the Tang *ge* was interchangeable with characters that pronounced *ghat* or *kat* in translating foreign names (see, e.g., *ZZTJ* 246.7946). Another appearance of the word *geluo* was in the remnants of a poem among the Dunhuang manuscripts (Chen Yinke, *Jianzheng gao*, p. 242). The poem, by an unknown author, was part of "Wang Zhaojun *bianwen*" (Transformation text about Wang Zhaojun—Wang was the famous Hàn dynasty palace attendant who volunteered to marry the Xiongnu *Chanyu* to help mitigate the enmity between the Hàn and the Xiongnu)" and contained quite a few non-Chinese words. See Guo Zaiyi et al., *Dunhuang bianwenji jiaoyi* (*Emendations and Discussions of the Collection of Dunhuang Bianwen Texts*), p. 81.

116. Chen Yinke, *Jianzheng gao*, pp. 241–42. See also Zhu, *Jianjiao*, pp. 232.

117. The best Turkic equation would seem to be the word *qïšlaq*. However, in addition to the phoneme *š*, by its etymology *kis*, "winter," the word refers primarily to "winter

quarters." Clauson, *Etymological Dictionary of Pre-thirteenth-century Turkish*, p. 672. This can hardly be reconciled with the "thick and luxuriant" pastures Bai wrote about. Another possibility is the uncommon word *kalap* mentioned in al-Kašɣarī's *Divan* to refer to a plant species that could be used as fodder. See *Compendium of the Turkic*, vol. 3, p. 101. But in addition to the term's possible Hebrew origin (Jastrow, *Dictionary of the Targumim, the Talmud Babli and Yerushalmi, and the Midrashic Literature*, p. 664), a word without the meaning of "pasture" is difficult to fit in Bai's poem.

118. MacKenzie, *Concise Pahlavi Dictionary*, p. 21; and Boyce, *Word-List of Manichaean Middle Persian and Parthian*, p. 31.

119. See, e.g., Bartholomae, *Altiranisches Wörterbuch*, pp. 1866–67; Bailey, *Dictionary of Khotan Saka*, p. 504; Boyce, *Word-List of Manichaean Middle Persian and Parthian*, pp. 100–101; and Gershevitch, *Grammar of Manichean Sogdian*, pp. 36 and 85.

120. It nevertheless was used for "human food" in Christian Sogdian. See Sims-Williams, *Christian Sogdian Manuscript C2*, p. 169. Also compare with Tokharian *çwal* ("meat" in dialect A; "bait" in dialect B), < *çwa-* ("to eat.") See Windekens, *Le tokharien confronté avec les autre langues indo-européenes*, vol. 2, p. 32. On the other hand, the notion of "water and grass" in the context of animal husbandry was not an infrequent topic in ancient Iranian texts. See, for instance, Gershevitch, "Bactrian fragment in Manichean script."

121. For example, see *Ta'rikj-i-jahan-gusha of 'Ala'u d-Din 'Ata Malik-i-Juwayni* (*The History of the World-Conqueror by 'Ala-ad-Din 'Ata-Malik Juvaini*), part I, p. 194, line 18, and the "Zij-i-Ilkhani" text, as quoted in Boyle, "Longer introduction to the 'Zij-i-Ilkhani' of Nasir-ad-Din Tusi," the last line of the original text on p. 247.

122. Lane, *Arabic-English Lexicon*, part 7, p. 2624, has fairly early authorities on this word.

123. Vladimir Minorsky, "Tamin ibn Bahr's Journey to the Uyghurs," pp. 279 and 283.

124. The close correlation here is a strong hint that Tamin's visit might not have missed Bai Juyi's letter (and the poem) by far, which suggests Minorsky's second guess 805-8. Minorsky, "Tamin ibn Bahr's journey to the Uyghurs," pp. 300–303, thought his third guess, namely early 821, was the most likely largely because of his erroneous contention that the "golden tent" of the Uighur *qaghan* was part of the dowry of Princess Taihe. On "the golden tent," see, e.g., *ZZTJ* 246.7947.

125. For Arab mercenaries during the An Lushan Rebellion, see Ouyang et al., *Xin Tang shu*, 217a.6115 (Mackerras's translation, p. 59). See also Edwin Pulleyblank, "The An Lu-shan rebellion and the origins of chronic militarism in Late T'ang China," particularly p. 44.

126. Liu X. et al., *Jiu Tang shu* 195.5200; and Ouyang et al., *Xin Tang shu* 217a.6116 (Mackerras's translation, pp. 62–63).

127. Gibb, *Arab Conquests in Central Asia*, p. 98.

128. According to the ninth-century Arab writer Ibn-Khurdadhbih, the Radhanite Jewish merchants traded from "the land of the Franks" all the way to China and spoke

Arabic, Persian, Roman, and various other languages See Rabinowitz, *Jewish Merchant Adventurers: A Study of the Radanites*, pp. 9–10.

129. *Kar* had an "animal" etymology. See Gesenius, *Hebrew and English Lexicon of the Old Testament*, p. 499. *Kala'* appeared to come from a botanical pedigree. Note that the standard Arabic version of the Old Testament uses the word *marah,* "pasture," to translate the term *kar.*

130. Young, *Analytical Concordance to the Holy Bible*, p. 734.

131. Koehler, *Lexicon in Veteris Testamenti libros*, p. 453; and Gordon, *Ugaritic Handbook*, vol. 3, p. 240. Due to the strong Semitic influence including the Semitic origin of the Pahlavi alphabet, the word is also attested in Pahlavi in the form of the word *kalyâ,* "ram," "sheep," "goat." See Haug, *Old Pahlavi-Pazand Glossary*, p. 138.

132. See, e.g., Dunlop, *History of the Jewish Khazars*, pp. 34–40. Recently Senga cast doubt upon this theory due to the lack of tangible evidence ("Toquz Oghuz problem and the origin of the Khazars").

133. Roth and Wigoder, *Encyclopaedia Judaica*, vol. 10, p. 947. Dunlop, *History of the Jewish Khazars*, p. 91, further qualifies it as no later than 809. The latter was exactly the year Bai was supposed to have composed his "Yinshan dao." That the conversion reached a culminating point in the early ninth century is supported by Peter Golden's recent discussion of the subject, "Conversion of the Khazars to Judaism."

134. Quoted in Senga, "Toquz Oghuz problem and the origin of the Khazars," p. 63n21. Note that Róna-Tas's dates apparently allow such interchanges to happen after the Khazars' conversion to Judaism.

135. For example, the once popular pursuit of the "Chinese connection" in the study of the Old Testament in Hebrew as surveyed by Katz, "The Chinese Jews and the problem of biblical authority in eighteenth- and nineteenth-century England."

136. Sinor, "Horse and pasture in Inner Asian history."

137. The once much-touted *Kanman'er's Anthology* of Bai Juyi has been found to be a modern forgery. See Yang L., "Kanman'er shijian bianwei" (On the forgery of the Kanman'er Anthology).

138. See also the interesting story in *Xuanshi zhi* (*Journal at the Chamber for Discussing the Supernatural*), 1.2–3) by the Tang author Zhang Du, about a Hu merchant speaking of the Tang policy of "striking the four uncivilized corners culturally."

139. There is this famed and oft-cited "old washerwoman story" about Bai's concern over the comprehensibility of his poetry to the common folk. The authenticity of the story has been challenged by many authors. But they all seem to have missed the real point here: According to his exchanges with Yuan Zhen and Yuan's foreword to his collected works, Bai had apparently taken pride in his poems' being widely read by all walks of society, including "sing-song girls" and cowboys. The "old washerwoman story" is a fitting reflection of this sentiment, and whether it actually happened is not really relevant. In this sense, a recent Bai poetry selection is quite correct in stressing this folklore. Zhu and Zhu, *Bai Juyi shiji daodu* (*A Guide to the Poetry Anthology of Bai Juyi*), p. 36.

140. Mair, "Buddhism and the rise of the written vernacular in East Asia."

141. Luo Xianglin, *Tang Yuan erdai zhi Jingjiao*, pp. 193-224.

142. Zhu and Zhu, *Bai Juyi shiji daodu* (appendices), contains a good selection of these comments.

143. Li Guanghua in his article "Bai Juyi xue Fo xinlu licheng" (The spiritual path of Bai Juyi in becoming a Buddhist) also concludes that Bai Juyi's writing style was motivated by his conscious efforts to spread Buddhism among the uneducated masses.

144. Wu-chi Liu, *Introduction to Chinese Literature*, p. 149.

145. See, e.g., Zhou X., "Yuanhe wentan de xin fengmao" (The new atmosphere and styles of the literary world of the Yuanhe era).

146. See, e.g., Zhu Jincheng, *Bai Juyi Yanjiu*, 155–58.

147. As suggested earlier, one cannot help speculating on the truthfulness of yet another claim by Bai on his family's relation to a noted Chinese clan. In particular, the prefecture of Changli happened to be in the frontier district of Yingzhou, famed for its ethnic population, with the Turco-Sogdian general An Lushan as its most prominent local son.

148. Read, e.g., Kawai, "Kan Yu to Haku Kyoi," and Yu S., "Han-Bai shifeng de chayi. . . ."

149. *Han Yü and the T'ang Search for Unity*, p. 322n46.

Appendix

This appendix is essentially my article of the same title, published in the *Central Asiatic Journal* 49: 161–74.

1. Sinor, *Introduction à l'étude de l'Eurasie centrale*, p. 224.

2. Pelliot's opinion on this was most forcefully conveyed in Barthold, *Zwölf Vorlesungen über die Geschichte der Türken Mittelasiens*, p. 25 (French translation pp. 18–19). Boodberg's conclusion was found on p. 185 of his article "The Language of the T'o-Pa Wei." For Clauson's view, see his *Turkish and Mongolian Studies*, pp. 37 and 39–40, as well as *An Etymological Dictionary of Pre-thirteenth-century Turkish*, preface.

3. Eberhard, *Das Toba-Reich Nordchinas*, p. 328.

4. Aydemir, "Altaic etymologies," p.123.

5. For instance, see Róna-Tas, "Periodization and sources of Chuvash linguistic history," p. 139; Pearce, "Status, labor and law: Special service households under the Northern dynasties," p. 89; and Hess, "Manchu exegesis of the *Lunyu*," p. 417.

6. Read, e.g., Viatkin, *Materialy po istorii kochevykh narodov v Kitae, III–V vv*, vol. 3, introduction.

7. See my 1996 article "A-gan revisited" for other criticisms of Ligeti's study.

8. As I noted in Chapter 1, there is an interesting historical parallel was the Jurchen emperor Wanyan Liang (reign 1150–61).

9. Wei Shou, *Wei shu* 21a.536 and 14.360; *ZZTJ* 140.4386 and 141.4408.

10. In his superb study of "Barbarian" surnames in the Northern dynasties, *Beichao huxing kao*, Yao Weiyuan has also made this explicit distinction.

11. Eberhard, *Conquerors and Rulers: Social Forces in Medieval China*, pp. 116–18.

12. Boodberg, "Language of the T'o-pa Wei," was the first to make these two identifications, which Bazin followed in "Recherches sur les parlers T'o-pa."

13. See Yao W., "Dugu ji Tuge kao," for an elegant exposition of a Dugu = Liu equation. Eberhard in his *Lokalkulturen im alten China* also mentions this equation.

14. Menges, *Turkic Languages and Peoples*, p. 74.

15. See Chapter 2. It should be pointed out that many, if not most, "entering-tone" characters still transcribe a full syllable. Examples abound and include ancient Chinese names for both Turks and Uighurs.

16. Mathematically, this follows what is called conditional inference in statistics. See, e.g., Berger and Wolpert, *Likelihood Principle*; or Casella and Berger, *Statistical Inference*.

17. Statistical significance was calculated using two statistical packages: SPSS for Windows, Version 7.5 (Chi-square and Fisher's Exact tests) and Statxact Version 2.0 (CYTEL Software Corp., Cambridge, Mass., for binomial distribution calculation).

18. Sinor, *Introduction à l'étude de l'Eurasie centrale*, p. 186. The original essay, published in an Uppsala University periodical, is not accessible to me.

19. Embleton, *Statistics in Historical Linguistics*. This text is itself part of the general series *Quantitative Linguistics*. There is another series, *Travaux de linguistique quantitative*, published by Slatkine in Geneva. The methodology William Baxter uses in his study of the Old Chinese rhyme classes (*Handbook of Old Chinese Phonology*, pp. 87–137) is the closest to mine.

20. Menges, *Turkic Languages and Peoples*, p. 74.

21. Collinder, *Comparative Grammar of the Uralic Languages*, p. 208.

22. Hangin, *Basic Course in Mongolian*, p. 22.

23. Bosson, *Modern Mongolian*, p. 21.

24. See, e.g., Poppe, *Mongolian Language Handbook*, p. 47.

25. Poppe, *Introduction to Mongolian Comparative Studies*, pp. 16, 59–60, and 76.

26. Ibid., p. 15.

27. Cited by Poppe, *Introduction to Altaic Linguistics*, p. 79.

28. Schmidt, *Grammatik der mongolischen Sprache*, p. 14.

29. Menges, *Turkic Languages and Peoples*, p. 74. See also Bazin, "Structures et tendances communes des langues turques (Sprachbau)," p. 14; and Johanson, "Wie entsteht ein türkische Wort?" pp. 112–13. Johanson points out, in particular, that such exceptions tend to be a relatively recent development.

30. Von Gabain, *Alttürkische Grammatik*, p. 42; Menges, *Turkic Languages and Peoples*, p. 74.

31. Tekin, *Grammar of Orkhon Turkic*, p. 102.

32. Collinder, *Comparative Grammar of the Uralic Languages*, pp. 206–7.

33. The migration of Turkic tribes from the Baikal region to Yakutia may have started as early as the sixth century. See, for instance, Gogolev, "Basic stages of the formation of the Yakut people," p. 65. Using the sometimes controversial glottochronological method, S. E. Iakhontov even calculated that the Yakut language separated from the Common Turkic roughly 1,500 to 1,600 years ago, as quoted in Gogolev (p. 67). Based on modern DNA

analysis, Brigitte Pakendorf et al. not only find (p. 349) "clear evidence of a southern origin of Yakuts" but also provide two possible dates of the initial migration as 880 (±440) and 1,286 (±800) years ago, respectively, or in general "the period between the sixth and thirteenth century AD."

34. Mongolian, not Russian, heads Menges's list (*Turkic Languages and Peoples*, p. 66) of languages that influenced the Yakut lexicon. Gogolev (p. 67) states categorically that "the Mongolian languages played a special role in the formation of the Yakut language." One may also read Stanislaw Kaluzynski's special study of this issue, *Mongolische Elemente in der jakutischen Sprache*.

35. Böhtlingk, *Uber die Sprache der Jakuten*, p. 151, claimed this was always (*immer*) the case. According to John Krueger (*Yakut Manual*, p. 70), there are a few exceptions to this rule.

36. Benzing, "Das Tschuwaschische," p. 713. See also Krueger, *Chuvash Manual*, p. 86.

37. Poppe, *Introduction to Altaic Linguistics*, p. 33; Krueger, *Chuvash Manual*, p. 56.

38. Proto-Bulgarian is as old as the Tuoba and has been universally considered an *l/r*-language, if not the direct ancestor of modern Chuvash. See, for instance, Poppe, *Introduction to Altaic Linguistics*, p. 58.

39. Clauson, *Etymological Dictionary of Pre-thirteenth-century Turkish*, preface, paragraph 2.

40. Read, e.g., Menges, *Turkic Languages and Peoples*, p. 17.

41. This was cited in Chapter 1. See Robert Dankoff's translation of *Compendium of the Turkic Dialects*, vol. 1, p. 341.

42. Keightley, "*Bamboo Annals* and Shang-Chou chronology," p. 425.

Bibliography

Adshead, Samuel A. M. *China in World History.* 2nd ed. London: Macmillan, 1995.

Albertz, Rainer. *Persönliche Frömmigkeit und offizielle Religion: Religionsinterner Pluralismus in Israel und Babylon.* Stuttgart: Calwer Verlag, 1978.

Alderson, Anthony D. *The Structure of the Ottoman Dynasty.* Oxford: Clarendon Press, 1956.

Asia Society. "Monks and merchants: Silk Road treasures from northwest China, Gansu and Ningxia, 4th–7th century." http://www.asiasociety.org/arts/monksandmerchants/merchants.htm. Accessed July 16, 2006.

Aydemir, Hakan. "Altaic etymologies." *Turkic Languages* 7 (2003), 105–43.

Bael, Samuel. *The Life of Hiuen-Tsiang.* London: K. Paul, 1911.

Bagchi, Prabodh Chandra. *Deux lexiques sanskrit-chinois.* 2 vols. Paris: P. Geuthner, 1929/1937.

Bai Juyi. *Bai Juyi ji (Collected Works of Bai Juyi).* Ed. and punctuated by Gu Xuejie. Beijing: Zhonghua shuju, 1979.

Bailey, Harold. *Culture of the Sakas.* Delmar, N.Y.: Caravan Books, 1982.

———. *Dictionary of Khotan Saka.* Cambridge: Cambridge University Press, 1979.

———. "Hvatanica." *Bulletin of the School of Oriental Studies* 8 (1935–37), 923–34.

———. "Irano-Indica II." *Bulletin of the School of Oriental and African Studies* 13 (1949–51), 121–39.

———. *Khotanese Texts IV.* Cambridge: Cambridge University Press, 1961.

———. *Khotanese Texts VII.* Cambridge: Cambridge University Press, 1985.

Bai Shouyi. "Cong Daluosi zhanyi shuodao Yisilan zhi zuizao de Huawen jilu" (The battle of Talas and the earliest Chinese records on Islam). In *Zhongguo Yisilan shi cungao (Saved Draft on the History of Islam in China).* Yinchuan: Ningxia renmin chubashe, 1982. Pp. 56–103.

Balsdon, J. "The 'divinity' of Alexander." *Historia* 1 (1950), 380–82.

Bang, W. "Über die türkischen Namen einiger Großkatzen." *Keleti Szemle* 17 (1917), 112–46.

Bang W., and A. von Gabain. "Türkische Turfan-Texte." *Sitzungsberichte der Preussischen Akademie der Wissenschaften (Philosophisch-historische Klasse)* 22 (1929), 411–30.

Ban Gu. *Hàn shu (History of the [Former] Hàn Dynasty).* Beijing: Zhonghua shuju, 1962.

Barakat, Halim. *The Arab World: Society, Culture, and State.* Berkeley: University of California Press, 1993.

Barfield, Thomas J. *The Perilous Frontier.* Cambridge Mass.: Basil Blackwell, 1989.

Barthold, W. *Turkestan Down to the Mongol Invasion.* 3rd ed. E. J. W. Gibb Memorial Series 5. London: Luzac, 1958.

———. *Zwölf Vorlesungen über die Geschichte der Türken Mittelasiens. Die Welt des Islams,* Bd. IV. Berlin: Deutsche gesellschaft für Islamkunde, 1935. Rpt., Hildesheim G. Olms, 1962. French tr. by M. Donskis, *Histoire des Turcs d'Asie centrale* (Paris: Adrien-Maisonneuve, 1945).

Bartholomae, Christian. *Altiranisches Wörterbuch.* Strassburg: K. J. Trübner, 1904. Rpt., Berlin: Walter de Gruyter, 1961.

Bauer, Wolfgang, *Der chinesische Personenname: Die Bildungsgesetze und hauptsachlichsten Bedeutungsinhalte von Ming, Tzu und Hsiao-Ming.* Wiesbaden: O. Harrassowitz, 1959.

Bawden, Charles R., tr. and annot. *The Mongol Chronicle Altan tobci.* Wiesbaden: O. Harrassowitz, 1955.

Baxter, William H. *A Handbook of Old Chinese Phonology.* Berlin: Mouton de Gruyter, 1992.

Bazin, Louis. "Man and the concept of history in Turkish Central Asia." *Diogenes* 42 (1962), 81–97.

———. "Pre-Islamic Turkic borrowings in Upper Asia: Some crucial semantic fields." *Diogenes* 43 (1995), 35–44.

———. "Recherches sur les parlers T'o-pa." *T'oung Pao* 39 (1951), 228–327.

———. "Structures et tendances communes des langues turques (Sprachbau)." In *Philologiae Turcicae fundamenta,* vol. 1. Aquis Mattiacis: Steiner, 1959. Pp. 11–19.

———. *Les systèmes chronologiques dans le monde turc ancien.* Paris: Editions du CNRS, 1991.

Beckwith, Christopher. "The Frankish name of the king of the Turks." *Archivum Eurasiae Medii Aevi* 15 (2007), 5–11.

———. "On the Chinese names for Tibet, Tabghatch, and the Turks." *Archivum Eurasiae Medii Aevi* 14 (2005), 5–20.

Benedict, Paul. *Sino-Tibetan: A Conspectus.* London: Cambridge University Press, 1972.

Benveniste, Émile. *Titres et noms propres en iranien ancien.* Paris: C. Klincksieck, 1966.

Benz, Frank L. *Personal Names in the Phoenician and Punic Inscriptions.* Rome: Biblical Institute Press, 1972.

Benzing, Johannes. "Das Tschuwaschische." In *Philologiae Turcicae fundamenta,* vol. 1. Aquis Mattiacis: Steiner, 1959. Pp. 695–751.

Berger, James O., and Robert L. Wolpert. *The Likelihood Principle.* Hayward, Calif.: Institute of Mathematical Statistics, 1984.

Bittles, A. H., A. Radha Rama Devi, et al. "Consanguineous marriage and postnatal mortality in Karnataka, South India." *Man,* n.s., 22 (1987), 736–45.

Böhtlingk, Otto. *Uber die Sprache der Jakuten.* St. Petersburg: Buchdruckerei der Kaiserlichen Akademie der Wissenschaften, 1851. Rpt., The Hague: Mouton, 1964.

Boodberg, Peter A. "An early Mongolian toponym." *Harvard Journal of Asiatic Studies* 19 (1956), 407–8.

———. *Hu Tien Han Yüeh Fang Chu*, no. 1 (March 1932). In *Selected Works of Peter A. Boodberg.* Berkeley: University of California Press, 1979. Pp. 74–82.

———. *Hu Tien Han Yüeh Fang Chu*, no. 5 (January 1933). In *Selected Works of Peter A. Boodberg.* Berkeley: University of California Press, 1979. Pp. 94–109.

———. *Hu T'ien Han Yüeh Fang Chu*, no. 9 (May 1935). In *Selected Works of Peter A. Boodberg.* Berkeley: University of California Press, 1979. P. 132.

———. "The language of the T'o-pa Wei." *Harvard Journal of Asiatic Studies* 1 (1936), 167–85.

———. "Marginalia to the histories of the Northern dynasties." *Harvard Journal of Asiatic Studies* 4 (1939), 230–83.

———. "Marginalia to the histories of the Northern dynasties," II. *Harvard Journal of Asiatic Studies* 3 (1938), 225–35.

———. "Turk, Aryan and Chinese in ancient Asia." In *Selected Works of Peter A. Boodberg.* Berkeley: University of California Press, 1979. Pp. 1–21.

———. "Two notes on the history of the Chinese frontier. II. The Bulgars of Mongolia." *Harvard Journal of Asiatic Studies* 1 (1936), 291–307.

Bosson, James E. *Modern Mongolian: A Primer and Reader.* Bloomington: Indiana University Press, 1964.

Bosworth, Clifford E. *The Ghaznavids: Their Empire in Afghanistan and Eastern Iran, 994–1040.* Edinburgh: University Press, 1963.

———. *The Later Ghaznavids: Splendour and Decay; The Dynasty in Afghanistan and Northern India, 1040–1186.* New York: Columbia University Press, 1977.

Boyce, Mary. *A History of Zoroastrianism.* Vol. 1. Leiden: Brill, 1975.

———. *A History of Zoroastrianism.* Vol. 2. Leiden: E. J. Brill, 1982.

———. *A Word-List of Manichaean Middle Persian and Parthian.* Acta Iranica 9a. Leiden: E. J. Brill, 1977.

Boyle, John A. "The longer introduction to the 'Zij-i-Ilkhani' of Nasir-ad-Din Tusi." *Journal of Semitic Studies* 8 (1963), 244–54.

Braun, Hellmut. "Iran under the Safavids and in the 18th century." In B. Spuler, ed., *The Muslim World: A Historical Survey*, vol. 3. Leiden: E. J. Brill, 1969. Pp. 181-218.

Carroll, Thomas D. *Account of the T'u-yü-hun in the History of the Chin Dynasty.* Berkeley: University of California Press, 1953,

Casella, George, and Roger L. Berger. *Statistical Inference.* Pacific Grove, Calif.: Wadsworth & Brooks, 1990.

Cefu yuangui (Prime Tortoise of the Record Bureau). Beijing: Zhonghua shuju, 1960.

Cen Zhongmian. "Lun Li Deyu wudang . . ." (On that Li Deyu did not form a clique . . .). In *Cen Zhongmian shixue lunwenji (Collected Papers on History by Cen Zhongmian).* Beijing: Zhonghua shuju, 1990. Pp. 462–76.

————. *Sui Tang shi* (*History of the Sui and Tang Dynasties*). Beijing: Gaodeng jiaoyu chubanshe, 1957.

Chavannes, Edouard. *Documents sur les Tou-Kieu (Turcs) occidentaux*. Paris: Librairie d'Amérique et d'Orient, 1903. Rpt., Paris: Adrien-Maisonneuve, 1942.

————. "Les pays d'Occident d'après le *Heou Han chou*." *T'oung Pao* 8 (1907), 149–234.

Chen, Jo-shui. *Liu Tsung-yüan and Intellectual Change in T'ang China, 773–819*. Cambridge: Cambridge University Press, 1992.

Chen Mengjia. *Yinxu buci zongshu* (*Summation of Divinatory Inscriptions from the Ruins of Yin*). Beijing: Kexue chubanshe, 1956.

Chen Qiaoyi. *Li Daoyuan yu Shuijing zhu* (*Li Daoyuan and the Commentary on the Water Classic*). Shanghai: Shanghai renmin chubanshe, 1987.

Chen, Sanping, "A-gan revisited: The Tuoba's cultural and political heritage." *Journal of Asia History* 30 (1996), 46–78.

————. "From Azerbaijan to Dunhuang: A Zoroastrianism note." *Central Asiatic Journal* 47 (2003), 183–97.

————. "From Mulan to unicorn." *Journal of Asian History* 39 (2005), 23–43.

————. "Sino-Tokharico-Altaica: Two linguistic notes." *Central Asiatic Journal* 42 (1998), 24–43.

————. "Some remarks on the Chinese 'Bulgar.'" *Acta Orientalia Academiae Scientiarum Hungaricae* 51 (1998), 69–83.

————. "Son of heaven and son of god: Interactions among ancient Asiatic cultures regarding sacral kingship and theophoric names." *Journal of the Royal Asiatic Society*, ser. 3, 12 (2002), 289–325.

————. "Succession struggle and the ethnic identity of the Tang imperial house." *Journal of the Royal Asiatic Society*, ser. 3, 6 (1996), 379–405.

————. "Turkic or Proto-Mongolian? A note on the Tuoba language." *Central Asiatic Journal* 49 (2005), 161–74.

————. "Yuan Hong: A case of premature death by historians?" *Journal of the American Oriental Society* 123 (2003), 841–46.

Chen, Sanping, and Chung-mo Kwok. "*Nucai* as a proto-Mongolic word: An etymological study." In Chinese with an English abstract. *Journal of Oriental Studies* 34 (1996), 82–92.

Chen Shou. *Sanguo zhi* (*History of the Three Kingdoms*). Beijing: Zhonghua shuju, 1959.

Chen Yinke, *Chen Yinke xiansheng lunwenji* (*Collected Papers of Master Chen Yinke*). 2 vols. Taipei: Sanrenxing chubanshe, 1974.

————. "Huchou yu huchou" (Fox-smell and bromhidrosis). *Yuyan yu wenxue* (*Language and Literature*) (1936), 109–13. Rpt. in *Chen Yinke xiansheng lunwenji* (*Collected Papers of Master Chen Yinke*), vol. 2. Taipei: Sanrenxing chubanshe, 1974. Pp. 505–8.

————. "Lianhuaseni chujia yinyuan ba" (Afterword on Lianhuaseni becoming a Buddhist nun). 1932. Rpt. in *Collected Papers,* vol. 2. Pp. 719–24.

————. "Lun Tangdai zhi Fanjiang yu fubing" (On the foreign generals and militia of the Tang era). Rpt. in *Chen Yinke xiansheng lunwenji,* vol. 1. Taipei: Sanrenxing chubanshe, 1974. Pp. 665–77.

————. "Sisheng sanwen" (Three questions on the four tones). *Qinghua xuebao* 9 (1934), 275–87. Rpt., *Collected Papers,* vol. 2, pp. 441–54.

————. *Sui Tang zhidu yuanyuan lüelun gao* (*A Draft Exploration of the Origins of the Sui-Tang Institutions*). Chongqing/Shanghai: Commercial Press, 1944/1946.

————. *Tangdai zhengzhishi shulun gao* (*A Draft Treatise on the Political History of the Tang Era*). ChongqingShanghai: Commercial Press, 1944/1947.

————. *Yuan-Bai shi jianzheng gao* (*Draft Commentaries and Researches on the Poetry of Yuan Zhen and Bai Juyi*). Beijing: Wenxue guji, 1955.

Chen Yuan. "The Ch'ieh-yün and its Hsien-pi authorship." *Monumenta Serica* 1 (1935–36), 245–52.

————. *Tongjian Huzhu biaowei* (*Uncovering the Subtleties in Hu Sanxing's Commentaries on Comprehensive Mirror for Aid in Government*). Beijing: Kexue chubanshe, 1958.

Ching, Julia. "Son of heaven: Sacral kingship in ancient China." *T'oung Pao* 83 (1997), 2–41.

Choi Chiwon. *Gewon bilkyung rok* (*Records of Ploughing with Pens in the Cinnamon Garden*). Shanghai: Commercial Press, 1934.

Chun, Allen J. "Conceptions of kinship and kingship in classical Chou China." *T'oung Pao* 76 (1990), 16–48.

Chunqiu Zuoshi zhuan (*The Commentary of Mr. Zuo on the Spring and Autumn Annals*). *Chunqiu Jingzhuan jijie* ed. Shanghai: Shanghai guji chubanshe, 1988.

Cihai (*Sea of Words*). Shanghai: Shanghai cishu chubanshe, 1988.

Ciyuan (*Origins of Words*). Beijing: Commercial Press, 1988.

Clauson, Sir Gerard. *An Etymological Dictionary of Pre-thirteenth-century Turkish.* London: Oxford University Press, 1972.

————. "The foreign elements in Early Turkish." In L. Ligeti, ed., *Researches in Altaic Languages.* Budapest: kadémiai Kiadó, 1975. Pp. 43–49.

————. *Turkish and Mongolian Studies.* London: Royal Asiatic Society, 1962.

Coblin, W. South. "Comparative studies on some Tang-time dialects of Shazhou." *Monumenta Serica* 40 (1992), 269–361.

————. "Remarks on some early Buddhist transcriptional data from northwest China." *Monumenta Serica* 42 (1994), 151–69.

Codrington, K. De B. "A geographic introduction to the history of Central Asia." *Geographical Journal* 104 (1944), 27–40.

Collinder, Björn. *Comparative Grammar of the Uralic Languages.* Stockholm: Almqvist, 1960.

————. *Fenno-Ugric Vocabulary: An Etymological Dictionary of the Uralic Languages.* 2nd ed. Hamburg: H. Buske, 1977.

Constantin, G. I. *Were the Hiung-nu's Turks or Mongols: Regarding Some Etymologies Proposed by Shiratori.* Bucharest: Association d'études orientales, 1958.

Converse, H. S. "The Agnicayana rite: Indigenous origin?" *History of Religions* 14 (1974), 81–95.

Dankoff, Robert. See al-Kašγarī.

Creel, Herrlee G. (see also under his synonym Gu Liya). *The Origins of Statecraft in China.* Vol. 1. Chicago: University of Chicago Press, 1970.

Crossley, Pamela K. "Thinking about ethnicity in early modern China." *Late Imperial China* 11 (1990), 1–34.

Davids, Caroline A. F. Rhys. *The Milinda-Questions.* London: Routledge, 1930.

Deng Xinyue and Huang Qufei. "Bai Juyi shengping kaobian santi" (Three questions regarding the life of Bai Juyi). *Yumeng xuekan* 2001.4, 67–70.

Detschev, Dimiter. "Der germanische Ursprung des bulgarischen Volksnamens." *Zeitschr. F. Ortsnamenforschung* 2 (1927), 199–216.

Dickens, Arthur. *The Courts of Europe: Politics, Patronage and Royalty, 1400–1800.* London: Thames and Hudson, 1977.

Di Cosmo, Nicola. "Ancient Inner Asian nomads: Their economic basis and its significance in Chinese history." *Journal of Asian Studies* 53 (1994), 1092–1126.

Dien, Albert E. *Yen Chih-T'ui (531–91+), His Life and Thought.* Dissertation, University of California, 1962.

Dodge, Bayard, ed. and tr. *The Fihrist of al-Nadim: A Tenth-century Survey of Muslim Culture.* 2 vols. New York: Columbia University Press, 1970.

Doerfer, Gerhard. *Türkische und mongolische Elemente im Neupersischen*, Band 2 und 4. Wiesbaden: F. Steiner, 1965/1975.

Drompp, Michael R. *Tang China and the collapse of the Uighur Empire: a Documentary History.* Leiden: Brill, 2005.

———. "Turks, Sogdians, and the founding of the T'ang Dynasty." *Annual Conference of the Central Eurasian Studies Society*, September–October 2000.

Duan Yucai. *Shuowen jiezi zhu (An Annotated Edition of the Explanation of Simple and Compound Graphs).* Shanghai: Shanghai shudian, 1992.

Dubs, Homer H., tr. and annot. *The History of the Former Han Dynasty.* Vol. 2. Baltimore: Waverly, 1944.

Dunhuang Institute, comp. *Dunhuang Mogaoku gongyangren tiji (Inscriptions by Benefactors of Mogao Caverns at Dunhuang).* Beijing: Wenwu chubanshe, 1986.

Dunlop, D. M. *The History of the Jewish Khazars.* Princeton, N.J.: Princeton University Press, 1954.

Du Wenlan, comp. *Gu Yaoyan (Ancient Ballades and Aphorisms).* Beijing: Zhonghua shuju, 1958.

Du You. *Tong dian (The Comprehensive Statutes).* Shanghai: Commercial Press, 1935.

Eberhard, Wolfram. *Conquerors and Rulers: Social Forces in Medieval China.* 2nd ed. Leiden: E. J. Brill, 1965.

———. *A History of China.* 4th ed. London: Routledge and Kegan Paul, 1977.

———. *Lokalkulturen im alten China.* Leiden: E. J. Brill, 1942.

————. *Das Toba-Reich Nordchinas: Eine soziologische Untersuchung.* Leiden: E. J. Brill, 1949.

Ecsedy, Ildikó. "Ancient Turk (T'u-chüeh) burial customs." *Acta Orientalia Academiae Scientiarum Hungaricae* 38 (1984), 263–87.

Eide, Elling. "On Li Po." In Arthur F. Wright and Denis Twitchett, eds., *Perspectives on the T'ang.* New Haven, Conn.: Yale University Press, 1973. Pp. 367–403.

Embleton, Sheila M. *Statistics in Historical Linguistics.* Bochum: Studienverlag Brockmeyer, 1986.

Engnell, Ivan. *Studies in Divine Kingship in the Ancient Near East.* 1943. Rpt., London: Blackwell, 1967.

Eno, Robert. "Was there a high god *Ti* in Shang religion?" *Early China* 15 (1990), 1–26.

Ernits, Enn. "Folktales of Meanash, the mythic Sami reindeer." Part 1. *Electronic Journal of Folklore* (ISSN 1406–0949) 11 (1999), available online at http://haldjas.folklore.ee/folklore/vol11/meandash.htm. Accessed June 30, 2006.

Ershiwushi renming suoyin (*Index of Personal Names in the Twenty-four Histories*). Beijing: Zhonghua shuju, 1956.

Etiemble, Réné. *Les Jésuites en Chine: La querelle des rites (1551–1773).* Paris: Réné Julliard, 1966.

Fairbank, John King. "A Preliminary Framework." In John King Fairbank, ed., *The Chinese World Order: Traditional China's Foreign Relations.* Cambridge, Mass.: Harvard University Press, 1968. Pp. 1–19.

Fang Xuanling. *Jin shu* (*History of the Jin Dynasty*). Beijing: Zhonghua shuju, 1974.

Fan Xiangyong, emend. and annot. *Luoyang qielanji jiaozhu* (*An Emended and Annotated Edition of the Records of the Monasteries of Luoyang*). Shanghai: Shanghai guji chubanshe, 1978.

Fan Ye. *Hou Han shu* (*History of the Later Han Dynasty*). Beijing: Zhonghua shuju, 1965.

Fan Zuyu. *Tang jian* (*Reflections on the Tang*). Shanghai: Commercial Press, 1937.

Feifel, Eugene. *Po Chü-i as a Censor.* 'S-Gravenhage: Mouton, 1961.

Feng Chengjun. *Xiyu diming* (*Toponyms of the Western Regions*). 2nd ed. Beijing: Zhonghua shuju, 1980.

Feng Erkang, *Yongzheng zhuan* (*A Biography of Emperor Yongzheng*). Beijing: Renmin chubanshe, 1985.

Feng, Han-Yi (Feng Han-chi). *The Chinese Kinship System.* Ph.D. thesis, University of Pennsylvania, 1936. 1948. Rpt., Cambridge, Mass.: Harvard University Press, 1967.

Feng Yan. *Fengshi wenjian ji* (*Feng's Personal Perceptions and Observations*). Beijing: Zhonghua shuju, 1985.

Ferrand, Gabriel. "Les grands rois du monde." *Bulletin of the School of Oriental Studies* 11 (1930–32), 329–39.

————. *Relations de voyages et textes géographiques arabes, persans et turks relatifs à L'Extrême Orient du VIIIe au XVIIIe siecles.* Paris: E. Leroux, 1913.

Fletcher, Joseph. "Blood tanistry: Authority and succession in the Ottoman, Indian Muslim, and Later Chinese empires." *Conference on the Theory of Democracy and Popular Participation*, Bellagio, Italy, 1978.

———. "The Mongols: Ecological and social perspectives." *Harvard Journal of Asiatic Studies* 46 (1986), 11–50.

———. "Turco-Mongolian monarchic tradition in the Ottoman Empire." *Harvard Ukrainian Studies* 3–4 (1979–80), 236–51.

Forte, A. "Iranians in China: Buddhism, Zoroastrianism, and bureaus of commerce." *Cahiers d'Extrême-Asie* 11 (1999–2000).

———. "The Sabao question." In *The Silk Roads Nara International Symposium '97*. Record no. 4. 1999. Pp. 80–106.

Franke, Herbert. *From Tribal Chieftain to Universal Emperor and God: The Legitimation of the Yüan Dynasty*. Munich: Verlag der Baerischen Akademie der Wissenschaften, 1978.

Frankel, Hans H. *The Flowering Plum and the Palace Lady: Interpretations of Chinese Poetry*. New Haven, Conn.: Yale University Press, 1976.

———. "Yüeh-fu poetry." In Cyril Birch, ed., *Studies in Chinese Literary Genres*. Berkeley: University of California Press, 1974.

Fraser, P. M., and E. Matthews. *A Lexicon of Greek Personal Names*. 2 vols. Oxford: Clarendon Press, 1987.

Frazer, Sir James G. *The Golden Bough: A Study in Magic and Religion*. 3rd ed. 10 vols. New York: Macmillan, 1935.

———. "The killing of the Khazar kings." *Folklore* 28 (1917), 382–407.

Frye, Richard N., ed. *The Cambridge History of Iran*. Vol. 4. London: Cambridge University Press, 1975.

———. "The fate of Zoroastrians in eastern Iran." In Rika Gyselen, ed., *Au Carrefour des religions: Mélanges offerts à Philippe Gignoux*. Bures-sur-Yvette: Group pour l'Étude de la Civilisation du Moyen-Orient, 1995. Pp. 67–72.

———. *History of Ancient Iran*. Munich: Beck, 1983.

———. "Remarks on kingship in ancient Iran." *Acta Antiqua* 25 (1977), 75–82.

Frye, Richard N., and Aydin M. Sayili. "Turks in the Middle East before the Saljuqs." *Journal of the American Oriental Society* 52 (1943), 194–207.

Fu Sinian. "Yi-Xia dongxi shuo" (The East-West conflicts between the Yi and the Xia: A theory). Rpt. in *Minzu yu gudai zhongguo shi* (*Ethnicities and the Ancient History of China*). Shijiazhuang: Hebei jiaoyu chubanshe, 2002. Pp. 1–49.

Gabain, Annemarie von. *Alttürkische Grammatik*, 3. Auflage. Wiesbaden: Harrassowitz, 1974.

Gandhi, Maneka. *The Penguin Book of Hindu Names*. New Delhi: Penguin Books, 1992.

Gao Dianshi, comp. *Zhongguo lidai tongyao jizhu* (*An Annotated Compilation of Chinese Children Ballads through the Ages*). Jinan: Shangdong University Press, 1990.

Gao Guofan. *Dunhuang minsu xue* (*Studies of Folk Customs in Dunhuang*). Shanghai: Shanghai wenyi chubanshe, 1989.

Gardner, Percy. *The Coins of the Greek and Scythic Kings of Bactria and India in the British Museum*. Rpt., Chicago: Argonaut, 1964.

Gershevitch, Ilya. "The Bactrian fragment in Manichean script." In J. Harmatta, ed., *From Hecataeus to al-Hurarizmi*. Budapest: Akadémiai Kiadó, 1984. Pp. 273–80.

———. *A Grammar of Manichean Sogdian*. Oxford: B. Blackwell, 1954.

———. "Island-Bay and lion." *Bulletin of the School of Oriental and African Studies* 33 (1970), 82–91.

Gesenius, William. *Hebrew and English Lexicon of the Old Testament*. Tr. Edward Robinson. Oxford: Clarendon Press, 1908.

Gibb, H. A. R. *The Arab Conquests in Central Asia*. Rpt., New York: AMS Press, 1970.

Gibb, H. A. R., et al., eds. *The Encyclopaedia of Islam*. New ed. Vol. 1. Leiden: E. J. Brill, 1960.

Gignoux, Phillipe. "Le dieu Baga en Iran." *Acta Antiqua* 25 (1977), 119–27.

———. *Iranisches Personennamenbuch*. Band 2, Fasz. 2, *Noms propres sassanides en moyen-perse épigraphique*. Wien: Österreichischen Akademie der Wissenschaften, 1986.

———. "Les noms propres en moyen-perse épigraphique: Étude typologique." In Phillipe Gignoux, ed., *Pad Nām i Yazdān: Études d'épigraphie, de numismatique et d'histoire de l'Iran ancien*. Paris: C. Klincksieck, 1979. Pp. 35–106.

Givens, Benjamin P., and Charles Hirschman. "Modernization and consanguineous marriage in Iran." *Journal of Marriage and Family* 56 (1994), 820–34.

Gogolev, A. I. "Basic stages of the formation of the Yakut people." *Anthropology and Archeology of Eurasia* 31 (1992), 63–83.

Gökalp, Ziya. *The Principles of Turkism*. Tr. R. Devereux. Leiden: E. J. Brill, 1968.

Golden, Peter. "The conversion of the Khazars to Judaism." In *The World of the Khazars: New Perspectives*, ed. P. B. Golden et al. Leiden: Brill, 2007. Pp. 123–62.

———. *An Introduction to the History of the Turkic Peoples: Ethnogenesis and State-formation in Medieval and Early Modern Eurasia and the Middle East*. Wiesbaden: O. Harrassowitz, 1992.

———. *Khazar Studies.* 2 vols. Budapest: Akadémiai Kiadó, 1980.

Gonda, Jan. *Notes on Names and the Name of God in Ancient India*. Amsterdam: North-Holland Publishing Co., 1970.

Goodrich, Chauncey S. "Riding astride and the saddle in ancient China." *Harvard Journal of Asiatic Studies* 44 (1984), 279–306.

Goody, Jack, ed. *Succession to High Office*. Cambridge: Cambridge University Press, 1966.

Goody, Jack, and Ian Watt. "The consequence of literacy." *Comparative Studies in Society and History* 5 (1963), 304–45.

Gordon, Cyrus H. *Ugaritic Handbook*. Vol. 3. Rome: Pontificium Institutum Biblicum, 1947.

Grenet, Frantz. "The Pre-Islamic civilization of the Sogdians (seventh century BCE to eighth century CE): A bibliographic essay." *Silkroad Foundation Newsletter*, http://

silkroadfoundation.org/newsletter/december/pre-islamic.htm. Accessed May 20, 2005.

Grenet, Frantz, and Zhang Guangda. "The last refuge of the Sogdian religion: Dunhuang in the ninth and tenth centuries." *Bulletin of the Asia Institute*, n.s., 10 (*Studies in Honor of Vladimir A. Livshits*) (1996), 175–86.

Grønbech, Kaare. "The Turkish System of Kinship." In *Studia Orientalia Ioanni Pedersen*. Copenhagen: Einar Munksgaard, 1953. Pp. 124–29.

Gu Liya (H. G. Creel). "Shi *Tian*" (Interpreting Tian). *Yanjing xuebao* 18 (1935), 59–71.

Gulik, Robert van. *Sexual Life in Ancient China*. Leiden: E. J. Brill, 1961.

Guo Moruo (under pen name Guo Dingtang). *Xian-Qin tiandaoguan zhi jinzhan* (*Progression of the Concept of Heaven Divine Orders in Pre-Qin Times*). Shanghai: Commercial Press, 1936.

Guo Moruo et al., comps. and eds. *Jiaguwen heji* (*Complete Collection of Oracle Bone Texts*). 13 vols. Beijing: Zhonghua shuju, 1978–82.

Guo Zaiyi et al. *Dunhuang bianwenji jiaoyi* (*Emendations and Discussions of the Collection of Dunhuang Bianwen Texts*). Changsha: Yuelu shushe, 1990.

Guo Zhufeng, ed. *Hanyu da cidian* (*A Great Dictionary of Han Chinese*). Shanghai: Hanyu da cidian chubanshe, 1990.

Hangin, (John) Gombojab. *Basic Course in Mongolian*. Bloomington: Indiana University Press, 1968.

Harmatta, J. "The archaeological evidence for the date of the Sogdian letters." In J. Harmatta, ed., *Studies in the Sources of the History of Pre-Islamic Central Asia*. Budapest: kadémiai Kiadó, 1979. Pp. 75–90.

———. "Irano-Turcica." *Acta Orientalia Academiae Scientiarum Hungaricae* 25 (1972), 263–73.

———. "Sino-Iranica." *Acta Orientalia Academiae Scientiarum Hungaricae* 19 (1971), 113–43.

———. "Sogdian sources for the history of pre-Islamic Central Asia." In J. Harmatta, ed., *Prolegomena to the Sources on the History of Pre-Islamic Central Asia*. Budapest: kadémiai Kiadó, 1979. Pp. 153–65.

Hartman, Charles. *Han Yü and the T'ang Search for Unity*. Princeton, N.J.: Princeton University Press, 1986.

Haug, Martin. *An Old Pahlavi-Pazand Glossary*. Osnabrück: Biblio, 1973.

He Genhai. "Nuo and the fertility cult." (In Chinese.) *Journal of Oriental Studies* 34 (1996), 70–81.

Heiler, Friedrich. *Erscheinungsformen und Wesen der Religion*. Stuttgart: W. Kohlhammer, 1961.

Henning, W. B. "Argi and the 'Tokharians.'" *Bulletin of the School of Oriental and African Studies* 9 (1938), 545–71.

———. "The date of the Sogdian ancient letters." *Bulletin of the School of Oriental and African Studies* 12 (1948), 601–15.

————. "A Sogdian god." *Bulletin of the School of Oriental and African Studies* 28 (1965), 242–54.

————. "Sogdian loan-words in New Persian." *Bulletin of the School of Oriental and African Studies* 10 (1939–42), 93–106.

Herodotus. *The Histories*. Tr. Aubrey de Sélincourt. New York: Penguin Books, 1972.

Hess, Laura E. "The Manchu exegesis of the *Lunyu*." *Journal of the American Oriental Society* 113 (1993), 402–17.

Hirth, Friedrich. *Ancient History of China, to the End of the Chou Dynasty*. New York: Columbia University Press, 1908. Rpt., New York: AMS Press, 1975.

Holmgren, Jennifer. "Politics of the inner court under the Hou-chu (Last Lord) of the Northern Ch'i (ca. 565–73)." In A. E. Dien, ed., *State and Society in Early Medieval China*. Stanford, Calif.: Stanford University Press, 1990. Pp. 269–330.

Holt, Frank L. *Alexander the Great and Bactria: The Formation of a Greek Frontier in Central Asia*. Leiden: E. J. Brill, 1988.

Holt, Peter Malcolm et al., eds. *The Cambridge History of Islam*. Vol. 1. Cambridge: Cambridge University Press, 1970.

Honey, David. "Stripping off felt and fur: An essay on nomadic signification." *Papers on Inner Asia, Ancient Inner Asia* 21 (1992).

Hong Hao. *Songmo jiwen (Recollections about the Pine Deserts)*. Changchun: Jilin wen-shi chubanshe, 1986.

Hookham, Hilda. *Tamburlaine the Conqueror*. London: Hodder and Stoughton, 1962.

Hsu, Cho-yun, and Kathryn Linduff. *Western Chou Civilization*. New Haven, Conn.: Yale University Press, 1988.

Huang Qiurun. "Qiantan Quanzhou Huizu fengsu" (Preliminary discussions of Muslim special customs in Quanzhou). In *Quanzhou Yisilanjiao yanjiu lunwen xuan (Studies of Islam in Quanzhou: Selected Papers)*. Fuzhou: Fujian renmin, 1983. Pp. 177–200.

Hu Daojing. *Mengxi bitan jiaozheng (An Emended and Annotated Edition of Brush Talks from Dream Brook)*. Shanghai: Shanghai guji chubanshe, 1987.

Hu Houxuan. *Jiaguxue Shangshi luncong chuji (Studies of Oracle Bone Texts and Shang History, Premier Collection)*. Chengdu: Qi-Lu University Press, 1944. Rpt., Shijia-zhuang: Hebei jiaoyu chubanshe, 2002.

Hu Ji. *Wu Zetian benzhuan (A Proper Biography of Wu Zetian)*. Xi'an: Sanqin chuban-she, 1986.

Hulsewé, A. F. P. *China in Central Asia, the Early Stage: 125 B.C.–A.D. 23*. Leiden: E. J. Brill, 1979.

Humbach, Helmut. "Die Pahlavi-Chinesische bilingue von Xi'an." In *A Green Leaf: Papers in Honour of Professor Jes P. Asmussen*. Leiden: E. J. Brill, 1988. Pp. 73–82.

Hume, Robert E., tr. *The Thirteen Principal Upanishads: Translated from the Sanskrit*. London: Oxford University Press, 1921.

Hummel, Arthur William, ed. *Eminent Chinese of the Ch'ing Period (1644–1912)*. Washington, D.C.: U.S. Government Printing Office, 1943–44.

Huntington, John C. "The range of the 'cosmic' deer." Web presentation. http://www
.kaladarshan.arts.ohio-state.edu/Deer%20Discussion/PDF%20Files/Deer%20
Presentation.pdf. Accessed July 14, 2006.

Hu Rulei. *Li Shimin zhuan* (*A Biography of Li Shimin*). Beijing: Zhonghua shuju, 1984.

Jackson, Peter, and Laurence Lockhart, eds. *The Cambridge History of Iran*. Vol. 4.
Cambridge: Cambridge University Press, 1986.

Jacobsen, Thorkild. *The Treasures of Darkness: A History of Mesopotamian Religion*.
New Haven, Conn.: Yale University Press, 1976.

Jacobson, Esther. *The Deer Goddess of Ancient Siberia: A Study in the Ecology of Belief*.
Leiden: E. J. Brill, 1993.

Jacoby, Felix, ed. *Die Fragmente der griechischen Historiker*. Zweiter Teil A. Leiden: E.
J. Brill, 1961.

Jastrow, Marcus. *A Dictionary of the Targumim, the Talmud Babli and Yerushalmi, and
the Midrashic Literature*. Brooklyn: P. Shalom, 1967.

Jarring, Gunnar. *Eastern Turki-English Dialect Dictionary*. Lund: CWK Gleerup, 1964.

Ji Xianlin, ed. *Da Tang xiyuji xiaozhu* (*An Emended and Annotated Edition of Records
of the Western World of the Great Tang*). 2 vols. Beijing: Zhonghua shuju, 1985.

Johanson, Lars. "Wie entsteht ein türkische Wort?" In Barbara Kellner-Heinkele and
Marek Stachowski, eds., *Laut- und Wortgeschichte der Turksprachen*. Wiesbaden:
Harrassowitz, 1995. Pp. 97–121.

Joki, Aulis J. "Die lehnwörter des Sajansamojedischen." *Mémoires de la Société Finno-
ougrienne* 103 (1952).

Jong, J. W. de. "L'Épisode d'Asita dans le Lalitavistara." In J. Schuvert and U. Schneider, eds.,
Asiatica: Festschrift Friedrich Weller. Leipzig: Otto Harrassowitz, 1954. Pp. 312–25.

Justi, Ferdinand. *Iranisches Namenbuch*. Marburg: N. G. Elwert, 1895. Rpt., Hildesheim:
G. Olms, 1963.

Juvaini, 'Ala-ad-Din 'Ata-Malik. *Ta'rikj-i-jahan-gusha of 'Ala'u d-Din 'Ata Malik-i-Juwayni*
(*The History of the World-Conqueror by 'Ala-ad-Din 'Ata-Malik Juvaini*). Part I. London: Luzac, 1912.

Kaluzynski, Stanislaw. *Mongolische Elemente in der jakutischen Sprache*. Warsaw: Pol-
ish Academy of Sciences, 1961.

Kane, Daniel. *The Sino-Jurchen Vocabulary of the Bureau of Interpreters*. Bloomington: Indiana University Press, 1989.

Karlgren, Bernhard. *Grammata Serica Recensa*. Bulletin no. 29. Stockholm: Museum of
Far Eastern Antiquities, 1957. Rpt., Göteborg: Elanders Boktryckeri, 1964.

al-Kašγarī, Mahmud. *Compendium of the Turkic Dialects* (*Türk Siveleri Lügati*). Ed.
and tr. Robert Dankoff and James Kelly. 3 vols. Cambridge, Mass.: Harvard University Press, 1982–85.

Katayama Tetsu. *Taishu shijin Haku Rakuten* (*Popular Poet Bai Letian*). Tokyo: Iwanami
shoten, 1961.

Katz, David S. "The Chinese Jews and the problem of biblical authority in eighteenth-
and nineteenth-century England." *English Historical Review* 105 (1990), 893–919.

Katzschmann, Michael, and Janos Pusztay. *Jenissej-Samojedisches Wörterverzeichnis.* Hamburg: H. Buske, 1978.

Kawai Kozo. "Kan Yu to Haku Kyoi" (Han Yu and Bai Juyi). *Chugoku bungakuho* 41 (1990), 66–100.

Keightley, David N. "The *Bamboo Annals* and Shang-Chou chronology." *Harvard Journal of Asiatic Studies* 38 (1978), 423–38.

Klyashtorny (Kljaštornyj), S. G., and V. A. Livshitz (Livšic). "The Sogdian inscription of Bugut revised." *Acta Orientalia Academiae Scientiarum Hungaricae* 26 (1972), 69–102.

Koehler, Ludwig. *Lexicon in Veteris Testamenti libros.* Leiden: E. J. Brill, 1953.

Konow, Sten. *Kharoshthi Inscriptions with the Exception of Those of Aśoka.* Calcutta: Government of India Central Publication Branch, 1929. Rpt., Varanasi: Indological Book House, 1969.

Korotayev, Andrey. "Parallel-cousin (FBD) marriage, Islamization, and Arabization." *Ethnology* 39 (2000), 395–407.

Kotwal, Firoze M., and Khojeste Mistree. "The court of the lord of rituals." In Pheroza J. Godrej and Firoza Punthakey Mistree, eds., *A Zoroastrian Tapestry: Art, Religion and Culture.* Usmanpura, India: Mapin, 2002. Pp. 366–83. Simultaneously published in the United States by Grantha.

Krader, Lawrence. *Social Organization of the Mongol-Turkic Pastoral Nomads.* The Hague: Mouton, 1963.

Krauze, Enrique. "The pride in Memin Pinguin." *Washington Post,* July 12, 2005, p. A21.

Krueger, John R. *Chuvash Manual: Introduction, Grammar, Reader, and Vocabulary.* Bloomington: Indiana University Press, 1961.

Krueger, John Richard. *Tuvan Manual.* Bloomington: Indiana University Press, 1977.

———. *Yakut Manual.* Bloomington: Indiana University Press, 1962.

Kurland, Stuart M. "Hamlet and the Scottish succession?" *Studies in English Literature, 1500–1900* 34 (1994), 279–300.

Lane, Edward William. *An Arabic-English Lexicon.* 8 vols. Rpt., Beirut: Librarie du Liban, 1968.

Laroche, Emmanuel. *Recueil d'onomastique Hittite.* Paris: C. Klincksieck, 1951.

Lattimore, Owen. *Inner Asian Frontiers of China.* 2nd ed. Irvington on Hudson, N.Y.: Capitol, 1951.

Laufer, Berthold. "The prefix *a-* in the Indo-Chinese languages." *Journal of the Royal Asiatic Society* (1915), 757–80.

———. *Sino-Iranica: Chinese Contributions to the History of Civilization in Ancient Iran, with Special Reference to the History of Cultivated Plants and Products.* Chicago: Field Museum of Natural History, 1919. Rpt., New York: Kraus Reprint, 1967.

Legge, James, tr. *The Four Books: Confucian Analects, the Great Learning, the Doctrine of the Mean, and the Works of Mencius.* Rpt., New York: Paragon, 1966.

Leslie, Donald D. *The Survival and the Chinese Jews.* Leiden: E. J. Brill, 1972.

Lévi, Sylvain. "Devaputra." *Journal asiatique* 204 (1934), 1–21.

Liang Zhangju. *Chengwei lu* (*Records of Names and Appellations*). Yangzhou: Guangling guji, 1989.

Liao Meiyun. *Yuan-Bai xinyuefu yanjiu* (*Studies of the New Folk-Songs by Yuan Zhen and Bai Juyi*). Taipei: Taiwan xuesheng shuju, 1989.

Li Baiyao. *Bei Qi shu* (*History of the Northern Qi*). Beijing: Zhonghua shuju, 1974.

Li Daoyuan (emended by Chen Qiaoyi). *Shuijing zhu* (*The Commentary on the Water Classic*). Shanghai: Shanghai guji, 1990.

Liddell, Henry G., Robert Scott, and Henry S. Jones. *A Greek-English Lexicon*. 9th ed. Oxford: Clarendon Press, 1951.

Lieu, Samuel N. C. *Manichaeism in the Later Roman Empire and Medieval China: A Historical Survey*. 2nd ed. Tübingen: J. C. B. Mohr, 1992.

———. "Polemics against Manichaeism as a subversive cult in Sung China." *Bulletin of the John Rylands University Library* 62, no. 1 (1979), 132–67.

Li Fang. *Taiping guangji* (*Extensive Records from the Reign of Great Tranquility*). Beijing: Zhonghua shuju, 1961.

Ligeti, Louis (Lajos). "Mots de civilization de Haute Asie en transcription chinoise." *Acta Orientalia Academiae Scientiarum Hungaricae* 1 (1950), 141–85.

———. "Le tabgatch, un dialecte de la langue sien-pi." In L. Ligeti, ed., *Mongolian Studies*. Budapest: Akadémiai Kiadó, 1970. Pp. 265–308.

Li Guanghua. "Bai Juyi xue Fo xinlu licheng" (The spiritual path of Bai Juyi in becoming a Buddhist). *Fojiao wenhua* (*Buddhist Cultures*) 1996.06, 41–43.

Li Guotao. "Erlangshen zhi Xianjiao laiyuan" (The Zoroastrian origin of the god Erlang). *Zongjiaoxue yanjiu* (*Studies in Religions*) 2004.02, 78–83.

Li Jingde, comp. *Zhuzi yulei* (*Teachings of Master Zhu Xi Categorized*). Beijing: Zhonghua shuju, 1986.

Limet, Henri. *L'Anthroponymie sumérienne dans les documents de la 3e dynastie d'Ur*. Paris: les Belles lettres, 1968.

Lin Gan, ed. *Xiongnu shiliao huibian* (*Compilation of Historical Sources on the Xiongnu*). 2 vols. Beijing: Zhonghua shuju, 1988.

———, ed. *Xiongnu shi lunwen xuanji, 1919–1979* (*Selected Papers on the History of the Xiongnu, 1919–1979*). Beijing: Zhonghua shuju, 1983.

Linghu Defen. *Zhou shu* (*History of the [Northern] Zhou*). Beijing: Zhonghua shuju, 1971.

Lin Meicun. "Cong Chen Shuozhen qiyi kan Huoxian jiao dui Tangdai minjian de yingxiang (The Zoroastrian influence in the Tang population based on the Chen Shuozhen uprising)." *Zhongguo shi yanjiu* (*Studies of Chinese History*) 1993.2, 140–42.

———. "Yingshan Bi Sheng bei yu Huainan Moni jiao" (The tomb inscription of Bi Sheng at Yingshan and Manichaeism in Huainan). In *Hang-Tang Xiyu yu Zhongguo wenming* (*The Western Regions during the Han and Tang and Chinese Civilization*). Beijing: Wenwu chubanshe, 1998. Pp. 393–419. Originally published in *Beijing daxue xuebao* 1997.2.

Lin Wushu. "Tangren feng Huoxian jiao bian" (Arguments for the Zoroastrian faith among the Tang population). *Wenshi* 30 (1988), 101–7.

Liu Huiqin and Chen Haitao. "Cong tonghun de bianhua kan Tangdai ru-Hua Sute ren de Hanhua" (The sinification of Sogdians who came to China during the Tang era based on the changes of intermarriages). *Huxia kaogu*, 2003.4, 55–61.

Liu Pansui. "Li-Tang wei fanxing kao" (Evidence that the imperial Li house of the Tang was of foreign origin). *Nü shida xueshu jikan* 1, no. 4 (n.d.), 1–5.

———. *Da Tang xinyu* (*New Talks of the Great Tang*). Beijing: Zhonghua shuju, 1984.

Liu Su. *Da Tang xinyu* (*New Talks of the Great Tang*). Beijing: Zhonghua shuju, 1984.

———. *Sui-Tang jiahua* (*Enjoyable Tales of the Sui and Tang*). Beijing: Zhonghua shuju, 1979.

Liu, Wu-chi. *An Introduction to Chinese Literature*. Bloomington: Indiana University Press, 1966.

Liu Xu. *Jiu Tang shu* (*Old History of the Tang Dynasty*). Beijing: Zhonghua shuju, 1975.

Li Yanshou. *Bei shi* (*History of the Northern Dynasties*). Beijing: Zhonghua shuju, 1974.

———. *Nan shi* (*History of the Southern Dynasties*). Beijing: Zhonghua shuju, 1975.

Li Zhengyu. "Dunhuang nuo sanlun" (Three discussions of Nuo in Dunhuang). *Dunhuang Yanjiu* 1993.2, 111–22.

Lockhart, Laurence. *The Fall of the Safavi Dynasty and the Afghan Occupation of Persia*. Cambridge: Cambridge University Press, 1958.

Lubotsky, Alexander. "Early contacts between Uralic and Indo-European: Linguistic and archaeological considerations." In C. Carpelan, A. Parpola, and P. Koskikallio, eds., *Papers presented at an International Symposium Held at the Tvärminne Research Station of the University of Helsinki, 8–10 January 1999*. Mémoires de la Société Finno-ougrienne 242. Helsinki: Suomalais-Ugrilainen Seura, 2001. Pp. 301–17.

Lu Deming. *Jingdian shiwen* (*Interpreting the Text of the Confucian Canon*). Beijing: Zhonghua shuju, 1983.

Lu Qinli, comp. *Xian-Qin Han Wei Nanbeichao shi* (*Anthology of Poems of the Pre-Qin Era, the Han, the Wei and the Southern and Northern Dynasties*). Han volume. Beijing: Zhonghua shuju, 1983.

Luo Changpei. *Tang Wudai xibei fangyin* (*Northwest Dialectal Accents from the Tang to Five Dynasties*). Shanghai: Academia Sinica, 1933.

Luo Xianglin. *Tang Yuan erdai zhi Jingjiao* (*Nestorianism during the Tang and the Yuan Dynasties*). Hong Kong: Zhongguo xueshe, 1966.

Luo Xin. "Bei Wei zhiqin kao" (A study of *zhiqin* [*tekin*] of the Northern Wei). *Lishi Yanjiu* 2004.05, 24–38.

Luoyang qielan ji (*A Catalog of Buddhist Monasteries in Luoyang*). See Fan Xiangyong (also Taisho T2092 V51).

Lu You. *Weinan wenji* (*Collected Works of [the Earl of] Weinan*). Taipei: Commercial Press, 1965.

Luo Zhenyu. *Hou dingwu gao* (*Second Manuscript of Years 1927–1928*). In *Zhensong laoren yigao jia ji* (*Posthumous Manuscript of Old Man Zhensong—Collection A*). Shangyu: Luo's family edition, 1941.

MacKenzie, David N. *A Concise Pahlavi Dictionary.* London: Oxford University Press, 1971.

Mackerras, Colin, ed. and tr. *The Uighur Empire according to the T'ang Dynastic Histories.* Canberra: Australian National University Press, 1972.

Ma Duanlin. *Wenxian tongkao (Comprehensive Examination of Source Materials).* Shanghai: Commercial Press, 1936.

Maenchen-Helfen, Otto. "Huns and Hsiung-nu." *Byzantion* 17 (1944–45), 222–43.

———. "A Parthian coin-legend on a Chinese bronze." *Asia Major* 3 (1952), 1–6.

———. "Pseudo-Huns." *Central Asiatic Journal* 1 (1955), 101–6.

———. "The Ting-ling." *Harvard Journal of Asiatic Studies* 4 (1939), 77–86.

———. *The World of the Huns: Studies in Their History and Culture.* Berkeley: University of California Press, 1973.

Mair, Victor H. "Buddhism and the rise of the written vernacular in East Asia: The making of national languages." *Journal of Asian Studies* 53 (1994), 707–51.

———. "Canine conundrums: Eurasian dog ancestor myths in historical and ethnic perspective." *Sino-Plantonic Papers*, no. 87 (1998).

———, ed. *The Columbia Anthology of Traditional Chinese Literature.* New York: Columbia University Press, 1994.

———. "Old Sinitic *Mᵍag, Old Persian Maguš, and English 'magician.'" *Early China* 15 (1990), 27–48.

———. *T'ang Transformation Texts.* Cambridge, Mass.: Harvard University Press, 1989.

———. *Tun-huang Popular Narratives.* Cambridge: Cambridge University Press, 1983.

Malalasekera, G. P. *Dictionary of Pāli Proper Names.* 1937. Rpt., London: Luzac, 1960.

Malov, S. E. *Pamiatniki drevnetiurkskoi pis'mennosti.* Moskva: Izd-vo Akademii nauk SSSR, 1951.

Manz, Beatrice F. *The Rise and Rule of Tamerlane.* Cambridge: Cambridge University Press, 1989.

Marcellinus, Ammianus. *Ammianus Marcellinus.* 3 vols. Cambridge, Mass.: Harvard University Press, 1950–52.

Marquart, J. "Über das Volkstum der Komanen." *Abhandlungen der Königlichen Gesellschaft de Wissenschaften: Philologisch-Historische Klasse* 8 (1914), 25–157.

Ma Shutian. *Huaxia zhushen (The Chinese Pantheon of Gods).* Beijing: Beijing Yanshan chubanshe, 1990.

Maspero, Henri. "Sur quelques texts anciens du chinois parlé." *Bulletin de l'Ecole Française d'Extrême Orient* 14 (1914), 1–36.

Masson, Olivier, "Remarques sur quelques anthroponymes myceniens." *Acta Mycenaea* (1972), 281–93.

———. "Une inscription éphebique de Plotemaïs (cyrenaïque)." In *Onomastica Graeca Selecta*, Tome 1. Nanterre: Université de Paris X, 1990. Pp. 243–56.

al-Mas'udi, Abu-l Hassan. *Muru-j al-Dhahab wa Ma'adin al-Jawhar (The Meadows of Gold).* Ed. with a French translation by C. B. de Maynard and P. de Courteill. 9 vols. Paris: Imprimerie impériale, 1861–1917.

Mayrhofer, Manfred, ed. *Iranisches Personennamenbuch*. Wien: Österreichischen Akademie der Wissenschaften, 1977–90.

Mazzaoui, Michel M. *The Origins of the Safawids: Ši'ism, Sufism, and the Gulat*. Wiesbaden: F. Steiner, 1972.

Meng Fanren. "Taiyuan Bai Juyi kao" (A study of Bai Juyi of Taiyuan). *Jinyang xuekan* 1996.4, 98–103.

Meng Sen. "Haining Chenjia" (The Chen Family of Haining). In *Ming-Qing shi lunzhu jikan xubian* (*Collected Works on the History of the Ming and Qing, Supplementary Volume*). Beijing: Zhonghua shuju, 1986. Pp. 324–26.

Menges, Karl. "Altaic elements in the proto-Bulgarian inscriptions." *Byzantion* 21 (1951), 85–118.

————. "Titles and organizational terms of the Qytan (Liao) and Qara-Qytaj (Śi-Liao)." *Rocznik Orientalistyczny* 17 (1951–52), 68–79.

————. *The Turkic Languages and Peoples: An Introduction to Turkic Studies*. 2nd ed. Wiesbaden: Harrassowitz, 1995.

————. "Die Wörter für 'Kamel' und einige seiner Kreuzungsformen im Türkischen." *Ungarische Jahrbücher* 15 (1935), 517–28.

Meskoob, Shahrokh. *Iranian Nationality and the Persian Language* (Translation of *Milliyat va zaban*). Washington, D.C.: Mage, 1992.

Miao Yue. *Dushi cungao* (*Saved Reflections on Reading History*). Beijing: Sanlian shudian, 1963.

Minorsky, Vladimir. "Tamin ibn Bahr's journey to the Uyghurs." *Bulletin of the School of Oriental and African Studies* 12 (1948), 275–305.

Mi Wenping. "Qiangu zhi mi Da Xianbei shan" (The Great Xianbei Mountain: A millennium-old enigma). *Guangming Daily*, May 19, 2000.

————. "Xianbei shishi de faxian yu chubu yanjiu (The discovery of the Xianbei rock chamber and it preliminary study). *Wenwu* 1981.2, 1–7.

Miyakawa Hisayuki. "Rikucho jinmei ni arawaretaru Bukkyogo" (Buddhist terms shown by the personal names of the six dynasties). *Toyoshi Kenkyu* 3, no. 6 (1938), 41; 4, no. 1 (1939), 71; no. 2, 94; no. 6, 78–79.

Molè, Gabriella. *The T'u-yü-hun from the Northern Wei to the Time of the Five Dynasties*. Rome: Istituto italiano per il Medio ed Estremo Oriente, 1970.

Morgan, David. *Medieval Persia, 1040–1797*. London: Longman, 1988.

Mukherjee, B. N. "The title Devaputra on Kushana coins." *Journal of the Numismatic Society of India* 20 (1968), 190–93.

Müller, Karl, ed. *Fragmenta historicorum Graecorum*. 5 vols. Paris: Ambrosio Firmin Didot, 1853–70.

Mungello, David E. *Curious Land: Jesuit Accommodation and the Origins of Sinology*. Stuttgart: Franz Steiner, 1985.

Nattier, J. "The heart sutra: A Chinese apocryphal text?" *Journal of the International Association of Buddhist Studies* 15(1992), 153–223.

Needham, Joseph. *Science and Civilisation in China*. Vol. 1. Cambridge: Cambridge University Press, 1954.

———. *Science and Civilisation in China*. Vol. 3. Cambridge: Cambridge University Press, 1959.

Németh, Gyula (Julius). *A honfoglaló magyarság kialakulása* (*The Shaping of the Hungarians of the Conquest Era*). Budapest, 1930. Rpt., Budapest: Akadémia Kiadó, 1991.

———. "The Meaning of the Ethnonym Bulgar." In A. Róna-Tas, ed., *Studies in Chuvash Etymology*. Vol. 1. Szeged: Universitas Szegediensis de Attila József Nominata, 1982. Pp. 7–13.

———. "Noms ethniques turcs d'origine totémistique." In L. Ligeti, ed., *Studia Turcica*. Budapest: Akadémiai Kiadó, 1971. Pp. 349–59.

Nigosian, Solomon Alexander. *The Zoroastrian Faith: Tradition and Modern Research*. Montréal: McGill-Queen's University Press, 1993.

Ningxia Huizu Zizhiqu Bowuguan. "Ningxia Guyuan Bei-Zhou Li Xian fufu mu fajue jianbao" (A brief report on the excavation of the Northern Zhou tombs of Li Xian and his wife at Gu yuan in Ningxia). *Wenwu* 1985.11, 1–20.

Norman, Jerry. *A Concise Manchu-English Lexicon*. Seattle: University of Washington Press, 1978.

———. "A Note on the Origin of the Chinese Duodenary Cycle." In G. Thurgood, J. Matisoff, and D. Bradley, eds., *Linguistics of the Sino-Tibetan Area: The State of the Art; Papers Presented to Paul K. Benedict for His 71st Birthday*. Canberra: Australian National University, 1985. Pp. 85–89.

Okladnikov, A. P. "Inner Asia at the dawn of history." In Denis Sinor, ed., *The Cambridge History of Early Inner Asia*. Cambridge: Cambridge University Press, 1990. Pp. 41–96.

Oldenberg, Hermann. *Buddha: Sein Leben, Seine Lehre, Seine Gemeinde*. Stuttgart: Cotta, 1921.

Ouyang Xiu and Song Qi. *Xin Tang shu* (*New History of the Tang Dynasty*). Beijing: Zhonghua shuju, 1975.

Ouyang Xun et al., comps. *Yiwen leiju* (*Anthology of Literature by Genre*). Shanghai: Zhonghua shuju, 1965.

Pakendorf, Brigitte, I. N. Novgorodov, V. L Osakovskij, A. P. Danilova, A. P. Protod'jakonov, and M. Stoneking. "Investigating the effects of prehistoric migrations in Siberia: Genetic variation and the origins of Yakuts." *Human Genetics* 120 (2006), 334–53.

Palandri, Angela. *Yüan Chen*. Boston: Twayne, 1977.

Pallisen, N. "Die alte Religion der Mongolen und der Kultus Tschingis-Chans." *Numen* 3 (1956), 178–229.

Parker, Edward. *A Thousand Years of the Tartars*. 2nd ed. London: K. Paul, 1924.

Pearce, Scott. "Status, labor and law: Special service households under the Northern dynasties." *Harvard Journal of Asiatic Studies* 51 (1991), 89–138.

Pelliot, Paul. "À propos des Comans." *Journal asiatique* 15 (1920), 125–85.

———. "Des artisans chinois à la capitale abbasside en 751–762." *T'oung Pao* 26 (1928), 110–12.

———. "L'édition collective des œuvres de Wang Kouo-wei." *T'oung Pao* 26 (1929), 113–82.

———. "Neuf notes sur des questions d'Asie centrale." *T'oung Pao* 26 (1929), 201–66.

———. *Notes on Marco Polo*. 3 vols. Paris: Imprimerie Nationale, 1959–73.

———. "Notes sur les T'ou-yu-houen and les Sou-p'i." *T'oung Pao* 20 (1920–21), 323–31.

———. "Notes sur le 'Turkestan' de M. W. Barthold." *T'oung Pao* 27 (1930), 2–56.

———. *Notes sur l'histoire de la horde d'or*. Paris: Adrien-Maisonneuve, 1949.

———. "La théorie des quartre Fils du Ciel." *T'oung Pao* 22 (1923), 97–125.

———. "Le Sa-pao." *Bulletin de l'École francaise d'Extrème-orient* 3 (1903), 665–71.

———. "Tängrim > tärim." *T'oung Pao* 36 (1944), 165–85.

Penzer, Norman Mosley. *The Harem*. London: Harrap, 1936.

Picken, Lawrence. *Music from the Tang Court*. Vol. 2. London: Cambridge University Press, 1985.

Pokrovskaia, L. A. "Terminy rodstva v tiurkskikh iazykakh." In E. I. Ubriatova, ed., *Istoricheskoe razvitie leksiki tiurkskikh iazykov*. Moskva: Izd-vo Akademii nauk SSSR, 1961. Pp. 11–81.

Pollak, Michael. *Mandarins, Jews, and Missionaries*. Philadelphia: Jewish Publication Society, 1980.

Polo, Marco. *The Description of the World*. Ed. A. C. Moule and Paul Pelliot. London: Routledge, 1938.

Popov, A. A. "Semeinaia zhizn' u dolgan." *Sovetskaia Etnografiia* 1946.4, 50–74.

Poppe, Nicholas. *Introduction to Altaic Linguistics*. Wiesbaden: Harrassowitz, 1965.

———. *Introduction to Mongolian Comparative Studies*. Helsinki: Suomalais-ugrilainen Seura, 1955.

———. *Mongolian Language Handbook*. Washington, D.C.: Center for Applied Linguistics, 1970.

Pritsak, Omeljian. *Die Bulgarische Fürstenliste und die Sprache der Protobulgaren*. Wiesbaden: Harrassowitz, 1955.

Prušek, Jaroslav. *Chinese Statelets and the Northern Barbarians in the Period 1400–300 B.C.* Dordrecht: D. Reidel, 1971.

Pulleyblank, Edwin G. "The An Lu-shan Rebellion and the origins of chronic militarism in Late T'ang China." In J. C. Perry and B. L. Smith, eds., *Essays on T'ang Society*. Leiden: E. J. Brill, 1976. Pp. 32–60.

———. *The Background of the Rebellion of An Lu-shan*. London: Oxford University Press, 1955.

———. "Chinese and Indo-Europeans." *Journal of the Royal Asiatic Society* (1966), 9–39.

———. "The Chinese and their neighbours in prehistoric and early historic times." In David N. Keightley, ed., *The Origins of Chinese Civilization*. Berkeley: University of California Press, 1983. Pp. 411–66.

———. "The Chinese name for the Turks." *Journal of American Oriental Society* 85 (1965), 121–25.

———. "The consonantal system of Old Chinese: Part II." *Asia Major*, n.s., 9 (1963), 206–65.

———. "The 'High Carts': A Turkish-speaking people before the Turks." *Asia Major*, 3rd ser., 3 (1990), 21–26.

———. *Lexicon of Reconstructed Pronunciation in Early Middle Chinese, Late Middle Chinese, and Early Mandarin.* Vancouver: University of British Columbia Press, 1990.

———. "A Sogdian colony in Inner Mongolia." *T'oung Pao* 41 (1952), 317–56.

Qian Boquan. "Han-Tang Qiuci ren de neiqian jiqi luosan" (The immigration and dispersion of the Qiuci people during the Han and Tang). *Xiyu yanjiu* 2001.1, 11–18.

Qian Daxin. *Hen yan lu* (*Notes on Perpetual Words*). Changsha: Commercial Press, 1939.

———. *Shijiazhai yangxin lu* (*Records of New Cultivations at the Ten-Horse Studio*). Shanghai: Commercial Press, 1937. Rpt., Shanghai: Shanghai shudian, 1983.

Qian Yi. *Nanbu xinshu* (*New Book from the South*). Shanghai: Commercial Press, 1936.

Qiu Xigui. "Guanyu Shangdai de zongzu zuzhi yu guizu he pingmin liangge jieji de chubu yanjiu" (A preliminary study of clan organizations and the noble versus commoner classification of the Shang era). *Wenshi* 17 (1983), 1–26.

Quan Tangshi (*A Complete Anthology of Tang Poems*). Shanghai: Shanghai guji chubanshe, 1986.

Quan Tang wen (*A Complete Collection of Tang Prose*). Beijing: Zhonghua shuju, 1983.

Rabinowitz, Louis I. *Jewish Merchant Adventurers: A Study of the Radanites.* London: E. Goldston, 1948.

Radloff, Wilhelm. *Die Alttürkischen Inschriften der Mongolei.* St. Petersburg, 1894–99. Rpt., Osnarbrück: Otto Zeller, 1987.

———. *Opyt slovaria tiurkskikh narechii* (*Versuch eines Worterbuches der Türk-Dialecte*). Vol. 1. St. Petersburg, 1893. Rpt., 's-Gravenhage: Mouton, 1960; Moskva: Izd-vo vostochnoĭ lit-ry, 1963.

Ramstedt, Gustaf J. *Kalmückisches Wörterbuch.* Helsinki: Suomalais-ugrilainen Seura, 1935.

Ranke, Hermann. *Die ägyptischen Personennamen.* Band 1–3. Glückstadt: J. J. Augustin, 1935–52.

Räsänen, Matti. "Uralaltaische Forschungen." *Ural-Altaische Jahrbücher* 25 (1953), 19–27.

———. *Versuch eines etymologischen Wörterbuchs der Türksprachen.* Helsinki: Suomalais-Ugrilainen Seura, 1969.

Redhouse, Sir James W. *A Turkish and English Lexicon.* Constantinople: A. H. Boyajian, 1890.

Ren Bantang. *Jiaofang ji jianding* (*An Emended Edition of the Records of the Palace Music School*). Shanghai: Zhonghua shuju, 1962.

———. *Tang xi nong* (*Tang Plays and Music*). Beijing: Zuojia chubanshe, 1958.

Ren Fang. "Zaitan Bi Sheng bei de zongjiao secai" (Another discussion of the religious aspects of the tomb inscription of Bi Sheng). *Chuban kexue* 1995.3, 37–38.

Rhee, Song Nai. "Jewish Assimilation: The Case of the Chinese Jews." *Comparative Studies in Society and History* 15 (1973), 115–26.

Róna-Tas, András. "The periodization and sources of Chuvash linguistic history." In A. Róna-Tas, ed., *Chuvash Studies*. Wiesbaden: Harrassowitz, 1982. Pp. 113–69.

Rong Xinjiang (tr. Bruce Doar). "Research on Zoroastrianism in China (1923–2000)." *China Archaeology and Art Digest, IV.1: Zoroastrianism in China* (December 2000), 7–13.

Roth, Cecil, and Geoffrey Wigoder, eds. *Encyclopaedia Judaica*. New York: Macmillan, 1971.

Roux, Jean-Paul, "Le chameau en Asie centrale." *Central Asiatic Journal* 5 (1960), 35–76.

———. "L'origine céleste de la souveraineté dans les inscriptions paléo-turques de Mongolie et de Sibérie." In *The Sacral Kingship*. Leiden: E. J. Brill, 1959. Pp. 231–41.

———. "Tängri: Essai sur le ciel-dieu des peuples altaïcs." *Revue de l'histoire des religions* 149 (1956), 49–82, 197–320; 150 (1956), 27–54, 173–212.

Ruan Yuan, ed. *Shisanjing zhushu*. Beijing: Zhonghua, 1980.

Rudnickij, J. B. *An Etymological Dictionary of the Ukrainian Language*. Vol. 1. Winnipeg: Ukrainian Free Academy of Sciences, 1962–66.

Runciman, Steven. *A History of the First Bulgarian Empire*. London: G. Bell & Sons, 1930.

Schafer, Edward H. *The Golden Peaches of Samarkand: A Study of T'ang Exotics*. Berkeley: University of California Press, 1963.

Schmidt, Hans-Peter. "An Indo-Iranian etymological kaleidoscope." In G. Cardona and N. H. Zide, eds., *Festschrift for Henry Hoenigswald*. Tübingen: G. Narr, 1987. Pp. 355–62.

Schmidt, Isaac Jacob (Iakov Ivanovich). *Grammatik der mongolischen Sprache*. St. Petersburg: Kaiserlichen Akademie der issenschaften, 1831.

Schmitt, Rüdiger. *Iranisches Namen in den Indogermanischen Sprachen Kleinasiens (Iranisches Personennamenbuch*, Band V Faszikel 4). Vienna: Verlag der Österreichische Akademie der Wissenschaften, 1982.

Senga, T. "The Toquz Oghuz problem and the origin of the Khazars." *Journal of Asian History* 24 (1990), 57–69.

Serruys, Henry. "The office of Tayisi in Mongolia in the fifteenth century." *Harvard Journal of Asiatic Studies* 37 (1977), 353–80.

Sevortian, Ervand V. *Etimologicheskii slovar tiurkskikh iazykov*. Vol. 1. Moscow: "Nauka," 1974.

Shanghai Library, comp. *Zhongguo congshu zonglu*. 3 vols. Shanghai: Shanghai Guji. 1986.

Shapiro, Sidney. *Jews in Old China: Studies by Chinese Scholars*. New York: Hippocrene Books, 1984.

Shaughnessy, Edward L. "Historical perspectives on the introduction of chariots into China." *Harvard Journal of Asiatic Studies* 47 (1988), 189–237.

Shen Yue. *Song shu (History of the Song Dynasty)*. Beijing: Zhonghua shuju, 1974.

Shiratori, Kurakichi. "Sur l'origine de Hiong-nu." *Journal Asiatique* 202 (1923), 71–81.

Silk, Jonathan. "Riven by lust: Incest and schism in Indian Buddhist legend and historiography," book manuscript, September 2004. Since published: Honolulu: University of Hawaii Press, 2008.

Sima Guang et al. *Zizhi tongjian (Comprehensive Mirror for Aid in Government)*. Beijing: Zhonghua shuju, 1956.

Sima Qian. *Shiji (Records of the Grand Historian)*. Beijing: Zhonghua shuju, 1959.

Sims-Williams, Nicholas. *The Christian Sogdian Manuscript C2*. Berlin: Akademie, 1985.

Sinor, Denis. "Altaica and Uralica." In D. Sinor, ed., *Studies in Finno Ugric Linguistics in Honor of Alo Raun*. Bloomington: Indiana University Press, 1978. Pp. 319–32.

———. "À propos de la biographie ouigoure de Hiuan-tsang." *Journal Asiatique* 231 (1939), 543–90.

———, ed. *The Cambridge History of Early Inner Asia*. Cambridge: Cambridge University Press, 1990.

———. "The establishment and dissolution of the Türk Empire." In D. Sinor, ed., *Cambridge History of Early Inner Asia*. Cambridge: Cambridge University Press, 1990. Pp. 285–316.

———. "Horse and pasture in Inner Asian history." *Oriens Extremus* 19 (1972), 171–84.

———. *Introduction à l'étude de l'Eurasie centrale*. Wiesbaden: Harrassowitz, 1963.

———. "Mongol and Turkic words in the Latin versions of John of Plano Carpini's Journey to the Mongols (1245–1247)." In L. Ligeti, ed., *Mongolian Studies*. Budapest: Akadémiai Kiadó, 1975. Pp. 537–51.

———. "On some Ural-Altaic plural suffixes." *Asia Major*, n.s., 2 (1952), 203–30.

———. "Sur les noms altaiques de la licorne." *Wiener Zeitschrift für die Kunde des Morgenlandes* 61 (1960), 168–76.

———. "Western information on the Kitans and some related questions." *Journal of the American Oriental Society* 115 (1995), 262–69.

Skelton, Raleigh Ashlin, T. E. Marston, and G. D. Painter. *The Vinland Map and the Tartar Relation*. New Haven, Conn.: Yale University Press, 1965.

Slotkin, J. Sydney. "On a possible lack of incest regulations in old Iran." *American Anthropologist*, n.s., 49 (1947), 612–17.

Smith, W. Robertson. *Kinship and Marriage in Early Arabia*. Rpt., Boston: Beacon Press, 1963.

Song Lian. *Yuan shi (History of the Yuan Dynasty)*. Beijing: Zhonghua shuju, 1975.

Song Minqiu, comp. *Tang da zhaoling ji (Compilation of Tang Imperial Edicts and Decrees)*. Beijing: Zhonghua shuju, 1959.

Soothill, William Edward, and Lewis Hodous. *A Dictionary of Chinese Buddhist Terms*. London: K. Paul, 1937.

Sprenkel, Sybille van der. *Legal Institutions in Manchu China: A Sociological Analysis.* London: Athlone Press, 1962.

Starostin, Sergei A. "Gipoteza o geneticheskikh sviaziakh sinotibetskikh iazykov s eniseiskimii severnokavkazkimi iazykami." In *Lingvisticheskaia rekonstruktsiia i drevneishaia istoriia Vostoka: Tezisy i doklady konferentsii,* vol. 4. Moskva: Izd-vo "Nauka," 1984. Pp. 19–38.

———. "Praeniseiskaia rekonstruktsiia i vneshnie sviazi eniseiskikh iazykov." In E. A. Aleksenko et al., eds., *Ketsii sbornik,* vol. 3. Moskva: "Nauka," 1982. Pp. 144–237.

Starostin, Sergei A., Anna Dybo, and Oleg Mudrak. *Etymological Dictionary of the Altaic Languages.* 3 vols. Leiden: E. J. Brill, 2003.

Stein, Rolf. "Liao-Tche." *T'oung Pao* 35 (1940), 1–154.

Sundermann, W., and W. Thilo. "Zur mittelpersischen Grabinschrift aus Xi'an" (Volksrepublik China). *Mitteilungen des Instituts für Orientforschung* 11 (1966), 437–50.

Sun Guangxian. *Beimeng suoyan (Trifling Bits of Northern Reverie).* Shanghai: Shanghai guji chubanshe, 1981.

Sun Guodong. "Tang Song zhiji shehui mendi zhi xiaorong" (The disappearance of prestigious pedigrees during the Tang-Song transition). In *Tang Song shi luncong (Collected Historical Studies of the Tang and Song).* Hong Kong: Longmen shudian, 1980. Pp. 211–308.

———. "Tang Zhenguan Yonghui jian dangzheng shishi." *Xinya Shuyuan xueshu niankan* 7 (1965), 39–49.

Sun Qikang. "Bi Sheng mubei zhi niandai duanding yu bihui wenti" (The dating of the tomb inscription and the issue of tabo names). *Chuban kexu,* 1995.2, 37–38.

Szyszman, S. "Le roi Bulan et le problème de la conversion des Khazars." *Ephemerides Theologicae Lovanienses* 33(1957), 68–76.

Tada Toshio. *Retsuden Ajia no sanga ni (Biographies: In the Land of Asia).* Tokyo: Nihon Hoso shuppan kyokai, 1983.

Taiping guangji. See Li Fang.

Taishō Tripitaka (Taishō shinshū daizōkyō). See Takakusu and Watanabe.

Takakusu Junjirō and Watanabe Kaigyoku, eds. *Taishō shinshū Daizōkyō (The Tripitaka Newly Compiled during the Taishō Period).* Tokyo: Taishō Issaikyō Kankōkai, 1924–32.

Tallqvist, K. L. *Assyrian Personal Names.* Helsinki: Acta Societatis Scientiarum Fennicae, 1914.

Tanaka Katsumi. *Haku Rakuten (Bai Letian).* Tokyo: Shueisha, 1972.

Tang Changru. "Wei-Jin zahu kao" (A Study of the Zahu of the Wei-Jin Era). In *Wei-Jin Nanbeichao shi luncong (Collected Historical Studies of the Wei-Jin Period and the Southern and Northern Dynasties).* Beijing: Sanlian shudian, 1955. Pp. 382–450.

Tang Geng'ou and Lu Hongji, comps. *Dunhuang shehui jingji wenxian zhenji shilu* (Facsimiles and Interpretations of the Dunhuang Socioeconomic Documents). Beijing: Shumu wenxian chubanshe, 1986.

Tang huiyao. See Wang Pu.

Tang Yongtong. *Sui-Tang Fojiao shigao* (*Draft History of Buddhism of the Sui-Tang Era*). Beijing: Zhonghua shuju, 1982.

———. *Wangri zagao* (*Miscellaneous Manuscripts of Yore*). Beijing: Zhonghua shuju, 1962.

Tan Qixiang. "Jie kao" (On the Jie People). In *Changshui ji* (*A Long-River Collection*). 2 vols. Beijing: Renmin chubanshe, 1987. Pp. 224–33.

Tan Qixiang, et al. *Zhongguo lishi dituji* (*The Historical Atlas of China*). Vol. 4. Beijing: Zhongguo ditu chubanshe, 1982.

Tao, Jing-Shen. *Jurchen in Twelfth-century China: A Study of Sinicization*. Seattle: University of Washington Press, 1976.

Tao Xisheng, comp. "Tang huji bu congji" (Compilation of Tang household registrations). *Shihuo*, special issue, 1936.4–5, 1–38.

Tao Zongyi. *Nancun chuogeng lu* (*Notes Jotted down during Breaks of Plowing at the South Village*). Beijing: Zhonghua shuju, 1959.

Tarn, W. W. *The Greeks in Bactria and India*. 3rd ed. Chicago: Ares, 1985.

Tekin, Talat. *A Grammar of Orkhon Turkic*. Bloomington: Indiana University Press, 1968.

Thomas, F. W. "Tibetan documents concerning Chinese Turkestan." *Journal of the Royal Asiatic Society* (1927), 51–85.

Toktogh et al. *Liao shi* (*History of the Liao Dynasty*). Beijing: Zhonghua shuju, 1974.

Togan, Zeki Velidi. "Sur l'origine des Safavides." In *Melanges Louis Massignon*, vol. 3. Damascus: Institut d'études islamiques, 1957. Pp. 345–57.

Tulufan chutu wenshu (Documents Unearthed at Turfan). 10 vols. Beijing: Wenwu chubanshe, 1981–91.

Twitchett, Denis, ed. *The Cambridge History of China*. Vol. 3, part 1. Cambridge: Cambridge University Press, 1979.

———, ed. "The composition of the T'ang ruling class." In Arthur F. Wright and Denis Twitchett, eds., *Perspectives on the T'ang*. New Haven, Conn.: Yale University Press, 1973. Pp. 47–85.

———. *The Writing of Official History under the T'ang*. Cambridge: Cambridge University Press, 1992.

Vaissière, Etienne de la. *Histoire des marchands sogdiens*. 2nd ed. Paris: Collège de France, Institut des hautes études chinoise, 2005. English translation: *Sogdian Traders: A History*. Tr. James Ward. Leiden: E. J. Brill, 2005.

———. "Huns et Xiongnu." *Central Asiatic Journal* 49 (2005), 3–26.

Vaissière, Étienne de la, and Eric Trombert, eds. *Les Sogdiens en Chine*. Paris: École Francaise d'Extreme Orient, 2005.

Vandermeersch, Léon, *Wangdao ou la Voie Royale: Recherches sur l'esprit des institutions de la Chine archaïque*. Paris: École française d'Extrême-Orient, 1977.

Velze, Jacob van. *Names of Persons in Early Sanscrit Literature*. Utrecht: Utr. typ. ass., 1938.

Vetch, Hélène. "Lieou Sa-ho et les grottes de Mo-kao." In M. Soymié, ed., *Nouvelles contributions aux etudes de Touen-houang*. Geneva: Droz, 1981. Pp. 137–48.

Viatkin, R. V., ed. *Materialy po istorii kochevykh narodov v Kitae, III–V vv.* Vol. 3. *Muzhuny.* Moscow: "Nauka," 1992.

Vorländer, Hermann. *Mein Gott: Die Vorstellungen vom persönlische Gott im Alten Orient und im Alten Testament.* Kevelaer: Butzon and Bercker, 1975.

Vovin, Alexander A. "Did the Xiongnu speak a Yeniseian language?" *Central Asiatic Journal* 44 (2000), 87–104.

Waley, Arthur. *The Life and Times of Po Chü-I.* London: George Allen and Unwin, 1949.

Wang Dang. *Tang yulin* (*Anecdotes of the Tang*). Changsha: Commercial Press, 1939.

Wang Deyi, Li Rongcun, and Pan Bocheng, comps. *Yaunren zhuanji ziliao suoyin* (*Index of Bibliographical Materials of Yuan Personages*). Rpt., Beijing: Zhonghua shuju, 1987.

Wang Dingbao. *Tang zhiyan* (*Collected Anecdotes of the Tang*). Shanghai: Shanghai guji chubanshe, 1978.

Wang Guowei. *Guantang jilin* (*Collected Works from the Hall of Observations*). 4 vols. Beijing: Zhonghua shuju, 1961.

———. "Xihu kao" and "Xihu xukao." In *Guantang jilin*. Beijing, 1959. 13.606–19.

Wang Liqi, annot. *Yanshi jiaxun jijie* (*An Annotated Edition of Yan's Family Instructions*). Beijing: Zhonghua shuju, 1993.

Wang Meng'ou. "Bai Letian xianzu ji housi wenti" (On Bai Letian's ancestry and descendants). *Guoli Zhengzhi daxue xuebao* 10 (1964), 123–58.

Wang Pu. *Tang huiyao* (*Institutional History of the Tang*). Taipei: Shijie Shuju, 1963.

Wang Shiyi. *Bai Juyi zhuan* (*A Biography of Bai Juyi*). Xi'an: Shaanxi renmin chubanshe, 1983.

Wang Shumin. *Nian'ershi zhaji jiangzheng* (*An Emended Edition of Notes on the Twenty-two Dynastic Histories*). 2 vols. Beijing: Zhonghua, 1984.

Wang Tongling. "Yang-Sui Li-Tang xianshi xitong kao" (Examining the ancestry lines of the Sui and Tang imperial houses). *Nü shida xueshu jikan* 2.2 (n.d.), 1–23.

Wang Yongxing. "Dunhuang Tangdai chakebu kaoshi" (Examination and interpretation of Tang era corvée labor registrations in Dunhuang). *Lishi yanjiu* 1957.12. Rpt. in *Dunhuang Tulufan wenshu yanjiu* (*Studies of Dunhuang and Turfan Documents*). Lanzhou: Gansu renmin, 1984. Pp. 289–336.

———. "Tang Tianbao Dunhuang chakebu yanjiu" (Studies of Tang corvée labor registrations of the Tianbao period in Dunhuang). In *Dunhuang Tulufan wenxian yanjiu lunji* (*Collected Studies of Dunhuang and Turfan Documents*). Beijing: Zhonghua shuju, 1982. Pp. 63–166.

Wang Yuxin. *Xizhou jiagu tanlun* (*Exploratory Studies of Western Zhou Oracle Bones*). Beijing: Zhongguo shehui kexue chubanshe, 1984.

Wang Zhongluo. *Beizhou liudian* (*Statutes of the Northern Zhou*). 2 vols. Beijing: Zhonghua shuju, 1979.

———. *Wei-Jin nanbeichao shi* (*History of the Wei-Jin Era and the Southern and Northern Dynasties*). 2 vols. Shanghai: Shanghai renmin chubanshe, 1980.

Wechsler, Howard J. *Mirror to the Son of Heaven: Wei Cheng at the Court of T'ang T'aitsung.* New Haven, Conn.: Yale University Press, 1974.

————. *Offerings of Jade and Silk*. New Haven, Conn.: Yale University Press, 1985.

Wei Chengsi. *Zhongguo fojiao wenhua lun'gao* (*A Draft Treatise on Chinese Buddhist Cultures*). Shanghai: Shanghai renmin, 1991.

Weinstein, Stanley. *Buddhism under the T'ang*. London: Cambridge University Press, 1987.

Wei Shou. *Wei shu* (*History of the Wei Dynasty*). Beijing: Zhonghua shuju, 1974.

Wei Songshan et al, *Zhongguo lishi diming da cidian* (*The Grand Dictionary of Chinese Historical Toponyms*). Guangzhou: Guangdong jiaoyu chubanshe, 1995.

Wei Zheng. *Sui shu* (*History of the Sui Dynasty*). Beijing: Zhonghua shuju, 1973.

Wen Yucheng. "Bai Juyi guju chutu de jingchuang" (Sutra stele unearthed at the former residence of Bai Juyi). *Sichuan wenwu* 2001.3, 63–65.

White, William C. *Chinese Jews*. 2nd ed. New York: Paragon, 1966.

Winderkens, A. J. van. *Le tokharien confronté avec les autre langues indo-européenes*. Louvain: Université catholique néerlandaise de Louvain, 1979.

Winstanley, Lilian. *Hamlet and the Scottish Succession*. Cambridge: Cambridge University Press, 1921.

Wittfogel, Karl A., and Chia-sheng Feng. *History of Chinese Society: Liao*. Philadelphia: American Philosophical Society, 1949.

Wright, Arthur F. *Studies in Chinese Buddhism*. New Haven, Conn.: Yale University Press, 1990.

————. *The Sui Dynasty*. New York: Knopf, 1978.

————. "Sui Yang-ti: Personality and stereotype." In A. Wright, ed., *Confucianism and Chinese Civilization*. New York: Atheneum, 1964. Pp. 158–87.

————. "T'ang T'ai-tsung and Buddhism." In A. Wright and D. Twitchett, eds., *Perspectives on the T'ang*. New Haven, Conn.: Yale University Press, 1973. Pp. 239–63.

Wroth, Warwick. *Catalogue of the Greek Coins of Galatia, Cappadocia and Syria*. London: Trustees, 1899. Rpt., Bologna: A. Forni, 1964.

Wu Gang, comp. *Sui-Tang Wudai muzhi huibian Shaanxi juan* (*Collection of Tomb Inscription of the Sui, Tang and Five Dyanties—Shaanxi Volume*). Tianjin: Tianjin guji chubanshe, 1991.

Wu, Silas H. L. *Passage to Power: K'ang-hsi and His Heir Apparent, 1661–1722*. Cambridge, Mass.: Harvard University Press, 1979.

Wu Wenliang. *Quanzhou zongjiao shike (Religious Inscriptions at Quanzhou)*. Beijing: Kexue chubanshe, 1957.

Wu Xiaosong. "Bi Sheng mudi faxian ji xiangguan wenti chubu tantao" (The discovery of Bi Sheng's tomb and the preliminary exploration of related issues). *Zhongguo keji shiliao* 1994.2, 89–97.

Wu Xiaosong et al. "Yingshan xian faxian Bi Sheng jiqi houyi muzang kaozeng" (A study of the newly discovered tombs of Bi Sheng and his offspring). *Chuban kexue* 1994.1, 39–41.

Wu Yugui. "Bai Juyi zhanzhang shi yu Tangchao shehui de hufeng" (Bai Juyi's tent poems and the foreign customs in Tang society). *Tang yanjiu* 5 (1999), 401–20.

Xiamen University, ed. *Putonghua Minnan fangyan cidian* (*A Dictionary of Mandarin-Southern Fujian Dialect*). Hong Kong: Sanlian shudian, 1982.

Xiao Zixian. *Nan Qi shu* (*The History of the Southern Qi Dynasty*). Beijing: Zhonghua shuju, 1972.

Xiang Da. *Tangdai Chang'an yu Xiyu wenming* (*The Tang Chang'an and the Civilizations of the Western Regions*). Beijing: Sanlian shudian, 1957.

Xie Haiping. *Tangdai liu-Hua waiguoren shenghuo kaoshu* (*Examination of the Life of Aliens Who Stayed in China during the Tang*). Taipei: Commercial Press, 1978.

Xiong, Victor Cunrui. "Sui Yangdi and the building of Sui-Tang Luoyang." *Journal of Asian Studies* 52 (1993), 66–89.

Xu Daoxun and Zhao Keyao. *Tang Xuanzong zhuan* (*A Biography of Tang Emperor Xuanzong*). Beijing: Renmin chubanshe, 1993.

Xue Juzheng. *Jiu Wudai shi* (*The Old History of the Five Dynasties*). Beijing: Zhonghua shuju, 1976.

Xu Fu et al., eds. *Gu Hanyu dacidian* (*A Grand Dictionary of Old Chinese*). Shanghai: Shanghai cishu chubanshe, 2001.

Xu Zhen'e, ed. and annot. *Shishuo xinyu xiaojian* (*An Emended and Annotated Edition of a New Account of Tales of the World*). Beijing: Zhonghua shuju, 1984.

Yang Lian. "Kanman'er shijian bianwei" (On the forgery of the Kanman'er Anthology). *Wenxue pinglun* 1991.3, 4–16.

Yang Zhen. *Qingchao huangwei jicheng zhidu* (*The System of Imperial Succession of the Qing Dynasty*). Beijing: Xueyuan chubanshe, 2001.

Yang Zongying. *Bai Juyi yanjiu* (*Bai Juyi Studies*). Taipei: Wenjin chubanshe, 1985.

Yao Silian. *Chen shu* (*History of the Chen Dynasty*). Beijing: Zhonghua shuju, 1972.

———. *Liang shu* (*History of the Liang Dynasty*). Beijing: Zhonghua shuju, 1973.

Yao Weiyuan. *Beichao huxing kao* (*A Study of Alien Surnames of the Northern Dynasties*). Beijing: Kexue chubanshe, 1958.

———. "Dugu ji Tuge kao" (On the Equivalence of the Clan Names Dugu and Tuge). In Lin Gan, ed., *Xiongnu shi lunwen xuanji* (*Selected Papers on the History of the Xiongnu*). Beijing: Zhonghua shuju, 1983. Pp. 69–74.

Ye Dehui, ed. *Shuangmei jing'an congshu* (*Book Series under the Shadow of Double Plum Trees*). Changsha: Yeshi anyuan, 1903–14.

Yihong Pan. *Son of Heaven and Heavenly Qaghan*. Bellingham: University of Western Washington Press, 1997.

Yi Zhongtian. *Nihao, Weige* (*Hello, Viagra*). Nanjing: Jiangsu wenyi, 2000.

You Guo'en et al. *Zhongguo wenxue shi* (*A History of Chinese Literature*). Hong Kong: China Book Press, 1986.

Young, Robert. *Analytical Concordance to the Holy Bible*. London: Religious Tract Society, 1890.

Yue Shi. *Taiping huanyuji* (*Geographical Records of the Reign of Great Tranquility*). Taipei: Wenhai chubanshe, 1963.

Yule, Sir Henry, ed. *The Book of Ser Marco Polo*. 3 vols. London: London: J. Murray, 1920.

Yu Liang. "Bai Juyi fumu jixing hunpei shuo zhiyi" (Questioning the abnormal marriage of Bai Juyi's parents). *Zhongguo yunwen xuekan* 2002.2, 40–42.

Yu Shucheng. "Han-Bai shifeng de chayi . . ." (On the different poetry styles between Han Yu and Bai Juyi . . .). *Wenxue yichan* 1993.5, 41–50.

Zhai Hao. *Tongsu bian* (*Collection of Common Sayings*). Shanghai: Commercial Press, 1937.

Zhang Du. *Xuanshi zhi* (*Palace Chamber Journal*). Changsha: Commercial Press, 1939.

Zhang Naizhu. "Ji Luoyang chutu de liangjian Tangdai shike" (Notes on two Tang era stone inscriptions unearthed in Luoyang). *Henan Keji daxue xuebao* 2005.1, 20–22.

Zhang Qun. "Tangdai Fanjiang chutan" (A preliminary discussion of ethnic generals of the Tang era). *Journal of Oriental Studies* 19 (1981), 1–38.

———. *Tangdai fanjiang yanjiu* (*Studies of Foreign Generals of the Tang Era*). Taipei: Lianjing chuban Co., 1986.

———. *Tangdai fanjiang yanjiu xubian* (*Studies of Foreign Generals of the Tang Era: A Sequel*). Taipei: Lianjing chuban Co., 1990.

Zhangsun Wuji. *Tanglü shuyi* (*Tang Legal Code Interpreted*). Beijing: Zhonghua shuju, 1983.

Zhanguo ce (*Intrigues of the Warring States*). Shanghai: Shanghai guji chubanshe, 1985.

Zhang Zhuo. *Chaoye qianzai* (*Popular Records of the Court and Commonality*). Beijing: Zhonghua shuju, 1979.

Zhao Chao. *Han-Wei Nanbeichao muzhi huibian* (*A Compilation of Tomb Inscriptions of the Han-Wei Era and the Southern and Northern Dynasties*). Tianjin: Tianjin guji chubanshe, 1990.

Zhao Lin. *Yinhua lu* (*Old Talk Recorded*). Taipei: Shiji shuju, 1962.

Zhao Lüfu, ed. and annot. *Shitong xin jiaozhu* (*A New Emended and Annotated Edition of General Historiography*). Chongqing: Chongqing chubanshe, 1990.

Zhao Yi. *Gaiyu congkao* (*Miscellaneous Research after Walking the Steps*). Taipei: Shi-jie shuju, 1965.

———. *Nian'ershi zhaji* (*Notes on the Twenty-two Histories*). Annot. Du Weiyun. Tai-pei: Dingwen shuju, 1975.

Zheng Qiao. *Tongzhi* (*Comprehensive History of Institutions*). Shanghai: Commercial Press, 1935.

Zhou Xunchu. "Yuanhe wentan de xin fengmao" (The new atmosphere and styles of the literary world of the Yuanhe era). *Zhonghua wenshi luncong* (*Serialized Research in Chinese Literature and History*) 47 (1991), 137–52.

Zhou Yiliang. "Beichao de minzu wenti yu minzu zhengce" (The ethnic problem and ethic policies of the Northern dynasties). In *Wei-Jin Nanbeichao shi lunji* (*Collected Papers on the History of the Wei-Jin and Southern and Northern Dynasties Era*). Beijing: Zhonghua shuju, 1963. Pp. 116–76.

———. *Wei-Jin Nanbeichao shi zaji* (*Miscellaneous Notes on the History of the Wei-Jin and Southern and Northern Dynasties Era*). Beijing: Zhonghua shuju, 1985.

Zhuang Chuo. *Jile bian* (*Notes of Marginal Values*). Beijing: Zhonghua shuju, 1983.

Zhu Jincheng, ed. and annot. *Bai Juyi ji jianjiao* (*An Annotated and Emended Edition of Collected Works of Bai Juyi*). Shanghai: Shanghai guji chubanshe, 1988.

———. *Bai Juyi yanjiu* (*A Study of Bai Juyi*). Xi'an: Shaanxi renmin chubanshe, 1987.

Zhu Jincheng and Zhu Yi'an. *Bai Juyi shiji daodu* (*A Guide to the Poetry Anthology of Bai Juyi*). Chengdu: Ba-Shu shushe, 1988.

Zürcher, Erik. *The Buddhist Conquest of China*. Vol. 1. Leiden: E. J. Brill, 1972.

Index

Acknowledgments

After a long and rewarding journey, it is finally the time to write the acknowledgments for this book.

First of all, I thank my parents for having created an environment that facilitated my learning of Chinese classics and histories, even during a period when such learning was condemned. I thus managed to receive a self-directed education on the Confucian Canon, especially *Shi jing* (*The Book of Songs*) and *Shang shu* (*The Book of Documents*). Yet historiography remained my favorite subject. I remember vividly how the great Chinese chronicle *Zizhi tongjian* (*Comprehensive Mirror for Aid in Government*) became my beloved reading while a teenager. No less important, I was exposed early on to works by Western scholars like Paul Pelliot and thus learned that there were a lot more than just Sinitic sources on Asian history. Moreover, the Chinese calligraphy on the cover referring to the title of Chapter 2 was penned by my father.

Growing up during the height of the Cultural Revolution in China embedded me with a life-long distrust of official records and similarly one-sided sources, however less biased they might have been than their latter-day counterparts. Many segments of this book have been, at least partially, prompted by such suspicions and doubts.

Of all the scholars I have had the opportunity to be associated with, I would foremost like to thank the late Denis Sinor. He not only published my first study in English with kind encouragement, but also, befitting his own meticulous training under *Maître* Pelliot, demonstrated the rigor standards that one's research should be held up to. I have also handsomely benefited from his yet-to-be-surpassed *Introduction à l'étude de l'Eurasie centrale*.

I owe another great Denis, the late Denis Twitchett, whose personal letters were much more than just encouragement. A segment of Chapter 1 of this book was developed from his ideas. I also learned from these exchanges the intellectual openness and breadth of a true master in Sinology.

In addition to Giovanni Stary, who has always been supportive of my research by accepting my submissions within days or even hours, thanks are also due to the Royal Asiatic Society of Great Britain and Ireland, which bestowed upon me the 1996 Major Barwis-Holliday Award. Such an honor to a relative outsider greatly helped me continue my research in an environment not conducive to Asian studies.

The fact of the matter is that, during the entire research period for the materials covered in this book, I have always lived in a city that does not have an Asian library, much less the modern Western publications and journals indispensable to my research. Other than my own meagre bookshelves, for many years, almost all substantive references were procured via slow and cumbersome interlibrary loans from across North America. While the Internet has in recent years mitigated this situation significantly, I am still hampered by a lack of access to a research library in humanities, let alone one in Asian studies. Hence my advance apologies to readers of this book for any missed references.

I thank my wife for her understanding and support, and my son for helping secure many hard-to-find references during his four undergraduate years at Harvard.

Over the years, many people have provided help in securing important references. I would like to mention in particular Samuel Adshead for the late Joseph Fletcher's conference paper on blood tanistry, and Jonathan Silk for his book manuscript *Riven by Lust*.

I thank my good friend Chung-mo Kwok for years of stimulating outside-the-box discussions about medieval China, including the one leading to our joint paper on the proto-Mongolian origin of the popular Chinese slur word *nucai*. I also thank Paul Kroll for his detailed suggestions and comments on earlier drafts of the study that later becomes Chapter 7 of this book.

I acknowledge my debt and gratitude to several earlier masters, in particular Paul Pelliot, Berthold Laufer, and Peter Boodberg, who pioneered the modern study of ancient xeno-Sinitic exchanges. More admiringly, they set the example of conducting fruitful research on subjects whose source materials are patchy and sporadic, in sharp contrast to other areas in which the output is proportional to the quantity of available sources.

I am deeply indebted to reviewers of my manuscript, who helped to improve the book by correcting my many errors, inaccuracies, and insufficiently substantiated claims. I must in particular thank Peter Golden, whose repeated readings contributed so much to the book, not the least by adding numerous important and up-to-date references.

Thanks are also due to the editors and staff of the University of Pennsylvania Press, especially Peter Agree, Julia Rose Roberts, and Erica Ginsburg. Their meticulous and constructive work greatly enhanced the quality of the book.

Last but not least, my thanks go to the editor of this series, Victor Mair, who not only suggested this title several years ago but also patiently and painstakingly nurtured every step in its preparation: the current book would not be in readers' hands but for his persistent support, encouragement, and contributions.